SOUTH AFRICA
1991~92

OFFICIAL YEARBOOK

South Africa 1991/92
Official Yearbook of the
Republic of South Africa
Seventeenth edition
First English edition in the
new, shortened version

Editor
Elise Keyter

Assistant Editor
Minette Pietersen

Editing and layout
Minette Pietersen
Esté Koorts
Magda Schlesinger

Language editors
Jeanette McKenna
Diana Coetzee

Compiled, edited and published by the
South African Communication Service,
Private Bag X745, 0001 Pretoria
Telephone: (012) 314-2911, Telex: 322499, Fax: 3233831

Printed and bound in the Republic of South Africa
by CTP Book Printers, Cape Town
on behalf of the Government Printer, Pretoria

ISBN 0 7970 2272 4

ISSN 0302 0681
Library of Congress Catalogue Card Number: 57-40609

The Official Yearbook is compiled and edited by the Publications Division of the South African Communication Service. While the editorial staff has taken all reasonable care to ensure correctness of facts and statistics, any person requiring formal confirmation of any data in the Yearbook, or more detailed specific information, should consult the contributors. The news items at the end of each chapter were compiled from newspapers and is not necessarily a full account of the events which took place during the year.

Unless otherwise specified, the information contained in this book was the latest available in December 1990.

Table of contents

EMORY AND HENRY LIBRARY

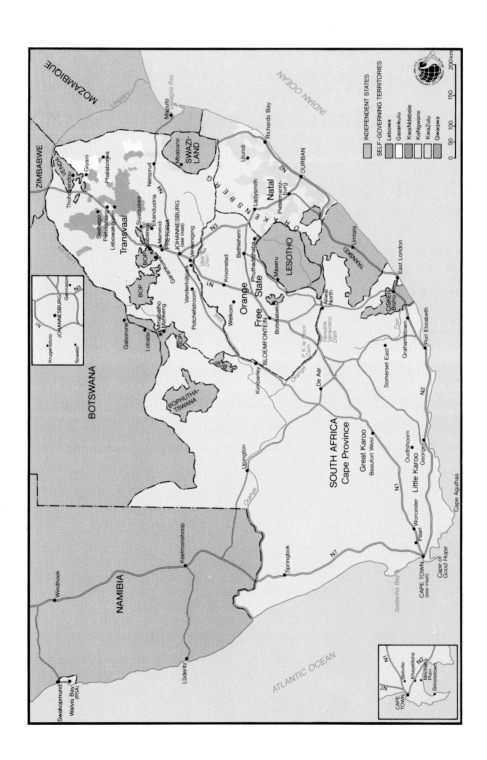

Physical features

South Africa occupies the southernmost part of the African continent, stretching latitudinally from 22°S to 35°S and longitudinally from 17°E to 33° E. In the north South Africa has common boundaries with Namibia, the Republic of Botswana and Zimbabwe, while the Republic of Mozambique and the Kingdom of Swaziland lie to the north-east. Completely enclosed by South African territory in the south-east are the Kingdom of Lesotho and the republics of Transkei and Ciskei. The separate territorial units of the republics of Bophuthatswana and Venda are similarly surrounded by South African territory in the north-central and far northern parts of the country respectively.

To the west, south and east South Africa borders on the South Atlantic and southern Indian oceans. Isolated in the great southern ocean 1 920 km south-east of Cape Town, lie Prince Edward and Marion islands. South Africa proclaimed its sovereignty over Prince Edward Island in 1947, actually annexing it in 1948. In 1947 South Africa proclaimed sovereignty of Marion Island and established a meteorological station in 1948.

South Africa consists of four provinces — the Cape Province, the Orange Free State, Natal and the Transvaal — with a surface area of 1 127 200 km^2 (347 860 sq miles). This excludes the territories of Transkei, Bophuthatswana, Ciskei and Venda, but is still almost five times the size of Britain and nearly equal to the combined areas of Germany, France and Italy. The distance from Cape Town to Pretoria is almost equal to that between Amsterdam and Rome.

The location of South Africa has had a great influence on many aspects of its geography and development. Thus its sunny, dry climate and the small variation between summer and winter daylight periods are both accounted for by its subtropical latitudinal position. The great isolation of South Africa's location has in turn largely determined the course of its history and economic development. Overland it is separated from Europe by large distances and natural barriers such as the Sahara Desert and the equatorial forest zone. In addition, thousands of kilometres of sea surround the country on three sides. For many centuries the region was therefore effectively isolated from the main currents of history and civilisation. This isolation was only broken during the great voyages of discovery in the late 15th century.

Oceans and coastlines

The seas
Surrounded by sea to the west, south and east, South Africa has a lengthy coastline. This coastline is swept by two major ocean currents - the Mozambique-Agulhas and the Benguela systems respectively. The former is a warm, south-flowing current skirting the east and south coasts as far as Cape Point. The Benguela current, on the other hand, is cold and flows northwards as far as southern Angola along the west coast. The average annual sea temperature for Muizenberg (Indian Ocean) is 16,6° C and that for the Cape Town harbour (Atlantic Ocean) only 12,8°C, even though they are situated only a few kilometres apart.

The contrast in temperature between these two currents partly accounts for important differences in climate and vegetation between the east and west coasts of South Africa. It also

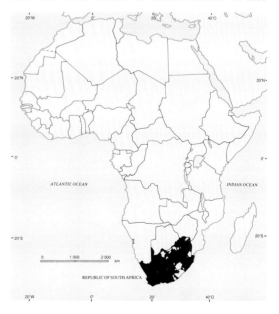

South Africa's location in Africa

Table 1 Length of coastline

Total length (Orange River to Ponta do Ouro)	2 954 km (1 836 miles)*
Orange River to Cape Point	872 km (542 miles)
Cape Point to Ponta do Ouro	2 082 km (1 294 miles)*

* The coastline of the Republics of Transkei and Ciskei included

causes big differences in marine life, with the waters of the west coast much richer in oxygen content, nitrates, phosphates and plankton than those of the east coast. For this reason the South African fishing industry centres on the west coast.

The coasts

The coastline itself is an even, closed one with few bays or indentations naturally suitable for harbours. This is a feature the country shares with the rest of the continent. Along the south coast there are a number of wide embayments which relieve the monotony of the coastline, but they are unsuitable as harbours.

The only good natural harbour along 2 954 km of coastline is Saldanha Bay in the south west. Unfortunately the bay area lacks fresh water and offers no natural lines of penetration to the interior. Because of this Table Bay, relatively unsheltered but with abundant freshwater supplies, was chosen as the site for the first White settlement.

Most South African river mouths are unsuitable as harbours because large sandbars block entry for most of the year. These bars are formed by the action of waves and currents and the episodic flow, heavy sediment load and steep gradients of most South African rivers. Only the largest rivers, such as the Orange and Limpopo, maintain narrow permanent channels through the bars. For much the same reasons the country has no navigable rivers.

The isolated west coast is rocky for the most part but quite even. Back from the coastline itself lie raised beaches and terraces covered by a layer of brown sand 6-10 m deep and stretching inland for 30 to 50 km.

This is the so-called 'Sandveld' of the western Cape which continues almost uninterruptedly as far south as the Cape Flats near Cape Town. The 'Sandveld' is covered by dwarf bush vegetation. Moving dunes, such as those found in the Namib Desert north of the Orange River, are seldom found.

The south coast stretches from Table Bay to Cape Padrone (east of Port Elizabeth). Between Cape Agulhas and Cape Padrone the coast has a simple pattern of capes and bays. Some of the finest beaches in the country are found here.

The east coast falls naturally into two sections: the remarkably straight coastline from Cape Padrone to the mouth of the Mhlalazi River south of Richards Bay, and the coast of Zululand and the Mozambique Plain beyond. Durban harbour is found in the former section. The even Zululand coastal zone is one of South Africa's few seismic areas and forms the southern continuation of the vast Mozambique Plain.

Geology

South Africa is underlain by rocks which differ in age from the oldest on earth (3,8 billion years) to the most recent.

A variety of highly transformed gneiss, greenstone and granite rocks can be found in the north-eastern parts of the country while similar rocks, 1,0 to 1,8 billion years in age, are found in the northwest (Namaqualand) and east (Natal). Sedimentary rocks (mainly sandstone/quartzite, shale and dolomite) are deposited on the older rockbases in different basins.

In the northern part of the country the famous gold-bearing Witwatersrand Basin is important, as are the Ventersdorp Basin which is filled mainly with lava and the Transvaal/Griqualand West Basin which yields the country's iron and manganese. In the south the Cape Basin along the southern and south-western edge of the subcontinent and the Karoo Basin, which covers 75 per cent of the central part of South Africa, with most of the country's coal resources in its northern part, are of the most important. Geologically South Africa is also well-known for the unique and economically important Bushveld complex in the north-central Transvaal. This consists of a layered succession of basic igneous rocks containing all the country's chrome and platinum.

Topography

The surface of South Africa falls naturally into two major physiographic provinces: The interior plateau, and the marginal lands between the plateau and the coast. Forming the boundary between these two areas is the Great Escarpment, the most prominent and continuous topographical feature in the country. In various regions it has different local names and it can be traced from the Drakensberg in the north-eastern Transvaal to Namaqualand in the west. Its height above sea level varies from 1 500 m in the latter area to a maximum of 3 482 m in the Natal Drakensberg.

Inland from the escarpment lies the interior plateau, which is the southern continuation of the great African plateau stretching north to the Sahara. Like that larger unit, it consists of a base of ancient rocks on which a succession of sedimentary and volcanic rock formations were deposited later. Due to subsequent uplifts, the outer edge of the plateau (the Great Escarpment) has over the course of millions of years gradually been displaced towards the interior through the headward erosion of scores of rivers draining its outer slopes.

The plateau itself is characterised by wide plains with an average height of 1 200 m above sea level surmounting the plateau in places and a number of well-defined upland blocks. Of these the dissected Lesotho plateau, which exceeds 3 000 m above sea level, is the most prominent. In general the escarpment forms the highest parts of the plateau. From there it slopes gradually inwards down to the Kalahari Basin which stretches northward into Botswana.

Climatic features

South Africa is blessed with a healthy and invigorating climate which favours outdoor living in all seasons. The subtropical location, on either side of 30°S, accounts for the warm temperate conditions so typical of South Africa. At the same time this position also means that it falls squarely within the subtropical belt of high pressure. Basically, the country is therefore a dry one, but with an abundance of sunshine.

The wide expanses of ocean on three sides have a certain moderating influence on the climate. More apparent, however, are the effects of the warm Agulhas and cold Benguela currents along the east and west coasts respectively. While Durban (east coast) and Port Nolloth (west coast) lie more or less on the same latitude, there is a difference of no less than 6°C in their mean annual temperatures.

Even more significant is the effect on rainfall. Because east coast air masses are warmer, they tend to be less stable and more likely to cause abundant rain. Indeed moist, hot air masses from the Indian Ocean are the chief source of rainfall for most of the country. Over the west coast, however, air masses are chilled from beneath by the cold waters of the Benguela current. Together with the strong subsidence and adiabatic heating of air in the upper layers of the offshore high-pressure cell, this produces a

sharp (about 6°C) and virtually permanent upper air inversion over the west coast, usually at a height of about 600 m. Under these conditions of exceptional stability, rain-forming processes are severely discouraged — hence Port Nolloth's meagre average annual rainfall total of only 63 mm. Durban (east coast), on the other hand, records 1 018 mm annually.

Pressure systems and general weather patterns
Over the interior, weather patterns are largely determined by the waxing and waning of the anticyclonic cell. Thus Tyson (1969) attributes the dry, sunny conditions so typical of plateau areas in winter to the combined influence of

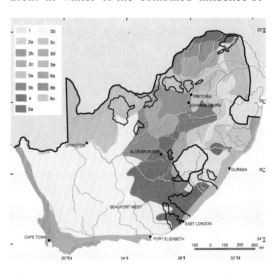

Soil map of South Africa

Source: Soil and Irrigation Research Institute, Pretoria
1. Dystrophic, red and yellow, well-drained clays with varying amounts of rock and lithosols
2. Red, yellow and grey soils in catenary association
   2a Dystrophic and mesotrophic sands, loams and clays with varying amounts of rock and lithosols
   2b Eutrophic sands and loams, red dominant with varying amounts of rock and lithosols
   2c Eutrophic sands and loams, yellow and grey dominant with varying amounts of rock and lithosols
3. Black and red clayey soils
   3a Black and red clay with varying amounts of rock and lithosols
   3b Black clays with varying amounts of rock and lithosols
4. Duplex and paraduplex soils with varying amounts of rock and lithosols
5. Weakly developed soils on rock
   5a Sands and loams with lime in upland and bottomland sites and much rocky land
   5b Loams and clays with lime in upland and bottomland sites and much rocky land
   5c Sands and loams with lime common in bottomland sites but absent in upland sites and much rocky land
   5d Loams and clays with lime common in bottomland sites but absent in upland sites and much rocky land
   5e Loams and clays with lime rare or absent and varying amounts of rock
6. Sandy soils
   6a Grey sands with varying amounts of rock and lithosols
   6b Red non-shifting sands with varying amounts of rock and lithosols
   6c Red and brown shifting sands with varying amounts of rock and lithosols

this cell and the height above sea level of the interior.

In summer, when surface heating weakens the high-pressure cell so that its base humid 'lifts' above plateau level, it is possible for east coast air to be transported inland. Such inflow is usually triggered by the west-east passage of a local anticyclonic cell along the south coast. Relief rains may fall as this air ascends the eastern plateau slopes and the escarpment. Over the plateau itself surface heating will yield abundant convection rains from this air if it is unstable and general weather conditions are otherwise favourable. Thus the plateau and the eastern plateau slopes, together covering the largest part of the country, have summer rain and a dry winter.

The exact opposite conditions, winter rain and dry summers, prevail in the south-western Cape and adjacent areas. In summer this area falls under the influence of the Atlantic high-pressure cell. As a result the weather is hot, cloudless and dry. It is often quite windy, however, and the Cape 'south-easter' frequently reaches gale strength.

In winter this area is affected by a succession of moving low-pressure systems and associated cold fronts moving in from the west. The sub-sequent influx of cool, moist subpolar air brings with it icy, rainy weather and frequently snow on the Cape mountain ranges. Occasionally the cold weather may succeed in surmounting the great escarpment, producing a sudden 'cold snap' over the interior with snow on the highlands.

Gale-force winds are frequent on the coasts, especially the south-western and southern coastal areas. Over the interior wind velocity is generally lower. However, both the highest average wind velocity (99 km/h) and the strongest squall (186 km/h) were recorded at Beaufort West in the interior. On hot summer days whirlwinds (dust devils) are common in the interior. Tornadoes are, however, a rare occurrence, averaging perhaps five a year.

Rainfall

South Africa has an average annual rainfall of only 464 mm, as against a world average of 857 mm. Twenty-one per cent of the country has a total rainfall of less than 200 mm annually, 48 per cent between 200 and 600 mm, while only 31 per cent records more than 600 mm. To summarise: 65 per cent of the country has an annual rainfall of less than 500 mm — usually regarded as the absolute minimum for successful dryland farming.

The lowest rainfall — even less than 50 mm in places — is found in Namaqualand on the west coast, while the highest totals occur on the windward slopes of the Cape mountain ranges, the Drakensberg and the eastern Transvaal escarpment. In the Wemmershoek and Jonkershoek mountains in the south-western Cape, annual figures as high as 3 200 mm have been recorded, while Broederstroom on the eastern Transvaal escarpment has an average annual rainfall of 2 088 mm.

Taking the period of maximum rainfall as a yardstick, three precipitation subregions can be distinguished. The winter rainfall region is a relatively small area along the Cape west and south-west coasts which has a Mediterranean rainfall regime with a prominent winter maximum. Rain is often long lasting and not very intense, except along the mountains. Hail and thunder occur only rarely in this region.

The summer rainfall region covers most of the rest of the country. Violent convection storms, accompanied by thunder, lightning, sudden squalls and often hail, are the source of most of the rainfall in this region. The intensity of these storms (which usually occur in the afternoon or early evening) is highest over the eastern parts of the plateau.

Between the winter and summer rainfall

Table 2 Average percentage of possible sunshine

	Year %	Maximum month %	Minimum month %
South Africa Cape Town	67	79	56
Durban	54	69	41
Kimberley	78	88	70
North Africa Khartoum	85	89	65
North America Washington	57	63	46
Phoenix (Arizona)	84	93	75
San Francisco	65	76	53
Ottawa	46	57	26
Europe London	33	42	17
Vienna	40	55	17
Rome	53	76	37
Australia Sydney	49	57	44
Perth	64	74	47
Asia Jericho	79	90	63

regions lies a transitional area where rain occurs in all seasons — neither in winter nor in summer is more than 60 per cent of the annual total recorded. There is in fact a clear double maximum in autumn and spring respectively. This transitional area can be divided into two subregions: a southern coastal belt with an annual total of 375 to 875 mm, and a drier inland corridor behind the mountain ranges with an annual total of 50 to 250 mm.

South Africa's rainfall is typified by its unreliability and unpredictability. Over the biggest part of the country large fluctuations in the average annual figure are the rule rather than the exception. Years with a below-average figure are more common than years with an above-average total however. As in other countries in similar latitudes, South Africa is in fact periodically afflicted by severe and prolonged droughts which often end in severe floods.

Temperatures
Temperature conditions show three main features. Firstly, temperatures tend to be lower than in other countries in similar latitudes, eg North Africa and Australia. This is primarily due to the subcontinent's greater elevation above sea level. Secondly, despite a latitudinal span of 13 degrees, average annual temperatures are remarkably uniform throughout the country. Due to the increase in the height of the plateau towards the north-east, there is hardly any increase in temperature from south to north as might be expected. For example, Cape Town's average annual temperature is 17°C, and Pretoria's 17,5°C. The third feature has already been mentioned, for example the striking contrast between temperatures on the east and west coasts, with the difference in average annual figures for Durban and Port Nolloth a full 6 °C.

Maximum temperatures above 32°C are fairly common during summer. In the lower Orange River valley and the Transvaal Lowveld they frequently exceed 38°C.

The highest temperatures ever recorded in South Africa were 47,8°C at Goodhouse on 20 January 1939 and 47,7°C at Komatipoort (12 December 1944).

Frost, relative humidity and fog
Frost often occurs in the cold, clear winter nights of the interior plateau, and ice forms on still pools and in water pipes. The frost season is longest (from April to October) over the eastern and southern plateau areas bordering on the escarpment. The period gradually decreases to the north, while the coasts are virtually frost-free.

Average annual relative humidity readings show that in general the air is driest over the western interior and over the plateau. Along the coast the humidity is much higher and at times may rise to 85 and even 90 per cent. On the warm east coast this high humidity causes sultry, muggy weather in summer.

Low stratus clouds and fog occur frequently over the cool west coast, particularly during summer. At night the fog tends to advance inland to a distance of 30 to 50 km over the coastal plain, receding again as the land heats up during the day. The only other area where fog is fairly common is in the 'mist belt' along the eastern foothills of the escarpment.

Table 3 The ten largest rivers in South Africa in order of volume of run-off

River	Catchment area (km^{2}x100)	Flow (million m^3)	Length of river	Run-off of catchment area 10^{6}m^3/km^2	Percentage of total run-off
Orange and Vaal	6 067	12 057	2 340	0,020	22,5
Tugela	290	4 589	520	0,158	8,6
Olifants (Letaba included)	683	3 103	760	0,045	5,8
Umzimvubu	198	2 968	470	0,150	5,5
Komati (Crocodile included)	217	2 681	340	0,124	5,0
Limpopo main basin	1 096	2 290	960	0,121	4,3
Greater Usutu	167	2 005	290	0,120	3,1
Breede	126	1 785	310	0,140	3,3
Umzimkulu	67	1 472	380	0,220	2,8
Pongola	118	1 253	440	0,106	2,3

Sunshine

South Africa's abundant sunshine is famous. In general the total amount increases as one moves to the interior and rainfall and the occurrence of cloud and fog decreases. Minimum hours of sunshine coincide with the rainy seasons, but even then most days will still have some sun because the rain comes mainly in brief, sharp showers.

To summarise: April and May are usually the most pleasant months. The rainy season over the summer rainfall region has ended, while it has not yet really begun in the south-western Cape.

The hot summer weather is over its worst and the winds, which can be quite unpleasant at the coast, are lighter than during the rest of the year. In certain areas, notably the Natal coast and the eastern and northern Lowveld, June and July are the ideal holiday months.

Drainage and hydrology

Worldwide, 31 per cent of all rainfall is returned to the sea via rivers. In South Africa, with its

The Richtersveld where patches of wildflowers appear after the big rains every six or seven years

abundant sunshine and therefore high evaporation rate, the figure is a mere 9 per cent.

The combined annual run-off of all South African rivers (including the rivers of the republics of Transkei, Bophuthatswana, Venda and Ciskei) amounts to 53 500 million m^3. This is only half that of the Zambesi and roughly equal to that of the Nile at Aswan and the Rhine at Rotterdam. The eastern plateau slopes which cover 13 per cent of the area of South Africa, account for nearly 43 per cent of the total run-off. The Orange River system, on the other hand, which drains almost the entire plateau — 48 per cent of the total area of the country — accounts for only 22,5 per cent (about 12 060 million m^3) of the total annual run-off to the sea.

Truly perennial rivers are only found over one quarter of South Africa's surface area — mainly in the south and south-western Cape and on the eastern plateau slopes. Rivers whose flow is restricted to the rainy season are found over a further quarter of the surface area. Over the entire western interior rivers are episodic in nature, which means they flow only sporadically after infrequent storms, while their beds are dry for the rest of the year.

Lakes and pans

With the exception of Lake Fundudzi in the Soutpansberg, formed by a huge landslide, there are no true lakes in the country. The 'lakes' at the Wilderness on the south coast and at St Lucia, Sibayi and Kosi Bay on the Zululand coast, are actually freshwater lagoons. 'Lakes' Chrissie and Banagher on the Transvaal Highveld near Ermelo, differ little in other respects from the innumerable 'pans' to be found in a wide belt from the northern Cape through the western Free State to the southern Transvaal.

Ground water resources

Nearly 13 per cent of all water used in South Africa is obtained from underground sources. Apart from its contribution to river flow, and fossil water derived from non-renewable sources, the maximum quantity of ground water which can be developed economically is estimated at about 5 400 million m^3 a year. More than 70 per cent of the country, including more than a hundred medium-sized towns, are dependent on ground water.

Natural vegetation

Five primary communities of natural vegetation are recognised: desert and semi-desert vegeta-

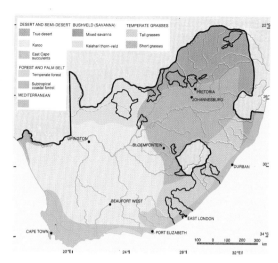

The major vegetation regions of South Africa (generalised)

tion, the Cape floral kingdom, bushveld or savanna, temperate grassland and forests. The map gives a general picture of their distribution.

Soils

Six major soil associations are recognised and shown on the map. All the map units include varying amounts of rock and lithosols (shallow and stony soils) and are numbered from 1 to 6.

The total soil loss through erosion for the world as a whole was calculated at half a ton a year per person while in South Africa this figure was 12 tons. The amount of sediment carried off by rivers in the country was calculated at between 233 and 363 million tons a year.

Natural disasters

Natural disasters such as floods, hail, snowfalls and storms are common occurrences in South Africa. Some of the biggest disasters experienced by the country during the past decade include the following:

1981: On 25 January a total of 104 people drown when Laingsburg is flooded. Only 23 of the town's total of 208 houses survive and the home for the aged is destroyed. Damage and loss of life are also reported at Montagu, Ashton, Robertson and Ladismith.

1981: On 1 March ten people are killed in a violent rain storm that sweeps through Johannesburg, Henley on Klip and Vereeniging.

1981: On 26 March damage of more than R50 million is done and 17 people drown when Port Elizabeth is flooded. The Gamtoos Valley is declared a disaster area.

1984: On 29 January tropical cyclone Domoina sweeps through Mozambique, Swaziland, eastern Transvaal and north-eastern Natal killing 200 people. Damage amounts to R150 million.

1984: On 17 February tropical cyclone Imboa hits the Natal north coast, killing four people.

1985: On 1 November a hailstorm hits Pretoria causing damage of more than R150 million.

1986: On 27 December Piet Retief is hit by a tornado causing damage of more than R12 million. A total of 132 houses are damaged. A second tornado hits the town on 7 January 1987.

1987: On 27 September Natal experiences a devastating disaster when floods kill approximately 388 people, leaving 65 000 homeless. Damage amounts to more than R1 500 million.

1988: On 20 February floods sweep across the Orange Free State, western Transvaal, the Karoo and northern Cape, causing the main route to Namibia to be closed at Viooslsdrif.

1988: On 8 March floods ravage southern and central Free State. Damage is estimated at R1 000 million.

1990: On 20 March a tornado hits Welkom, causing damage of R130 million. Three suburbs are destroyed. Loss of life, however, numbers only two, but 110 people are injured.

News items: 1990

The Cape Peninsula experienced its wettest April in 25 years, with almost 130 mm of rain recorded at D F Malan Airport. The average is 49 mm.

The winter of 1990 brought some of the coldest weather experienced in decades. On 23 May Buffelsfontein in the eastern Cape recorded -15°C, three degrees colder than on the same day in 1980, the previous record. Somerset East recorded -1,6°C, previously registered on 23 May 1941.

Geologists of the Rand Afrikaans University and the Soviet Union signed an agreement to co-operate in research on the development of the earth's archaic crust.

South Africa had one of its driest years in 1990. Some areas experienced the lowest rainfall in 87 years with the north-western, west and south-western Transvaal being the worst hit regions. Over the rest of the country the situation ranged from barely adequate to serious and critical, according to the South African Agricultural Union.

Acknowledgements:
Mr M K R van Huysteen, Department of Geography, University of Stellenbosch

Discoveries at Taung (in Bophuthatswana), Klasies River mouth (between Plettenberg Bay and Port Elizabeth), Sterkfontein (near Krugersdorp) and other sites in the Transvaal, bear witness to the fact that prehistoric man lived about one and a half million years ago in what is today known as South Africa.

The San were the first people to settle here. About 2 000 years ago they were followed by the Khoikhoi who settled at the Cape. Disease, displacement by new inhabitants and miscegenation gradually caused these groups to become extinct.

The first Black population groups arrived during the Iron Age. There is doubt about the order in which the various Black groups moved from Central Africa to present-day South Africa. It is, however, clear that the Black population can be divided into four main language groups, the Nguni, Sotho, Tsonga and Venda.

With the exception of the Venda all the Black groups were affected, in various ways, by the so-called 'mfecane' (in Nguni) or 'difaqane' (in Sotho). These words mean 'pulverisation', 'crushing' or 'forced migration' and indicate a sequence of conflicts within and between the various groups in the early 19th century. This conflict led to greater differentiation between the main groupings and to consolidation of sub-groupings. Examples of this are the way in which Shaka blended the different Nguni tribes into the Zulu nation and Moshweshwe's bonding of the South Sotho tribes into the Basotho nation.

The first contact between Europe and South Africa took place in 1488 when Bartholomeu Dias, a Portuguese who was looking for a sea route to India, sailed round the Cape of Good Hope and soon afterwards round the southernmost point of Africa. Nine years later his compatriot, Vasco da Gama, sailed the same route on a voyage which opened the way to India and to wealth for Portugal. On this voyage he visited the east coast of southern Africa and gave Natal its name on Christmas Day 1497.

By 1600 England, France and Holland had started challenging the Portuguese monopoly of the Eastern trade. Table Bay became a halfway station for their commercial fleets to the East. However, only in 1652 the Vereenighde Oostindische Compagnie (VOC) decided to establish a settlement in Table Valley where its fleet could take in fresh supplies and hospitalise sick crew members.

On 6 April 1652 Jan van Riebeeck, the first commander of the refreshment station, arrived in Table Bay. The Council of Seventeen, the board of directors of the VOC, sent him with 90 men to build a fort and a hospital and to provide meat and fresh vegetables for passing ships. He was also to maintain peace with the Khoikhoi herdsmen with whom he would have to trade for meat.

In 1657 soldiers released from service were allowed to farm to supplement the crop of the company gardens and the uncertain yield of the cattle trade. These so-called 'free burghers' started an agricultural tradition in what was soon to become a land of farmers.

Initially the intention was that the colonists would practise agriculture rather than cattle-farming, but a significant and spontaneous outward movement became noticeable at the beginning of the 18th century while Adriaan Van der Stel was governor (1699-1707).

Cattle farmers in search of water and good grazing followed the trail blazed by hunters and cattle traders. This process of expansion into the interior did not cease until well into the 19th century when the borders of present-day South Africa were fixed.

Van der Stel was dismissed from office as a result of a clash with farmers who accused him of monopolising an already restricted market for his own farm produce and that of his friends. It was during this conflict that it became clear that the colonists had begun to think of themselves as 'Afrikaners'. The term boer (farmer), which Van der Stel had used contemptuously to describe his enemies, was elevated by them to a name of honour. Boer and Afrikaner became synonymous. The word denoted a people imbued with patriotism rooted in their new fatherland.

Meanwhile, the cattle farmers continued their trek eastward into the interior. In 1770, along the Great Fish River, they encountered the vanguard of the Bantu (Black) peoples who, during the course of centuries, had slowly been migrating southwards over a broad transcontinental front.

The clash between White and Black cattle

farmers in the vicinity of the Fish River led to no fewer than nine frontier wars in the course of a century, the first of which was fought in 1779.

At the same time political storm clouds disturbed the older, settled districts of the Cape, and in 1795 the districts of Swellendam and Graaff-Reinet both experienced bloodless revolts. Shortly afterwards, in September of the same year, a British expeditionary force took over the Cape of Good Hope.

This force was sent to occupy the Dutch colony on behalf of the Prince of Orange. The prince had been an exile in England since his country became the Batavian Republic under French guardianship during the Napoleonic wars. At the Peace of Amiens (1803) the Cape was handed back to the Batavian Republic.

By this time the settled White population had come to identify completely with South Africa, despite their European origin. They had developed a new vernacular, Afrikaans, the only Germanic language to have originated outside Europe.

In January 1806 the British occupied the Cape temporarily pending the outcome of the war against Napoleon. At the Congress of Vienna of 1815 the Cape was formally ceded to Britain. Thus the Cape became a British crown colony as part of the British Empire.

For some decades the most pressing problem of the British government at the Cape remained the Fish River frontier. Conflict with the Xhosas gradually developed into a series of campaigns which involved the Xhosa both west and east of the Kei River. In 1820 some 5 000 British immigrants were settled on the eastern frontier to alleviate the problem. The pioneer cattle ranchers and other farmers, both Boer and British, regarded the protection offered by the British as no better than that during the days of the VOC.

During the years 1834—36 White Boers, thoroughly disillusioned with British policy on the eastern frontier, started north in what is known as the Great Trek, an important event in South African history. The Voortrekkers (pioneers), as they became known, crossed the Orange River and the highveld plateau south and north of the Vaal River and trekked as far north as the Limpopo River (today the northern border of the Republic), as well as east to subtropical Natal where they decided to establish a republic. Through their leader, Piet Retief, they made an accord with Dingaan, the Zulu king, but Retief and his company of unarmed men were murdered in Dingaan's kraal. Consequent attacks on parties of Voortrekkers led to the Battle

of Blood River on 16 December 1838 where the Voortrekkers defeated the Zulus. A week earlier the Voortrekkers had made a covenant with God that they would always commemorate 16 December if they should be victorious.

Britain, however, still considered all emigrant Voortrekkers beyond the borders of the Cape Colony subjects of the Crown and refused to recognise the Republic of Natalia. An expeditionary force was sent to Port Natal to subjugate the republic. At first the Voortrekkers under Andries Pretorius easily repulsed the British assault at Congella but a month later the republic capitulated and most Natal Voortrekkers retraced their steps across the Drakensberg to rejoin their fellows in the interior.

In the early 1850s Britain decided to free herself from some of her colonial responsibilities. Thus in 1852 a convention was signed with Transvaal Boer leaders recognising their independence. Continuing its policy of withdrawal, Britain granted independence to the land between the Orange and the Vaal rivers in a convention signed at Bloemfontein in February 1854. This became the independent Republic of the Orange Free State (OFS).

In fewer than 20 years the events set in motion by the Great Trek had 'balkanised' South Africa into two independent Boer republics, one north and one south of the Vaal River, and two British colonies, the Cape and Natal.

The most significant 19th century event after the Great Trek was the discovery in 1886 of the world's richest gold fields on the Witwatersrand, about 50 km south of Pretoria, capital of the Zuid-Afrikaansche Republiek (ZAR). This attracted thousands of fortune hunters from all corners of the world and within ten years one third of the 200 000 White inhabitants of the Transvaal were *uitlanders* (foreigners).

The discovery of the Witwatersrand gold fields gave new impetus to British imperialist designs in Southern Africa. The grievances of the *uitlanders,* both real and imagined, were seized upon by men like Sir Alfred Milner, British High Commissioner in South Africa, and Cecil Rhodes, diamond magnate of Kimberley and Prime Minister of the Cape Colony from 1890 to 1895, as a means of realising their dream of subjugating the entire subcontinent to British rule. Gradually Britain, by treaty, conquest or annexation, encircled the ZAR with hostile territory. The only exceptions were the OFS in the south and Portuguese East Africa in the east.

In 1897 a non-aggression treaty was concluded between the ZAR and OFS. On 11 October 1899 Kruger's ultimatum regarding British troop movements near the borders was rejected by Britain and war broke out between the two republics and the British Empire.

Britain's war against 'Krugerism' lasted 32 months. Peace came on 31 May 1902 with the signing of the Treaty of Vereeniging.

The Anglo-Boer War, like the Great Trek, was of crucial importance in shaping the course of South African history. The entire subcontinent now constituted British South Africa. For the first time since the Voortrekkers had occupied the northern interior the map (excluding South-West Africa) was coloured a uniform British red.

The new Liberal government in Britain, which had ousted Lord Salisbury's Tories in 1906, granted responsible government to the Transvaal in December 1906 and to the Orange River Colony six months later.

The government institutions were not much different from those in the Cape and in Natal. It became evident that a closer union of the four colonies was bound to follow.

A draft constitution for the Union of South Africa was submitted to the British Parliament in 1909 and adopted without amendment as the South Africa Act, 1909. It served as the constitution of the Union of South Africa, which was founded on 31 May 1910. The Union's first general election was held on 15 September 1910.

The historic Balfour Declaration of 1927 defined the dominions as autonomous communities within the British Empire, equal in status, in no way subordinate to one another.

The Purified National Party (NP), established in 1934 by Dr D F Malan, won the general election held in May 1948. From the mid-1940s until the early 1980s the NP's strength at the polls, relative to other political parties, could at least partly be attributed to the fact that the party became the embodiment of the broad political ideals of Afrikanerdom.

When Mr J G Strijdom died in 1958 he was succeeded as Prime Minister by Dr H F Verwoerd. Shortly after the election on 6 September 1966 Dr Verwoerd was assassinated in Parliament. Mr B J Vorster was elected leader of the NP and consequently Prime Minister. He retired on 20 September 1978. Mr P W Botha became Prime Minister.

The most significant development during Mr Botha's term of office was the introduction in 1984 of South Africa's new constitution which represented a complete break with the Westminster system. It provided for three Houses of Parliament, one each for Whites, Coloureds (people of mixed descent) and Indians, who share in decisions on general or na-

tional matters. Decisions on own affairs — those affecting a specific population group — are made separately.

The recurrence of Black opposition to the White government reached a climax in 1985 and 1986. The opposition, in the form of widespread unrest and school boycotts in various Black townships, compelled the government to declare a state of emergency in 36 magisterial districts in 1985. In June 1986 the state of emergency was extended to the whole of South Africa.

At the same time the government started dismantling the apartheid system systematically. The Group Areas Act was amended in 1984 to open central business districts to all races. The Prohibition of Mixed Marriages Act and section 16 of the Immorality Act were repealed in 1985. Legislation was also promulgated to revoke all race restrictions in hotels, restaurants and accommodation establishments.

In 1989 Mr Botha separated the offices of the leader of the National Party and State President, traditionally vested in one person, in an attempt to devote all his attention to the office of State President. On 2 February 1989 the NP caucus appointed Mr F W de Klerk, Minister of National Education, leader of the NP — placing him in a unique position in South African politics. On 15 August tradition was restored when Mr de Klerk was inaugurated as acting State President after Mr Botha had retired mainly for health reasons. In the general election held on 6 September, the NP was re-elected governing party. Mr de Klerk was inaugurated as State President on 20 September. In this capacity he devoted his attention to consideration and execution of measures to bring about orderly but dramatic changes in South Africa, involving all South Africans in the process of government.

An important step was the State President's announcement on 16 November 1989 that South Africa's beaches were to be opened to all population groups. This was welcomed abroad, but the Official Opposition, the Conservative Party, saw it as the beginning of the end of an own White community life.

At the opening of Parliament on 2 February 1990 (exactly a year after Mr de Klerk had been chosen leader of the National Party), in line with his policy of orderly, dramatic change, he announced far-reaching measures which immediately came into force. The ban on the African National Congress (ANC), the South African Communist Party (SACP), the Pan-Africanist Congress (PAC) and a number of minor organisations was immediately lifted; the unconditional release of Mr Nelson Mandela, former leader of the ANC, was announced and took place on 11 February 1990; persons serving prison sentences because they were members of prohibited organisations were released; the restrictions imposed on 33 organisations — among which the United Democratic Front (UDF), Congress of South African Trade Unions (Cosatu), the National Education Crisis Committee (NECC) and the *Blanke Bevrydingsbeweging* — in terms of the emergency regulations, were revoked; emergency regulations pertaining to the media as well as education, were scrapped; all executions were stayed until a final decision on new proposals on executions had been made by Parliament; the restrictions placed on 374 persons at the time of their release in terms of the security regulations were revoked and the regulations providing for such restrictions were scrapped. The period of detention in terms of security regulations would henceforth be limited to six months.

Heads of state since establishment of the Republic
1961 Mr C R Swart — first State President
       Dr H F Verwoerd — Prime Minister (since 1958)
1966 Mr B J Vorster — Prime Minister
1968 Mr J J Fouché — second State President
1975 Dr N Diederichs — third State President
1978 Mr B J Vorster — fourth State President
       Mr P W Botha — Prime Minister
1979 Mr Marais Viljoen — fifth State President
1984 Mr P W Botha — first executive State President
1989 Mr F W de Klerk — second executive State President

Historical milestones
1485 Diego Cão lands at Cape Cross north of Walvis Bay.
1487 On 8 December Bartholomeu Dias lands at Walvis Bay and soon afterwards at Lüderitz.
1488 Bartholomeu Dias rounds the Cape.
1497 Vasco da Gama lands at St Helena Bay on 7 November. In the first encounter between Europeans and Khoikhoi, Da Gama and three of his companions are wounded. On 26 November Da Gama anchors at Mossel Bay. On Christmas Day he names the Pondoland coast Natal.
1498 On 6 January Da Gama lands at the mouth of the Limpopo River. This is the first time the Portuguese see Black people.
1503 Saldanha discovers Table Bay and climbs Table Mountain.
1510 D'Almeida, first viceroy of the new Portuguese possessions in India, and 65 of his men

are killed in a skirmish with Khoikhoi on the shore of Table Bay. After this incident the Portuguese fleets avoid landing at the Cape and proceed straight to Mozambique.
1580 Sir Francis Drake sails around the Cape.
1595 First voyage by Hollanders to India under Houtman.
1602 Dutch East India Company *(Vereenighde Oostindische Compagnie)* established.
1652 On 6 April Jan van Riebeeck lands at the Cape to establish the first White settlement.
1654 Birth of South Africa's industry signalled when 60 000 bricks are baked.
1657 First free burghers start farming at Rondebosch. First navigational aid installed on Robben Island.
1658 Nearly 400 slaves imported from West Africa.
1659 On 2 February the first wine pressed at the Cape. Soon afterwards, wine is exported to Batavia. First beer brewed.
1666 Building of the Castle at Cape Town commences.
1679 Stellenbosch founded by Simon van der Stel.
1685 Copper discovered in Namaqualand. First astronomical observations made by Father Tachard, a Jesuit missionary en route to Siam.
1688 Arrival of the first Huguenot settlers.
1713 First known smallpox epidemic.
1760 Coetzee crosses the Orange River. Expeditions under Hendrik Hop and Willem van Reenen penetrate Namaqualand as far as Walvis Bay and Keetmanshoop.
1774 First mission station south of the Limpopo established at Genadendal by Georg Schmidt of the Moravian Mission Society.
1778 Fish River declared the eastern boundary of the Cape Colony.
1779 Xhosas, after crossing the Fish River and invading the Cape Colony, driven back in the First Frontier War.
1780-83 War between Holland and England. Decline of the Dutch East India Company.
1781 First British attempt to annex the Cape. French troops land to protect the Cape against the British. They are withdrawn in 1784.
1782 First paper rixdollars issued. The *Grosvenor* wrecked.
1789 First Spanish merinos — four ewes and two rams — imported. First official overseas mail service.
1795—1803 First British occupation of the Cape.
1803—06 Cape given back to Batavian Republic. Janssens and De Mist joint governors. First inland postal service as far as Algoa Bay.
1806 Second British occupation of the Cape.

1814 Holland cedes the Cape to Britain.

1819 Cape border extended to Keiskamma River.

1820 Arrival of 5 000 British settlers. Port Elizabeth founded by them. Cape Observatory established.

1821 Samuel and Richard Bradshaw, two 1820 Settlers, and the carpenter Isaac Wiggall build the first textile mill near Bathurst. Destroyed by Xhosas in 1835.

1825 First steamship arrives in Table Bay. Birth of Paul Kruger, later president of the ZAR.

1826 First vocabulary of an indigenous language (Xhosa) published by the missionary John Bennie.

1827 First medical society established in Cape Town.

1828 Death of the Zulu king Shaka. English becomes the official language of the Cape. Passes for Hottentots abolished. All free Blacks in Cape put on equal political footing with Whites.

1829 South African College opened in Cape Town (1 October).

1834 Slavery abolished. First grammar of an indigenous language (Xhosa), written by William B Boyce and published by the Wesleyan Mission Press, Grahamstown.

1835 Durban founded. Beginning of the Trichardt Trek.

1837 Ndebele, defeated by the Voortrekkers, cross the Limpopo into Rhodesia. Retief Trek to Natal.

1838 Great Trek from the Cape Colony. Retief's treaty with Dingaan, successor to Shaka. Massacre by Dingaan of Boers under Retief. Trekkers under Andries Pretorius win Battle of Blood River. Dingaan overthrown. Republic of Natal founded.

1839 Temporary British occupation of Durban. Pietermaritzburg and Potchefstroom founded.

1843 Natal proclaimed a British colony.

1844 Majority of Voortrekkers leave Natal, which is incorporated with Cape Colony.

1845 Natal separated from Cape Colony.

1846 Bloemfontein founded.

1847 East London founded. British rule extended over Kaffraria (Ciskei). Gaslighting introduced in Cape Town.

1848 British sovereignty proclaimed over territory between Orange and Vaal rivers. Skirmish between British troops and Boers at Boomplaats.

1850 Attempts to make the Cape a penal settlement successfully opposed. Rustenburg founded.

1852 Copper mining at Springbokfontein. Britain recognises the Transvaal's independence in the Sand River Convention. In January Edmund Morewood hands the editor of the *Times of Natal,* Port Natal, a packet of sugar he manufactured from cane brought from Réunion. Coffee trees imported to Natal.

1853 First postage stamp issued in Cape Colony.

1854 Britain recognises independence of Orange Free State (OFS) in Convention of Bloemfontein. First Cape Parliament in session.

1855 Pretoria founded.

1856 Natal becomes a separate colony. Lydenburg secedes from the ZAR. Famine among Xhosa tribes after the slaughter of all their cattle at instigation of a 'prophet'.

1857-59 Settlement of the German Legion in Kaffraria.

1858 First war between OFS and Basutos.

1860 First railway — a link of 3 km between the Point and Port Natal (Durban) — in operation. First telegraph line — between Cape Town and Simon's Town — in operation. Lighthouse built at Cape Point — at that stage the highest in the world. Pretoria established as seat of the Transvaal government. First Indian labourers imported for sugar plantations in Natal. Inauguration of Cape docks. The first weather service established on 26 October.

1861 Purchase of Griqua territory by OFS and migration of Adam Kok and his people to Griqualand East.

1863 Railway line between Cape Town and Wellington opened.

1865 Kaffraria incorporated with Cape Colony. Chrome ore found in Rustenburg district by Carl Mauch.

1867 First diamond discovered near Hopetown.

1868 Britain intervenes in Basutoland and annexes the territory.

1869 Diamonds discovered near Kimberley. Treaty of Aliwal North defines borders between OFS and Basutoland.

1870 Diamond fields annexed by Britain. Gold discovered in Murchison mountain range.

1871 Gold discovered at Eersteling near Potgietersrus. Goodman Household of Karkloof, Natal, flies nearly 1,5 km in a self-built glider.

1872 Responsible parliamentary government granted to Cape Colony.

1873 Gold discovered in Lydenburg district. Griqualand West becomes a Crown colony.

1875 Formation of Die Genootskap van Regte Afrikaanders (Association of True Afrikaners) in the Cape to campaign for full recognition of the Afrikaans language. President Burgers takes iron ore samples from Pretoria to Europe, but fails to evoke any interest.

1876 First Afrikaans magazine, *Di Afrikaanse*

Patriot (the Afrikaans patriot), issued. First eucalyptus plantation planted at Worcester by Joseph Store Lister.

1877 Transvaal annexed for Britain by Lord Shepstone.

1878 Walvis Bay proclaimed British territory.

1879 Anglo-Zulu War. Cetshwayo exiled. Britain occupies Zululand. On 31 July South Africa is linked by cable to Europe, via Aden.

1880 Founding of Afrikanerbond. First Anglo-Boer War breaks out.

1881 Transvaal regains independence under British suzerainty. Use of Dutch permitted in Cape Parliament.

1882 First telephone exchange opened in Port Elizabeth (1 May). Kimberley becomes the first urban community to use electricity.

1883 Paul Kruger sworn in as President of the ZAR. Republics of Stellaland and Goshen founded along western border of ZAR.

1884 South-West Africa becomes a German protectorate. Barberton gold fields opened. Treaty of London (27 February) grants ZAR full independence except for the right to make treaties with foreign states. Basutoland becomes a Crown protectorate. The Cape Parliament recognises Dutch as an official language.

1885 Dissolution of republics of Goshen and Stellaland. Southern Bechuanaland becomes a Crown colony and northern Bechuanaland a British protectorate. St Lucia annexed by Britain. Cape Town-Kimberley railway line opened.

1886 Johannesburg founded. Opening of Witwatersrand gold fields.

1887 Johannesburg Stock Exchange established. Zululand and Tongaland proclaimed British territories.

1888 British South Africa Company established. First mining concessions granted by Lobengula. Matabeleland and Mashonaland declared British spheres of influence.

1889 Defensive alliance between OFS and ZAR.

1890 Cecil Rhodes becomes Prime Minister of Cape Colony. British troops occupy Mashonaland. German-British treaty fixes borders of SWA.

1892 Cape Town-Johannesburg railway line completed.

1893 Self-government for Natal.

1894 Pondoland annexed and incorporated into Cape Colony. Separate administration for Transkei in terms of Glen Grey Act.

1895 British Bechuanaland annexed to Cape Colony. Jameson's raid into the Transvaal.

1896 Surrender and trial of Jameson. Rhodes resigns as Premier of Cape Colony. Outbreak of rinderpest.

1897 Railway line opened from Cape Town to Bulawayo.

1898 Paul Kruger elected President of the ZAR for the fourth time.

1899—1902 War between Britain and the two Boer republics — Anglo-Boer War.

1902 Peace of Vereeniging concluded on 31 May. The Transvaal (previously the ZAR) and OFS become British colonies. Premier diamond mine opened near Pretoria.

1904 President Kruger dies in Clarens, Switzerland. Chinese labourers imported for the Transvaal gold mines.

1905 Abdullah Abdurahman becomes president of African Political (later People's) Organisation (APO) which had been founded in 1902. Beginning of second Afrikaans language movement. Cullinan diamond (3 106 carats) discovered at Premier Mine.

1906 Victoria Falls Power Company founded. Self-government granted to the Transvaal. Cabinet constituted by Louis Botha. Rebellion under Bambatha in Natal. Copper mining started at Messina.

1907 Self-government granted to Orange River Colony. Import of Chinese mine labourers stopped. First oil company, Vacuum Oil, founded and first clothing factory built in Cape Town. *Industry and Trade* established in Cape Town as the first mouthpiece of South African industries. South African Native Congress meets in Queenstown to discuss Black reaction to proposed Union.

1908 National Convention in Durban, followed by meetings in Cape Town and Bloemfontein in 1909. The small laboratory established for Arnold Theiler at Daspoort by the former ZAR moves to Onderstepoort. This hails the beginning of South Africa's famous veterinary services.

1909 Native Congress of OFS calls for a convention of Blacks. South African Native Convention meets in Bloemfontein. Eight Coloured and Black politicians visit London to protest against draft South Africa Act. The South Africa Act passed by the British Parliament. First flight with power-driven aeroplane by Albert Kimmerling of East London (28 December).

1910 South Africa becomes a Union on 31 May. Lord Gladstone becomes Governor-General and Gen Louis Botha Prime Minister. Mahatma Gandhi acquires Tolstoy Farm in the Transvaal to house families of arrested protesters. The foundation stone of the Union Buildings, Pretoria laid by the Duke of Connaught. Wireless telegraph station opened in Durban. First census taken. Population of Union: 1,2 million

Whites, 4,6 million Blacks, Coloureds and Asians.

1911 Wireless telegraph station opened at Slangkop in the Cape Peninsula. South African Party (SAP) founded.

1912 South African Native National Congress (SANNC) founded in Bloemfontein. Defence system of Union established in terms of Defence Act. Gen Botha resigns and forms a new Cabinet excluding Gen J B M Hertzog. Union Land and Agricultural Bank and Union Steel Corporation founded.

1913 Strikes by both White and Black mineworkers on the Witwatersrand. Indian riots in Natal. Natal Indians march into the Transvaal. Unveiling of National Women's Monument in Bloemfontein (16 December) in memory of the 26 251 Afrikaans women and children who died in concentration camps during the Anglo-Boer War (1899—1902). Natives' Land Act passed to reserve traditional territories for Blacks and largest part of land for Whites.

1914 Industrial unrest on Witwatersrand and elsewhere: martial law proclaimed. Gen Hertzog founds the National Party (NP). Outbreak of World War I. South Africa accepts responsibility for its own defence and Imperial troops deployed for service in Europe. On 10 September Parliament decides by 91 votes to 12 in favour of entering the war. Union forces invade German SWA and occupy Lüderitzbucht. Rebellion against participation in war suppressed. SANNC deputation visits London to protest against Natives' Land Act. Gandhi returns to India.

1915 German forces in SWA surrender to Gen Botha. Union government recruits volunteers for service in Europe.

1916 Union expeditionary force under Gen Smuts dispatched to German East Africa. Battle of Delville Wood. South African Native College (later University of Fort Hare) opened.

1917 Gen Smuts returns from East Africa and departs for London to attend the meeting of the Imperial War Cabinet. Anglo American Corporation, today one of the country's largest companies, founded.

1918 Universities of South Africa, Cape Town and Stellenbosch constituted. Ceasefire announced on 11 November. Influenza epidemic (with pneumonia) claims an estimated 11 726 Whites and 127 745 people of colour. Founding of Afrikaner Broederbond.

1919 Union granted mandate over SWA Protectorate. Treaty of Versailles signed with Germany on 28 June. SANNC deputation attends signing. Generals Botha and Smuts sign treaty on behalf of the Union to end World War I. Death of Gen Botha. Gen Smuts appointed Prime Minister. Department of Health established. Industrial and Commercial Workers' Union (ICU) founded by Clements Kadalie.

1920 Strike by Black workers on the Rand. Transvaal Native Congress launches campaign against carrying passes. Col (later Sir) Pierre van Ryneveld and Maj (later Sir) Quintin Brand complete a flight from Cairo to Cape Town.

1921 Board of Trade and Industry established. Reserve Bank brought into operation. Defence of South Africa completely taken over by the Union government. Diamond mines closed in Kimberley; economic depression deepens. Comrades Marathon, now one of South Africa's biggest sporting events, held for the first time.

1922 Strike on gold and coal mines, in steel industry and at Victoria Falls Power Company on the Witwatersrand, followed by violence in various places. General strike called, followed by widespread revolutionary disruption in mining districts; martial law proclaimed and government forces mobilised (214 casualties). Eskom founded. Witwatersrand University inaugurated on 4 October. Bondelswarts rebellion suppressed in South-West Africa.

1923 Platinum is discovered in Waterberg district, Transvaal. First radio broadcast made on 18 December. Natives (Urban Areas) Act extends segregation to cities. SANNC changes its name to ANC.

1924 One-day flight by military aircraft from Cape Town to Pretoria. National Party/Labour Party Pact wins general election (17 June). Gen Hertzog becomes Prime Minister. Industrial Conciliation Act lays down strict procedures for collective bargaining.

1925 Union reverts to gold standard. Afrikaans recognised as official language, equal to English and Dutch. Rich platinum deposits discovered. Some 25 000 ICU supporters stay away from work in Bloemfontein.

1926 New agreement for repatriation of Indians concluded between South Africa and India. Dominions granted status equal to Britain. The Mines and Works Act amended to empower Minister of Mines to extend job reservation.

1927 Radio-telegraphic communication set up with Britain. Diamonds are discovered in Little Namaqualand. Iscor founded. A Moth aircraft, piloted by Lt R Bently, flies from England to Johannesburg in 26 days. Compulsory segregation announced in 26 urban areas; 64 locations are proclaimed in terms of Natives (Urban Areas) Act. Department of Foreign Affairs established.

1928 The diamond cutting industry is established

in Kimberley. A trade and customs convention signed between Mozambique and the Union.

1929 Airmail service established. Alfred Beit Bridge (road and rail) over Limpopo opened to connect Union with Southern Rhodesia. Afrikaans version of the four Gospels and Psalms published. Communists form African League of Rights, fight two seats in Parliament and suffer a defeat.

1930 University of Pretoria attains independent status. White women get the vote. Communists launch pass-burning campaign. Communist leader Johannes Nkosi killed during protest in Durban.

1931 Pretoria proclaimed a city. Statute of Westminster passed by British Parliament. South Africa given freedom of legislation on any matter.

1932 Diamond mining industry closed down temporarily owing to depression. Airmail service between Union and Britain inaugurated. Radio telephone communication established with Britain. South Africa renounces gold standard.

1933 Severe drought broken. Afrikaans Bible published. Coke-oven fired at Iscor in Pretoria.

1934 Union Airways taken over by government. Discovery of gold at Odendaalsrus. Hertzog and Smuts form the United South African National Party; DF Malan breaks away to form the Purified National Party; dissatisfied former SAP Members of Parliament form Dominion Party.

1935 Pan-African postal conference held in Pretoria. All-African Convention founded.

1936 Native Trust and Land Act passed to reserve more land for Blacks. Natives' Representation Act brings an end to the Cape Black franchise. South African Broadcasting Corporation (SABC) founded.

1937 Sir Patrick Duncan becomes first South African citizen to be appointed Governor-General. First regular Afrikaans service introduced by the SABC. Council for Non-European Trade Unions founded.

1938 Inauguration of South African Press Association (Sapa) providing general news service within Union. Railway line between Randfontein and Springs and between Germiston and Pretoria electrified. Centenary celebration of the Great Trek (symbolic ox-wagon trek). Foundation stone of Voortrekker Monument in Pretoria laid on 16 December. *Die Stem van Suid-Afrika* and *God Save the King* adopted as national anthems.

1939 Resignation of Gen Hertzog whose motion that Union should remain neutral in war is defeated in Parliament. New Cabinet sworn in with Gen Smuts as Prime Minister. South Africa declares war on Germany. A total of 334 324 South Africans fought in the war and 12 046 lost their lives. Ossewabrandwag founded.

1940 Active Citizen Force (ACF) reorganised on the basis of volunteers undertaking to serve anywhere in Africa. South Africa declares war on Italy (12 June). Alfred Xuma becomes president of the ANC.

1941 South African Mint Act promulgated. Import and Export Control Board established. Union declares war on Japan (8 December). Founding of African Mineworkers' Union.

1942 Introduction of petrol rationing as well as commodity control. Death of Gen Hertzog. Government relaxes influx control measures.

1943 United Party wins general election. Parliament approves employment of South African forces on a voluntary basis beyond the continent. Leading middle class Blacks formulate Black political demands in a document titled *African claims in South Africa*. Founding of ANC Youth League or Congress Youth League (CYL).

1944 James Mpanza starts the *Sofasonke* squatter movement in Johannesburg.

1945 SA Air Council and Civil Aviation Board appointed.

1946 Gold discovered in OFS. First South African-born Governor-General, Gideon Brand van Zyl, appointed. Strike by Black mineworkers on the Witwatersrand. Asiatic Land Tenure Act adopted which prevented further acquisition of land by Indians in Natal and the Transvaal.

1947 The King and Queen and the princesses Elizabeth and Margaret visit the Union.

1948 General election. National Party comes into power. Dr D F Malan Prime Minister. Marion and Prince Edward islands annexed by the Union.

1949 University of Natal constituted. Voortrekker Monument, Pretoria, inaugurated. Import control introduced. Militant CYL inspired action programme adopted at ANC congress.

1950 The University of the OFS attains independent status. Suppression of Communism Act passed. Death of Field-Marshal J C Smuts. Springbok Radio (commercial service) on the air. Establishment of the South African Coal, Oil and Gas Corporation (Sasol). Communist Party of SA dissolves in anticipation of Suppression of Communism Act. Population Registration, Immorality and Group Areas acts adopted; also Suppression of Communism Act.

1951 OFS's first two gold mines commence production. Dr E G Jansen is appointed Governor-General. Temporary withdrawal of Union from UN. Separate Representation of Voters Act takes effect and is disputed in court. Torch

Commando hold several rallies in support of Coloured voters.

1952 Riots in Black townships at Port Elizabeth and East London in the eastern Cape; countrywide defiance campaign after adoption of Act abolishing passes and introducing reference book for Blacks. Coelacanth, which had supposedly been extinct for 70 million years, caught. The Union's first uranium plant opened on West Rand.

1953 Black Education Act passed to create separate Black education system. Government wins election with mandate to remove Coloured voters from common voters' roll. Separate Amenities Act and Bantu Education Act passed. Jan Smuts Airport put into operation.

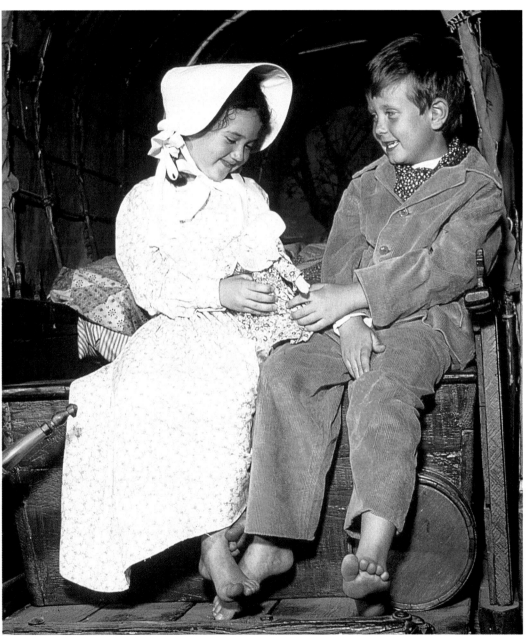

Voortrekker children used to wear clothes that were a replica of those of their parents

1954 Mr J G Strijdom becomes Prime Minister. First oil refinery opened at Wentworth, Durban.
1955 Sasol produces its first petrol from coal. First phosphate concentrates produced at Phalaborwa. Senate Act passed to increase the number of senators from 49 to 89. Freedom Charter adopted by Congress of the People. Countrywide swoop by security police on extra-parliamentary organisations.
1956 Joint sitting of both Houses of Parliament passes a bill placing Coloured voters on a separate voters' roll. Unprecedented activity in Union ports after the closure of the Suez Canal.
1957 The Union flag becomes the only official flag and *Die Stem van Suid-Afrika* the only national anthem. Simon's Town naval base officially handed to Union government.
1958 South Africa resumes full participation in UN activities. Prime Minister J G Strijdom dies. Dr H F Verwoerd elected sixth Prime Minister.
1959 Mr C R Swart appointed Governor-General. Extension of University Education Act prepares the way for Non-White universities. Pan-Africanist Congress (PAC) founded under Robert Sobukwe. Progressive Party founded under Dr Jan Steytler.
1960 At Sharpeville a large number of Blacks protesting 'pass laws' advance on the police station. Police shoot 69. Parliament passes Unlawful Organisations Act to outlaw the ANC and PAC. Worst mine disaster in history occurs at Coalbrook in north shaft of Clydesdale Collieries. Visit of Mr H Macmillan, British Prime Minister. Attempted assassination of Dr Verwoerd in Johannesburg. In referendum 850 458 vote in favour of a republican form of government, 775 878 against.
1961 New decimal coinage system introduced. Republic of South Africa founded outside the Commonwealth. Mr C R Swart elected first State President. Nelson Mandela proposes armed struggle; start of sabotage campaign. Albert Luthuli receives Nobel Peace Prize.
1963 Transkei granted self-government. 90 Day Detention Act passed to suppress *Poqo* and *Umkhonto we Sizwe,* military wing of the ANC. Police raid on Rivonia base of *Umkhonto;* Rivonia trial starts.
1964 Government announces the formation of the Coloured Persons' Representative Council to give limited self-government to Coloured community. National African Federated Chamber of Commerce (NAFCOC) established to promote Black business enterprises.
1965 Registration of the Suidelike Olie-eksplorasiekorporasie (Soekor). Atlas Aircraft Corporation founded.

1966 Dr Verwoerd assassinated in the House of Assembly by Dimitri Tsafendas, a deranged parliamentary messenger. Mr B J Vorster becomes new Prime Minister. The World Court rejects Ethiopian and Liberian complaints against South African rule over SWA. District Six, Cape Town, traditionally a Coloured area, proclaimed a White area.
1967 World's first heart transplant performed by Prof Chris Barnard on Mr Louis Washkansky at Groote Schuur Hospital in Cape Town.
1968 Mr J J Fouché sworn in as State President.
1969 Petroleum gas struck on the continental shelf off Plettenberg Bay. South African Students' Organisation established under Steve Biko. Establishment of Herstigte Nasionale Party under Dr Albert Hertzog.
1970 New uranium enrichment process developed by South African scientists.
1971 Internal self-government granted to the Zulu nation.
1972 Envoy of the Secretary-General of the UN, Dr A Escher, tours SWA and holds talks with Prime Minister in an effort to resolve the SWA issue. Opening of Hendrik Verwoerd Dam, largest dam in South Africa. Black People's Convention founded to co-ordinate supporters of Black Consciousness Movement.
1973 Black territories of Gazankulu and Venda granted self-government. Seats in Parliament increased from 165 to 171 with one additional seat in the Senate.
1974 First meeting between Prime Minister John Vorster and leaders of eight self-governing territories. 1820 Settlers' Monument opened at Grahamstown.
1975 Dr N Diederichs succeeds Mr J J Fouché as State President. Minister M C Botha retains Afrikaans as medium of instruction in Black education.
1976 South Africa involved in Angolan civil war following the precipitate granting of independence by Portugal. Unrest in Soweto spreads to other Black residential areas; hundreds die in riots. Transkei gains independence.
1977 Bophuthatswana gains independence. UN Security Council imposes mandatory arms embargo against South Africa. Armaments Corporation of South Africa (Armscor) established. Steve Biko, leader of the Black Consciousness Movement, dies in detention.
1978 The Western Five release their 'final' proposals to solve problem in SWA: accepted by South Africa, but Swapo rejects it conditionally. Death of the State President, Dr N Diederichs. Mr B J Vorster is the new State President and Mr P W Botha Prime Minister. Dr C P Mulder

resigns after the Information scandal. Sobukwe dies.

1979 Mr B J Vorster resigns as State President. He is succeeded by Mr Marais Viljoen. Republic of Venda gains independence.

1980 Parliament approves the establishment of a President's Council to advise government on constitutional reform. The government lifts restrictions on the employment of skilled Black workers in White areas.

1981 A total of 790 obsolete laws removed from the Statute Book. Ciskei becomes the fourth independent Black state. SABC introduces first television broadcasts in Black languages.

1982 Trade links between South Africa and the Republic of China strengthened. Foreign Minister R F Botha meets US Secretary of State George Shultz in Washington to discuss SWA negotiations. Population Registration Amendment Bill passed to introduce uniform identity documents for all South Africans. South Africa, the four independent states and six self-governing territories implement a new regional industrial development policy. Atomic Energy Corporation established. Sasol 3, at Secunda, produces its first marketable fuels. Venda independent. Conservative Party founded under Dr A P Treurnicht.

1983 Two thirds of White electorate approves the new constitution. Death of former State President, Mr B J Vorster. ANC car bomb kill 19 and wound 216 in Pretoria. Heads of state of governments of South Africa, Transkei, Bophuthatswana, Venda and Ciskei sign an agreement which provides for establishment of Development Bank of Southern Africa. United Democratic Front (UDF) founded outside Cape Town. Coloured Labour Party decides to participate in tricameral Parliament.

1984 Group Areas Act amended to open central business districts to all races. New constitution providing for a tricameral Parliament implemented. Mr P W Botha unanimously elected first executive State President. Widespread unrest in several Black townships. Accord of Nkomati signed with Mozambique. National Union of Mineworkers (NUM) formed.

1985 First full session of the new tricameral Parliament opens. Prohibition of Mixed Marriages Act and section 16 of the Immorality Act repealed. Abolishment of four provincial councils announced. The Prohibition of Political Interference Act which prevented multiracial membership of political parties abolished. The RSA accepted as member of the World Trade Centre Association. Black unrest continues. State of emergency delared in 36 magisterial

districts. The ANC indicates that it will draw no distinction between 'soft' (civilian) and other targets in the 'armed struggle'. Four PAC members convicted of high treason 20 years previously released after State President's offer of conditional release. Congress of SA Trade Unions (Cosatu) founded. Black, Coloured and Indian public service staff organisations represented on the Public Service Advisory Council for the first time.

1986 Legislation promulgated to repeal race restrictions in hotels, restaurants and accommodation establishments, subject only to the owner's right to reserve admission. Of the 20 members of the four new provincial executives appointed to replace the elected provincial councils and administrations, three are Black, three Indian and four Coloured. Regional Services Councils introduced. The unrest situation worsens. In June a national state of emergency is declared.

1987 Two South Africans of colour appointed ambassadors — Dr Frank Quint to the Netherlands and Dr Bhadra Ranchod to the European Community in Brussels. Mr N M Ramodike elected Chief Minister of Lebowa after the death of Dr Cedric Phatudi. Thirteen Portuguese and four South African sailors set sail from Lisbon in a replica of the caravelle in which Bartholomeu Dias discovered the sea route around the Cape 500 years ago. The NP wins 123 of the 166 seats of the House of Assembly in the general election, while the CP becomes the Official Opposition. Mr Govan Mbeki, former national chairman of the ANC, released from prison on 5 November.

1988 Soekor announces its most promising oil strike to date — about 120 km south-west of Mossel Bay. The RSA, Cuba and Angola sign the Brazzaville Protocol which provided for, among other things, implementation of Resolution 435 on 1 April 1989.

1989 State President P W Botha resigns mainly for health reasons. After the general election on 6 September he is succeeded by the Minister of National Education, Mr F W de Klerk. Democratic Party founded as successor to the PFP. The Republic's armed forces are withdrawn from SWA in view of the implementation of Resolution 435 of the UN, aiming at independence for the region. Swapo wins the independence election on 6 November.

News items: 1990

The State President, Mr de Klerk, in his opening speech in Parliament on 2 February, announced the release of Mr Nelson Mandela and the lifting of the ban on all unlawful organisations, including all restrictions on organisations in terms of the emergency regulations, thereby opening the door for negotiations.

Mr Mandela was elected Deputy President and spokesman of the ANC. During the year he visited various countries. In June for example, he embarked on a 13-nation tour of Europe, the USA and Africa and later in the year he visited Japan, India, Australia, Indonesia and Malaysia.

President de Klerk also paid various visits to countries such as Spain, Portugal and Morocco. In September he was the first South African State President to pay an official visit to the USA. He met Mrs Margaret Thatcher of Britain for the third time in 15 months at the end of October.

These political developments have resulted in the ban on new investment and promotion of tourism being lifted by the UK government. Hungary lifted all sanctions, Spain revoked certain sanctions and SAA was granted landing rights in Kenya and Madagascar.

Other developments include the transformation of the Inkatha cultural movement into a political party on 14 July 1990. All four provincial congresses of the National Party as well as the federal congress decided to open party membership to all South Africans. The South African Communist Party held its first public rally in 40 years. The Reservation of Separate Amenities Act was scrapped on 15 October 1990. The national state of emergency was lifted in June with the exception of Natal (including KwaZulu).

Negotiations between the government and the ANC resulted in the signing of the Groote Schuur Minute in May. Both parties committed themselves to the attainment of a new constitution by peaceful means. The Pretoria Minute followed on 6 August. The ANC agreed to an immediate suspension of its armed struggle and the government agreed to consider lifting the state of emergency in Natal. The government revoked the emergency measures on 19 October.

Violence and unrest erupted at the beginning of the year and spread throughout the country within months. According to a report released by the Institute of Race Relations in April, Black-on-Black violence was at its highest level in many years. In August alone, violence in Black residential areas on the Reef claimed more lives than during the whole of the 1976 unrest period.

In an effort to stem the violence, the SAP employed countermeasures such as curfews, roadblocks and rewards for information on illegal possession of firearms.

In September 1990, the SAP announced the implementation of Operation Iron Fist to curb unrest in Black residential areas on the Witwatersrand. Unrest areas were declared in parts of the Cape Province in November and extended in the Transvaal to include two Black residential areas in Pretoria.

A one-man Commission of Inquiry into Certain Alleged Murders chaired by Mr Justice Harms into allegations of SAP hit squads and political violence led to the disbandment of the Civil Co-Operation Bureau (CCB).

Extremist right-wing groups either declared 'open war' on the government and the ANC or engaged in violent acts.

At midnight on 20 March 1990 the former mandated territory of South-West Africa became independent under the name of Namibia. This followed months of supervision by Untag forces after which Swapo won the elections overwhelmingly. The leader of Swapo, Mr Sam Nujoma, became President of Namibia. Thus ended what was regarded as the last vestige of colonialism in Southern Africa.

President de Klerk and the deputy leader of the ANC, Mr Nelson Mandela, discussed the violence in Black residential areas, the destruction of property and the destabilisation of communities on 8 December 1990.

After 30 years the President of the ANC, Mr Oliver Tambo, arrived in South Africa on 13 December 1990.

Acknowledgements:

Division: Social Development, Group: Social Dynamics, Human Sciences Research Council

Peoples and languages 3

Throughout its history, South Africa has been a geographic designation rather than a reflection of a national reality. In fact, the country came into being not because of any natural affinity between its peoples, but by artificial lines drawn on the map of Africa by imperial administrations in Britain. Apart from the White community, of both Dutch and British descent, these lines arbitrarily incorporated in South Africa a number of disparate Black peoples, such as the Xhosa and Zulu, with their own clearly defined territories. Just as arbitrarily, segments of other Black peoples on the subcontinent were excluded from South Africa while other segments of the same peoples were included. Examples are the Swazi, Basuto and Tswana.

There is also a large racially-mixed community, the Coloureds, mostly the product of miscegenation between the indigenous Khoikhoi, White settlers and Blacks. In 1860 the imperial authorities agreed to the introduction of a contingent of indentured labourers from India — the origin of the current Indian community in South Africa.

The result is that today the Republic of South Africa (RSA) has one of the most complex and diversified population mixes in the world, a rich mosaic of distinctive minorities. This is underscored by the fact that not one of RSA's 11 major languages is spoken by a majority of all the people.

Black peoples

The four major ethnic divisions are the Nguni, Sotho, Shangaan-Tsonga and Venda. Together, the Nguni and Sotho account for the largest percentage of the total Black population. The number of Black people in RSA totalled 21,6 million in June 1990.

Nguni

The Nguni language group comprises three subgroups within which a number of ramifications and a large number of subramifications can be distinguished:
— The **Zulu-speaking peoples** comprise about 300 tribes (approximately 7,6 million people) who live in the self-governing territory of Kwa-

Zulu, in Natal and in some of the urban areas, as well as the Swazi-speaking peoples (approximately 1,2 million) who live mainly in the self-governing territory of KaNgwane in the eastern Transvaal (excluding the Swazi-speaking peoples in Swaziland beyond the borders of South Africa.)
— The **Xhosa-speaking tribes** comprise the Xhosa, Pondo, Pondomise, Hlangwini, Xesibe, Bomvana, Hlubi, Fingo, Bhaca and Ngqika (approximately 3 million people.) Xhosa is one of the most heterogeneous languages with a number of dialects of which many are not directly linked to the original Xhosa on which the written language is based. In 1834 Xhosa became the first African language in South Africa for which its own grammar was composed.
— The **South Ndebele** is a smaller group who live in the central Transvaal. The group includes the Manala and Ndundza peoples, commonly known as the Mapoch. (The northern group has largely been assimilated by the Sotho.)

Sotho

Like the Nguni, the Sotho group (7,6 million) within the RSA comprises three subgroups, each with its own ramifications:
— The **North Sotho's** geopolitical domain is Lebowa in the northern Transvaal. This group includes the Pedi, Pulana, Pai, Kutswe, Kgaga-Kone, Phalaborwa, Nareng, Tlou, Gananwa, Hlaloga and the Kolobe (including the Lobedu).
— The **South Sotho** are found in the Kingdom of Lesotho and the Orange Free State. Other tribes belonging to this group are the Fokeng, Tlokwa, Kwena, Phetla, Phuti and Pulana.
— The **Tswana-speaking peoples** live in independent Bophuthatswana among other places, and include tribes such as the Thlaping and Koni.

Tsonga

The Tsonga (1,5 million) are related to the Tsonga of Mozambique. They are also known as the Shangaan-Tsonga. However, not all the subgroups involved accept this designation. As a language Tsonga is divided into related dialects and it is the Nkuna dialect which is primarily used as written language. The geopolitical base of the Tsonga is Gazankulu in the north-eastern

Transvaal. A small group, however, live at Kosi Bay in KwaZulu.

Venda

The Venda (200 000) are a largely homogeneous people, although they include the distinguishable Lemba, who evidently have a Semitic origin and regard themselves as nobility. The Venda currently live primarily in the independent Republic of Venda in the far north-eastern Transvaal as well as in the urban areas of the Transvaal.

Whites

Of the total of 5 million Whites in the RSA, an estimated 56 per cent are Afrikaans-speaking. This group traces its origins to the Dutch East India Company settlement at the Cape in 1652.

The ethnic composition of the Afrikaners is difficult to quantify but a reasonable estimate would be 40 per cent Dutch, 40 per cent German, 7,5 per cent French, 7,5 per cent English and Scots and 5 per cent other.

Approximately 38 per cent of the 5 million Whites are English-speaking. One of the earliest recorded landings of Englishmen in South Africa was in Natal rather than the Cape. This was in 1699 when the English ship, *Fidelity*, put ashore three crew members in what was to become known as Port Natal (afterwards Durban) to trade for ivory, but never returned for them.

Only in 1795, with the first British occupation of the Cape, was an English-speaking community established in South Africa. It had grown to between 70 and 80 people when, in 1803, the Batavian Republic took over the Cape. Under a scheme to protect the Cape Colony against persistent incursions by the Xhosa, the British government in 1820 encouraged the settlement of the eastern frontier by groups from various parts of England, Ireland, Scotland and Wales.

Table 1 Population figures (mid-year estimates)*

Population group	1970	1980	1990
	1 000	1 000	1 000
Whites	3 864	4 520	5 018
Coloureds	2 170	2 693	3 214
Asians	652	806	956
Blacks	13 450	17 062	21 609
TOTAL	20 136	25 081	80 797

* Excluding the republics of Transkei, Bophuthatswana, Venda and Ciskei
Source: Central Statistical Service

Large-scale British immigration into the territories north of the Orange River followed only after the discovery of diamonds near Kimberley in 1867 and gold on the Witwatersrand in 1886.

Apart from these two language groups in the White population, there are also other language groups such as the Dutch, Scandinavians, Germans, French, Flemish, Portuguese, Spanish, Italians, Poles, Croatians, Hungarians, Czechoslovakians, Lebanese, Greeks, Armenians, Serbians, Russians and Jews in the country.

The Chinese whose forebears arrived in the 1920s, form a small group of growing importance. (See chapter on Cultural diversity in South Africa.)

The Coloureds

Of the 3,2 million Coloureds approximately 85 per cent live in the Cape Province, mainly in the Cape Peninsula and neighbouring districts.

The Coloured people also include two subcultural groups — the Griquas and Cape Malays.

The **Griquas**, largely of Hottentot (Khoikhoin)-European ancestry, settled in the northwestern and north-eastern parts of the Cape Province. They have developed a culture of their own, characterised linguistically by a broken form of Dutch-Afrikaans with a peculiar yet dignified power of expression. Their religion, love of sacred song and choirs are the chief cultural features of this dwindling community which is gradually being absorbed by the rest of the Coloured population.

Most of the **Cape Malays** live in the Cape Peninsula, particularly in the well-known Malay Quarter in Cape Town. They are descendants of the early Muslim people brought to the Cape by the Dutch East India Company. Despite bondage and isolation they remained faithful to Islam. This is manifest in all their traditional ceremonies at feasts, weddings, funerals and pilgrimages to Mecca.

The history of the approximately 109 000 Coloureds in Natal goes back more than 150 years. Their heterogeneity is due to contact and assimilation between various racial groups. Excluding the immigrants from the Cape and other provinces who settled there over the years, they differ in ancestry from the bulk of the Coloureds in the rest of South Africa. They are descendants of three main subgroups — Euro-Africans, St Helenians and Mauritians.

Until a few decades ago, fishing, agriculture and the service industries were the main avenues of employment for the Coloured community.

Communication across cultural borders is an everyday occurrence

Most of these people, except for those on farms and rural settlements, have been fully integrated into the country's free-enterprise industrial economy.

Today members of this group serve in the highest legislative structure, hold positions as heads of government departments, educational institutions and faculties; there are several industrialists; merchants, owners of prosperous businesses, medical doctors, jurists, engineers, technicians, artisans and teachers.

The Asians

There are approximately 956 000 Asians in South Africa of which 938 700 are estimated to be Indians, 12 600 Chinese, 500 Japanese and 4 200 other Asians.

The first **Indians** came to South Africa in 1860 as indentured labourers of the Natal colonial government for Natal's sugar plantations. At the end of this period they could renew their original contract, return to India at government expense or accept a piece of Crown land. The majority chose to stay in South Africa.

For many decades the idea was that the Indians (both the Hindus and later the Muslims) should eventually be repatriated. It was only in 1961, after South Africa became a republic, that this notion was abandoned and the Indian community was allowed to stay as a permanent part of the South African population.

The largest percentage of the Indians still live in Natal, with other significant communities in Cape Town, Johannesburg and Pretoria. Most are fluent in English and a small percentage also speak Afrikaans. Their original mother tongues of Tamil, Telugu, Hindi, Gujarati and Urdu are still maintained within the different language groups. These languages are offered as part of the arts curriculum of the University of Durban-Westville and within the formal school curriculum at school, under the jurisdiction of the House of Delegates. In 1990 a total of 36 497 pupils studied Indian languages and Arabic.

Most of the **Muslims** in South Africa are of Indian ancestry. Their forebears arrived when some people left India on their own initiative in the last decade of the 19th century. Today they are scattered all over South Africa with the largest concentration in Natal. Most are fluent in English, but a small percentage also speak Afrikaans. Mother tongues such as Urdu, Gujarati and Marathi are still used. Arabic, as the language of Islam, plays an important role.

The major part of the **Chinese** population is found in Johannesburg and vicinity with smaller communities in Port Elizabeth, Pretoria, East London, Cape Town, Durban and Kimberley. The Chinese are fluent in English and often in Afrikaans, while some families still use Hakka or Cantonese or even Mandarin at home.

The small Japanese community communicates in English, but fully retains their language and cultural identity. Most of the Japanese live in Johannesburg where there is a school for their children.

Official languagues

English and Afrikaans are the country's two official languages. They are compulsory subjects in all schools for all population groups. They enjoy equal status and rights, which are entrenched in the Constitution.

Like the Afrikaners, **Afrikaans** had its beginning in 1652 when the Dutch language was transplanted to the new colony at the southern tip of Africa where it became the language of the government, cultural life and social intercourse. However, within the relatively short period of 150 years it was supplanted — at least as a spoken language — by Afrikaans, the only Germanic language to have originated outside Europe.

By the end of the 18th century the language spoken by the Boer-Afrikaners differed so markedly from Dutch in pronunciation, accent, syntax and vocabulary that it was quite unintelligible to new arrivals from Holland.

In written form, Afrikaans was probably first consciously used about 1795 in a satirical poem about the action at Muizenberg during the first British occupation of the Cape. After 1828, when press freedom was firmly established at the Cape, Afrikaans began to appear regularly in published form.

Publishing in Afrikaans became fairly common after 1850 and sources show that by that time the vernacular at the Cape had developed into 'Cape Dutch', vastly different from European Dutch. Many words were taken over from Malay, Portuguese, Khoikhoin, German, French, English and the African languages.

Afrikaans did not gain recognition as a medium of cultural exchange until the last quarter of the 19th century. This was due mainly to the supremacy of English over other languages and became the language of government and administration in 1822.

The latter half of the 19th century saw the rise of a conscious language movement to win recognition for Afrikaans as a literary and official medium of communication as well. This coincided with renewed Afrikaner political awareness.

Die Genootskap van Regte Afrikaanders (Association of True Afrikaners) was formed in

1875. Its aim was to strive for the full recognition of Afrikaans and to unite Afrikaners in all parts of the country. Soon a periodical was issued, *Di Afrikaanse Patriot*. The leading figure was S J du Toit, a clergyman and writer.

This movement was succeeded at the beginning of the 20th century by the far stronger second language movement, characterised by a literary revival which produced the language's first great poets such as Eugène Marais, Louis Leipoldt and Totius, son of S J du Toit of the first language movement.

Afrikaans gradually came to be recognised generally as a cultural language with exciting possibilities. Rules of spelling for Afrikaans were laid down by the *Akademie vir Taal, Lettere en Kuns* (Academy for Language, Literature and Arts) — a body which was to co-ordinate and direct Afrikaans cultural and scientific endeavour.

One of the major ideals of the first language movement was achieved in 1933 when the Bible was translated into Afrikaans. This was followed about a decade later by the psalm and hymnbook.

Afrikaans was accepted as an official language by an Act of Parliament in 1925. The first regular Afrikaans service was introduced by the South African Broadcasting Corporation (SABC) in 1937. A sustained effort is being made to preserve the purity of Afrikaans vis-à-vis English and to extend its capacity for expression into all areas.

Although the history of **English** in South Africa only began in 1795, the language had begun to be influenced long before that by other languages spoken in South Africa, more especially Cape Dutch. English explorers, naturalists and scientists who visited the Cape used words from those languages to name the many new things they encountered among the inhabitants, especially indigenous flora and fauna, topographical features and customs.

Once isolated from its source, English in South Africa (SAE) developed into a regional version of the language, characterised not merely by its vocabulary, but also by pronunciation, idiom and other usages.

In spite of a marked influx of Americanisms and 'Queen's English' into SAE, British rather than American usage is observed in the spelling and grammar of SAE, just as British elements in the vocabulary finds greater favour than their American equivalents.

In 1961 the English Academy of Southern Africa was established to promote English culture and language, the mother tongue of one of South Africa's major communities and a second language to other South Africans.

African languages

In Southern Africa the Bantu-speaking population represents four main major language groups, namely the Nguni, Sotho, Tsonga and Venda. (See population groups above.)

Colloquial languages of urban areas
With so many languages spoken within one country, compromises are inevitable, especially in the Black residential areas on the fringes of the main industrial centres where all ethnic groups and widely differing languages live in close contact with each other.

Widely differing languages such as the Nguni and Sotho languages have so far resisted large-scale intermixing, but pure Northern or Southern Sotho, Tswana, Zulu or Xhosa are now encountered only in the self-governing territories. The common tongue used in most Black residential areas is either a hybrid form of Zulu and Xhosa or some Sotho variation often larded with Zulu words. These colloquial languages are fast becoming the most powerful communication links among the majority of Black people.

Fanakalo
Fanakalo is a pidgin language developed on the mines where the many different tongues spoken by the Black workers soon created a need for a common language that could easily be learnt by both Black and White speakers. It is based on the vocabularies of Zulu, English and Afrikaans and has a very limited syntax. Blacks regard it as an inferior and undignified medium of communication.

Foreign influences
Western civilisation has affected traditional Black lifestyles and cultures in many important ways, not least with regard to their languages. These languages, rich as they are in vocabulary and flexible as they may be in expression, could not define all the new things brought by the White man's civilisation. Many English and Afrikaans words have been therefore incorporated into the various African languages.

A language board has been established for each of the African languages. These boards use the mechanisms of the African languages themselves to find, adapt and even coin words to suit the changed conditions of Black life. Blacks have shown themselves to be very resourceful in creating new words. In Northern Sotho for instance, a car is known as a land-eater, a revolver as a drumstick, while condensed milk is known as a cow-in-the-tin! In many cases the flexible nature of the African languages made coining unnecessary, as existing words could easily be adapted to new circumstances.

An example is 'writing', and 'reading', formerly unknown to Blacks. Denoting these in the various Sotho languages presented no serious problem as the words 'to scratch' or, 'make marks', could be used to express writing, while the word 'count' could be adapted to express the idea of reading.

Acknowledgements:
Administration: House of Delegates
Administration: House of Representatives
Central Statistical Service
Prof J B Hartman, Department of Anthropology and Archaeology, University of Pretoria

Cultural diversity is an everyday reality within the South African context. This can be attributed to the complexity of the country's population, since many cultural groups have immigrated to South Africa over the years, introducing their traditions in the process.

These cultural heritages are mutually respected and there is extensive communication and cultural interchange, although each cultural group is still clearly distinguishable.

Black population

More than half of South Africa's total Black population still upholds traditional values. These values derive from a distinctive African cosmology characterised by, among other things

- acceptance of a masculine supreme entity as a creator, and acceptance of the belief in ancestral spirits and supernatural powers (sorcery);
- the right of primogeniture; polygymous marriage; forbidden or preferential marriages; patrilineal descent;
- a subsistence economy and division of work according to sex;
- art as a functional activity.

In respect of language the Black population can be divided into four main groups, namely the Nguni, the Sotho, the Tsonga and the Venda.

Nguni

The Nguni language group comprises three subgroups which are further subdivided:

The Zulu-speaking peoples

According to traditional Zulu belief, Unkulunkulu (old, old man) is the creator of life. His daughter, uNomkubulwana, is, however, closer to man. She is associated with rain and thus economic prosperity depends on her. Regular feasts are held in her honour and beer is poured as a sacrifice. In times of drought a field has to be planted specially for her. There is also a belief that girls can persuade her to send rain by donning their brothers' clothes and taking over their jobs as herdsmen.

Ancestral spirits are very important to the patriarchal Zulu. They are believed to control everyday life and must be appeased with sacrifices. Cattle are a link with the ancestral spirits, while the medicine man has an important ritual role.

Many Zulus have been converted to the Christian faith and some to Islam. Soweto, the Black city near Johannesburg, has its own mosque.

The political unity of the Zulu was broken at the end of the 19th century, but the chieftainship of the king was later reaccepted. Today King Goodwill Zwelithini is the constitutional monarch of KwaZulu. The king forms the apex of a neatly defined structure of authority consisting of tribal chiefs and ward headmen as well as lineage and family heads.

Zulu marriage is traditionally polygymous to enable the man to extend more family ties. Marriage arrangements are made by senior members of the respective families. After marriage non-related people are linked religiously, politically and economically.

Transition from childhood to adulthood is ceremoniously accomplished by initiation rites. These ceremonies differ from tribe to tribe, but mainly involve a period of seclusion, formal education concerning rules of conduct, subjection to physical hardship, and wearing of special clothing.

The Zulu's traditional economic system is subsidiary and based on the family, which is a self-sustaining unit. Family means do not differ greatly because any surplus is offered to the spirits of the ancestors. Time is not regarded as a factor and the Zulu focusses more on the present than on the future.

Both men and women are economically active. The men control the valuable possessions, namely cattle — also used as dowry or 'lobolo'. Lobolo is an institution among Black peoples in terms of which a young girl can be obtained as a wife by handing over a number of cattle to the prospective bride's family, thus creating mutual obligations and a permanent bond between the two families. Other goods — today even money — may sometimes be used as lobolo. Women are responsible for household chores and till the fields. Cattle are slaughtered mainly for sacrificial purposes.

The rural Zulu people live in a circular settlement, or kraal, surrounding round beehive-shaped huts of differing sizes. The circular form symbolises unity, while hierarchical differences are expressed by the varying sizes of the huts as well as their position in the kraal. To emphasise the social importance of each, the right half of the hut is reserved for the men and the left for women. The rear is reserved for ancestral spirits and reflects the importance of religion. The hearth in the centre of the hut symbolises unity within the family.

Dress and beadwork reflect social status. A girl may, for example, only wear the black leather skirt of a married woman once she is about to get married. Newly-wed women show respect for their in-laws by wearing strings of beads over their eyes to cover their faces. The abdomen of a pregnant woman must be covered by a fur-tanned buckskin which indicates her status.

To the Zulu, beadwork is not merely decorative. Before the existence of written language, it was a primary form of communication. Different colours carry different meanings which vary from region to region. These messages often pertain to the social status of the individual, so that one can see if a woman is married and how many children she has. New, brightly coloured beads are added to the headdress of a fertile woman.

Other crafts practised by the Zulu include basket weaving, pottery, woodwork and fashioning bone and ivory ornaments. Most of these objects have a practical use.

Acting, dancing and music traditionally centre on ritual sacrifices, during which parts are enacted. Repeated sounds and movements gradually unite the group. Even in this unit there is hierarchic differentiation as formations are based on seniority.

Within the context of urbanisation traditional architecture has made way for western-style buildings. Today Zulus wear western clothing sometimes decorated with traditional beadwork or with aprons and headrings. Handmade articles are made mostly for the tourist market.

Zulu artists came into contact with western graphic art, painting and sculpture which they incorporated into their new life-style. The result is a strong, expressive addition to South African art in which religion, social conditions, political protest and community projects play an important part.

The Swazi

The Swazi are not ruled by their king alone, but also by his mother. Traditionally he is associated with the lion and she with the elephant cow. This matriarchal element is not isolated, but is also found in other facets of Swazi culture. The mothers of kraal heads and tribal chiefs are held in equally high esteem. There is less emphasis on military power, while female rituals — such as the reed dance of the maidens — have an important part. The importance of female activities such as preparation of food and tilling of the fields is clearly visible in the layout of the kraal.

The harvest festival of the women serves to strengthen the position of the king. Dress reflects unique Swazi traditions and the similarities between the traditions for men and women. Swazis of both sexes use neckerchiefs of printed material. Those of the women are usually red and those of the men brown.

The hairstyles of both men and women are exceptional. Women wear their hair high on their heads, held in position with a hairnet and band. Men use soap or mix the ashes of aloe leaves with clay to sculpt a solid form with their hair. During ceremonies men wear head-dresses made from the tailfeathers of the black finch or sakabula. The red wingfeathers of the lourie are worn by both men and women and usually indicate royal descent. Porcupine quills are worn in the hair.

The Xhosa-speaking peoples

Two groups are identified among the Xhosa. The group known as the 'school people' has become christianised and westernised. The other group, known as the 'red people', has maintained the traditional way of life.

Within the context of the Xhosa the 'amagqirha' or traditional healers are regarded as chosen by the ancestors and they play an important role in the 'treatment' of disease and misfortune. Misfortune is regarded as the work of witches and sorcerers who work through confidants and henchmen. Uthikoloshe, believed to be a small hairy man who loves playing with children and who can harm women, is greatly feared. So is a fantasy bird which sheds its own fat in a fire to create lightning. Witches ride on baboons and water creatures are responsible for drownings.

The traditional political system is characterised by paramount chiefs, tribal chiefs, and ward headmen, assisted by a number of advisors. Hierarchy is less strict and huts are loosely arranged around a cattle-kraal with no definite fencing.

The Xhosa have a deep-rooted fear of incest and therefore prefer exogamic marriages. Initiation on reaching puberty is very important, involving a complex system of taboos. Great emphasis is placed on marriage, the solemnisation of which can last for up to ten days. The marriage ceremony is held at the groom's kraal. The bride and other young people from her own kraal live in guest huts for the duration of the festivities. The bride may show no signs of joy. She must grieve because she is leaving her family.

Xhosa dress reflects unique customs. The uncovered breasts of women indicate that they are nubile. Men, women and older boys wear tanned skins or blankets which are dyed with red ochre, while white clothes are worn only by the 'amagqirha' and at festivals. Also characteristic of the 'red people' are the large, folded headcloths of married women and clay-painted faces. These customs are believed to derive from contact with the hats and make-up worn by the early British settlers in the eastern Cape. Long-stemmed pipes — only for women with a certain number of children — and tobacco pouches decorated with beads, are also characteristic of the Xhosa.

The Ndebele of the Transvaal

Ndebele women shave their heads so that only a few tufts remain. Before marriage a bride's head is shaved clean. During the marriage ceremony she carries a doll which symbolises her fertility, and she also remains disguised until all the female members of her husband's kraal have welcomed her.

Ndebele art has made a unique contribution to South African cultural life. The Ndebele are well-known for their decorative murals and beadwork. Beadwork is used on women's clothing, each garment reflecting a certain status. A well-dressed Ndebele girl can wear up to 25 kilograms of copper, leather and beads. Men and boys wear western clothing only.

Contact between the Ndebele and Westerners has recently resulted in the incorporation of new motifs, such as cars, aeroplanes, trains, letters and numbers in murals and beadwork.

Because of increasing contact with Whites, the original round huts of the Ndebele have gradually made way for rectangular ones. The Ndebele have, however, also had their influence on western architecture. In recent years postmodern architecture in cities has often featured the characteristic forms of Ndebele murals with their typical blue, pink and purple colours.

The Sotho language groups

The Sotho language group consists of three subgroups and a number of subdivisions.

The North Sotho

The different North Sotho tribes do not form a political entity. Although there are many cultural differences, they have much in common.

Characteristic of the Lobedu — one of the North Sotho tribes — is veneration of Modjadji, the Rain Queen. According to tradition, she can create rain and was formerly greatly feared and respected. Modjadji may not marry, but she may have children so that one of her daughters can succeed her after her ritual suicide.

The North Sotho — like other Sotho — live in large units or 'kgoros' which consist of a merging of households divided by reed fences or clay walls. The area in the middle of the 'kgoro' serves as a meeting place while the men gather in a secluded section for purposes of politics and justice.

The identity of the respective tribes is indicated by totems or emblems. The totems bear the emblem of an animal and within each tribe that particular animal is sacred and may not be killed. Thus the Pedi are known by the sign of the porcupine; the Pulana by the lion; the Nareng by the buffalo; and the Thlou by the wild pig.

Like all Sotho the North Sotho believe in endogamous marriages, which mean that people marry into their own family group. A man should, for example, preferably first marry the daughter of his mother's brother. Such marriages are economically motivated because the cattle given as the dowry remain in the family.

The North Sotho use grass for bracelets and ladies' petticoats. Sometimes these petticoats are worn under western skirts.

South Sotho

More than 70 per cent of the South Sotho are Christians, about half of them Catholic.

The South Sotho, mainly a mountain people, are known as excellent horsemen. They are easily identified by their ponies as well as their brightly-coloured blankets and cone-shaped hats. Cattle are not important to their culture with sheep and angora goats being more suited to their environment.

Tswana

The Tswana are sometimes also called the 'West Sotho'. This grouping consists of more than 60 tribes, each with its own chief and tribal council. Their large settlements are divided into wards under the authority of hereditary heads. Matters of common concern are discussed with all the men and a majority of votes is decisive.

Unique to the Tswana is the custom that only the groom's parents decide how many head of cattle should form the dowry to be given to the parents of his bride.

The Tswana are also known for their traditional clay pots and large clay granaries. Today they make pots in bright colours, sculpt ceramic totem animals and make clothing which combines traditional and western elements very effectively.

Tsonga

The Tsonga are related to the Tsonga of Mozambique. They are also known as Shangana Tsonga, a term which refers to Soshangane, a former Zulu war chief, who subjugated some of the Tsonga tribes. Not all subgroups accept this term. Tsonga as a language is divided into related dialects.

The political system of these people changed considerably because of the Shangana influence. Today tribal chiefs (tikosi) and ward headmen (tindhuna), acting within a framework based on descent and social status, exercise authority.

The Tsonga economy includes hunting and fishing. Other Black groupings sometimes disparagingly refer to the Tsonga as 'fish-eaters'.

The Tsonga recognise a few preferential marriages with women belonging to related clans and the bond between the bride's family and that of the groom is sealed when the dowry (lobolo) is handed over. The marriage contract becomes binding as soon as the bride is delivered to the groom's family.

Overhanging roofs forming a cool porch are characteristic of Tsonga architecture. Women traditionally wear a short skirt, completely covered with beads. The Tsonga are well known for their mine dances, carried out to the beat of drums and horns and a wide variety of musical instruments such as the mbila.

Venda

The Venda form a relatively homogeneous group, which includes the distinctive Lemba who are probably of Semitic descent.

Venda culture is matriarchal and female ancestral spirits are worshipped, while women also act as high priestesses. Mixing of male and female principles is manifest in the 'domba' (python dance), a fertility rite during puberty. Girls perform the dance while the boys attend.

The Venda have sacred objects such as black bulls, black she-goats and large stones which are all connected with the worship of ancestral spirits. They also have sacred places, such as Lake Fundudzi and the Thathe Vondo rain forest. Many legends have originated from this, like that of the girls who were allegedly sacrificed in the lake after the 'domba', or the uncircumcised chiefs who were buried in the forest. Also unique to the religion of the Venda is the traditional healer's use of multiform astragali and floating

seeds in a bowl of water for purposes of divining. As there have been missionaries among them since 1860, many Venda have been christianised.

On the political level the Venda are divided among approximately 30 independent chieftains. Historically they benefitted from this, since attackers like the Swazi in 1839 could subjugate only one chieftaincy at a time.

Cattle are not very important to the Venda because of the tsetsefly which is prevalent in this region. Iron hoes, rather than cattle, served as dowry in the past. Men and women work their own individual fields and do not use each others' without permission. The Lemba are traders, while the Venda as a whole provided the first migrant workers to cities.

According to anthropologists the Lemba, recognisable by their Semitic features, are probably a blend of Arabs and Blacks. They do not eat pork, or the meat of any animal which has not bled to death.

The Venda are known for their extensive use of stone walls, textured leather and beadwork, for their grain vessels which are actually 'sculptures', for decorating their huts with charcoal, white clay and ochre, for brightly-coloured dolls, and for kudu-horn music.

Unique to the Venda are 'play kraals', miniatures of a real kraal. Children build these kraals and play there while their parents work. This ancient form of the modern 'nursery school' is an example of South Africa's fascinating cultural puzzle.

Whites

South Africa's White population is largely heterogeneous and is scattered over the country. Although Afrikaans and English are the country's two official languages, and most of those speaking a different language speak English and sometimes also Afrikaans, most immigrants retain their language identity.

With the exception of Afrikaans and English speakers, the figures henceforth used for each White cultural group, are those obtained from leaders within the cultural group. These figures also include non-South African residents.

Most Whites in South Africa share these variables to some extent. In this respect only the most important points are covered in this chapter.

The English-speaking Whites

White South Africans with English as home language include the English, Irish, Scots, Welsh,

Australians, Americans and Canadians. English-speaking South Africans brought with them a world language and literature and some of the earliest settlers were poets and newspaper editors. The English-speaking expanded their capitalist tradition in the country thus contributing much to the free market economy.

Other contributions of the English to South African culture include the establishment of exclusive clubs, Africana paintings by artists such as Baines and Bowler, Victorian and Edwardian architecture, Scottish music and Welsh singing, and place names such as Carletonville (named after the Canadian engineer R Carleton-Jones).

English-speaking South Africans are mostly Christian Protestants (Anglican, Presbyterian and Methodist) and have contributed towards both christianisation and to church architecture in the country.

Afrikaners

The Afrikaans language was developed locally.

Following the Depression of the early 1930s the Afrikaner played an increasingly important role in the economy and today holds positions on the executive of most private companies. Since 1948 the Afrikaner has taken the political lead and has been responsible for the most important organisational structures in the country, as is now the case with the emergence of so-called 'negotiation politics'.

The Afrikaner is also known for his pioneering spirit, desire for independence, adaptability and hospitality. According to Professor P J Nel of the Department of History, University of Pretoria, the Afrikaner community is unity-conscious, strongly bound to its culture, nation, country, language, religion, institutions and organisations.

Dutch

About 30 000 Dutch reside in South Africa. Most are Protestants who still use Dutch as home language. The background of the Dutch in South Africa goes back to 1652 since which time their language has been the primary source of Afrikaans.

Today the South African Dutch are totally integrated in the economy, professions and other trades. They preserve their own traditions informally, while their characteristic critical approach plays a corrective and directive role in many fields.

Scandinavians

Scandinavians in South Africa include Swedes, Finns, Danes and Norwegians. The members of this small Nordic community (only about 1 000 on the Witwatersrand) share the Protestant Lutheran Nordic Church of St Johannes, which was consecrated in Johannesburg in 1976.

Like the other Scandinavians, the Swedes brought with them a proud tradition of applied arts. Glassware, design in silver and stainless steel and furniture design are a few examples of how the Scandinavian tradition has manifested itself in South Africa.

The Finns brought with them the 'sauna' and the work of world renowned artist Karin Jaroszynska became part of the South African scene. The Danes contributed to the processing of semi-precious stones, while the Norwegians with their Viking background experimented with ship-building.

German-speaking peoples

In South Africa about 33 000 Germans, 20 000 Austrians and 7 000 German-speaking Swiss speak German at home. German South Africans are mostly members of the Lutheran Church, although a number are Catholics. Missionaries such as Merensky, Leipoldt, Schmolke and Strassberger made their mark on religious life in South Africa.

The German community has contributed much to industry and technology. German opera and German beer festivals are reminders of the German presence in the country.

There are a number of Austrian clubs in South Africa which organise rose balls and performances of typical Austrian music. Steyr Guedes and Martini rifles are both of Austrian origin. After World War II Lippizaner horses were imported from Austria and their performances are still enjoyed at Kyalami.

While the Austrian community is predominantly Catholic, the German-speaking Swiss in South Africa are mostly Protestant.

Like other immigrant groups, the Swiss have been fully integrated into the South African economy. They have contributed greatly to industry, manufacture of precision instruments and jewellery. They still practise traditional sports such as schwingen, play the alpenhorn and yodel.

French-speaking peoples

The small number of French-speaking people in South Africa include French, Walloons, French Canadians and Swiss. Where the earliest French immigrants and their descendants — most of whom have been completely assimilated — were and still are Protestant, the French who arrived later were mainly Catholic.

French presence in South Africa has contributed to the wine industry, motoring technology (after the establishment of Citroën in the country in 1938), closer contact with international haute couture, the perfume industry and haute cuisine, and has provided contact for South African graphic artists. With regard to culture and language, the Alliance-Française has over the years played an important role in strengthening the French presence in South Africa.

Flemings

A number of Flemings came to the Cape with Jan van Riebeeck in 1652. The first brewer and brandy distiller at the Cape was a Fleming from Geel, Jan van Passel. The oldest written account and route map of the Cape interior were compiled and drawn by Flemings.

Other signs of Flemish presence in South Africa are the Flemish Oblate, Brothers of Love, Sisters of Love and Marist Brothers who came to South Africa as missionaries and contributed to the process of christianisation. The Flemish literature of Gezelle and Streuvels influenced the work of Jan Cilliers, Totius and C M van den Heever, while Tine Balder, a Flemish elocutionist, set a standard in this field. Flemish graphic artists such as Maurice van Essche and Father Frans Claerhout enriched the arts and the tradition of Flemish lace is still an inspiration to South African lace makers.

Today the Flemish in South Africa are mainly Catholic. They maintain and strengthen bonds between South Africa and Belgium through the Afrikaans-Flemish Association. They have been completely integrated into the South African economy.

South Americans

Representatives of virtually all the South American countries reside in South Africa today, and are making a considerable contribution in various fields. Seven of the South American countries have either embassies or consulates in South Africa. The University of South Africa has established a Centre for Latin American Studies with the specific object of promoting a greater awareness of Latin America in South Africa, but also to foster mutual understanding and to strengthen cultural and trade ties between South African and Latin American countries.

Portuguese

The Portuguese community claims to represent one fifth of the White community of South Africa, although official statistics estimate it to be only about 35 000.

Currently there are approximately 30 Portuguese community centres on the Witwatersrand alone, the *Associacia da Colonia Portuguesa* having been established as early as 1938. These centres feature traditional Portuguese music, dances and dishes. Most of the Portuguese in South Africa are Catholic. They have made a major contribution to cultivation of fruit and vegetables, crafts, professions, the restaurant industry and soccer. Traditional needlework, ceramics and pewter ware are other Portuguese contributions to the cultural goods of the country.

There is a noticeable Portuguese influence in Johannesburg's southern suburbs such as La Rochelle, Troyeville, Bertrams and Bezuidenhout Valley where the traditional Portuguese architecture with its bright colours, balconies, tiles and typical ornaments are a familiar sight.

Spaniards

The Spanish community in South Africa is small (less than 1 000) and is centered mainly in Cape Town. This Catholic community has contributed to South Africa's cultural diversity in two main areas, firstly Spanish domestic architecture — characterised by thick white walls and small windows and used widely because it is suited to the South African climate — and secondly Spanish dancing which has become part of the repertoire of many dancing teachers in the country.

Italians

Community leaders estimate that there are approximately 60 000 Italian-speaking people in South Africa, who are mostly Catholic. They play an important role in industry, commerce, engineering, the textile industry and paper manufacturing. The *Club Dante Alighieri* was founded to preserve Italian literature and film tradition. Italian car designs, ceramic tiles, leather goods, glassware and traditional cuisine have also become part of South Africa.

Polish

The Polish in South Africa are Catholic, well educated and integrated into the professional life and economy of South Africa. They have erected the Katynian Memorial in Melrose Park, Johannesburg where a service is held annually in memory of the 14 000 Polish officers who died at Katyn and elsewhere in the Soviet Union in 1940.

There are several creative architects, engineers and artists among the South African Polish community. Particularly worthy of mention are artists Krystyna Romanowicz, Tadeusz Jaroszynski and Stanislav Kors.

Greeks

About 60 000 Greeks live in South Africa and are members of the Greek Orthodox Church.

With the church, Greek schools like Saheti in Johannesburg, Hellenic Associations and newspapers like *Nea Hellas, Afrikanis* and *Akropolis* preserve Greek traditions. Religion and the church play a prime role. Church festivals such as Passover, Christmas and the Festival of the Holy are celebrated with emphasis on tradition. Language is important and still spoken by third and fourth generation South African Greeks.

The Greek community in South Africa makes and owns beautiful lace and embroidery work. A small Cyprian subgroup is also known for silver filigree and paintings made of cocoons on velvet.

Croatians

Approximately 7 000 Croatians originating from Yugoslavia speak Serbo-Croatian as a home language and live in South Africa. Many of them came to South Africa in the 20th century to escape communist rule.

Hungarians

South Africa's Hungarian-speaking community is about 4 000 strong. Most South African Hungarians speak English and celebrate traditional feasts and the 1956 uprising against the Russian invasion of Budapest. This small Catholic community has its own church in Johannesburg and celebrates its national day on 15 March.

Czechoslovakians

Between 1620 and 1640 Protestants in Czechoslovakia were forced to flee to countries such as Holland. A few came to South Africa, bringing with them surnames like Horak. The Bata Company from Czechoslovakia was founded in Port Elizabeth and Pinetown and attracted immigrants. After the Russian invasion of Czechoslovakia in 1968 the SA government gave permission to another 6 000 Czechoslovakians to immigrate. Today this Catholic community has nearly 8 000 members. The Czechoslovakians have been integrated into the South African economy. They brought Bohemian crystal to the country. Most of the beads used by Blacks in their works of art come from Czecho-slovakia.

Lebanese

There are nearly 18 000 Lebanese in South Africa. They practise the Maronite rite of the Catholic religion. The Lebanese speak English or Afrikaans while some still speak Syrian and Aramaic. The Lebanese brought a rich cultural heritage with them. Although they have been fully integrated into the South African economy, they preserve their cultural identity. The Maronitic church plays an important role in this.

Armenians

The Armenian community in South Africa is active and true to its traditions, although it has only 120 members. The Armenians became integrated in the economy, but retained and promoted their culture. The Armenian Orthodox Church is very important to them. They are very proud of their language. Music, dancing, dress and food with a distinctive character are some of the contributions the Armenians have made towards the culture of South Africa.

Serbians

There are approximately 5 000 Serbians in South Africa who originate from what is today known as Yugoslavia. The Serbians share their land of birth with the Croatians and in South Africa they are traditionally a totally separate cultural group. They speak Serbo-Croatian, but use the Cyrillic alphabet characteristic of the Slavian culture of people belonging to the Eastern Orthodox Church. In religion the Serbians also differ from the Catholic Croatians. Even their traditional dress, dances and music vary from the Croatian cultural group.

Russians

A small group (approximately 100) of Russians live in South Africa. They belong to the Russian Orthodox Church and practise their religion in the Chapel of St Nicholas in Johannesburg where most are resident.

Jews

The Jewish community in South Africa is approximately 120 000 strong and practises Judaism. There is a small group of Ultra Orthodox Jews and a larger group of Reform Jews but the major group is Orthodox.

The South African Zionist Federation handles international Jewish interests in South Africa and the South African Jewish Board of Deputies deals with the affairs of South African Jews. Many organisations are affiliated to the latter to maintain Jewish traditions, education and charity work. In this regard Jewish schools play an important role.

Jews have always been prominent in the South African economy and surnames such as Mosenthal, Schlesinger and Oppenheimer are well known. The Jews made a major contribution to the ostrich feather industry, the diamond and gold industries and the banking sector.

South African art has greatly benefitted from the presence of Jews in the country. Examples are the contributions of Sidney Clouts and Ruth Miller to English literature, Olga Kirsch and the Lion-Cachets' contributions to Afrikaans, the creativity of Lippy Lipshitz, Moses Kottler and Irma Stern in fine arts, Betty Pack's role in music teaching and Barry Simon's contribution to the local Black theatre. Johannesburg's Civic Theatre and Cape Town's Baxter Theatre were both designed by Jewish architects.

Ali Bacher and Ilana Kloss are two South African Jews who excelled in sport. The familiar 'Computicket' system in common use was the brainchild of Percy Tucker.

Hebrew is spoken, written and studied in South Africa, as was Yiddish after the foundation of *The Dorem Afrikaner Yiddische Kultur Federatzie* in 1946.

Coloureds

The Coloureds number approximately three million. Eighty five per cent of them (including the Malays) live in the western Cape with smaller but significant communities in the northern Cape (the Griquas) and Natal. The remainder are scattered over the country.

The Coloureds per se, are of Euro-African descent, the Griquas are mainly of Hottentot-European descent and the origin of both dates back to the arrival of the Whites in South Africa. The Malays are descendants of the early Muslims who came from India, Ceylon, China, Indonesia and Malagasy and became assimilated into the eastern colonies of the Netherlands from where they were imported to the Cape by the Dutch East India Company. The Malays preserve their own traditions in respect of dress and food. Some members of the Natal Coloured community are descendants of the inhabitants of St Helena and Mauritius.

Ninety per cent of all Coloureds speak Afrikaans while the remainder speak English. Adam Small and S V Petersen made a major contribution to Afrikaans literature. The Coloureds are known for their sense of humour and wit. Eighty seven per cent are Christian and 7 per cent (mostly Malays) are Muslim.

Most Coloureds identify strongly with western norms and customs. This trend became stronger as more Coloureds moved away from fishing, farming and the trades to professions and the academic. Today the University of the Western Cape serves the Coloureds and most staff members are Coloureds.

The establishment of the parliamentary House of Representatives for Coloureds in the 1980s also served to move the Coloureds closer to western structures.

Asians

South Africa has some 930 000 Asians. Nearly 917 500 of them are Indians who, according to cultural diversity, may be divided into the larger Hindu group (70 per cent) and a smaller Muslim group (20 per cent). The remainder consists of approximately 12 000 Chinese and 500 Japanese.

Hindus

The Hindus have been fully integrated into the South African economy. The women often wear the traditional sari, a six meter length of brightly coloured silk draped around them.

Both the Hindus and Muslim have in recent years been prominent in politics in the House of Delegates. Indians such as Professor Bhai Parmanand and Mahatma Ghandi, who visited South Africa earlier in this century, contributed largely to cultural self-confidence within the Hindu community.

Hinduism is essentially monotheistic by nature. Second to this monotheism is a complex polytheism which in the Hindu religion consists firstly of the trinity of Brahma the creator, Vishnu the conserver and Shiva the destroyer. Each has a female companion, reincarnations and aspects which are symbolised by animals, physical characteristics, actions, instruments, objects and attributes. Thus the Hindu religion reflects a complex cosmology within which each subdivision of the Absolute finds a rightful place.

The Hindu religion tolerantly inclines towards assimilation rather than exclusion, accepting the value of all other religions and even incorporating certain of their aspects. Neither does it draw any important distinction between men and women. Its character is dramatic and this is reflected in ornamented temples, bright colours, a variety of textures and aromas (such as those of camphor and incense burnt in temples during festivals).

The *Vedas* and *Bhagavad Gita* are important texts within the Hindu religion and gurus and Swamis practise transcendental meditation which is also recommended for believers striving to become one with the Absolute.

The most important Hindu festival is *Deepavali* which celebrates the new year of the Hindu calender. During the festivities food, clothing and other necessities are distributed to the needy in the community, but as is the custom, there is no beef, as cattle are sacred to the Hindu.

Lamps are lit during *Deepavali* as light symbolises the victory of good over evil to the Hindu. Light also plays an important part at weddings which are celebrated lavishly in temples. The symbolic nature of light similarly comes to the fore in the Hindu fire dance while the golden thread in the women's costumes reflects light when traditional dances are performed. These dances are accompanied by the exotic sounds of Hindu musical intruments such as the sitar.

Muslims

With the exception of the Malays — of whom the 17th century Sheik Yusuf is regarded as the founder of Islam in South Africa and whose grave can be seen at Faure — and a small White Muslim community centered around the Muslim Dawah Society in Johannesburg, most of South Africa's Muslims are of Indian descent. Their forebears came to South Africa at the end of the 19th century when people fled on their own initiative from India. Today these Muslims are scattered over the whole of South Africa, with the largest concentration in Natal.

The Muslims have been fully integrated into South Africa's economy. The women wear slacks (izar) under a long straight dress (qamis) and a long scarf (dawni) around their heads. Orthodox women wear long wide black dresses and a veil.

In suburbs such as Lenasia and Laudium, Muslim houses can often be identified by a grey or sandy colour and a simple, large block shape. This relates to the so-called 'kutum', which is an extensive system of family relationships. A son

and his wife are, for example, expected to live with his parents as a sign of respect.

Islam involves monolithic recognition of Allah as the Supreme Being and the laws of the Koran. According to Professor J A Naudé of the Department of Semitic Languages at the Rand Afrikaans University, these questions are negotiable and not open to any syncretic mixing. Muslims in South Africa observe their religion strictly with regular times of prayer, halaal food and a firm family structure. Decoration of their houses and mosques is in abstract, geometric patterns.

The Jumma Masjid in Durban is the largest mosque in the southern hemisphere. It is a gathering place for believers who want to pray and always faces Mecca, the centre of Islam. Inside certain areas are reserved for men and women and ablution facilities are used for physical cleansing before entering the mosque. The 'imam' leads the ceremony after the 'muezzin' has called believers to prayer from a tower.

Muslims do not eat pork and their most important time of year is *Ramadan* , a month during which they avoid food, liquids and sexual activity from sunrise to sunset. Directly after this follows the feast of *Eid al Fitr*. Another important occasion is *Eid-U-Adha* which recalls Abraham's willingness to sacrifice his son to God.

Austerity characterises Muslim art. The literature of the Koran is central to this and the singing and recitation of its contents in the mosque is very important.

Chinese

Most Chinese are Catholic, with a small number belonging to the Baptist Church. Some older

Table 1 Migration by occupational group

Occupational group	Nov 1988 to Oct 1989			Nov1989 to Oct 1990		
	Immi-grants	Emigrants	Net gain/loss	Immi-grants	Emigrants	Net gain/loss
Professional, semi-professional and technical occupations	1 346	1 041	+305	1 865	1 038	+827
Managerial, executive and administrative occupations	674	204	+470	842	250	+592
Clerical and sales occupations	1 252	449	+803	1 892	583	+1 309
Transport, delivery and communications occupations	26	16	+10	45	20	+25
Service occupations	186	55	+131	258	63	+195
Farming and related occupations	54	16	+38	73	13	+60
Artisans, apprentice and related occupations	767	280	+487	1 173	389	+784
Production foreman and supervisor, miner and quarry worker, operator, production and related worker	181	44	+ 137	282	88	+ 194
Occupation unspecified and not elsewhere classified	483	269	+ 214	300	132	+ 168
Not economically active	5 959	2 619	+ 3 340	7 662	2 315	+ 5 347
TOTAL	10 928	4 993	+ 5 935	14 392	4 891	+ 9 501

Source: Central Statistical Service

Chinese, however, still believe in ancestral and other forms of traditional worship.

South African Chinese are capitalistically inclined and seem to identify themselves more with the Republic of China (Taiwan) than with communist China. They have been fully integrated into the South African economy.

The Chinese Society of SA aims to maintain and promote Chinese culture. The society is the mouthpiece of the nearly 13 000 Chinese in the country. The Chinese new year and 'double ten' (10 October) are celebrated and on such occasions the lion dance, the feather dance and the ribbon dance are performed. Children learn these dances at schools like the Chinese Kuo Ting School in Johannesburg. The Chinese community in South Africa owns a so-called 'culture chest', which contains a large number of replicas of valuable Chinese works of art. From time to time these prints of high quality are displayed to give South Africans an opportunity of admiring the Chinese tradition of sculpture, paintings, calligraphy, porcelain, pottery and objects in bronze.

Japanese
The Japanese maintain a low profile, but they nevertheless contribute to the large cultural diversity which characterises South Africa.

Migration

There has been a steady increase in the number of immigrants to South Africa, 70 per cent from 1986 to 1989. The majority of immigrants come from Europe and the United Kingdom, but many also come from former eastern bloc countries.

From 1986 to 1989 there was a 60 per cent decrease in the number of emigrants. The average rate of emigration among graduates has been an annual 4 500 since 1980 — 25 per cent of the total number of graduates from South African universities.

News items: 1990

Despite a strict selection process, 5 167 people were allowed permanent residence in South Africa from 1 January to 31 May 1990.

SA's foreign missions and embassies received 48 630 inquiries from people in eastern bloc countries and 375 passport holders from these countries entered SA during the year.

An Institute for Jewish Learning for adults was established in July, offering six lectures a week at Temple Shalom and Temple Emmanuel.

In September the Minister of Finance, Mr Barend du Plessis, announced that immigrants would in future be allowed to bring into the country a total amount of 500 000 instead of the former amount of 200 000 financial rand. After five years they could import the remainder of their assets in financial rand. The former period was three years.

Polish citizens living in the Pretoria-Witwatersrand-Vereeniging (PWV) area were allowed to vote in Poland's first direct presidential election on 25 November.

Acknowledgements:
Prof J B Hartman, Department of Anthropology and Archeology, University of Pretoria

Government systems

The Constitution, which was formally put into effect in September 1984, provides for an executive President, a Parliament with three Houses, a central Cabinet and a Ministers' Council for each House as well as a joint President's Council. A fundamental premise of the Constitution is government by consensus rather than the confrontational politics of the Westminster system, which was the basis of government for more than 70 years (1910-84).

In the preamble to the Constitution the legislators solemnly declare their conviction that unity is essential;
— to uphold Christian values and civilised norms and recognise and protect freedom of worship;
— to safeguard the integrity of the country and the freedom of its people;
— to uphold the independence of the judiciary and the equality of all before the law;
— to maintain law and order;
— to promote the happiness and spiritual and material welfare of all;
— to respect and protect the human dignity, life, liberty and property of all;
— to respect and promote the right to self-determination of all population groups; and
— to promote private enterprise and effective competition.

The State President is elected every five years by an electoral college drawn from the three Houses of Parliament. The same electoral college thereafter also elects the Speaker of Parliament from among the ranks of the members of all three Houses. The State President is a member and chairman of the Cabinet, i.e. chief executive officer of the country as a whole. He is not a member of Parliament but no one may be a candidate for the State Presidency unless he is qualified to be an elected or nominated member of any one of the three Houses. The State President may speak in any one of the three Houses or during a joint sitting of all three Houses, but he does not have a vote.

The State President's term of office coincides with the life of a Parliament, which is a maximum of five years. The State President must be elected within the first seven days of the new session of Parliament after a general election for members of all three Houses. The State President may be removed from office on the grounds of misconduct or incapacity to perform his duties. The State President must resign or call a general election when all three Houses pass a motion of no confidence in the Cabinet within any one period of 14 days, or reject his budget.

The State President is Commander-in-Chief of the South African Defence Force; he declares war and makes peace; proclaims and terminates martial law; and enters into and ratifies international treaties, conventions and agreements. He also appoints South African ambassadors and other diplomatic representatives abroad and receives and accredits similar representatives of other countries in South Africa. He is empowered to pardon and reprieve offenders.

At his own discretion the State President appoints members of the Cabinet and deputy ministers. In exercising all other powers the State President acts either in consultation with the Cabinet or on the advice of the Ministers' Councils.

Own and general affairs

One of the fundamental premises of the 1983 Constitution is the distinction between own and general affairs. Legislation affecting the interests of one group alone is handled by the appropriate House, while legislation on general affairs is dealt with by all three Houses.

In case of doubt whether a certain matter affects the interests of a particular population group or is a general affair on which all three Houses of Parliament must deliberate and decide, a decision is taken by the State President.

In general affairs, executive authority is vested in the State President and the central Cabinet, which may comprise White, Coloured and Indian members; and in own affairs in the State President and a Ministers' Council designated from among the majority ranks of the members of the appropriate House. All Bills on general affairs must be deliberated and passed by all three Houses.

Own Affairs are those affecting the maintenance, upholding or furtherance of the identity, lifestyle, culture, traditions and customs of each population group. The matters listed in

Schedule 1 to the Constitution, which are the own affairs of each population group, include health and welfare services, education at all levels, matters relating to and facilities for recreation and cultural activities, community development — including housing, local government, agricultural services — including assistance to farmers, training and extension services, water supplies, the appointment of marriage officers under any general law, and election of members of the House of Parliament in question.

Legislature

Legislative authority is vested in the State President and Parliament. In April 1988 Parliament passed the Constitution Second Amendment Act to give effect to certain proposals of the joint committee on the revision of the Standing Rules and Orders of Parliament. Probably the most important proposal was one providing for joint sitting by all three Houses of Parliament. At the conclusion of each such joint sitting the three Houses vote separately on the issue before them. The number of joint sittings has increased appreciably since the introduction of the present Constitution.

The State President
The State President decides whether an issue is an own or general affair. In the event of an irreconcilable dispute among the three Houses regarding a Bill relating to general affairs, the State President has the discretion to refer it to the President's Council for a decision. Before any Bill can become legislation, the State President has to give his consent, which may only be withheld if the State President is satisfied that the Bill has not been dealt with as provided in the Constitution.

Parliament
Secretary to Parliament: Mr G P C de Kock. Tel: (021) 403-2600; 403-2599.
Speaker: Mr L le Grange. Tel: (021) 403-2595/6
Parliament comprises three Houses — the House of Assembly (Whites), the House of Representatives (Coloureds) and the House of Delegates (Indians).
The **House of Assembly** consists of 178 members, of whom 166 are elected by simple majority in single-member geographic constituencies, while four (one for each of the four provinces) are nominated by the State President, and eight are elected by the 166 directly elected members on the basis of the proportional representation

of the various political parties. The allocation by province of the 166 constituencies is: Transvaal 76, Cape Province 56, Natal 20 and Orange Free State (OFS) 14.
The **House of Representatives** consists of 85 members, of whom 80 are elected by Coloured voters in constituencies allocated as follows to the provinces: Cape 60, Transvaal 10, and OFS and Natal five each. Two more are appointed by the State President and three are elected by the 80 directly elected members.
The **House of Delegates** consists of 45 members, of whom 40 are directly elected by Indian voters in constituencies allocated as follows: 29 to Natal, eight to the Transvaal and three to the Cape Province. Two more members are nominated by the State President and three are elected by the 40 directly elected members.
The life of any one Parliament may not exceed five years. In consultation with the Cabinet, the State President may convene joint sittings of all three Houses of Parliament. He is also obliged to convene such a joint sitting when requested to do so by all three Houses. The State President determines the times for the sessions of Parliament in consultation with the Cabinet. Parliament must meet at least once a year and the first session following a general election must be held within 30 days after polling day.

President's Council

Of the 60 members of the President's Council, 20 are designated by majority vote by the House of Assembly, 10 by the House of Representatives and five by the House of Delegates. The remaining 25 members are nominated by the State President.
The President's Council advises the State President on matters of national importance, either on its own initiative or at the request of the State President. The council may also be asked by the State President to give a binding ruling when the three Houses disagree on legislation on general affairs.
When a Bill is passed by one or two Houses and rejected by the other House(s), the State President has the discretion to refer it to the President's Council for a decision, or not. If he decides not to, the Bill simply lapses. The State President may withdraw the Bill before the Council has reached a decision, but must accept its decision once it has been made. The President's Council can only give a ruling on decisions taken by the three Houses because it is not empowered to amend the legislation itself.

Executive

There are two components to the executive authority. The first is the Cabinet, comprising the State President and an unspecified number of ministers who deal with matters of common concern. Members of the Cabinet may be appointed from the ranks of all three population groups. Every member of the Cabinet heads one or more central government department, but the State President is empowered to include ministers without portfolios as well. A member of the Cabinet may sit and speak in any one of the three Houses but may only vote in the House of which he is a member.

The principle of joint responsibility applies to all Cabinet members. This means that any Cabinet member who disagrees fundamentally with a Cabinet decision will be expected to accept joint responsibility for that decision, unless he clears his position with the chairman and a joint statement setting out his position is issued.

Cabinet

On 8 April 1991 the members of the Cabinet were as follows:

Mr F W de Klerk: State President
Mr R F Botha: Minister of Foreign Affairs
Dr G van N Viljoen: Minister of Constitutional Development
Gen M A de M Malan: Minister of Defence
Dr D J de Villiers: Minister of Economic Co-ordination and Public Enterprises
Mr H J Coetsee: Minister of Justice and of Correctional Services
Mr B J du Plessis: Minister of Finance
Mr A A Venter: Minister of State Expenditure and for Regional Development
Mr E van der M Louw: Minister of Manpower
Mr A J Vlok: Minister of Law and Order
Mr G J Kotzé: Minister of Water Affairs and Forestry
Dr C J van der Merwe: Minister of Education and Training
Mr E (Gene) Louw: Minister of Home Affairs
Mr G S Bartlett: Minister of Mineral and Energy Affairs
Dr A I van Niekerk: Minister of Agriculture
Dr E H Venter: Minister of National Health
Mr H J Kriel: Minister of Planning, Provincial Affairs and National Housing
Mr J de Villiers: Minister of Public Works and Land Affairs and of Development Aid
Mr L A Pienaar: Minister of National Education and of Environment Affairs

Dr G Marais: Minister of Trade and Industry and Tourism
Dr P J Welgemoed: Minister of Transport

Ministers' Councils

The second component of the executive is a Ministers' Council appointed for each of the three Houses to serve the interests of the population group concerned and administer the government departments established for that particular group. Only members enjoying the support of the majority in their respective Houses may be appointed chairmen of the Ministers' Councils. On 8 April 1991 the Chairmen and members of the Ministers' Councils were as follows:

House of Assembly
Mr H J Coetsee: Chairman
Mr P J Clase: Minister of Education and Culture
Mr S J de Beer: Minister of the Budget and of Welfare, Housing and Works
Dr A I van Niekerk: Minister of Agricultural Development
Dr E H Venter: Minister of Health Services
Mr H J Kriel: Minister of Local Government
Mr A T Meyer: Deputy Minister of Agricultural Development

House of Representatives
Mr H J Hendrickse: Chairman, Minister of Education and Culture
Mr A A Julies: Minister of Local Government and Agriculture
Mr D M G Curry: Minister of Housing
Mr C J April: Minister of Health Services and Welfare
Mr I Richards: Minister of the Budget
Mr A Williams: Deputy Minister of Education and Culture

House of Delegates
Dr J N Reddy: Chairman, Minister of Housing
Mr B Dookie: Minister of Health Services and Welfare
Mr R Bhana: Minister of the Budget and Auxiliary Services
Mr Y Moolla: Minister of Local Government and Agriculture
Dr K Rajoo: Minister of Education and Culture
Mr S V Naicker: Deputy Minister of Local Government, Housing and Agriculture

Deputy Ministers

The State President may also appoint a number of deputy ministers. There are two categories of deputy ministers — those appointed to assist members of the Cabinet, but who are not themselves members of the Cabinet, while those appointed to assist members of the Ministers' Councils of the various Houses automatically become members of these councils. On 8 April 1991 the following Deputy Ministers were in office:

Mr R P Meyer: Deputy Minister of Constitutional Development and for Information Services

Mr W N Breytenbach: Deputy Minister of Defence

Mr J A van Wyk: Deputy Minister of Finance, of Water Affairs and of Land Affairs

Dr T G Alant: Deputy Minister of Finance and of National Education

Mr L Wessels: Deputy Minister of Foreign Affairs

Mr A Fourie: Deputy Minister of Planning

Mr D P A Schutte: Deputy Minister of Justice and of Correctional Services

Mr P G Marais: Deputy Minister of Education and of Development Aid

Dr J T Delport: Deputy Minister of Constitutional Development and of Provincial Affairs

Mr J H L Scheepers: Deputy Minister of Law and Order

Mr A T Meyer: Deputy Minister of Agriculture

Mr D de V Graaff: Deputy Minister of Trade and Industry and Tourism

Government departments

The departments are as follows:
— State President's Office. Director-General: Dr J P Roux. Tel: (012) 325-2000
— Administration: House of Assembly. Director-General: Mr I H Robson. Tel: (012) 314-5911
— Administration: House of Delegates. Director-General: Dr C F Scheepers. Tel: (031) 327-0911
— Administration: House of Representatives. Director-General: Mr P D McEnery. Tel: (021) 461-6070
— Agriculture. Director-General: Mr H S Hattingh. Tel: (012) 206 -9111
— Commission for Administration. Director-General: Mr L R Kluever. Tel: (012) 314-7911
— Constitutional Development Service. Constitutional Advisor: Mr S S van der Merwe. Tel: (012) 341-2400
— Correctional Services. Commissioner of Correctional Services: Lieutenant-General W H Willemse. Tel: 207-9111
— Development Aid. Director-General: Mr L K van Gass. Tel: (012) 312-8911
— Education and Training. Director-General: Dr J B Z Louw. Tel: (012) 312-5911

— Environment Affairs. Director-General: Mr W F Visagie. Tel: (012) 310-3911
— Finance. Director-General: Mr G P Croeser. Tel: (012) 315-5111
— Central Economic Advisory Services. Head: Mr J P Dreyer. Tel: (012) 325-1545
— Foreign Affairs. Director-General: Mr N P van Heerden. Tel: (012) 323-0527
— Home Affairs. Director-General: Mr P J Colyn. Tel: (012) 314-8911
— Central Statistical Service. Head: Dr A P T du Toit. Tel: (012) 310-8911
— Justice. Director-General: Adv J J Noeth. Tel: (012) 315-1111
— Manpower. Director-General: Adv J D Fourie. Tel: (012) 310-6911
— Mineral and Energy Affairs. Director-General: Dr P J Hugo (acting Director-General). Tel: (012) 322-8561
— National Education. Director-General: Dr J G Garbers. Tel: (012) 314-6911
— National Health and Population Development. Director-General: Dr C F Slabber. Tel: (012) 325-5100
— National Intelligence Service. Director-General: Dr L D Barnard. Tel: (012) 323-8133
— Office of the Auditor-General. Auditor-General: Mr R P Wronsley. Tel: (012) 32-44100
— Public Works and Land Affairs. Director-General: Mr C W van Niekerk. Tel: (012) 205-9111
— South African Communication Service. Head: Mr D W Steward. Tel: (012) 314-2911
— South African Defence Force. Chief of the SADF: Gen A J Liebenberg. Tel: (012) 291-9111
— South African Police. Commissioner: Gen J V van der Merwe. Tel: (012) 310-1911
— Trade and Industry. Director-General: Dr S J Naudé. Tel: (012) 310-9791
— Transport. Director-General: Mr R G Meyer. Tel: (012) 290-9111
— Water Affairs and Forestry. Director-General: Mr G C D Claassens. Tel: (012) 299-9111

Political parties

Only the major political parties in the three Houses are discussed.

House of Assembly

National Party

Leader: Mr F W de Klerk. The NP's policy may

be summarised as follows: South Africa is a single undivided state with single citizenship for all and the right of every South African to political participation on all government levels where his interests are affected, taking into account the principle of non-domination and protection of groups. Other principles are protection of human and group rights, an independent judiciary, enhancement of human dignity and development of civilised norms, repeal of regulations based on race, a free economic system, an effective security system which secures order and safety and maintenance of good relations with the international community.

ConservativeParty
Leader: Dr A P Treurnicht. The major policy platform of the CP is a geographical division of South Africa to serve as a basis for separate political self-realisation and sovereignty of the country's different peoples - Whites, Coloureds, Indians and Blacks. The CP maintains that the Whites has an inalienable right to self-rule. The party is opposed to racial integration in any form whatsoever. It endorses equal rights for Afrikaans and English as official languages, as well as Christian national principles, especially in education, while upholding the right of all to religious freedom.

Democratic Party
Leader: Dr Z J de Beer. Some of the major policy principles of the Democratic Party as set out before the general election of 1989, are:
— Protection of the fundamental rights and freedoms of all South Africans.
— Representative government based on universal suffrage for all South African citizens.
— An independent judiciary and sovereignty of justice.
— Limitation of central government's authority by establishing government on different levels.
— Negotiation to bring about the orderly transition to a true democracy in South Africa in which all people can share and in which the different cultural groups can co-exist in harmony as a single South African nation.
— Rejection of violence as a political instrument.
— Sound labour relations based on concerted bargaining.

House of Representatives
Labour Party
Leader: Rev H J Hendrickse. The Labour Party totally dominates the political scene in the House of Representatives and won both elections since 1983. The party's policy is a non-racial federal South Africa with a bill of human rights to protect the individual, an independent judiciary, a country without apartheid and discrimination and a country with franchise for all its citizens.

House of Delegates
Solidarity
Leader: Dr J N Reddy. Solidarity's policy is that participation in the tricameral parliament is meaningful/significant in abolishing apartheid; that there should be a striving for a united South Africa without discrimination and apartheid; that all South Africans must have the right to vote; that a system of free market economy should lead to upliftment of all its citizens; that supremacy of the judicial system with an independent judiciary should be recognised.

National Peoples' Party
Leader: Mr A Rajbansi. The National Peoples Party maintains that South Africa is indivisible and belongs to all its inhabitants; that there should be a free press, freedom of speech and religion must be pursued at all times; an independent judiciary is important to maintain law and order and to secure justice for all citizens; and wants franchise for all.

Elections

The chief electoral officer prepares a list, based on the population register, of all people entitled to be registered as voters, i.e. those over 18 years of age in each constituency of all three Houses of Parliament. On polling day every registered voter must identify himself by producing one of several official documents.

Election results, 1989
The registered voters numbered 3 170 667 and the number of votes cast 2 176 481, or 68,64 per cent. Position of political parties on 31 January 1991:

House of Assembly
National Party — 91 seats
Conservative Party — 39 seats
Democratic Party — 33 seats
Vacancies — 3 seats

House of Representatives
Labour Party — 69 seats
Democratic Reform Party — 5 seats

United Democratic Party — 3 seats
Freedom Party — 1 seat
Independents — 2 seats

House of Delegates
Solidarity — 20 seats
National Peoples Party — 13 seats
Democratic Party — 3 seats
National Federal Party — 1 seat
Peoples Party of SA — 1 seat
Independents — 2 seats

Provincial government

Administrator of the Orange Free State: Mr L J Botha
Administrator of Natal: Mr C J van R Botha
Administrator of the Cape Province: Mr J W H Meiring
Administrator of the Transvaal: Mr D J Hough

Under Act 32 of 1961, before it was replaced by Act 69 of 1986, each province had an elected provincial council consisting of White persons, an Administrator appointed by the State President, a provincial executive committee, which was in effect the 'cabinet' of the province concerned, and a provincial administration to administer the affairs of the province. On 1 July 1986 the provincial legislatures were abolished and replaced by executive authorities appointed by the State President.

The elected provincial councils were abolished by the introduction of the Provincial Government Act, 1986. Executive committees, the members of which are appointed by the State President, were retained. These committees are multiracial. The Administrator continues to be appointed by the State President and, in consultation with his executive committee, has legislative powers to enact certain legislation.

Current provincial structures are responsible for 'general' affairs only. As far as local government is concerned, this means that the new provincial bodies exercise control over Black local authorities. Other bodies, from among which the membership of the regional services councils is constituted, are controlled by 'own' affairs ministers of local government in the three Houses of Parliament.

During 1987 and 1988 the provincial administrations were given greater powers and increased responsibilities in a number of areas. These include housing and community development for Blacks, physical development planning, including guide plans for the development of metropolitan cities, environmental protection

and conservation measures, and health services, including hospitals. Most general state hospitals for the different population groups are now administered by the provincial governments.

Local government

The Promotion of Local Government Affairs Act, 1983, laid the foundation for full participation by all population groups in local government and provides for a forum for consultation on local government matters among all communities.

The Act provides for uniform criteria for constitution of various types of local authorities for all population groups. Apart from laying down minimum standards for basic services such as water and electricity, reticulation, sewerage and streets, the Act also provides that the wishes of the community concerned should be taken into account when a decision is taken on the constitution of a new local authority. Financial viability is an important consideration, as is the capacity of the community concerned to provide from among its own members the councillors needed to ensure a viable administration.

The main functions of larger local authorities are: Construction and maintenance of streets; traffic control; provision of water and electricity; provision of housing, especially for people in the lower income groups; city and town planning and building control; parks and recreation services; cemeteries and crematoria; health services and the inspection of food and meat; transport services; abattoirs; public library services; trade and other licences; fire fighting; rubbish and sanitary removal and sewerage.

Under this Act the Council for the Co-ordination of Local Government Affairs was established to inform and advise government on issues relating to development of local government. In 1986 the Joint Parliamentary Committee on Constitutional Affairs requested the Co-ordinating Council to investigate the replacement of the existing different systems and structures of local government by a uniform Act — that is legislation for a common system of local government for South Africa.

On 25 October 1990 a Manifesto on Local Government was adopted by all members of the Co-ordinating Council, identifying the following points of departure as the basic principles on which a workable and acceptable new democratic and non-racial system of local government for South Africa should be built.

— Local government is an independent form

and tier of government consisting of autonomous, directly elected local authorities which are fully-fledged government institutions with legislative and executive powers.
— Any new system of local government should provide for democratic political participation, elimination and prevention of domination, effective participation of minorities, free and independent community life, elimination of discrimination, freedom of association, and commitment to negotiation as a method of change.
— Local authorities should be endowed with maximal powers and functions, as well as sufficient sources of income. Devolution of power should therefore be accompanied by devolution of financial sources and financial responsibility.
— Existing and new sources of income of local government, as well as intergovernmental grants, must be utilised in an effective and non-discriminatory manner to promote sound economic development and financial independence of a town or city and to eliminate historical disadvantages urgently and systematically.
— The citizens of South Africa have the right to play an important role at local level in determining the future of their towns and cities.

Extra-parliamentary groups

Black resentment was substantially increased after the Union of South Africa enacted legislation of a discriminatory nature, and in 1912, on the initiative of a Durban advocate, Dr Pixley Ka Isaka Seme, prominent Blacks from all over the country met in Bloemfontein and established the South African Native National Congress, renamed the **African National Congress** (ANC) in 1925.

The activities of the ANC, according to Prof Thomas Karis, reflect six different reactions (marking as many periods) to official policy: The ANC retained liberal expectations, became more militant, attempted passive resistance, with the adoption of the Freedom Charter in 1956 it became a multiracial front which became popular among all population groups, was overtaken by impatient Black nationalism and moved underground.

Umkhonto we Sizwe, the military wing of the ANC, was established in 1961 by leaders of the ANC and the SACP, including Nelson Mandela.

Nelson Mandela, a prominent leader of the ANC, was taken captive in 1962. Other ANC leaders were arrested in Rivonia in 1963. They were all convicted on charges of sabotage and

sentenced. Eight of these prisoners were released unconditionally by the end of 1989 and Mr Mandela on 11 February 1990.

The **Pan Africanist Congress** (PAC), a radical resistance organisation, developed from the ANC.

Because of the activities of the ANC and the PAC during the 1950s, they were declared unlawful organisations in 1960. The Communist Party of South Africa (CPSA) was declared an unlawful organisation as early as 1950 and appeared much later as the **South African Communist Party** (SACP).

Black Consciousness made its appearance in the late 1960s. This ideology exalted Blacks and Black nationalism and denied Whites any part in the 'freedom struggle'. The umbrella organisation is the **Black Consciousness Movement** (BCM) whose largest component is the **Azanian People's Organisation** (Azapo). The best known leader of the BCM was Mr Steve Biko, who died on 12 September 1977 while in police custody. The BCM and Azapo declare themselves opposed to 'colonialism and capitalism' and they lean strongly towards socialism. The external wing of the BCM is located in Zimbabwe and is known as the Black Consciousness Movement of Azania (BCMA). The military wing of the BCMA is called Azanian National Liberation Army (Azanla).

The **South African Students' Organisation** (Saso), established in 1968, was one of the first organisations devoted to this ideology. Similar organisations such as the **Black People's Convention** (BPC) and the **South African Student Movement** (SASM) were established in the early 1970s to foster a strong consciousness of being Black among the young.

The **United Democratic Front** (UDF) was established in 1983. This organisation, established solely to put forward objections to the government's constitutional plans, welcomes members of all population groups who endorse the principles of the Freedom Charter.

Student movements affiliated to the UDF include the South African National Student Congress (SANSCO), the National Union of South African Students (Nusas) and the Congress of South African Students (Cosas). The Congress of South African Trade Unions (Cosatu) is probably the most militant of all.

The **Mass Democratic Movement** (MDM) is the most comprehensive umbrella organisation ever to be mobilised against racial discrimination and political exclusion.

Most of the MDM's support is from the Black community. This movement has no constitution and there is no record of its membership. There is also no national or regional governing body and it has no office-bearers. A characteristic of groups in the MDM is that they all accept the provisions of the Freedom Charter.

The MDM's approach is that the masses, rather than the individual, can bring about change. Thus groups affiliated to the MDM strive to work at grassroots level.

The MDM was established after the UDF clashed with the government and was banned in terms of the emergency regulations in 1988. Since the inception of Cosatu in 1985, these two organisations have worked together. This relationship led to the establishment of the MDM.

In 1989 the MDM became prominent when it launched its 'defiance campaign' and hundreds of Blacks arrived at White hospitals and insisted on being treated.

Inkatha Freedom Party (IFP) is a political party under the leadership of Dr M G Buthelezi. The IFP claims a membership of 1,7 million members, most of them being Zulu. During the IFP's first congress the following principles were accepted: The IFP is a non-racial party which endorses equal opportunities for all individuals in a reconciliatory community with democratic rights and protection of all people; the wealth of the country must be utilised to counter poverty and joblessness; redistribution of wealth and creation of structures (political and economical) to generate wealth and maintenance of peace and stability. Both Dr Buthelezi and the Inkatha Freedom Party are committed to negotiation and a peaceful transition to a new political dispensation for South Africa. They are also strongly opposed to the disinvestment campaign.

The **Afrikaner-Weerstandsbeweging**(AWB) is a conservative cultural resistance organisation formed in 1973 for a section of the Afrikaners who identified themselves as the 'Boers' ('Boerevolk'). Their leader is Mr Eugene Terre'-Blanche. The aims of the AWB include: searching for a solution to the problems of the Republic, protecting the national identity and reuniting the Afrikaner nation. The AWB strives after a 'unitary state' modelled on the Boer republics, in which White Christianity, irrespective of language differences, will be reunited without any interference from party politics. The AWB wants to cultivate an awareness among Afrikaners of their White origin and heritage, blood relationships and racial purity. It also wants to institute 'effective security measures' to maintain and protect the Afrikaner state or so-called 'Boerestaat'.

The **Boere-Vryheidsbeweging**(BVB), a right-wing extra parliamentary movement was established by a splinter group of the AWB early in 1989. Its immediate task was to work for a nation state. Former members of the AWB are prominent in this movement.

News items: 1990

(Official overseas visits by the State President and other government officials are discussed in chapter 9: Foreign relations.)

At the end of 1989 there were 3 156 643 White South Africans registered as voters — 1 695 150 in the Transvaal, 855 616 in the Cape Province, 368 307 in Natal and 237 570 in the Orange Free State.

In the House of Representatives, statistics showed that 1 563 286 Coloureds were registered as voters.

The number of Indians registered as voters totalled 532 915.

The September 1989 election cost R18 million, the Minister of Home Affairs announced.

On 26 January Nelson Mandela affirmed the ANC's aim to nationalise mines and monopolistic industries.

When young ANC members and members of the National Party Jeugkrag (youth movement) met in Lusaka for a two-day conference early in 1990 they agreed that there should be rapid and fundamental change in South Africa.

The 30-year-old ban on the ANC and the more radical PAC and the 40-year-old ban on the SACP was lifted on 2 February.

Johannesburg's municipal buses were opened to all races in February.

Dr Stoffel van der Merwe was appointed chairman of the National Party's Federal Information Service in February. He succeeded Mr Barend du Plessis.

The ANC opened its first office in South Africa in Stanger on 13 February with former Robben Island detainee Mr Justice Mpanza as its head.

ANC and Inkatha met for the first time on 22 February to hold discussions to bring about peace in the strife-torn Natal.

In February Mr Nelson Mandela met a representative of the Swedish Legation, Mr Jan Lundvik, and 15 chiefs from Tembuland in Transkei in separate meetings at his home in Soweto.

Mr Nelson Mandela was elected deputy president of the ANC in March.

President de Klerk announced Cabinet changes on 7 March to strengthen the roles of Ministers charged with constitutional reform and with economic renewal.

Natal's 12th Administrator, Mr Con Botha, was sworn in by the Judge President, Mr Justice JA Howard, on 2 April.

The Democratic Party took over control of the Johannesburg City Council from the National Party in April.

Dr Beyers Naudé, former minister of the NG Church and previously restricted member of the ANC, was included in the ANC's negotiation team in April.

Mr Alfred Nzo, Mr Joe Slovo, Mr Joe Modise, Mr Thabo Mbeki and Miss Ruth Mompati of the ANC returned to South Africa in April.

In an agreement reached between the government and the ANC in May, known as the Groote Schuur Minute, both parties committed themselves to achieving a new constitution by peaceful means.

Mr Nelson Mandela left on a 12-day African trip on 9 May. He met with Palestine Liberation Organisation (PLO) chairman Mr Yasser Arafat on 20 May.

Former State President P W Botha announced his intention to sever all ties with the National Party in May.

In May Prof Albie Sachs, exiled member of the ANC, returned to South Africa after spending 24 years abroad.

Dr Oscar Dhlomo, Inkatha's general secretary and Minister of Education and Culture in Kwa-Zulu, announced his resignation from politics on 1 June.

Mr Nelson Mandela and President de Klerk met at the Union Buildings in June in an attempt to reduce violence in the country.

Mr Nelson Mandela and his wife, Mrs Winnie Mandela, left in June for Botswana on the first leg of a 13-nation tour of Europe, the US and Africa.

After Inkatha became a political party on 14 July about 100 Whites, 20 Indians and a few Coloured people joined the party.

The SACP had its first public rally in South Africa in 40 years on 29 July, at which it declared its commitment to peaceful negotiations.

In July a powerful bomb exploded at the NP's head office in Bloemfontein.

The government and the ANC issued a joint statement, known as the Pretoria Minute, on 6 August in which, inter alia, the government agreed to review security legislation to ensure free political activity. The ANC, in turn, agreed to suspend its armed struggle with immediate effect.

The State President paid an impromptu visit to Soweto on 4 September.

Dr Zach de Beer was elected sole leader of the Democratic Party on 7 September.

Mr F W de Klerk celebrated his first year as State President on 20 September.

By October the NP Congress in all four provinces had decided to open party membership to all races.

The Pretoria City Council opened its buses and public amenities to all population groups on 15 October.

The 37-year-old Reservation of Separate Amenities Act, scrapped by Parliament earlier this year, was finally erased from the country's law books on 15 October.

Pan Africanist Congress leader, Mr Zeph Mothopeng, died in Johannesburg in October.

In October residents of Vosloorus Township rejected their local authority demand of R70 as a flat rate for rent per household, electing instead to continue their six-month rental boycott until the council agreed to accept their final offer of R50.

Essential services, including electricity, water and sewerage were cut in several eastern Transvaal Black residential areas on 16 October. These areas are in arrears to the White local authority supplying bulk services for amounts up to R1 million.

All forms of discrimination on the basis of race and colour ended on 19 October with the commencement of the Discriminatory Legislation regarding Public Amenities Repeal Act.

By the end of October only about 30 per cent of Black residents in the Orange Free State were paying service charges to local authorities.

Changes to the Cabinet were announced in November, including two new ministers and a new deputy minister. A number of deputy ministers were given new responsibilities.

A total of 40 per cent of the country's 262 Black local authorities collapsed. Eighty councillors resigned nationwide in November alone.

The ANC started its countrywide mass campaign with marches in Johannesburg and Pretoria on 6 December.

In December the Afrikaner-Volkswag (AV) of Prof Carel Boshoff was ousted from the mainstream of the right-wing cultural movement by a new organisation, the Afrikaner-Kultuurbond.

At a two-day UN debate in December the ANC urged the world community to keep up the pressure on South Africa despite significant changes in government policy.

Mr Clarence Makwetu was elected as the

president of the Pan Africanist Congress during the organisation's December Congress in Johannesburg.

Mr Oliver Tambo, president of the ANC, returned to South Africa on 13 December after 30 years of self-imposed exile. On the national consultative conference the following day Mr Tambo questioned the advisability of continuing the demand for the maintenance of sanctions.

The ANC proclaimed 1991 a year of mass action to step up pressure on the government for the transfer of power. The ANC also gave government an ultimatum that it would reconsider its participation in the negotiation process if all undertakings of the Groote Schuur and Pretoria minutes were not met by 30 April 1991.

The first ANC congress in South Africa in 31 years was held outside Johannesburg in December.

Almost 800 political exiles were granted indemnity in December.

President de Klerk and Mr Tambo met at the Union Buildings in December. Both agreed that violence and intimidation should end in order to enable proper negotiations to start.

Acknowledgements:

Mr Theo Bekker, Department of Political Science and International Politics, University of Pretoria
Commission for Administration
Constitutional Development Service
Department of Planning, Provincial Affairs and National Housing
Office of the State President
South African Police

National symbols and honours   6

National anthem

Die Stem van Suid-Afrika was composed as a poem by C J Langenhoven in 1918. Originally there were three verses, but a fourth was added by popular request. The final version is:

1

Uit die blou van onse hemel, uit die diepte van ons see,
Oor ons ewige gebergtes waar die kranse antwoord gee,
Deur ons vér-verlate vlaktes met die kreun van ossewa —
Ruis die stem van ons geliefde, van ons land Suid-Afrika.
Ons sal antwoord op jou roepstem, ons sal offer wat jy vra:
Ons sal lewe, ons sal sterwe — ons vir jou, Suid-Afrika.

2

In die merg van ons gebeente, in ons hart en siel en gees,
In ons roem op ons verlede, in ons hoop op wat sal wees,
In ons wil en werk en wandel, van ons wieg tot aan ons graf —
Deel geen ander land ons liefde, trek geen ander trou ons af.
Vaderland! ons sal die adel van jou naam met ere dra:
Waar en trou as Afrikaners — kinders van Suid-Afrika.

3

In die songloed van ons somer, in ons winternag se kou,
In die lente van ons liefde, in die lanfer van ons rou.
By die klink van huw'liks-klokkies, by die kluitklap op die kis —
Streel jou stem ons nooit verniet nie, weet jy waar jou kinders is.
Op jou roep sê ons nooit nee nie, sê ons altyd, altyd ja:
Om te lewe, om te sterwe — ja, ons kom, Suid-Afrika.

4

Op U Almag vas vertrouend, het ons vadere gebou:
Skenk ook ons die krag, o Here! om te handhaaf en te hou —
Dat die erwe van ons vaad're vir ons kinders erwe bly:
Knegte van die Allerhoogste, teen die hele wêreld vry.
Soos ons vadere vertrou het, leer ook ons vertrou, o Heer —
Met ons land en met ons nasie sal dit wel wees, God regeer.

Langenhoven's own melody drew strong criticism and the Cape newspaper *Die Burger* sponsored a national competition to find more suitable music. After several unsuccessful attempts, the Rev M L de Villiers of Paarl produced an acceptable melody in 1921.

Die *Stem van Suid-Afrika* was first sung publically at the official hoisting of the national flag in Cape Town on 31 May 1928. Rev de Villiers conducted a mass choir of schoolchildren. In 1938 the Prime Minister, Gen J B M Hertzog, decided that *Die Stem* should be played with *God save the King* at the opening of Parliament. It was not until 2 May 1957, however, that the then Prime Minister, Mr J G Strijdom, announced in Parliament that the Government had adopted *Die Stem* as South Africa's official national anthem. The Government obtained copyright on *Die Stem* in the same year, and this was confirmed by legislation in 1959.

Official acceptance of the national anthem intensified the need for a suitable English translation. In 1952 a special committee of eminent South Africans recommended a translation drawn from 220 submitted. In the same year the national anthem was sung in English for the first time during the Van Riebeeck tercentenary festival in Cape Town. The words are as follows:

1

Ringing out from our blue heavens, from our deep seas breaking round;
Over everlasting mountains where the echoing crags resound;

From our plains where creaking wagons cut their
  trails into the earth —
Calls the spirit of our Country, of the land that
  gave us birth.
At thy call we shall not falter, firm and steadfast
  we shall stand.
At thy will to live or perish, O South Africa, dear
  land.

2

In our body and our spirit, in our inmost heart
  held fast;
In the promise of our future and the glory of the
  past;
In our will, our work, our striving, from the cradle
  to the grave —
There's no land that shares our loving, and no
  bond that can enslave.
Thou hast borne us and we know thee. May our
  deeds to all proclaim
Our enduring love and service to thy honour and
  thy name.

3

In the golden warmth of summer, in the chill of
  winter's air,
In the surging life of springtime, in the autumn
  of despair;
When the wedding bells are chiming, or when
  those we love depart,
Thou dost know us for thy children and dost take
  us to thy heart.
Loudly peals the answering chorus: We are
  thine, and we shall stand,
Be it life or death, to answer to thy call, beloved
  land.

4

In Thy power, Almighty, trusting, did our fathers
  build of old;
Strengthen then, O Lord, their children to
  defend, to love, to hold —
That the heritage they gave us for our children
  yet may be:
Bondsmen only to the Highest and before the
  whole world free.
As our fathers trusted humbly, teach us, Lord, to
  trust Thee still:
Guard our land and guide our people in Thy way
  to do Thy will.

Coats of arms

When the Republic of South Africa came into
being on 31 May 1961, it retained the coat of arms
of the former Union of South Africa. These arms

were designed at the time of the establishment
of the Union on 31 May 1910 and contain elements from the coats of arms of the Cape Colony,
Natal, the Republic of the Orange Free State and
the Zuid-Afrikaansche Republic (Transvaal).

Symbols for each province were placed in a
quartered shield:

The Lady of Good Hope (Cape Province), two
black wildebeest (Natal), an orange tree
(Orange Free State) and an ox-wagon
(Transvaal). A wavy horizontal partition line
symbolises the Orange River flowing through the
country. A lion *passant guardant,* holding four
bound staves representing the unity of the four
provinces, was chosen for the crest. This unity is
also expressed in the motto *Ex Unitate Vires* —
Unity is strength — the Latin translation of the
Zuid-Afrikaansche Republic's motto *Eendragt
maakt Magt.* The supporters are a springbok and
an oryx ('gemsbok'). The original version of
these arms was used until 1930. In that year it was
largely replaced by an 'improved' rendition. At
the same time the London artist Kruger Gray
prepared an 'embellished' version of the coat of
arms, which was recorded by the College of
Arms in London on 21 September 1932. This
embellished version of the national arms has a
helmet above the shield with red and silver mant-
ling. Two protea species appear on the grass
compartment beneath the shield.

The embellished coat of arms is now in general
use, although it has not entirely replaced the
earlier versions. When used by the State President of the Republic of South Africa, the letters
'SP' are added above the crest.

Coats of arms have also been registered for the
Black self-governing territories, and the independent republics which were formerly part of
the RSA.

National flag

At the time of union, South Africa acquired a
number of flags on the British colonial pattern,
largely similar to those of the other Dominions.
In 1926 an official committee was appointed to
consider the design of a distinctive national flag
for the Union of South Africa. It soon became
apparent that there were two opposing points of
view which were difficult to reconcile; one held
that the Union Jack should be included and the
other that it should be omitted. This was an
emotional issue and feelings ran high on both
sides.

A new commission was then appointed under
the chairmanship of Prof W Blommaert. It

proposed the use, as the basis of the national flag, of the old Netherlands orange, white and blue — probably the flag of the oldest administration in South Africa. It was proposed that on this 'Van Riebeeck flag', there should be placed a quartered shield consisting of the Union Jack, *Vierkleur,* OFS flag and, in the remaining quarter, four white stars on a blue field. Ultimately this shield was replaced by the three flags mentioned. The national flag was adopted in terms of the Union Nationality and Flags Act of 1927 and was flown for the first time on 31 May 1928. For nearly 30 years the national flag was flown together with the Union Jack. This arrangement was abandoned in March 1957 when the Flags Amendment Act proclaimed the national flag to be 'the Flag of the Union', and scrapped all references to the use of the Union Jack in South Africa. When South Africa became a republic on 31 May 1961, the 'Flag of the Union' continued unchanged as the national flag of the Republic of South Africa.

A flag for Transkei was introduced in 1963, and in 1971 provision was made for the introduction of a flag for each of the Black self-governing territories.

The mace

The 'colonial' mace, which had been used in the Cape Legislative Assembly and then in the Union House of Assembly after 1910, was replaced by a new mace when South Africa became a republic in 1961.

The head of the republican mace is encircled by the escutcheons of the two former Boer republics (Transvaal and Orange Free State) and two former British colonies (Cape and Natal) which now constitute the four provinces of the RSA. It is heightened with three embellished national coats of arms issuant from a circlet bearing the motto: *Ex Unitate Vires* — Unity is Strength — *Eendrag maak Mag.* Within the circle of coats of arms is the ground plan of the Castle of Good Hope, the oldest seat of authority in South Africa. Inside the ground plan is a representation of the *Drommedaris*, flagship of Jan van Riebeeck, founder of the first settlement at the Cape. The arrival of the British Settlers in 1820 is commemorated by the sailing-ship *Chapman* and the Great Trek is symbolised by a circle of ox-wagons at the bottom of the mace. The protea, South Africa's national flower, is engraved in various motifs on the staff, while the head of the mace is supported by four blue cranes (the national bird).

When the Constitution was introduced to establish a tricameral Parliament, it was decided to make three replicas of the mace, one for each of the three Houses. These new maces, which were made by the South African Mint, were presented to Parliament on 26 August 1987. The original mace, previously used in the House of Assembly, is now used on ceremonial occasions and also in the new Chamber of Parliament during joint meetings of all three Houses, when the Speaker is in the Chair.

Emblems

National flower: Giant or King Protea
        (*Protea cynaroides*)
National tree: Real Yellowwood
        (*Podocarpus latifolius*)
National bird: Blue Crane
        (*Anthropoides paradisea*)
National animal: Springbok
        (*Antidorcas marsupialis*)
National fish: Galjoen
        (*Coracinus capensis*)

The emblems of the Cape Province are the Red Disa (*Disa uniflora*), Silver Tree (*Leucadendron argenteum*), Knysna Lourie (*Tauraco corythaix*) and the Bontebok (Damaliscus dorcas dorcas).

Natal has the Crane Flower (*Strelitzia reginae*), Flat-crown tree (*Albizia adianthifolia*), Lammergeier or Bearded Vulture (*Gypaetus barbatus*) and the Black Wildebeest (*Connochaetes gnou*).

The Orange Free State's provincial emblems are the River Lily (*Crinum bulbispermum*), Wild Olive (*Olea europaea* subsp. *africana*), Black Korhaan (*Eupodotis afra*) and the Black Wildebeest (*Connochaetes gnou*).

The Yellow Arum Lily (*Zantedeschia pentlandii*), Baobab (*Adansonia digitata*), Bokmakierie (*Telophorus zeylonus*) and the Impala (*Aepyceros melampus*) are the provincial emblems of the Transvaal.

National honours

The Chancery of Orders was established in the State President's Office in 1986 to administer The Woltemade Cross for Bravery and the National Orders of the Republic of South Africa. The Director-General of the State President's Office acts as Chancellor of Orders.

National honours are awarded to recognise distinguished service to the Republic of South

Africa by both South African citizens and foreigners.

An Advisory Council for Orders, appointed by the State President, recommends nominations for national orders and advises the State President on related matters.

The national honours, in order of precedence, are:

The Woltemade Cross for Bravery
This decoration is awarded to South African citizens and other persons within or outside the Republic of South Africa in the following categories:
— **Gold:** South African citizens who have distinguished themselves by outstanding bravery through which their lives were in great danger while trying to save the life of another person or by saving or protecting property belonging to the State, in or outside the RSA; or other persons who have distinguished themselves by outstanding bravery through which their lives were in great danger while trying to save the life of a South African citizen or by saving or protecting property belonging to the State, in or outside the RSA.
— **Silver:** South African citizens who have distinguished themselves by exceptional bravery while trying to save the life of another person or by saving or protecting property belonging to the State, in or outside the RSA; or other persons who have distinguished themselves by exceptional bravery while trying to save the life of a South African citizen or by saving or protecting property belonging to the State, in or outside the RSA.

The Order of the Southern Cross
The order is awarded in two classes to South African citizens:
— **Gold:** Those whose unique achievement of the highest standard has served the interest of the RSA.
— **Silver:** Those whose outstanding achievement of a high standard has served the interest of the RSA.

The Order of the Star of South Africa (Military)
The order is awarded in two categories to officers of the South African Defence Force:
— **Gold:** Major-generals and higher officers or officers of comparable rank who distinguished themselves by meritorious military service promoting the efficiency and preparedness of the South African Defence Force and contributing lastingly to the security of the Republic of South Africa.
— **Silver:** Brigadiers and higher officers or officers of comparable rank who distinguished themselves by exceptionally meritorious service of major military importance.

The Order of the Star of South Africa (Non-Military)
The order is awarded in the following categories to officers of the various service departments (except the South African Defence Force) or persons of comparable rank in other departments or institutions, as well as other South African citizens:
— **Grand Cross (Gold):** Major-generals and higher officers or persons of equivalent ranks and other South African citizens who distinguished themselves by excellent meritorious service contributing lastingly to the security and/or general national interest of the RSA.
— **Grand Officer (Silver):** Brigadiers and higher officers or persons of equivalent ranks and other South African citizens who distinguished themselves by outstanding meritorious service contributing significantly to the security and/or general national interest of the RSA.
— **Commander:** South African citizens who distinguished themselves by exceptionally

Table 1 Number of national honours
awarded, 1990

The Woltemade Cross for Bravery	
Gold	8
Silver	7
The Order of the Southern Cross	
Gold	2
Silver	0
The Order of the Star of South Africa (Military)	
Gold	0
Silver	0
The Order of the Star of South Africa (Non-military)	
Grand Cross (Gold)	0
Grand Officer (Silver)	1
Commander	1
Officer	1
Member	0
The Order for Meritorious Service	
Gold	8
Silver	15
The Order of Good Hope	
Grand Cross (Gold)	0
Grand Officer (Silver)	1
Commander	6
Officer	0
Member	1

Stamps depicting some of the national honours

meritorious service contributing meaningfully to the security and/or general national interest of the RSA.

— **Officer:** South African citizens who distinguished themselves by rendering meritorious service contributing to the security and/or general national interest of the RSA.

— **Member:** South African citizens who distinguished themselves by exceptional service contributing to the security and/or general national interest of the RSA.

The Order for Meritorious Service

The order is awarded in two classes to South African citizens:

— **Gold:** South African citizens who have distinguished themselves by rendering exceptionally meritorious service in the general public interest.

— **Silver:** South African citizens who have distinguished themselves by rendering meritorious service in the general public interest.

This order was awarded for the first time in 1986. It replaces the Decoration for Meritorious Service established in 1970. The order and the decoration enjoy the same precedence and the

Decoration for Meritorious Service may still be worn by recipients.

The Order of Good Hope

This order is awarded in five classes to citizens of foreign countries who have distinguished themselves by their services in the mutual promotion of our international relations or have promoted the interest of the Republic of South Africa:

— **Grand Cross (Gold):** Heads of State and, in special cases heads of government and other persons who have promoted the interests of the RSA through excellent meritorious service.

— **Grand Officer (Silver):** Heads of government and other ministers of state, Supreme Court judges, presidents of legislative bodies, secretaries of state, ambassadors extraordinary and plenipotentiary, commanders in chief of armed forces, other functionaries and persons of comparable rank and station according to the rules and practices of each country, who have promoted the interests of the RSA through outstanding meritorious service.

— **Commander:** Members of legislative bodies,

envoys extraordinary and ministers plenipotentiary, general officers of the armed forces other than commanders in chief, other functionaries and persons of comparable rank and station according to the rules and practices of each country, who have promoted the interests of the RSA through exceptionally meritorious service.

— **Officer:** Chargés d'affaires, counsellors of diplomatic missions, consuls general, colonels and lieutenant-colonels or persons of equivalent rank, other functionaries and persons of comparable rank and station, according to the rules and practices of each country, who have promoted the interests of the RSA through meritorious service.

— **Member:** Secretaries of diplomatic missions, consuls, lower ranking officers of the armed forces, other functionaries and persons of comparable rank and station according to the rules and practices of each country, who have promoted the interests of the RSA through exceptional service.

Acknowledgements:
Bureau for Heraldry
Department of Environment Affairs
Office of the State President

South African law is based on the principles of the Roman-Dutch law, but has since 1806 been influenced by English law — legislation and judgments/verdicts. This influence can best be seen in our statutory law and the establishment of criminal procedure law.

South African legislation is constantly revised, developed, adapted and supplemented to meet changing circumstances in a dynamic and developing society. This is done by Parliament on advice of the legal sections of various departments, but primarily by the South African Law Commission.

The commission undertakes research in all branches of the law of the Republic and makes recommendations on the development, improvement, modernisation or reform of the law. This includes repeal of obsolete and unnecessary provisions; removal of anomalies; promotion of uniformity in the law in force in various parts of the Republic; consolidation or codification of any branch of the law; and steps to make common law more readily available.

Sovereign legislative authority is vested in the State President and Parliament, which comprises the House of Assembly, the House of Representatives and the House of Delegates. The Republic of South Africa Constitution Act, 1983, imposes certain rules for passing of laws.

Administration of Justice

Authority to initiate and observe legal proceedings in the case of a crime falling under the jurisdiction of a lower court or a Supreme Court is vested in the state.

Attorneys-General, appointed by the State President, direct public prosecution within their areas of jurisdiction subject to the control of the Minister of Justice. This authority of the Attorney-General is delegated to public prosecutors to conduct prosecutions in the lower courts.

An Attorney-General has the power to prosecute anybody on behalf of the state in a court that has jurisdiction, for an offence committed in the area over which he was appointed. This also includes the power to continue an appeal, arising from criminal proceedings, in any court.

Among other things an Attorney-General closely examines inquiries into mining accidents and fatal accidents at factories, investigations under the Explosives Act, as well as records of certain other inquests to determine whether prosecution should be instituted.

Private prosecution is instituted in the same way as prosecution by the state, except that all costs and expenses of the defence must be paid by the litigant, subject to any order by the court when the prosecution has been completed.

An Attorney-General can at any stage of a private prosecution take up the prosecution and continue in the name of the state.

The Supreme Court

Decisions of the various divisions of the Supreme Court of South Africa are an important source of law. The function of a judge is not to make new laws, but to interpret, to explain and to apply existing common law, rules and legislation. In many cases a judicial decision establishes a new rule of law by interpretation and is thus termed judge-made law. Decisions of the Appellate Division of the Supreme Court are binding on all courts of a lower order and the decisions of the provincial and local divisions are binding on magistrates' courts within their respective areas of jurisdiction.

Judges and acting judges are appointed by the State President. Judges are appointed from the bar. The Chief Justice of South Africa is the Hon M M Corbett. The judges president are the Hon J A Howard (Natal); the Hon J J Kriek (acting) (Northern Cape); the Hon F S Smuts (OFS); the Hon D D V Kannemeyer (Eastern Cape); the Hon G G A Munnik (Cape of Good Hope); and the Hon H H Moll (Transvaal).

The Supreme Court is constituted as follows:

Appellate Division
The Appellate Division is the highest court and is seated in Bloemfontein, the judicial capital. It is composed of the Chief Justice and as many judges of appeal as the State President may determine from time to time.

The Appellate Division has jurisdiction to hear and determine an appeal against any decision of the court of a provincial or local division. An accused who has been sentenced to death may appeal against his conviction or sentence to the Appellate Division of the Supreme Court without applying for leave to appeal. In a case in which a person has been sentenced to death, the Minister of Justice may refer the case record to the Appellate Division to revise the proceedings in the Supreme Court.

Provincial and local divisions

There are six provincial divisions: Cape of Good Hope, with its seat in Cape Town; Eastern Cape (Grahamstown); Northern Cape (Kimberley); Orange Free State (Bloemfontein); Natal (Pietermaritzburg); and Transvaal (Pretoria). Each of these divisions is composed of a judge president and, if the State President so determines, one or more deputy judge president and as many puisne judges as the State President may determine from time to time.

The local divisions are the Witwatersrand Division, with its seat in Johannesburg; Durban and Coast (Durban); and South-Eastern Cape (Port Elizabeth). These courts are presided over by judges of the provincial division concerned.

A provincial or local division has jurisdiction in its own area, as specified in the Supreme Court Act, 1959, over all persons residing or being in that area, and in all causes arising and all offences triable within that area, and over all other matters of which it may take cognisance according to law. These divisions hear matters that are usually of such a serious nature that the magistrate's or regional court would not be competent to impose an appropriate penalty. Except where minimum or maximum sentences are laid down by law, their punitive jurisdiction is unlimited and includes the death sentence as well as life imprisonment in certain specified cases.

Circuit local divisions

These are itinerant courts, each presided over by a judge of the provincial division. These courts periodically visit areas nominated by the judge president of the provincial division concerned.

Special superior courts

When an Attorney-General decides to arraign an accused upon a charge which relates to the security of the state or maintenance of public order, and the Minister of Justice is of the opinion that the circumstances are such that the interests of justice or of public order would be better served were the accused tried by a superior court specially constituted for the trial, the State President may constitute such a court which consists of three judges.

Regional courts

The Minister may divide the country into districts and may create regional districts consisting of a number of districts. Regional courts are then established at one or more places in each regional division to hear matters within their jurisdiction. Unlike the Supreme Court, the regional courts' punitive jurisdiction is limited by legislation.

Magistrates' courts

Each magisterial district is under the control of a magistrate who is responsible for aspects of state administration within his district. When a state department has no local office in a district, the magistrate acts as its representative. In most country districts the magistrate performs a number of administrative duties on behalf of these departments. Although district courts are subordinate to regional courts with regard to punitive jurisdiction, an accused cannot appeal to the regional court against the decision of a district court. There are 309 magistrates' offices in the Republic with 956 magistrates, 1 164 prosecutors and 3 531 officers of other ranks.

Civil jurisdiction

Except when otherwise provided by law, the area of civil jurisdiction of a magistrate's court is the district, subdistrict or area for which the court is established. Roman-Dutch law as applied in the Cape Province is in force on Prince Edward and Marion islands which, for the purpose of the administration of justice, are deemed to be part of the Cape Town magisterial district.

Unless all parties in a case consent to higher jurisdiction, the magistrate's court's jurisdiction is limited to cases in which the claim value does not exceed R10 000, or in the case of claims based upon liquid documents, R30 000.

Criminal jurisdiction

Apart from differently worded specific provisions of the Magistrates' Courts Act or any other Act, jurisdiction with regard to sentences in district courts is limited to a period of not more than 12 months' imprisonment or a fine not exceeding R4 000. The regional court can impose a sentence of not more than 10 years' imprisonment or a fine of R40 000.

Any person charged with any offence committed within any district or regional division may be tried either by the court of that district or the court of the regional division. When it is uncertain in which of several jurisdictions an offence has been committed, it may be tried in any of such jurisdictions.

Where by any special provision of law a magistrate's court has jurisdiction over an offence committed beyond the local limits of the district or of the regional division, the court shall not be deprived of this jurisdiction unless the accused lodges an objection.

Where an accused is alleged to have committed various offences within different districts within the areas of jurisdiction of two or more attorneys-general, the Minister of Justice may in writing direct criminal proceedings to any court with jurisdiction.

A magistrate's court (district court) has jurisdiction over all offences, except treason, murder and rape. The court of a regional division has jurisdiction over all offences except treason. The Supreme Court, however, may try all offences. Depending on the gravity of the offence and circumstances pertaining to the offender, the attorney-general decides in which court a matter will be heard. He may even decide on a summary trial in the Supreme Court.

Prosecutions are usually disposed of summarily by magistrate's courts and judgment and sentence passed. The following sentences may, where provided for by law, be passed upon a convicted person: Imprisonment, periodical imprisonment, declaration as an habitual criminal, committal to any institution established by law, a fine with or without imprisonment as alternative, whipping, conditional or unconditional reprieve or a suspended sentence, and a warning or caution and discharge.

Sentencing 'petty' offenders to serve community service, in fitting circumstances, has become a part of an alternative sentence instead of direct imprisonment. Only the Supreme Court may pass the death sentence.

The State President, acting on the advice of the Executive Council, is by law empowered to commute a death sentence.

Where a court convicts a person of any offence, other than one for which any law prescribes a minimum punishment, the court may, in its discretion, postpone the passing of sentence for a period not exceeding five years and release the person convicted on one or more conditions or pass sentence but suspend it. If the conditions of suspension or postponement are not fulfilled, the offender may be arrested and made to undergo the sentence, provided that the court may grant an order further suspending the operation of the sentence, if the offender proves that circumstances beyond his control or any other good and sufficient reason prevented him from complying with the conditions of suspension.

Small Claims Court

Cases involving civil claims not exceeding R1 500 in value are heard by a commissioner in the Small Claims Court. The commissioner is usually a practising advocate or attorney, a law academic or another competent person who offers his or her services free of charge. Neither the plaintiff nor the defendant may be represented or assisted by counsel at the hearing. The commissioner's decision is final and there is no appeal to a higher court. By 1 March 1990 small claims courts had been established in 72 regions consisting of 110 districts (from a total of 267 magistrate's districts countrywide), with 11 seats of hearing.

Civil courts

An authorised Black chief or captain or his deputy may hear and determine civil claims arising out of indigenous law and custom and brought before him by a Black person against another Black person within his area of jurisdiction. Courts constituted in this way are commonly known as chiefs' courts. Litigants have the right to choose whether to institute an action in the chief's court or in a magistrate's court. Proceedings in a chief's court are informal. An appeal against a judgment of a chief's court can be heard in a magistrate's court.

Other criminal courts

In terms of the Black Administration Act, 1927, the Minister of Constitutional Development and Planning may confer upon a Black chief or headman or his deputy, jurisdiction to try and to punish a Black person who has committed an offence under common law or indigenous law and custom, with the exception of certain serious offences specified in the Act. The procedure at such trials is in accordance with indigenous law and custom. The jurisdiction conferred upon a chief and a magistrate does not affect the jurisdiction of other courts competent to try criminal cases.

Rules Board

The Rules Board for courts of law comprises experts from all facets of the legal profession. The board may, from time to time, review existing rules of court and, subject to the approval of the Minister of Justice, make, amend or repeal rules for the Supreme Court and lower courts. The board is empowered to advise the Minister of Justice on the monetary jurisdiction limits of lower courts, the limitation of the costs of litigation and any other matter referred to the board by the Minister.

The Palace of Justice designed by Sytze Wierda in the Italian Renaissance style and erected at the turn of the century

Legal aid

The **Legal Aid Board**, an independent statutory body, renders or makes available legal aid to indigent persons and has the power to engage legal practitioners and lay down conditions for granting legal aid.

Free legal aid is also offered by the advice centres and legal aid clinics of some universities. These clinics are staffed by final year students under the guidance of a qualified attorney.

An official of the Department of Justice acts as a **Prisoner's Friend** at each of the larger magistrate's courts. He helps those who have been fined or allowed bail to raise the required funds. He does this by assisting prisoners to enlist the aid of relatives, employers or friends.

In the larger magisterial districts, officials of the Department of Justice are appointed as **witness friends** in order to assist witnesses who have to appear in court. The witness friends arrange for the timely appearance of the witness in the correct court and assist in obtaining payment of the witness' expenses.

The **National Institute for Crime Prevention and Rehabilitation of Offenders** (Nicro) is a non-sectarian welfare organisation striving to prevent crime and rehabilitate offenders. The Institute strives for successful reintegration of the offender into the community and assists his family during his imprisonment. It undertakes and promotes research on deviant behavioural patterns, analyses the causes of crime and promotes effective preventive measures. It seeks to foster public awareness and concern by disseminating information on crime, its causes and consequences.

Legal practitioners

The legal profession is divided into two branches — advocates and attorneys — who are subject to a strict ethical code.

Advocates are organised in bar associations or societies, one each at the seat of the various divisions of the Supreme Court. The General Council of the Bar of South Africa is the co-ordinating body of the various independent bar associations.

For attorneys there is a law society in each of the four provinces. A practising attorney is ipso jure member of at least one of these societies, which seek to promote the interests of the profession. The Association of Law Societies is the co-ordinating body of the various independent law societies.

State law advisers give legal advice to ministers, government departments and provincial administrations, as well as a number of statutory bodies. In addition, they draft Bills and assist the Minister concerned in their passage through Parliament. They also assist in criminal and constitutional matters. State attorneys render attorney services to the government. They also defend government officials in criminal courts on charges arising from the performance of their official duties. State attorneys have only one client — the government, represented by its various departments and administrations. Any fees that a state attorney may earn are paid into the Consolidated Revenue Fund.

There are three basic law degrees — LL.B., B.Proc. and B.Iuris. These qualifications may be obtained through full-time or part-time study at 15 residential universities, or by correspondence from the University of South Africa (Unisa). Comprehensive law libraries are accessible to all students and practitioners, while new developments are covered in numerous law journals and textbooks.

The Department of Justice offers special courses for prospective public prosecutors. Courses for more experienced officials are also offered.

Department of Correctional Services

The Department of Correctional Services has at its aim promotion of order and security in the community through control of, detention and/or handling of persons/prisoners in the most effective and least restrictive way.

While the department is currently responsible for prisoners who are detained in prisons, the department will in future also be responsible for those persons who are placed under correctional supervision outside prisons.

The department's headquarters is the policy-making body while regional commissioners co-ordinate activities in their regions, which are divided according to geographic boundaries.

The 202 prisons countrywide consist of 188 prisons for men (13 maximum and 175 medium security prisons) and 14 prisons for women. These also include two prisons for juveniles. Some of the above-mentioned prisons are situated on the department's 16 prison farms and in 103 of the prisons for men there are separate sections in which women prisoners can be detained.

The department has a personnel corps of approximately 22 600 men and women who form a countrywide team striving for a common goal, each in his own field of occupation and speciality. They are equipped for their task by extensive training at the beginning of their careers as well as at different stages later. Further studies at tertiary institutions are encouraged and supported.

In South African prisons there are currently four categories of prisoners, namely:
— Unsentenced prisoners (mainly people who are standing trial on a charge and who are detained in prison pending their hearing or sentence);
— short-term prisoners (sentenced prisoners serving a sentence of less than two years);
— long-term prisoners (sentenced prisoners serving sentences of two years and longer); and
— juvenile prisoners (sentenced prisoners under the age of 21).

The **detention** and **physical care** of the approximately 95 300 prisoners in South African prisons is the most important responsibility of the management of any prison. A high standard of health care and hygiene is maintained in all prisons according to international accepted norms. District surgeons assisted by nurses in the employ of the Department of Correctional Services, are responsible for the medical care of prisoners. When necessary, prisoners are referred to other medical practitioners, specialists or public hospitals.

Long-term prisoners undergo security classification upon admission to determine their security classification, based, inter alia, on their type of crime, length of sentence and previous convictions. Prisoners are then detained in either a medium or maximum security prison. The security classification of a prisoner is reviewed regularly.

A goal-oriented programme approach is followed in dealing with prisoners. The needs of the individual are determined, after which he/she can follow a suitable programme.

Provision of education includes literacy tuition for illiterate prisoners, primary, secondary and tertiary education, as well as preparedness and recreation programmes.

Training of prisoners implies:
— Vocational training in a variety of trades in which a prisoner can obtain a diploma or a certificate;
— training in skills which do not confer artisan status, but which require special training, for example training as cooks, waiters, training in clothing manufacturing and in a variety of agricultural fields; and
— constructive unskilled labour by means of which prisoners who cannot receive formal training can take part in a variety of other

work opportunities such as elementary farming activities, gardening work, maintenance of prison premises, etc.

Labour performance by and training of prisoners not only aims to keep prisoners constructively and sensibly occupied during their detention, but also to allow better equipped individuals to return to the community more able to enjoy independent and productive life after their release.

Social work services are case work and group work, and are aimed at effective social functioning of the prisoner. These services are provided in close co-operation and consultation with ex-

A uniform penal and prison policy is followed by all four provinces

in which they turn 16, but are not called up for service before the year in which they turn 18.

The initial service commitment is a continuous period of service not exceeding 24 months followed by subsequent periods of service (Citizen Force camps) during six cycles of two years, none exceeding an average of 120 days.

Due to concessions by the State President and Minister of Defence, the initial period of service was reduced in 1990 from 24 months to 12 months and the Citizen Force/Commando Force call up period from 60 days per cycle to 30 days. It should be noted that the Defence Act provides for maximum periods of service, within which these reductions can be accommodated. The reduced periods are possible for as long as the security situation permits.

Non-Whites are not liable for military service but thousands of volunteers are accepted annually at special units and training establishments. In 1974 the SADF established its first Black Permanent Force unit, 21 Battalion. At present the SADF has nine Black battalions.

Since 1970 women have been appointed in 65 musterings in the SADF. They serve in the Permanent Force, the Citizen Force and in the Commandos. Women are not used in a combat role.

SADF decorations

The Castle of Good Hope Decoration (CGH) may be awarded to all ranks in the SADF for conspicuous heroism in the field. Instituted with effect retrospective to 6 April 1952, this is the highest SADF award for bravery. To date it has never been awarded.

Other decorations include four Honoris Crux decorations, the Southern Cross Decoration (SD), the Pro Merito Decoration (PMD), the Southern Cross Medal (SM), the Pro Merito Medal (PMM) and the SADF Good Service Medal (different periods). Good service medals also include the John Chard Decoration (JCD), John Chard Medal (JCM) and the De Wet Decoration (DWD). Other medals include the Chief of the SADF Commendation Medal, the Danie Theron Medal and the Pro Patria Medal.

Altogether 164 decorations and 11 496 medals were awarded by the SADF during 1990.

Armaments

The **Armaments Corporation of South Africa** (Armscor) meets South Africa's armaments requirements, including those of the SADF, to a large extent.

Established in 1964, Armscor has assets of about R2,1 billion and employs about 20 000 people from all population groups. There are 12 manufacturing subsidiaries as well as a number of service facilities.

The private sector has been involved in armaments development and production from the start. It is, in fact, Armscor's policy not to duplicate within its own organisation facilities which already exist in the private sector. Today Armscor is associated with a large number of private contractors which account for about 70 per cent of all armaments and ammunition manufactured in the country.

Not only is South Africa virtually self-sufficient regarding armaments, but Armscor and its subsidiaries have reached a level of production and expertise which has meant successful competition on the international armaments market.

South African Police

The South African Police (SAP) was founded on 1 April 1913 after the establishment of the Union of South Africa in 1910. Since then the SAP has developed into one of the most formidable police forces in the world even though it is one of the smallest, considering the ratio of its numerical strength to the total population of the Republic (2 per 1 000 of the population).

Since 1 January 1990 the SAP has been divided into 11 regions for administration and execution of its task, which is to protect the internal security of the RSA, to maintain law and order, to prevent crime and to investigate alleged offences.

A Regional Commissioner heads each region. The regions are subdivided into districts, each under command of a district commissioner who oversees the work of the different police stations.

Command and control of the SAP is vested in the Commissioner of Police, with the rank of general.

The South African Police executes its task in accordance with internationally accepted principles of policing, which include the principle of correct application of the legal force and minimum use of violence to handle any given situation. For the execution of its task the SA Police, like any other police force in the world, depends on thorough training, efficient legislation and the support of the public, which it serves.

Ten management functions within the SAP, each under the command of a lieutenant-general, carry out the task of the force.

Uniformed Branch

On completion of their training at any one of four training colleges, student constables normally join the Uniformed Branch in which the majority

Table 1 Major crimes in South Africa (as portrayed by number of incidents reported to the SA Police)

Crime	1988	1989	% of change in incidence
Theft (not mentioned elsewhere) including shoplifting	257 717	261 447	+ 2,84
Burglary	182 754	187 946	+ 2,84
Assault with the intent to do bodily harm	125 571	128 887	+ 2,64
Theft from motor vehicles	116 813	122 385	+ 4,77
Theft (of motor vehicles and bicycles)	83 863	84 087	+ 0,27
Malicious injury to property	74 399	82 487	+10,87
Robbery	45 847	50 636	+ 10,45
All fraud, forgery, misappropriation, embezzlement, etc	37 032	43 321	+ 16,98
Driving under the influence of alcohol or narcotics	25 682	30 744	+ 19,71
Rape	19 368	20 458	+ 5,62
Murder	10 631	11 750	+ 10,52
Public violence	1 368	3 173	+ 131,94

of Force members serve. This branch is concerned with administration of the force, prevention of crime, investigation of certain types of crimes and other police duties not incorporated into any of the other branches of the Force.

Detective Branch
Before becoming a detective, a policeman must normally have served in the Uniformed Branch long enough to gain the necessary experience.

Special investigation units of the Detective Branch include the diamond and gold branch, the SA Narcotics Bureau and the units for murder and robbery, vehicle theft and stock theft, child protection, commercial crimes, protection of endangered species and theft from trains.

Security Branch
This branch is primarily responsible for investigation of all matters relating to protection of the internal security of the RSA. This is done not only through investigation of any person or instance which threatens the country's security, but also by applying the provisions of all security legislation.

Operational Branch
This branch is divided into different special services. It is firstly responsible for all counter-insurgency services. This branch must therefore also react to information on planned internal unrest and riots, gathered by the security branch.

The Special Guard Unit is responsible for protection of all VIPs, as well as all fixed property under the control of the South African Police and other state institutions.

Units for special constables and the municipal police are also seen as part of the Operational Branch. Unlike other members of the Force the municipal police have legal powers only in the municipal areas in which they serve.

The unit for transport policing supplies specialised police services at airports and other places connected to South Africa's transport services which are of strategic importance to the country.

Scientific Technical Services
All activities of a scientific, technical nature are rendered by this branch. This includes the Criminal Records Centre (previously known as the SA Criminal Bureau), the Forensic Sciences Laboratory, the division Information Systems where electronic information technology is obtained and developed for the Force, the division for advanced communications systems, architectural services and other consulting services.

Personnel Services
This branch is responsible for recruiting members of the Force, their basic training at the four colleges (Pretoria, Hammanskraal, Bishop Lavis, near Cape Town, and Durban), for training members for special tasks, admission to the officers' corps and for management development at all levels. This branch is also responsible for administration of all personnel matters, excluding those regarding officers.

Management Services
Management Services include the division of the senior staff officer at head office who handles all matters regarding the administration and posting of officers.

It also includes the Public Relations Section, which is aimed at fulfilling all functions in order to gain the support and co-operation of the public and to keep it in attaining the Force's aims.

The Force's inspectorate is seated in the Division for Efficiency Services. Not only does the inspectorate ensure that services are in accordance with the needs of the public, but also that the Force has an efficient organisation and the necessary aids at its disposal to enable it to fulfil its task.

The Logistical Services division (previously the Quartermaster) obtains and distributes all physical aids such as uniforms, office equipment and stationery, vehicles, arms and ammunition, housing and office space for the Force throughout South Africa.

In the Legal Services division care is taken that

Policewomen were incorporated in the SAP in 1972. They proved themselves to be invaluable

investigations and police actions are initiated legally and are technically correct. Attention is also given to criminal and other charges against members of the Force and any legal action arising from such charges, whether against the member involved or against the Force.

Pastoral and Welfare Services
This branch sees to the spiritual needs of all members. The activities of the branch are not linked to those of any specific church, although chaplains of most of the major christian churches in the Republic serve in the Force.

Financial Services
This branch is responsible for all financial services including preparation of the SAP's annual budget which is tabled in Parliament.

Crime prevention
Crime prevention is one of the primary duties of the South African Police and enjoys very high priority.

Crime is a social phenomenon and its prevention is the co-responsibility of every member of society.

Nearly four years ago the SAP launched a campaign aimed at motivating the public to accept this responsibility. Nearly 3 million placards, pamphlets and other information material have been distributed to the public. Police officers addressed groups on crime prevention and security measures.

Exhibits of safety equipment are arranged in larger centres in collaboration with the manufacturers and distributors and general guidance in this regard is also provided.

Radio talks and television programmes including Police File are used to foster a greater awareness of crime. Editorial space in regional newspapers are used for regular columns in which the public is made aware of crime and where hints are given regarding security and general crime prevention.

A crime prevention room has recently been installed at the SA Police College in Pretoria. All types of safety equipment are installed and displayed here. Here trainee policemen and members of other organisations are trained and educated on all aspects of crime prevention.

Each police district has a crime prevention unit that consists of policemen and -women who concentrate on patrols, observation at points where certain types of crimes are common, and the general clearing up of places where layabouts and others meet or congregate under suspicious circumstances. The activities of these units are co-ordinated and controlled by a crime-prevention officer.

Other activities
The **Police Museum** was started in Pretoria in 1964. The cultural history division contains exhibits of historical significance, while the crime division contains objects used as exhibits in courts of law in notorious cases of murder, theft, sabotage and other crimes.

The **SA Police Band** was formed in 1902 as the SA Constabulary Band. The band has 85 members, including 16 women.

The **Reserve Police Force** consists of members of the public who volunteer for service to maintain law and order and combat crime. These reservists include members of all population groups as well as recent immigrants. Black, Coloured and Asian reservists generally serve their own communities.

A junior reserve corps was established in 1981. To date, some 2 921 young members have been inducted. The first female reservists were accepted in 1982.

The Police Reserve consists of ex-members of the SAP, divided into an active and an inactive group. Members of the former are those who have completed less than 10 years' permanent service in the SAP and can be called up for police duty for a maximum of 90 days a year.

Members of the inactive group have completed more than 10 years' permanent service in the SAP and have resigned before 1 January 1983 or have already performed the compulsory service outlined above. They may be called up for service in times of emergency.

Security legislation

The Internal Security Act empowers the Minister of Justice to declare any organisation unlawful if he is satisfied that it engages in activities which endanger or could endanger the security of the state or maintenance of law and order, or that the organisation promotes communism or spreads it. He may also prohibit printing, publication or circulation of any publication for the same reasons.

The Act also provides for the detention or restriction of people. The Minister may, if he is satisfied that a person engages in any of these activities, prohibit him from taking part in the activities of certain organisations; from attending any specified gathering; from being within any place or area or absenting himself from it; from performing certain specified acts and from communicating with certain categories of persons during a specified period.

The Act provides for appointment by the State President of a board of review or, if he deems it expedient, two or more boards of review to review the Minister's actions.

After the Minister has taken steps to detain or restrict a person, he must submit to the board of review a copy of the notice and a written statement giving reasons for the detention or restriction order for investigation and a recommendation. Upon a written application, the board of review is obliged to allow the person concerned to give oral evidence, unless the chairman deems it not to be in the public interest.

Since circumstances may change during the duration of an order, provision is made for periodic review by a board of the cases of restricted or detained persons. Anybody to whom an order applies may, at intervals of six months in the case of preventive detention and 12 months in the case of restricted persons, request that his case be reviewed. Such persons can, however, address representations to the Minister at any time.

The review procedure does not deprive anyone of his right to challenge the order in court, provided such proceedings are instituted within 14 days of the order being served. If a person does not succeed in such proceedings and the order therefore remains in force, he may request revision of the order six or 12 months after the judgment of the court and at similar intervals thereafter. This will depend on the nature of the order.

The Act also authorises detention for interrogation of a suspected terrorist or anybody suspected of subversion. Such a person may not be detained for more than 30 days, unless the Minister of Law and Order is satisfied that a longer period of detention is necessary for the purpose of interrogation and he personally authorises further detention in writing.

If a detainee has not been released after six months, the Commissioner of Police is obliged to give the board of review reasons why he should not be released. The board must thereafter submit to the Minister of Law and Order a written report on the proceedings and its findings.

The Act also provides that detainees shall be visited as frequently as possible by independent inspectors who must satisfy themselves of their wellbeing. Magistrates and district surgeons must also visit detainees once every fortnight.

A comprehensive set of directions on treatment of persons detained for interrogation has been issued in terms of the Act to ensure their wellbeing while in detention.

According to the Act the offence of terrorism, briefly, consists of the commission by a person, with intent to overthrow or endanger the state authority, or to achieve or promote any constitutional, political, industrial, social or economic objective or change in the Republic, of an act of violence, or in his threatening or attempting to commit such act, or in his performance of any act which is aimed at such act or threat of violence. The offence of subversion consists in the commission by a person, with the same intent as in the case of terrorism, of acts which endanger or prejudice the state or the community, or where a person conspires with or incites or encourages any other person to commit any one or more of such acts.

Sabotage consists of commission by a person of an act, or his attempting or conspiring with or inciting or encouraging any other person to commit an act, with the intent to destroy or damage vulnerable and strategic buildings and installations, or to impede essential services.

The Act does not provide for any minimum sentence but only prescribes a maximum sentence. The court, therefore, has the discretion to impose a sentence depending on the circumstances of each case.

The future role of security legislation

Widespread unrest since 1984 forced the government in 1985 to declare a partial state of emergency. After it was revoked for a few months, a countrywide state of emergency was declared in 1986 and thereafter from year to year until 8 June 1990, when a state of emergency was declared in the province of Natal only. This was lifted on 18 June 1990.

For years organisations such as the ANC and the PAC have justified the use of violence to achieve political aims because they were excluded from political processes, having been declared unlawful in terms of security legislation.

When he opened Parliament on 2 February 1990 the State President announced the lifting of restrictions on all existing unlawful organisations as well as all restrictions on organisations in terms of the then emergency regulations. These organisations are now in the position to practise politics in a normal and lawful manner free of any restrictions.

The government has thus opened the door for negotiations. Furthermore one of the most important ANC leaders, Mr Nelson Mandela, who received a lifelong sentence after being found guilty of sabotage, was released. Various other so-called political prisoners were also released.

After discussions between the government and the ANC at Groote Schuur, Cape Town, the government undertook to review existing security legislation to bring it into line with the new dynamic situation in South Africa, in order to ensure normal and free political activity.

After further discussions in August 1990 the government undertook to consider repealing certain provisions of the Internal Security Act, 1982, among others those prohibiting fostering of communism. The government further undertook to continue reviewing security legislation with a view to introducing amending legislation during the 1991 Parliamentary session.

The State President has, however, indicated that the process of negotiation will be conducted legally and in an orderly way. During the negotiation process some security legislation will still be relevant to maintain law and order.

News items: 1990

The Dangerous Weapons Amendment Act introduced during the year empowers the Minister of Law and Order to restrict or prohibit possession of dangerous weapons in public places and gatherings and enables the police to disarm people carrying such weapons. Possession of a prohibited weapon carries a maximum penalty of R4 000 or one year's imprisonment, or both.

The first attack helicopter to be built in the Southern Hemisphere, the Rooivalk XH-2 combat support helicopter, was unveiled by Armscor in January.

The South African Defence Force announced cutbacks on military spending in 1990. These included an 18,3 per cent reduction of Navy personnel and 10 per cent of Armscor personnel, disbanding of the Marine Corps, several Air Force squadrons and a number of Army units.

The period of community service for conscientious objectors to military service was halved, while under certain conditions the period of imprisonment served by those refusing to do military service was halved.

The appointment of a Commission of Inquiry into Certain Alleged Murders was announced in February. Mr Justice L T C Harms was the chairman and only commission member. His brief was to investigate the alleged occurrence of murders and other unlawful deeds in South Africa. The Commission found that the Civil Co-operation Bureau (CCB), which was part of the SADF, had been involved in hit squad activities but exonerated the SAP from any similar action. All activities of the CCB were suspended pending the conclusion of investigations by the SAP and the Harms Commission. It was also announced that Mr Anton Lubowski, the murdered Swapo legal adviser, had been a paid agent of Military Intelligence. The CCB was operationally disbanded in the latter half of 1990.

Mark Goodwin, (18) became the first Chinese South African to join the SA Police.

On 31 May 1990 the SA Police employed a total of 82 251 persons: 36 406 Whites (32 853 men and 3 553 women), 37 208 Blacks (35 736 men and 1 472 women), 5 819 Coloureds (5 415 men and 404 women) and 2 818 Indians (2 581 men and 237 women).

A total of 36 policemen were killed on duty in 1989 and 164 were seriously injured. A total of 91 policemen were killed on duty in 1990, 65 of them in unrest-related incidents.

From January to 15 August there were 1 223 attacks on policemen and police patrols, 522 on policemen's homes and families while 1 805 police vehicles were damaged or destroyed.

Police dogs sniffed out 96 812 kg of dagga in 1989, helped recover stolen property worth over R36 million and correctly identified bombs and dynamite in 83 cases.

The Deputy Chief of the Army, Lt-Gen Georg Meiring, became Chief of the Army on 1 March. His predecessor, Lt-Gen A J Liebenberg, succeeded Lt-Gen Ian Gleeson as Chief of Defence Force Staff. The Chief of the SADF, Gen Jannie Geldenhuys, retired at the end of October. He was succeeded by Gen A J Liebenberg.

The SADF presented 100 000 ration packs worth R1 million to the Mozambican Defence Force.

Rear Admiral L J Woodburne was promoted Vice-Admiral and succeeded Vice-Admiral A P Putter as Chief of the Navy on 1 July.

The Minister for Planning and Provincial Affairs allocated R250 000 in aid for war-ravaged Natal. Canada pledged R450 000 in emergency assistance.

A new salary deal for policemen, nurses, the SA Defence Force, the Prisons Service and some law enforcement officials in the Department of Justice was announced in April.

The Indemnity Act, which enables so-called political prisoners and other exiles to return to South Africa, was approved by Parliament.

Law and Order Minister Adriaan Vlok extended the ban on police joining the Afrikaner Weerstandsbeweging (AWB), a right-wing organisation, to all political parties or groups.

Drastic measures to defuse racial tension in Welkom was announced in May following an incident at the President Steyn Gold Mine in which two Whites were killed by Black mineworkers.

In the biggest ever police investigation into alleged irregularities concerning the financial rand, Commercial Branch detectives arrested three prominent businessmen in Johannesburg and Cape Town on alleged fraud involving more than R350 million in May.

Ruth Gerhardt, convicted for high treason in 1983, was freed in May. Her husband, Dieter, who was convicted with her, was the officer commanding Simon's Town Naval Base. He received a life sentence.

The state's contingency fund was doubled to R2 billion to pay for a plan of action to boost the strength of the security forces. This will cost R814 million in the present financial year to be appropriated as follows: SAP (R644 million), Police in self-governing areas (R48 million), SA Prisons Services (R88 million), Prisons Services in self-governing areas (R1 million) and legal services (R33 million).

Police launched a nationwide 'witch-hunt' to determine the extent of satanism in South Africa, probing the following crimes linked to satanism: Murder, sexual offences, drug abuse, violations of the Human Tissue Act, the Witchcraft Suppression Act, the Children's Act, the Child Care Act and the Animal Protection Act.

Police offered a R50 000 reward for information leading to the arrest of Boerestaat Party leader Piet 'Skiet' Rudolph after he released a video saying he would seek the 'bloody and violent' overthrow of the government. He was arrested in Pretoria in September and charged on six counts of terrorism.

The Graaff-Reinet College for Continued Education became a police academy for tertiary education at the beginning of 1991. The first rector is Gen Johan Coetzee, former Commissioner of Police.

Eight crew members from helicopters which were locked in battle with Swapo terrorists in Ovambo in April 1989 received Honoris Crux decorations in July. Another two soldiers received the medals for exceptional bravery under fire. Four of the medals were in the silver class and six were straight Crux decorations.

South African paratroopers carried out the biggest night-jump training exercise in the history of the famed 'Parabats' in July. More than 400 parabats, 70 tons of equipment and 24 vehicles were used in 'Exercise Iron Eagle'.

Lt Koomaresen Earganbram, the first Indian pupil pilot in the SAAF, received his pilot's insignia at a wings parade at Central Flying School Dunnottar, near Springs.

A municipal policeman from Sebokeng received the SA Police Cross for Bravery for courage and perseverance displayed while dealing with an armed robber.

After saving the life of his handler, Rinty, a seven-year-old police dog, became the 26th recipient since 1913 to be awarded the SAP Commemorative Medal for Bravery.

About 250 Naval combat officers received wings in July. The badges were presented to bridge watch-keepers and captains.

The State President's Unit, which performed ceremonial services at the State President's offices and homes, was disbanded.

Police smashed an ANC underground system in July. Access was obtained to a computer which produced documentary material exposing the existence of Operation Vula, which was aimed at establishing underground structures, revolutionary bases and expanding a revolutionary army in South Africa. Minutes of a secret meeting of the South African Communist Party in May revealed a plan to establish a people's militia under the guise of self-defence units. Members of the SACP allegedly planned to smuggle arms into the country after the Groote Schuur talks in May.

Government and the ANC signed the Pretoria Minute in August after four months of talks. The ANC undertook to suspend its armed struggle immediately while the government undertook to consider lifting the state of emergency in Natal as early as possible.

In September commuters were attacked by panga-wielding gangs on trains on the Reef. In one of these attacks 26 people were killed and 100 hurt, in another 36 were killed and at least 270 injured. A reward of R50 000 was offered by the SAP for information leading to the arrest and conviction of anyone responsible for the massacre on a Soweto-bound train on 13 September. Counter-measures taken by the police included cordoning of certain hostels in Black residential areas to control entry to and from these hostels, roadblocks, a curfew in seven Black residential areas on the Reef and a reward of up to R100 000 for information about illegal firearms.

A new anti-tank missile system claimed to surpass comparable European and American systems, the ZT-3, was introduced by the SADF.

Firearm licences increased from R2 to R50 in October.

South African spy Odile Harington was released from a Zimbabwean prison on 1 November after spending three years in jail for passing on intelligence about the ANC. She was sentenced by the Harare High Court to 25 years' imprisonment.

Captain Paul Booysen (26) from Air Force Base Ysterplaat became the first Coloured air traffic controller in the country.

The Supreme Court inquest into the deaths of 42 people killed during faction fighting and clashes between crowds and security forces in Sebokeng in September began in November.

The East Cape Murder and Robbery Squad launched a manhunt for the killers, armed with AK-47 rifles, who mowed down two members of the Police Riot Unit and an unidentified Black informer in an ambush in Zwide, a Black residential area in Port Elizabeth in November.

More than 3 500 people were killed in unrest-related incidents up to mid-December. Approximately 2 200 people were injured.

The SA Police withdrew from South African borders on 7 December and left border protection duties to the South African Defence Force. The aim was to free police to enable them to make maximum use of members in combating crime.

Three bags of heroin and 103 000 Mandrax tablets with a combined value of R17 million were seized at Jan Smuts Airport in December.

The ANC's marches for 'Peace and Freedom Now' took place in Pretoria and Johannesburg on 6 December.

Acknowledgements:
Department of Justice
South African Defence Force
South African Police

It is the Republic of South Africa's aim to strive towards world peace and sound relations with all peace-loving nations as a full and equal member of the community of nations. Despite political pressure to isolate South Africa internationally, South Africa maintains mutually beneficial relations with countries in its sphere of interest.

Liaison with foreign governments on all matters affecting official relations is conducted by the Ministry and Department of Foreign Affairs. Such liaison takes place either directly or through foreign representatives in South Africa or South Africa's accredited representatives abroad. There are more than 60 South African missions (embassies, legations, consulates and special missions) abroad.

SA and Africa

South Africa's foreign relations with Africa are important because the RSA is inextricably part of Africa. There are more than 50 countries in Africa, including South Africa and the four independent Black states, Transkei, Bophuthatswana, Venda and Ciskei. The four above-mentioned territories became independent republics in 1976, 1977, 1979 and 1981 respectively. Their independence is recognised only by South Africa and among themselves.

SA and Namibia

South Africa withdrew its troops from Namibia in 1989 during the implementation of UN Resolution 435, the start of Namibia's transition to independence. A historical highlight was reached when 10 political parties/alliances participated in the general election in Namibia from 7 to 11 November 1989. The election was won by Swapo. South Africa's mandate over the region ended when Namibia became independent on 21 March 1990.

SA and Southern Africa

South Africa's attention is mainly focussed on Southern Africa which, together with South Africa, consists of 14 countries, namely Angola, Mozambique, Malawi, Zambia, Zimbabwe, Botswana, Lesotho, Swaziland, Namibia, Transkei, Bophuthatswana, Venda and Ciskei. In area these countries cover some 6 million km^2. A considerable number of Southern African countries are dependent on South Africa's transportation, manufacturing industry, labour market, scientific and technical expertise, as well as her capital resources.

Transport

Long distances between the coast and the inland urban centres necessitate a well-developed transport system. The RSA's transport system provides the only reliable bulk trade link with the outside world for at least eight land-locked countries in the region. They are Botswana, Lesotho and Swaziland (the BLS states), Bophuthatswana, Venda, Zimbabwe, Zambia and Malawi. In addition Namibia, Transkei, Ciskei and the Shaba province of Zaïre are dependent on South Africa's transport system.

Located along the subcontinent's 8 500 km coastline are 12 major ports, seven in the RSA (including Walvis Bay), three in Mozambique and two in Angola. The subcontinental railway system is largely an extension of the South African railway grid. There are also pipelines conveying liquid cargo from Durban and Beira in Mozambique, to the interior.

Many countries in the region rely on South African air carriers to ferry in vital supplies. South African Airways (SAA) transports passengers and freight between Johannesburg and Zambia, Zimbabwe, the Comores, Kenya, Madagascar, Malawi, Mozambique, Mauritius, Reunion, Zaïre and the Côte d'Ivoire. Safair's fleet of freighters regularly ferries in urgent supplies to these and many other countries in sub-Saharan Africa.

Trade

If gold sales to the developed world are excluded, Africa, including the BLS countries, accounts for 20 per cent of South Africa's merchandise exports — mostly intermediate and final goods such as chemicals, textiles, rubberware, foodstuffs, clothing, vehicles and other machinery.

South Africa imports far less from the rest of the continent than it exports to African countries. However, South Africa is an important market for manufactured products from Zimbabwe, for cattle and sheep from Namibia and for beef from both Namibia and Botswana.

Employment
Africa has the highest population growth rate in the world (3,1 per cent a year) and the lowest average rate of economic development. Hundreds of thousands of migrant labourers make their way to South Africa every year — mainly from Lesotho, Mozambique, Malawi, Botswana and Swaziland. In recent years there were more than 1,2 million migrant workers and daily commuters from neighbouring countries (including the TBVC countries) legally employed in the RSA at any one time. Thousands were illegally employed or self-employed in the RSA.

Power and water
SAf's national power utility, Eskom, generates sufficient electricity for its own power needs and those of neighbouring countries such as the BLS states and Mozambique. SA is also the major market for hydro-electric power and water from neighbours with abundant water resources.

The largest water supply scheme ever undertaken in Africa is the Lesotho Highlands Water Project — a joint venture of the South African and Lesotho governments. The project will also be a source of electricity for Lesotho, which stands to benefit from income generated through transfer of its surplus water to the RSA.

Agriculture
SA is a member of the Southern African Regional Commission for the Conservation and Utilisation of the Soil (SARCCUS), founded to promote co-operation in the region on soil conservation and utilisation, as well as the conservation of natural vegetation and water resources.

South Africa shares its expertise and advanced technology related to animal husbandry and cultivation of subtropical crops and maize with most of its neighbours.

Financial affairs
Investment, development aid and loans by the South African private sector make a substantial contribution to the economies of many countries in the region. Many of the railways, roads, hospitals, factories and agro-industrial plants to process agricultural products were built with the aid of South African expertise.

The South African Reserve Bank renders banking services to Lesotho and Swaziland, which form the Common Monetary Area (CMA) with the RSA. Parity between the currencies of CMA members facilitates trade between them. CMA and Customs Union arrangements are applied by the RSA to the TBVC countries through bilateral agreements.

The Development Bank of Southern Africa (DBSA) was established to finance economic development projects in Southern Africa. (See chapter 18: Finance). The bank's borrowers are governments, development agencies and non-government organisations. By 31 December 1990 the bank had already approved loans to the value of over R5 000 million for more than 700 programmes and projects. The bank is also structured to administer grants from local or overseas public or private sources.

Science and technology
By employing and training migrant labourers, as well as workers in countries in which projects are undertaken, South African mining houses, construction and other companies operating in Southern Africa help to generate a pool of workers skilled in technologies previously unknown, but vital to the economic development of the countries concerned. In addition these activities create jobs.

Many Southern African countries freely draw on various technologies appropriate to African conditions developed by South African organisations such as the CSIR and the South African Bureau of Standards (SABS).

Health services
Most of the vaccines and other medicines used to prevent or control common diseases such as tuberculosis, poliomyelitis, diphtheria, tetanus, malaria, and measles in Southern Africa are supplied by South African laboratories. In any one year more than 1 000 patients from other African countries are treated in South African hospitals.

The private sector also helps to cast the lifeline of South African medical expertise to other countries in the region. Two national conglomerates sponsor regular visits to Lesotho and Swaziland by teams of South African physicians and nurses.

Tourism
The RSA, Lesotho, Swaziland, Malawi and the Comores have joined forces in the Southern African Regional Tourism Council (Sartoc) to promote and co-ordinate their tourist industries. Special efforts are being made to encourage

tourists from other continents to include most or all the Sartoc countries in their itineraries when visiting Southern Africa.

Customs Union

About half of SA's African export trade takes place within the long-established Southern African Customs Union, comprising the RSA, Botswana, Lesotho, Swaziland and Namibia. The bulk of the latter four countries' imports are supplied by the RSA. Allowing for the unrestricted flow of goods and services between its members, the Customs Union collects the levies on their imports from the rest of the world and apportions the amount among the member states according to an agreed formula. Earnings from the customs pool contribute substantially to the government revenues of Botswana, Lesotho and Swaziland.

The Economic Community of Southern Africa

Transkei, Bophuthatswana, Venda and Ciskei (previously known as the TBVC countries), with South Africa, are also known as the Economic Community of Southern Africa (Ecosa).

In accordance with an agreement concluded between SA and these states, an international organisation, the Secretariat for Multilateral Co-operation in Southern Africa (Secosaf), was established in 1988. It is funded and staffed by the five member states. Secosaf is a neutral, international organisation and its aim is to play a facilitating role in planned, accelerated socio-economic development in Southern Africa through multilateral and regional co-operation and to create a climate of mutual faith and aid.

Ecosa comprises nine economic development regions of which seven cover the areas of more than one state. Consultation across boundaries in these seven regions takes place in the forums of regional liaison committees.

Information centres

Private organisations concerned with SA's relations with the rest of the world fall into two categories. Those in the first category seek to promote a better understanding of SA's problems abroad by providing factual information and encouraging person-to-person contact. This is the approach and strategy of the South Africa Foundation, among others. Those in the second category are mainly academic research institutes which seek to inform the South African public on international issues. Included among these are the South African Institute of International Affairs in Johannesburg, the Institute for American Studies at the Rand Afrikaans University, the Institute for Strategic Studies at Pretoria University, the Institute for Latin American Studies at the Unisa, the Institute for Soviet Studies at Stellenbosch University and the Africa Institute of SA, based in Pretoria.

Representatives of the RSA abroad

Argentina (Buenos Aires)
Telephones: (0954) (1) 311-8991/8

Australia (Canberra)
Telephones: (0961) (62) 73-2424/5/6/7 and 73-3912

Austria (Vienna)
Telephone: (0943) (222) 32-6493 Serie 7

Belgium (Brussels)
Telephone: (0932) (2) 230-68-45

Bophuthatswana (Mmabatho)
Telephones: (0140) 32521/2/3

Brazil (Brasilia)
Telephone: (0955) (61) 223-4873

Brazil (Sao Paulo)
Telephone: (0955) (11) 285-0433

Brazil (Rio de Janeiro)
Telephone: (0955) (21) 542-6191

Bulgaria (Sofia)
Telephone: Not available

Canada (Ottawa)
Telephone: (091) (613) 744-0330

Canada (Montreal)
Telephones: (091) (514) 878-9231/2, 878-9217/8

Canada (Toronto)
Telephone: (091) (416) 364-0314

Chile (Santiago)
Telephones: (0956) (2) 231-3185, 231-3361, 231-2373, 231-2860/2/3

China (Republic of) (Taipei)
Telephones: (09886) (2) 715-3250/4

Ciskei (Republic of) (Bisho)
Telephones: (0433) 24525/6/7 or 24560/1/2

Comores (Moroni)
Telephones: 73-1812 via Paris

Côted'Ivoire (Abidjan)
Fax: (09225) 44-3878

Czechoslovakia (Prague)
Telephone: Not available

Denmark (Copenhagen)
Telephone: (0945) (31) 18-0155

Finland (Helsinki)
Telephone: (09358) (0) 65-8288

France (Paris)
Telephone: (0933) (1) 45-55-92-37

France (Marseilles)
Telephone: (0933) (91) 52-8169

Germany (Bonn)
Telephone: (0949) (228) 82010

Germany (Frankfurt)
Telephones: (0949) (69) 72-3741, 72-5647

Germany (Hamburg)
Telephones: (0949) (040) 41-2961/5

Germany (Munich)
Telephone: (0949) (89) 260-5081

Greece (Athens)
Telephone: (0930) (1) 692-2125

Guatemala (Guatemala City)
Telephones: (0900) (502-2) 36-2890, 34-1531/5

Hong Kong (Hong Kong)
Telephones: (09852) (5) 77-3279, 77-3463

Hungary (Budapest)
Telephone: (0936)(1)117 5122

Israel (Tel Aviv)
Telephone: (09972) (3) 25-6147

Italy (Rome)
Telephones: (0939) (6) 844-3246, 844-3252, 844-3254

Japan (Tokyo)
Telephones: (0981) (3) 265-3366/7/8/9

Lesotho (Maseru)
Telephones: (09266) 32-5758/9

Luxembourg (Luxemburg)
Telephone: (0932) (2) 230-6845

Malawi (Lilongwe)
Telephone: (09265) 73-0088

Malawi (Blantyre)
Telephone: (09265) 62-0444

Mauritius (Port Louis)
Telephone: 08-2811

Monaco (Monte Carlo)
Telephone: (0933) (93) 25-2426

Mozambique (Maputo)
Telephones: (012) 291-2587, 291-3568, 291-2088,

Namibia (Windhoek)
Telephone:: (061) 22-9765

The Netherlands (The Hague)
Telephones: (0931) (70) 92-4501/2/3/4

Norway (Oslo)
Telephone: (0947) (2) 53-5816

Paraguay (Asunción)
Telephones: (09595) (21) 44331/2, 96031

Poland (Warsaw)
Telephone: Not available

Portugal (Lisbon)
Telephones: (09351) (1) 53-5713, 53-5041/2/3/4/5

Portugal (Madeira)
Telephones: (09351) (91) 46825/6/7

Rumania (Bucharest)
Telephone: Not available

Spain (Madrid)
Telephones: (0934) (1) 227-3153/4/5/6

Swaziland (Mbabane)
Telephones: (09268) 44651/2/3/4

Sweden (Stockholm)
Telephone: (0946) (8) 24-3950

Switzerland (Berne)
Telephone: (0941) (31) 44-2011

Switzerland (Geneva)
Telephones: (0941) (22) 735-7801/2/3

Switzerland (Zurich)
Telephone: (0941) (1) 911-0606

Togo (Lome)
Telephone: (0900) 21-6590

Transkei (Umtata)
Telephone: (0471) 22191

United Kingdom of Great Britain and Northern Ireland
(London)
Telephone: (0944) (1) 930-4488

United Kingdom of Great Britain and Northern Ireland
(Glasgow)
Telephone: (0944) (41) 221-3114

United States of America (Washington)
Telephone: (091) (202) 232-4400

United States of America (Houston)
Telephones: (091) (713) 850-0150/1

United States of America (Chicago)
Telephones: (091) (312) 939-7929/32, 939-7143/
76, 939-7216

United States of America (Beverley Hills)
Telephone: (091) (213) 657-9200

Uruguay (Montevideo)
Telephones: (09598) (2) 955-058, 961-209,
952-425

Venda (Republic of) (Thohoyandou)
Telephones: (015581) 31023/4/5/6

Zaire (Kinshasa)
Telephones: (09243) 34-676/7

Zimbabwe (Harare)
Telephones: (09263) (4) 70-7901/6

International organisations

International Atomic Energy Agency (Vienna)
  Telephone: (0943) (222) 326493 Serie 7

International Monetary Fund & World Bank
(Washington)
  Telephone: (091) (202) 364-8320

United Nations (New York)
  Telephone: (091) (212) 371-8154

United Nations (Geneva)
  Telephones: (0941) (22) 735-7801/2/3

**Secretariat of the Economic Community of Southern
  Africa** (Secosaf) (Pretoria)
  Telephone: (012) 341-4313

Addresses of foreign missions in the RSA

Argentina (Johannesburg)
  Telephones: (011) 339-2382

Australia (Pretoria)
  Telephones: (012) 325-4315/24

Austria (Pretoria)
  Telephones: (012) 322-7790/1/2

Belgium (Pretoria)
  Telephones: (012) 44-3201/2

Bophuthatswana (Pretoria)
  Telephones: (012) 43-6001/4/5/6

Brazil (Pretoria)
  Telephones: (012) 43-5559/0

Canada (Pretoria)
  Telephone: (012) 28-7062

Chile (Pretoria)
  Telephones: (012) 26-9387/8/9

China (Republic of) (Pretoria)
  Telephones: (012) 43-6071/2/3

Ciskei (Pretoria)
  Telephones: (012) 343-2334/5/6/7

Denmark (Johannesburg)
  Telephones: (011) 804-3374/5

Finland (Pretoria)
  Telephones: (012) 343-0275/6

France (Pretoria)
  Telephones: (012) 43-5564/5

Germany (Pretoria)
  Telephones: (012) 344-3854/5/6/7/8/9

Greece (Pretoria)
  Telephone: (012) 43-7352

Guatemala (Cape Town)
  Telephone: (021) 418-2020

Ireland (Eire) (Johannesburg)
  Telephone: (011) 836-5869

Israel (Pretoria)
  Telephone: (012) 421-2222

Italy (Pretoria)
  Telephones: (012) 43-5541/2/3/4

Japan (Pretoria)
  Telephones: (012) 342-2100/5

Lesotho (Johannesburg)
  Telephone: (011) 29-0751

Malawi (Pretoria)
  Telephones: (012) 47-7827/8/9

Mozambique (Johannesburg)
  Telephones: (011) 234-907/8

The Netherlands (Pretoria)
  Telephones: (012) 344-3910/5

Norway (Cape Town)
  Telephone: (021) 25-1687

Paraguay (Pretoria)
  Telephones: (012) 45-1081/2

Portugal (Pretoria)
  Telephones: (012) 341-2340/1/2

Spain (Pretoria)
  Telephones: (012) 344-3875/6/7

Swaziland (Pretoria)
  Telephones: (011) 29-9776/7/8

Sweden (Pretoria)
  Telephone: (012) 21-1050

Switzerland (Pretoria)
  Telephones: (012) 43-7788/9

Transkei (Pretoria)
  Telephones: (012) 21-5626/7/8/9

**United Kingdom of Great Britain and Northern
  Ireland** (Pretoria)
  Telephone: (012) 43-3121

United States of America (Pretoria)
  Telephone: (012) 28-4266

Uruguay (Cape Town)
  Telephone: (021) 25-1847

Venda (Pretoria)
  Telephones: (012) 344-3950/1/2/3

Zimbabwe (Johannesburg)
  Telephones: (011) 838-2156/7/8/9

News items: 1990

January
Howard Wolpe, US Congressman and one of
South Africa's staunchest critics, visited South
Africa on a five day fact-finding trip.

South African Foreign Minister Mr R F Botha visited Hungary.

South Africa's trade mission on the Comores Island was upgraded to a consulate.

President F W de Klerk and Mr R F Botha, Minister of Foreign Affairs, held discussions with the leader of the Social Democratic Party in Britain, Dr David Owen.

The military leader of Transkei, Major-General Bantu Holomisa, and President de Klerk held talks in Transkei.

President de Klerk spoke to the people of the Soviet Union by way of an interview with the Soviet magazine *New Time*.

A Polish South African Friendship Association was formed in Warsaw, Poland.

February
Foreign Minister of the Côte d'Ivoire, Mr Simeon Ake, visited South Africa to meet President de Klerk.

The British government lifted the ban on new investments and promotion of tourism to SA.

The Rev Jesse Jackson, former US presidential candidate and civil rights leader, visited South Africa.

March
At midnight on 20 March the former mandated territory of South-West Africa became independent under the name of Namibia. During the independence celebrations President de Klerk held discussions with President Hosni Mubarak of Egypt, Chairman of the Organisation of African Unity (OAU) as well as with ten heads of state, six foreign affairs ministers and three other ministers from different countries regarding recent changes in South Africa.

Soviet Minister of Foreign Affairs, Mr Eduard Shevardnadse, and President de Klerk met in South-West Africa House.

Mr Leon Wessels, South African Deputy Minister of Foreign Affairs, held discussions with Mr Hans van den Broek, Minister of Foreign Affairs of the Netherlands.

President de Klerk met with Mr Douglas Hurd, British Foreign Secretary, Mr James Baker, US Secretary of State and members of the US Congress.

April
Dr Gerrit Viljoen, Minister of Constitutional Development, visited New York, Washington and London where he held discussions with government and business leaders and the media.

Mr Riaan Eksteen became South Africa's first representative to Namibia.

South Africa opened a permanent mission in Budapest, Hungary.

A Polish trade delegation to SA signed agreements to buy iron ore, set up a joint food venture and strengthen other economic ties.

May
Spain lifted certain trade sanctions against South Africa.

President F W de Klerk was well received on his nine-nation tour to Europe. He met with King Boudouin of Belgium, King Juan Carlos of Spain, presidents, prime ministers, foreign ministers and business policy-makers. He also visited the Côte d'Ivoire and the Cape Verde islands on his way back.

June
A United Nations delegation, in South Africa on a fact-finding mission, held talks with the PAC, ANC and the leader of the Boerestaat Party.

Dr Juergen Warnke, Minister of Economic Co-operation of former West Germany, visited SA to hold talks with Foreign Minister R F Botha and Finance Minister Barend du Plessis.

Poland established a Chamber of Commerce in Johannesburg.

July
Portuguese Foreign Affairs Minister, Dr João de Deus Pinheiro, visited South Africa for five days and met with government officials and leaders of the Portuguese community in South Africa.

Foreign Affairs Director-General, Mr Neil van Heerden, and his deputy, Mr Herbert Beukes, held informal talks in Moscow with their Soviet counterparts.

Gen Olusegun Obasanjo, former Nigerian head of state and member of the Eminent Persons Group of the Commonwealth, held discussions with President de Klerk on the role of the new South Africa in Africa.

August
Hungary lifted all anti-South African sanctions.

A South African delegation led by Mr Kent Durr, Minister of Trade, Industry and Tourism, visited the Soviet Union where they discussed possibilities for trade and investment.

South Africa re-establised commercial and economic relations with Madagascar after 15 years. South African Airways introduced a weekly flight to Antananarivo.

A group of 35 Italian industrialists spent three days in South Africa investigating investment opportunities in the country.

September

A group of Dutch MPs visited South Africa and met government officials, ANC leaders, church groups and other political leaders.

South Africa's Minister of Mineral and Energy Affairs, Dr Dawie de Villiers, held talks with President Jose Eduardo dos Santos of Angola in Luanda.

Officials from the Department of Foreign Affairs, South African Airways (SAA) and leading businessmen met President Didier Ratsiraka and other government officials of Madagascar.

Minister of Foreign Affairs, Mr R F Botha, attended the opening of the new basilica at Yamoussoukro, the Côte d'Ivoire by the Pope.

Mr de Klerk held discussions with Mrs Margaret Thatcher at Chequers.

Mr F W de Klerk paid the first-ever official visit by a State President of the RSA to the United States. He met President George Bush.

Manpower Minister Eli Louw was the first SA Cabinet Minister to attend the annual International Labour Organisation meeting in Geneva since SA/ILO links were severed in 1964.

Mauritius approved a South African trade office on the island.

October

President de Klerk visited the Portuguese Head of State, Dr Mario Soares, and Prime Minister, Dr Anibal Cavaco Silva. He met the British Prime Minister, Mrs Margaret Thatcher.

The South African Department of Veterinary Services announced it has informal links with 42 African states.

It was announced in October that between 16 million and 30 million doses of Onderstepoort Veterinary Research Institute vaccine are exported annually, mainly to neighbouring African states.

A Comoran delegation, led by the Comoran Minister of Tourism, Transport, Urban Planning and Housing, Mr Saidali Youssouf, visited SA.

Mr Leon Wessels, Deputy Minister of Foreign Affairs, received a visit from his Swedish counterpart, Mr Bengt Sare-Soderbergh and from the Italian Foreign Affairs Deputy Minister, Senator Ivo Butini.

President de Klerk visited Morocco, the Netherlands, Luxembourg and Senegal.

Mr Kent Durr, Minister of Trade and Industry and Tourism, and Mr Constantin Fota, his Rumanian counterpart, concluded a trade treaty. In a follow-up visit Mr R F Botha held talks with Rumanian President Ion Iliescu, Premier Petre Roman and Foreign Minister Adrian Nastase in Bucharest.

The leaders of the Yugoslavian republics of Slovenia and Croatia met Mr R F Botha in Munich for unofficial talks on the establishment of ties.

SA established official diplomatic relations with Poland.

November

Mr Harry Schwarz, was appointed South Africa's new ambassador to the US.

The government granted permission to Mr Nikolai Reshetnyak of the Moscow-based *New Times,* to open an office in Pretoria.

South Africa decided to close its consulate in Sydney and reduce staff at its embassy in Canberra. In return Australia refused a formal request to reduce its embassy in Pretoria.

Czechoslovakia and SA agreed to re-establish consular relations, which were severed 27 years ago.

Mr Marc Burger was appointed the new South African ambassador to France.

Diplomatic ties at consular level were established between South Africa and Bulgaria.

The first official delegation from the Soviet Union arrived for a meeting with President de Klerk. The delegation was led by a member of the Soviet Council of Ministers, Mr A V Chernuchin.

A Bulgarian trade mission, led by Prof Valentin Grosdanof, Bulgarian Deputy Minister of Industry and Technology, visited South Africa.

Minister of Trade and Industry and Tourism, Mr Kent Durr, was appointed South African ambassador to the Court of St James.

After midnight on 31 December 1990 persons crossing the border between SA and Namibia required a valid passport or travel document.

Minister of Foreign Affairs, Mr R F Botha, and Kenya's President Daniel Arap Moi had the first official high-level contact between Pretoria and Nairobi in 40 years.

December

A high-level Mauritian delegation arrived in South Africa to explore expanding trade between the two countries.

SA and Transkei held talks resolving their differences following alleged SA complicity in a coup attempt in Transkei on 22 November.

Mr de Klerk formally accepted the credentials of Mr I-Cheng Loh from the Republic of China.

Contracts amounting to R1,7 billion were signed in Lesotho for the construction of the first phase of the Highlands Water Project.

The European Community partially lifted sanctions against South Africa on 15 December.

Minister Dawie de Villiers visited four West African countries, during which he became the first South African cabinet minister to meet members of the Cameroon government in an official capacity.

A bomb exploded at the home of the US ambassador to South Africa. Relative little damage was caused.

Mr Pieter Swanepoel was appointed South Africa's new ambassador to Portugal.

Acknowledgements:
Central Economic Advisory Service
Department of Foreign Affairs
Department of Trade and Industry and Tourism
Development Bank of Southern Africa
Mr P W Esterhuysen, Africa Institute of South Africa

Agriculture

South Africa has a dualistic agricultural economy — a well-developed commercial sector and a predominantly subsistence-orientated sector in the Black self-governing territories.

As a result of implementation of research results and improved farm management, real agricultural production has more than doubled during the past 30 years. Today South Africa is not only self-sufficient in virtually all important agricultural products but in good seasons also one of only a few countries in the world which exports food. Although farming conditions are not ideal and the number of farming units for Whites has decreased from 100 000 to 67 010 during the past 20 years, food valued at R4 153 million was exported in 1989. This represents approximately 7 per cent of the country's total exports (excluding gold).

In monetary terms, agriculture's share in the economy has long since been outstripped by that of mining and secondary industry. In 1960 agriculture contributed R615 million (or 12,5 per cent) to the gross domestic product (GDP), as against about 20 per cent in the 1930s. By 1989, farming's share in the GDP had dropped to 6 per cent but the gross value of production in 1989/90 was more than R19 532 million.

Notwithstanding the farming industry's declining share in the GDP, it remains of vital importance to the economy as a whole and the development and stability of the Southern African region. The industry employs more than 1 000 000 people (mostly Blacks and Coloureds).

Only about 11 per cent of South Africa's surface is suitable for agricultural purposes. By world standards natural resources for agriculture are generally poor. Because rainfall is unreliable, the country as a whole is subject to severe recurrent droughts, which are sometimes broken by devastating floods.

The unreliability and variability of rainfall explains why irrigation farming is such a vital component of the agricultural industry. A large variety of crops such as sugar, citrus, vegetables and grain are grown under irrigation.

Agriculture, in particular irrigation, is the largest single user of surface water resources and the proportion of water resources used for irrigation is among the highest in the world. Areas under irrigation on state and irrigation board projects and other as yet unmeasured areas of irrigated land probably total about one million ha. Most of this land is situated in the sub-humid to semi-arid parts of the country.

On the basis of climate, natural vegetation, types of soil and the type of farming practised, the country may be subdivided into a number of farming regions. Agricultural land utilisation in these regions ranges from intensive crop production and mixed farming in winter rainfall and high summer rainfall areas, to extensive beef ranching in the bushveld and sheep farming in the arid areas.

Production

The steady increase in gross value over the past decade is accounted for by an increase in production and a general rise in producer prices. The prices of agricultural products generally increased by 4,8 per cent from 1988/89 to 1989/90. Prices of field crops increased by 9 per cent, those of horticultural products by 14,3 per cent while those of livestock products decreased by 1,6 per cent.

The net income of the 67 010 farmers in the country increased from R5 919 million in 1988/89 to R6 599 million in 1989/90.

Field crops and horticulture

Of the total cultivated area of 8 675 000 ha, about 40 per cent is planted with maize and 31 per cent with small grains. Together with oil seeds and grain sorghum, these crops occupy more than three-quarters of total arable land.

Maize is produced mainly in the south-western Transvaal, the north-western OFS, the eastern

Table 1 Agriculture's contribution to GDP, 1987—1990

Year	GDP (R mil)	Agriculture's contribution (R million)	percentage
1987	149 931	9 532	6,4
1988	178 277	11 011	6,2
1989	206 804	12 477	6,0
1990	234 716	10 794	4,6

Table 2 Gross value of agricultural production 1988/89—1989/90 (R million)

Products	1988/89	1989/90*
Field crops		
Maize	2 999	2 495
Wheat	1 217	880
Hay	977	1 102
Grain sorghum	104	82
Sugar cane	817	943
Groundnuts	120	90
Tobacco	346	346
Sunflower seed	252	403
Cotton	182	169
Other	329	426
TOTAL	7 343	6 936
Horticulture		
Viticulture	445	524
Citrus	400	372
Subtropical fruit	242	322
Deciduous and other fruit	853	995
Vegetables	697	854
Potatoes	395	457
Other	368	420
TOTAL	3 400	3 944
Livestock products		
Wool	875	745
Dressed poultry and eggs	2 589	2 561
Cattle and calves slaughtered	1 989	2 167
Sheep and goats slaughtered	769	832
Pigs slaughtered	355	371
Fresh milk	817	951
Dairy products	608	637
Other	382	387
TOTAL	8 384	8 651
GRAND TOTAL	19 127	19 532

* Preliminary

Table 3 Production** of important field
crops and horticultural products
1988/89—1989/90 ('000 t)

	1988/89*	1989/90*
Maize	11 587	8 794
Wheat	3 535	2 003
Grain sorghum	487	363
Groundnuts	114	79
Sunflower seed	435	609
Sugar cane	19 864	18 636
Deciduous fruit	1 015	1 067
Citrus	833	924
Subtropical fruit	568	500
Vegetables	1 907	1 793
Potatoes	1 259	1 257

*   Preliminary
** RSA - excluding self-governing territories

Transvaal highveld, the eastern OFS and the
Natal midlands.

Wheat is produced mainly in the winter rainfall
areas of the south-western Cape, in the OFS and
in certain areas of the Transvaal in the summer
rainfall area. The OFS is at present the major
producing area, but experiences considerable
annual fluctuations. The south-western Cape is
the most stable production area.

Barley is produced mainly in the southern
coastal plain of the south-western Cape, comprising more than 90 per cent of locally produced
malting barley.

Sorghum is grown mostly on drier soils in the
summer rainfall areas. Groundnuts are grown in
the northern, eastern and western Transvaal, the
OFS and the Vryburg area of the northern Cape.

Sunflower seed is produced in the eastern
Transvaal highveld, the western Transvaal and
the OFS.

About 10 per cent of the sugar crop is grown
under irrigation in the coastal regions of Natal
and the eastern Transvaal. The remainder is
produced in the frost-free coastal and midlands
areas of Natal.

Deciduous fruit is grown mainly in the western
Cape (78 per cent) and the Langkloof valley in
the eastern Cape (11 per cent). Smaller production areas are found along the Orange River, in
the OFS and the Transvaal.

In South Africa about 100 000 ha is covered by
vineyards. Of this approximately 90 per cent consists of wine grapes planted in the winter rainfall
region of the western Cape. Smaller plantings
occur in the north-western Cape (mainly grapes
for drying), northern Cape, Orange Free State
and the Transvaal.

Citrus is largely limited to the irrigation areas
of the northern, eastern and western Transvaal,
the eastern and western Cape and Natal.

Pineapples are grown in the eastern Cape and
northern Natal. Other subtropical crops such as
avocados, mangoes, bananas, litchis, guavas,
pawpaws, granadillas, and macadamia and
pecan nuts are produced mainly in the eastern
Transvaal and the subtropical coastal areas of
Natal and the eastern Cape.

Of the country's potato crop, about 40 per cent
is grown in the higher-lying areas of the OFS and
the Transvaal. The northern Transvaal, the eastern, western and northern Cape and the higher-
lying areas of Natal are other important areas of
production. About two thirds of the total potato
crop is produced under irrigation.

In terms of gross income to the grower,
tomatoes, onions and cabbages are probably the
most important vegetable crops. They contribute

respectively 28, 14 and 4 per cent to the income derived from vegetables. Tomatoes are produced countrywide, but mainly in the lowveld and middleveld of the Transvaal, the Pongola area of Natal and the south-eastern and western Cape. Onions are grown in the middleveld of the Transvaal, in the districts of Caledon, Ceres and Worcester in the Cape and at Venterstad and the adjoining areas of the southern OFS. Cabbages are also grown countrywide, but are more concentrated in the middleveld of the Transvaal, the Camperdown and Greytown districts of Natal and near the big cities.

Ornamental plants are produced throughout the country but are more concentrated in the central part of the Transvaal. Ornamental plant production includes nursery crops, cut flowers and potplants. The gross income of the flower industry increased from R47 million in 1981 to R350 million in 1988. The country's most important plant export products are gladioli, proteas, roses, bulbs and chrysanthemum cuttings.

Fynbos is not only a worldwide source of cut flowers, foliage and dried flowers for flower markets, but also serves as a source of genes for flowers such as fresias, Guernsey lilies and gladioli which are cultivated worldwide. Cultivation of fynbos earns the western Cape valuable foreign currency. This industry also creates jobs for about 15 000 people. Approximately 60 per cent of the genus *Protea* is cultivated while the foliage is mainly gathered in the veld. The relation between the veld crop and cultivated material is about 65:35. Dried flowers are an important section of the fynbos industry. A large variety of dry flower species such as the everlasting, tumbleweeds and other suitable types are produced for the market.

Livestock

Livestock is produced in most parts of South Africa. Numbers vary according to climatic conditions. Stock breeding concentrates mainly on the development of breeds that are well adapted to diverse climatic and environmental conditions. The latest estimates for cattle and sheep are 8,5 million and 28,6 million respectively.

Dairy farming is distributed over the entire country, with the largest concentrations in the metropolitan areas of the PWV (Pretoria-Witwatersrand-Vereeniging) area, the Natal midlands, the eastern and western Cape and the eastern and northern OFS.

Friesland (76 per cent) and Jerseys (16 per cent) are the predominant dairy breeds, with smaller numbers of Ayrshires and Guernseys. Average production of fat-corrected milk of officially recorded registered Friesland and Jersey cows is 5 369 kg and 4 533 kg respectively.

Extensive beef cattle farming is practised mainly in northern and eastern Cape, parts of the OFS, parts of Natal and the northern Transvaal. The indigenous Afrikaner, Bonsmara, Drakensberger and Nguni are popular beef breeds but British, European and American breeds such as the Hereford, Sussex, Simmentaler, Charolais, Brahman and Santa Gertrudis are maintained as pure breeds and used in cross-breeding. The Bonsmara, adapted to warmer climates and very fertile, was bred from the Afrikaner, Hereford and Shorthorn breeds.

The Taurus Livestock Improvement Co-op (Irene, Pretoria) annually provides the country's beef farmers with an average of 110 000 units of semen for use in artificial insemination. The co-op normally has 400 prime quality bulls and strives to improve South Africa's stock.

The feedlot industry has made great strides during the past few years. A total of 2,0 million head of cattle were slaughtered in controlled and uncontrolled areas during 1990.

The Karoo is the main sheep farming area of South Africa with the eastern Cape, the north-eastern OFS, western Natal and the eastern Transvaal highveld gaining in importance. Recently wooled sheep farming was introduced into the western marginal grain producing areas. The fine-wooled Merinos' numbers are highest (59,7 per cent), yielding 3,9 kg per sheep during the 1990 season. This represents 70 per cent of all the wool produced in the country. In 1990 Ermelo in the eastern Transvaal was the wool-producing district with the largest number of commercial Merino sheep.

During 1989/90 a total of 81,9 million kg of wool (greasy) was produced. The locally-developed Afrino (a wooled mutton breed adapted to arid conditions), the South African Mutton Merino, the Dohne Merino and Dormer sheep, the Merino Land Sheep and the Ile de France are other white-wooled breeds. They numbered 5 137 million in 1990, producing 12,5 million kg of wool at 2,4 kg per sheep. The total of 22 794 million white-woolled sheep (including the Merino) produced 81 864 million kg of wool (greasy) with an average yield of 3,6 kg per sheep.

These minor breeds and the Dorper, a highly productive locally developed mutton breed for arid regions, account for the RSA's mutton production.

The indigenous meat-producing Boer goat accounts for approximately 28 per cent of all goats and the Angora goat, used for mohair production, for the remaining 72 per cent. South Africa has about 4 000 Angora farmers with 2,5 million goats. It is estimated that they produce between 40 and 45 per cent of the total world mohair clip of about 19 million kg.

Compared with the predominantly extensive cattle and sheep industries, the poultry and pig industries are more intensive and are located on farms near metropolitan areas such as Johannesburg, Durban, Cape Town and Port Elizabeth. The predominant pig breeds are the South African Landrace and Large White.

Game farming

South Africa has more game and a wider specie variety than most other countries of the world.

Game farming has grown extensively in the past ten years and today it is a viable industry with great economic potential.

There are approximately 8 000 game farms in all parts of the country, covering millions of hectares and representing capital investment of millions of rands.

The main game areas are the northern, northwestern and eastern bushveld regions of the Transvaal, the central grass region of the OFS, the valley bushveld of the eastern Cape, the Karoo, the Kalahari in the north-western Cape and the thorn scrub of Zululand. Game is well adapted to dry conditions and can provide a means of income for farmers in arid regions. Despite prolonged droughts in the past, game numbers have increased consistently.

In 1990 the total turnover at game auctions was R14,5 million for approximately 13 000 head of game.

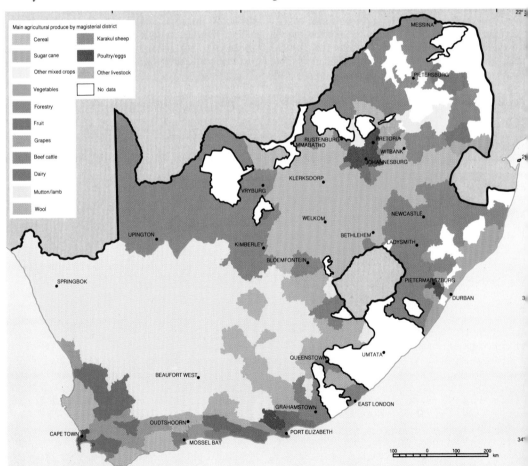

Agricultural regions of South Africa based on the dominant products sold per district

Aquaculture

The aquaculture industry in South Africa is now out of its infancy and produces approximately 5 per cent and 0,03 per cent of aquaculture produce in Africa and the world respectively. It has made, and is still making, meaningful progress in technology of cultivation, marketing strategy, marketing practice and scientific innovation. Production in 1980 was a mere 345 tons which increased to 3 094 tons in 1988. The estimated tonnage for 1990 is 4 300.

Mussels accounted for slightly more than half of the total production (1 575 t), followed by trout (739 t), oysters (299 t) and waterblommetjies (250 t).

Approximately 130 established producers produce 14 commercial species for human consumption with a value in exchange of about R46 million.

Veterinary services

(See also chapter 19: Research and development.) Most of the country's landward borders have stock or game-proof fences which are patrolled and kept in order to prevent straying of stock and game from neighbouring countries. Stock in the border areas is inspected at short intervals.

The Animal Diseases Act provides the necessary powers to combat and eradicate diseases such as foot-and-mouth disease, swine-fever, rabies and anthrax. About 16 200 herds are now free of bovine tuberculosis and more than 14 100 herds are free of bovine brucellosis.

The Animal Slaughter, Meat and Animal Products Hygiene Act stipulates that meat inspections and hygiene control must be carried out by qualified meat inspection personnel at abattoirs to prevent transmission of diseases through meat to humans and animals.

Marketing

The Marketing Act is an enabling measure in that it provides for the introduction and amendment of marketing schemes for agricultural products by proclamation instead of by specific parliamentary enactment for each product.

The principal objectives of the Marketing Act are to secure a greater measure of stability in the prices of farm products and to reduce the price differential between producer and consumer. Today 67,20 per cent of agricultural production

(in terms of gross value) is marketed through schemes introduced in terms of the Act, while five commodities (10,51 per cent of the gross value of agricultural production) are marketed in terms of other legislation. The balance (22,29 per cent) is not controlled.

The uncontrolled portion of agricultural production comprises mainly fresh fruit and vegetables sold through local markets. Although the greater part is sold on municipal markets, an increasing quantity is delivered to major supermarkets in terms of private contracts. Approximately 15 per cent of all vegetables are processed while the quantities exported are negligible.

Sales of fresh fruit and vegetables on municipal produce markets amounted to R1 116 million in 1989. National markets in major urban areas accounted for about 99 per cent of this.

Training

There are 19 specialised agricultural high schools for Whites or schools offering a comprehensive range of agricultural subjects. Prospective White farmers are trained at six agricultural colleges: Cedara (Pietermaritzburg), Glen (Bloemfontein), Grootfontein (Middelburg, Cape), Elsenburg (Stellenbosch), Potchefstroom and Lowveld (Nelspruit). Diploma courses are also presented at technikons. Degree courses are presented at the faculties of agriculture of the universities of Stellenbosch, Pretoria, Natal and the OFS.

Veterinary surgeons are trained at the Faculty of Veterinary Sciences at Onderstepoort and at the Medical University of Southern Africa.

The major institution for training of Coloureds is located at Kromme Rhee near Stellenbosch. The college has an annual enrolment of about 30 diploma students while approximately 1 300 students take the course for farmhands each year.

Most Black farmers in the self-governing ter-

Table 4 Livestock numbers, 1989—90
(million)

	1989	1990
Cattle	8,6	8,7
Sheep	29,6	30,0
Pigs	1,2	1,2
Goats	2,9	2,8
Laying hens for commercial purposes	10,9	10,8
Broilers	311,0	314,1

ritories are of the traditional peasant type but a growing number of highly-trained commercial farmers are being settled on irrigation schemes or on rain-fed farms. These commercial farmers and technical support staff are trained at, among others, an agricultural college in Lebowa and one in KwaZulu.

Training takes place at school level to prepare Black children for a career in the primary or secondary agricultural industry. Approximately 1 765 secondary schools offer agricultural science up to the junior secondary phase and a total of 1 487 schools up to the senior secondary phase (self-governing territories inclusive). There are three specialised agricultural high schools for Blacks and the fourth will be opened in 1993.

Black farm workers in the commercial sector outside the self-governing territories are trained at Boskop Training Centre, near Potchefstroom in the western Transvaal.

Agricultural Science has been introduced into the curriculum of the Shakaskraal Secondary School for Indians in Natal.

Credit

The agricultural sector is a net borrower in that it borrows more than it saves. In fact, the total debt of South African farmers has grown by about 21 per cent a year since 1980 — reaching R15 978 million by the end of 1990, compared with R1 402 million at the end of 1970.

The major sources of credit for farmers are, in order of importance: Commercial banks (28 per cent), agricultural co-operatives (25 per cent), the Land Bank (20 per cent), other financial institutions (13 per cent), private creditors (8 per cent) and the state through the Agricultural Credit Board (7 per cent).

While the Agricultural Credit Board has the smallest share in overall farming debts, the state gave assistance in some or other form to about 27 000 (or 43 per cent) of the country's 67 010 White farmers during the 10 years up to the end of 1990. In this period total state assistance amounted to R4 067 million (R1 983 million in loans and R2 084 million in subsidies in some or other form).

Included in these state aid figures are the following: R537,8 million for consolidation of debts, R824,5 million in crop production loans, R293,3 million in cattle feed loans and R1 000,2 million in subsidies for interest on carry-over debts and production credit. Excluded from these figures are R15,5 million in financial assis-

tance to the wood industry, R309 million for the maize industry and R900 million in government guarantees for carry-over debts.

Because South Africa often experiences prolonged droughts, the government has introduced drought-relief measures, in terms of which applicants must reduce their livestock, for which they receive an incentive. A rebate or transportation of approved fodder and licks is paid as are subsidies on stock-feed loans. Farmers can also claim a rebate on the cost of transporting livestock to leased grazing areas and a subsidy on the grazing fee.

Land and Agricultural Bank

The Land and Agricultural Bank of South Africa, generally known as the Land Bank, is a statutory body established to provide for the credit needs of farmers.

The bank advances money to farmers, agricultural co-operatives, control boards established under the provisions of the Marketing Act, 1968 and statutory agricultural institutions.

Long-term loans are granted to farmers against mortgage of land or the registration of a charge against land, whilst short and intermediate-term loans are granted in terms of section 34 of the Land Bank Act.

South African Agricultural Union

The SAAU is an independent organisation comprising all provincial agricultural unions, various commodity organisations and agricultural co-operatives.

The main objective of the union is to attain optimum economic and social dispensation for agricultural producers within the South African community. To this end, the union organises the farming population and agricultural co-operatives into a united front.

Agribusiness

Agribusiness organisations may be divided into two categories: Profit-motivated business ventures and service-orientated co-operative organisations.

Profit-motivated business ventures are involved in production and distribution of agricultural equipment and production requisites but co-operatives dominate the distribution of intermediate requisites and are also active in handling, processing and marketing of agricultural products.

Agricultural co-operatives are regarded as the farmers' own independent business organisations. There are 245 primary co-operatives with 1 300 branches throughout the country. These co-operatives supply their farmer members with all producer goods such as seed, fertiliser, fuel, repair services and credit and extension services and handle virtually all their members' produce. There are also 41 central co-operatives which provide the primary co-operatives with specific services such as processing and marketing of agricultural products, insurance services for crops and short-term damages and farming requisites.

Co-operative turnover was R20 929,2 million in 1989. Of this, produce accounted for R15 340 million, farming requisites for R4 720,5 million and services for R868,7 million.

Foreign relations

The Department of Agriculture and the Department of Agricultural Development are represented in the following cities by officials attached to the local South African embassy or mission: Geneva, Brussels, Buenos Aires, Canberra, London, Paris and Washington DC.

The main functions of the foreign representatives are to foster agricultural trade relations with the countries to which they are accredited, to provide South Africa with information on agricultural developments concerning mainly policy matters; and to liaise with all agricultural organisations in those countries on matters of mutual interest.

The Department of Agriculture is represented in organisations of the Southern African Customs Union and the Economic Community of Southern Africa (Ecosa) and handles matters concerning formal relations with Malawi, Zimbabwe and the Republic of China.

Aspects concerning South Africa's rights and obligations in terms of the General Agreement on Tariffs and Trade are handled by the Department of Agriculture in co-operation with other state departments.

On the agricultural terrain South Africa has bonds with a number of African states, including those who avoid overt relations. South Africa is a member country of the Southern African Regional Commission for the Conservation and Utilisation of the Soil (Sarccus) and is involved in the meetings of Ecosa which promotes socio-economic growth in the region.

The Veterinary Research Institute at Onderstepoort has been the world conference centre for bluetongue in sheep and African horse sickness for the International Office for Epizootic Diseases (OIE), of which South Africa is a member, for many years.

News items: 1990

A record 12,2 million cartons of grapes were produced during the 1989/90 season.

The maize crop for 1990 is estimated at 8,4 million tons as against 11,4 million tons for 1989.

Agreements providing for co-operation between agricultural scientists and institutions and for exchange of plant material were signed by the Republic of China and SA on 29 January.

History was made early in 1990 when South Africa exported its first frozen-dried embryos. Five embryos taken from Pinzgauer cows were sold to the president of the International Pinzgauer Association, a cattle farmer from Brazil.

Wool marketing in South Africa will enter a new era with the creation of a body that will market wool by means of an alternative marketing arm, to be known as a special central farmers' co-operation.

The biggest agricultural industry in the Cape Province, the deciduous fruit industry, has been partly privatised following the establishment of Unifruco, the industry's international marketing organisation, as a fully privatised public company.

A South African record price of R55 000 for a 75 per cent share in a merino ram was paid at the Merino Stud Breeders Society's ram sale. A South African record price for a yearling was set in April when a filly was sold for R540 000.

Zambia imported 2 500 tons South African wheat to ease increasing bread shortages in the country. Swaziland imported more than 17 000 metric tons of maize from South Africa.

The 1990 World Merino Conference was held in South Africa. It was attended by more than 600 delegates from all over the world.

The first yearbook of the Tea Association of Southern Africa was published in 1990.

KWV's 20-year-old brandy was judged the best brandy in the world at the 21st International Wine and Spirit Competition in Britain. Fourteen wines entered by the Bergkelder of Stellenbosch in the International Monde Selection Competition in Brussels won gold medals. A noble late harvest wine, produced by Neethlingshof Estate, was adjudged 1990's South African champion.

In June 12 584 farmers and tenants on farms in the Transvaal went to the polls in a referendum to determine the views of White land owners as to the retention of White land ownership in the Transvaal. A total of 94,52 per cent voted in favour of retention.

The export value of fresh deciduous fruits increased by more than R400 million (43 per cent) after the good season of 1990.

Stellenbosch Farmers' Wineries established an international division to promote the South African wine and spirits industry on world markets.

The first of two consignments of rooibos tea to the value of R1,5 million was exported to Japan in October.

Farmers throughout the country battled in the grip of severe drought and soaring temperatures. In certain parts of the eastern Cape conditions were compared to the great drought of 1933 while the northern Transvaal experienced its worst drought in three decades.

A record total of 3 878 tons of rooibos tea was sold during 1990.

Acknowledgements:

Administration: House of Assembly
Administration: House of Delegates
Administration: House of Representatives
Department of Agriculture
Department of Education and Training

Natural resources are classified as either renewable or non-renewable living resources. Because South Africa's resources of water, forest and marine fisheries are limited they must be 'mined' judiciously to keep numbers stable.

Water

South Africa lies in a drought belt. Rainfall is seasonal and influenced by the topography. A comparatively narrow belt along the eastern and southern coastlines is reasonably well watered but the greater part of the interior and western part of the country are arid or semi-arid.

The combined average annual flow of the rivers is about 53 500 million m^3. Much of this volume is, however, lost through flood spillage and evaporation, so that only about 33 000 million m^3 a year can be utilised economically. In addition, ground water supplies can yield about 5 400 million m^3 a year. Meanwhile, the demand for water by agriculture, industries and urban areas grows by about 1,6 per cent a year. If this trend should continue, the total demand for water will be about 25 900 million m^3 a year by the year 2010.

In terms of the Constitution, implemented in 1984, the Department of Water Affairs and Forestry retains responsibility for the development of the country's water resources at national level while a number of functions pertaining specifically to the White, Coloured and Indian communities have been transferred to the ministries concerned in the administrations of the three Houses of Parliament. These relate mainly to water supply for agricultural purposes.

The department regards itself as the custodian of a limited national resource in a society with a growing, diversified and competitive economy. Its major goal is to ensure the ongoing, equitable provision of adequate quantities and qualities of water to all competing users at acceptable degrees of risk and cost in changing conditions. They are therefore constantly investigating ways and means of increasing water supplies so that general economic development will not be impeded by shortages. These investigations include improved methods of developing and utilising existing resources, more efficient use of developed supplies and new sources, such as desalination of sea-water.

An important function of the department is planning the optimal utilisation of all water resources. This requires intensive evaluations of probable future water demands and the most economical means of meeting those demands, field investigations to find suitable dam sites and environmental implications of water projects. The high capital cost involved and the increasing need for regional and multi-purpose projects favour national development rather than private projects. Municipalities, town councils, local and statutory authorities are, however, encouraged to finance and carry out their own development in areas where this is compatible with overall planning.

Because planning is necessary, the department collects and compares hydrological data necessary to determine the quality and quantity of the surface water resources available. This work includes construction, operation and maintenance of river-flow gauging stations as well as processing and analysis of data obtained.

The Division of Geohydrology is concerned with quantitative assessment of ground water supplies and their development, while the department's Hydrological Research Institute (HRI) provides information on catchment areas and the water environment to manage water resources.

The HRI's laboratories for macro-constituents, trace metals, organic and biological elements provide the basis for the networks that monitor national and regional water quality for research projects and for many special surveys or problem investigations. Water quality monitoring networks are systematically planned by the HRI on the basis of the water quality requirements of different users and of the factors that have an influence on water quality. Satellite remote sensing is regarded as an effective way in which a large-scale and regularly updated information base can be provided for the planning and control of the land and water consumption of whole monitoring areas. The HRI makes use of image processing equipment, among other things to extract information on ground cover from satellite data.

The department undertakes research drilling

Open sluices at the Blyde Dam in the eastern Transvaal creates a magnificent sight

for water projects and drilling operations for other government departments. The department co-operates with local and statutory authorities such as Eskom, water boards and municipalities in design, construction and financing by private enterprise of projects needed to meet the water demands of these authorities.

The department manages, operates and maintains state irrigation and regional water supply projects. The Water Act does not inhibit development of private water supply projects but abstraction of water from public streams in government water control areas is subject to the approval of the Minister on the recommendation of his department. Control is also exercised over waterworks and ministerial approval is required if abstraction exceeds specified quantities.

To minimise damage to life and property, water is released from dams before, during and after floods, while the maximum amount is retained for use afterwards. During droughts water

restrictions are intensified as the drought worsens and are lifted when conditions improve. Quality has become a major consideration in the protection and conservation of water, especially with the increase in human interference in catchment areas. This aspect is discussed under Water pollution in chapter 26.

Forestry

The limited national forests in SA were heavily exploited in the 19th century. This led to their protection and the establishment of plantations of exotic trees. Today SA is almost self-sufficient in its timber needs and has been a net exporter of forest products since 1985. Imports consist of specialised timber products, certain high-quality paper and hardwood for the joinery industry.

The main products exported by South Africa are sawn timber, rayon pulp, newsprint, other pulp and paper products, pulpwood chips and wattle tanning extract. The total annual value of these products is R1 900 million.

Local production meets the country's needs for mining timber, firewood, poles, wooden boxes and crates, particle and fibre board and sawn timber for the building industry and industrial purposes. It takes care of 30 per cent of the sawn hardwood required for joinery and more than 80 per cent of paper requirements.

The capital investment in the forestry industry at current market prices amounts to R5 995 million, while an amount of R7 200 million has been invested in the forest products industry.

The major part of the indigenous high forest is controlled by the Forestry Branch of the Department of Water Affairs and Forestry. Forests are managed to allow gradual rehabilitation.

Mainly dead and moribund trees are felled in the production class (20 per cent of forest area)

and logs are sold by tender and/or on public auction. On average only about 3 750 m³ in round logs is exploited annually (200 m³ of stinkwood, 600 m³ of yellowwood, 2 700 m³ of Australian blackwood and 250 m³ of other species).

The Forestry Branch promotes optimal development of forestry and arboriculture in Southern Africa. It manages state forest under its control on multiple use principles, which include production of timber and forest products, conservation of natural ecosystems, setting aside of wilderness areas and nature reserves.

Indigenous forests
The indigenous forests consists of high and scrub forest and woodlands.

High forests
High forests, which cover only about 300 000 ha or 0,25 per cent of the country's surface, occur

Table 1 Distribution of plantations and timber species by zones, 30 June 1989

Zone	Pines and other softwoods (ha)	%	Eucalypts (ha)	%	Wattle (ha)	%	Other hardwoods (ha)	%	TOTAL (ha)	%
Transvaal and OFS	309 940	51,8	258 734	54,3	34 368	29,5	3 186	46,7	606 228	50,0
Northern Transvaal	24 605	4,1	33 586	7,0	231	0,2	928	13,6	—	—
Eastern Transvaal	172 667	28,9	95 965	20,1	37	—	1 052	15,4	15,4	
Central Transvaal and OFS	11 358	1,9	8 562	1,9	219	0,2	51	0,8	—	—
South-eastern Transvaal	101 301	16,9	120 621	25,3	33 881	29,1	1 155	16,9	—	—
Natal	170 521	28,6	210 953	44,2	81 421	69,9	2 793	40,9	465 688	38,9
Maputaland	14 152	2,4	5 393	1,1	0	0	3	—	—	—
Zululand	41 896	7,0	72 961	15,3	5 906	5,1	180	2,6	—	—
Natal Midlands	65 715	11,0	64 056	13,4	46 189	39,6	1 948	28,6	—	—
Northern Natal	9 571	1,6	20 962	4,4	20 426	17,5	67	1,0	—	—
Southern Natal	39 187	6,6	47 581	10,0	8 920	7,7	595	8,7	—	—
Cape	117 264	19,6	7 083	1,5	743	0,6	844	12,4	125 934	10,5
Eastern Cape	20 802	3,5	707	0,1	537	0,4	151	2,2	—	—
Southern Cape	70 496	11,8	5 049	1,1	163	0,2	538	7,9	—	—
Western Cape	25 966	4,3	1 327	0,3	43	—	155	2,3	—	—
TOTAL: RSA	597 725	100,0	476 770	100,0	116 532	100,0	6 823	100,0	1 197 850	100,0
Transkei	49 994	—	22 464	—	4 856	—	574	—	—	—
Ciskei	6 676	—	913	—	667	—	43	—	—	—
Venda	4 289	—	1 771	—	0	—	0	—	—	—
GRAND TOTAL	658 684	—	501 918	—	122 055	—	7 440	—	1 290 097	—

Table 2 Losses caused by plantation fires 1988/89

Forest region	Number of fires	Total damage per fire R	Total extinguishing cost (direct cost) R	Total afforested area damaged (ha)	Damage plus extinguishing cost R/ha
Western Cape	12	3 493	53 148	187,34	3,43
Southern Cape	11	108	4 294	2,95	0,11
Eastern Cape	10	46 052	17 815	276,83	4,96
Tsitsikamma	16	0	8 552	8,09	0,26
Natal	19	4 997	6 918	15,10	0,67
Zululand	28	727	6 812	18,10	0,22
Southern Transvaal	23	787 861	76 111	1 203,97	16,87
Eastern Transvaal	19	5 883	12 837	13,66	0,37
Northern Transvaal	1	0	795	2,50	0,06
TOTAL	139	849 121	187 282	1 728,54	—
Average	—	—	—	—	3,97

Source: Department of Environmental Affairs

mainly on the eastern and southern slopes of the mountain ranges from the Cape Peninsula to the Soutpansberg mountain range in the northern Transvaal. They are seldom continuous but are normally found in isolated sections, varying in size from only a few hectares to several thousand hectares.

The largest area of high forest (65 000 ha) lies within a strip some 180 km long and 16 km wide between the Outeniqua and Tsitsikamma mountain ranges and the sea, extending from Mossel Bay eastwards through Knysna to the Humansdorp district. High forest has virtually disappeared from the mountain ranges from Mossel Bay westwards to the Cape Peninsula, and survives only in small patches in inaccessible mountain kloofs. In the eastern Cape, indigenous forest is found on the coastal mountains but it is only of significant extent on the Amatola mountain range near King William's Town.

Natal forests are generally small and those easily accessible have in the past been heavily exploited. Although similar in composition to those of the eastern Cape, they also include more common species in the north. In the Transvaal, high forest, which in turn resembles the Natal forest in composition, occurs in patches in the mountain ranges along the eastern edge of the highveld. The largest areas are in the Woodbush and Soutpansberg ranges.

Annual auctions of limited quantities of indigenous timber are held in the southern Cape and Tsitsikamma Forest regions.

Scrub forests and woodlands
These cover extensive areas in the low-lying, drier areas of the Transvaal and Natal. Some areas of savanna and woodlands have been denuded for cultivation and firewood. Most species grow slowly and are small. The woodlands are, however, a valuable source of fuel, fencing material and other products and provide protection for the soil and shelter and fodder for stock. The tree growth along much of the coast is classified as coastal scrub. Large areas of this growth have been reserved as protection against drift-sand.

Exotic plantations
Two world wars showed that South Africa was heavily dependent on imported timber. These wars and the depression during the 1930s prompted the state to establish extensive plantations to make South Africa self-sufficient in its timber requirements and to provide more job opportunities in a diversified economy. Commercial plantations of exotic species proved to be sound investments and the private sector, especially since World War II, has established large plantations of pine, eucalyptus and wattle trees.

Plantation yields
Annual sales from 1,2 million ha of exotic plantations totalled about 15,3 million m^3 for 1988/89, made up of —
—4,5 million m^3 of sawlogs for conversion into structural and other timber;

— 7,6 million m^3 of pulpwood for the manufacture of paper, fibreboard and rayon pulp;
— 2,45 million m^3 of round mining timber;
— 403 000 m^3 of poles for preservation (fence, telephone and transmission poles);
— 34 000 m^3 of matchwood; and
— 298 000 m^3 of wood for charcoal, firewood and other uses.

Eucalyptus and wattle plantations, which are grown mainly for pulpwood, mining timber and wattle-bark, are usually felled after about eight to 12 years. Pine plantations are felled after about 19 years for pulpwood or about 25 to 30 years to produce sawlogs.

Plantation fires

The four main causes of plantation fires are incendiarism (25 per cent); burning (12 per cent); honey hunters (10 per cent) and lightning (8 per cent). Fires usually occur in June, July and August. From 1 April 1985 to 31 March 1989, 1 607 fires occurred on 383 plantations in the Transvaal and Natal and one in the southern Cape.

Roundwood processors

On 30 June 1989 there were 140 sawmilling, and six veneer and plywood manufacturing plants. The 15 pulp and board mills were all private sector owned, as were 32 plants for manufacture of mining timber. There were 37 pole preservation plants. Two match factories and seven charcoal factories brought the total of timber-related plants to 239.

The wattle-industry in Natal accounts for 70 per cent of the total area of the 117 000 ha of wattles in the RSA. The Transvaal, with 30 per cent of the total area under tan wattle cultivation, is the other major producer.

Training

The University of Stellenbosch in the Cape is the only university in the country that provides professional training in forestry and offers various degrees in forestry.

Foresters are trained at the School for Foresters at Saasveld near George in the southern Cape, while the Natal Technikon offers a national diploma in pulp and paper technology.

The Timber Industry Manpower Services offers courses in forestry and sawmilling.

The Commission for Administration provides bursaries for students wishing to enter the state forest service. A number of private bursaries are also available.

Marine fisheries

Fishing off a coastline of about 3 000 km, the South African industry landed 615 000 tons (live weight) of fish, shell-fish, mollusc, seaweed, guano and seals in 1989. About 22 000 people are employed in the fishing industry and its ancillary activities.

The total value of catching, collecting and culling for 1988 was estimated at R614 million and the wholesale value of total output at R1 175 million. Catches landed at Walvis Bay, the South African enclave in Namibia, are excluded, since these are mostly made along the coast of that territory. More than 90 per cent of the catch is taken from the productive cold waters off the west coast.

The government follows a strict conservation policy in a fisheries zone of 200 nautical miles. This policy is based on scientific research by the Sea Fisheries Research Institute and enforced by some 80 full-time fisheries control officers, 75 harbour personnel and 470 honorary officers, now under the control of the Cape Provincial Administration.

The South African Bureau of Standards (SABS) maintains compulsory standards for the seafood processing industry and the Fishing Industry Research Institute does research on processing technology. The Small Business Development Corporation (SBDC) gives financial aid to fishermen and smaller entrepreneurs.

Harbours

The Cape Provincial Administration supervises harbour facilities and provides fisheries control officers at 11 proclaimed fishing harbours. These are Lambert's Bay, the mouth of the Berg River, St Helena Bay, Saldanha Bay, Hout Bay, Kalk Bay, Gordon's Bay, Hermanus, Gansbaai, Arniston and Stilbaai. Other harbours, such as Port Nolloth, Cape Town, Mossel Bay, Knysna, Port Elizabeth, East London and Durban, are also used. Most are controlled by Transnet.

Fleet

The fishing fleet consists of about 4 219 vessels, licensed by the Department of Environment Affairs. These include 126 trawlers, 806 motor boats, 58 motor ski boats, 1 392 ski boats and 1 837 dinghies. The largest registered vessel is a factory trawler of 1 700 gross tons. Line-fishing vessels have been divided into two classes: commercial (class A) and semi-commercial (class B). Some 243 licence permits were issued in 1988 for the recently established squid jigging industry. Vessels register for participation in each fishery sector and many hold more than one licence.

Fishing methods
Fishing methods include purse seining (pelagic industry), bottom and mid-water trawling (demersal fish and shrimps), hoop-net and trap fishing (rock lobster industry), handlining (various linecaught fish), long-lining and Madeira pole fishing (tuna), jigging (squid), beach seining, set and stake netting (mullet and other migratory coastal fish), clubbing and shooting (seals), diving (abalone) and collecting, harvesting and cultivating (oysters, mussels, seaweed, guano).

Fishing industry
Volume-wise the multi-species shoal fishing by purse seine is the most important branch of the

The fishmarket at Hout Bay harbour is a beehive of activity

marine fishing industry, with the catch totalling 408 000 tons in 1989.

Catches of anchovy and pilchard are limited by quota. The anchovy quota was reduced from the high levels in 1987 and 1988 to a more traditional level as a result of scientific evaluation of the state of the stock. Anchovy, pilchard and round herring are processed into fish meal, fish body oil and canned fish. Together these products were valued at R216 million.

The major purse seine fishing areas are in the vicinity of Walker Bay and St Helena Bay, both on the West Coast of the Cape, up to 25 km offshore. Because of the high local demand for fish meal and the small catches of canning fish, this branch of the industry exports virtually no products.

Trawling remains the most important fishery branch of the industry economically. The wholesale value of processed products, from a catch of 220 000 tons, was R578 million in 1989. However, the catches of hake in offshore trawls, of hake and kingklip on demersal longlines and of hake and sole in inshore trawls are regulated by quota. About 75 per cent of the annual catch of rock lobsters is exported. The total wholesale value of rock lobster products (quota-restricted landings of 4 470 tons on the species of the west and east coasts) was estimated at over R131 million for the 1988/89 season.

Taking third place is line fishing, bringing 29 000 tons to shore in 1989, with a wholesale value of R177 million.

Important line fishing species are snoek (*Thyrsites atun*), kob (*Johnius hololepidotus*), silverfish (*Argyrozona argyrozona*), geelbek (*Atractoscion aequidens*), yellowtail (*Seriola lalandi*) and hottentot (*Pachymetopon blochii*).

Other exploited renewable sources are pink prawn (*Haliporoides triarthrus*), langoustine (*Nephrops andamanicus*), red crab (*Geryon quinquedens*), squid (*Loligo vulgaris*), abalone, (*Haliotis midae*), mullet (*Liza richardsoni*), elephant fish (*Callorhynchus capensis*), oysters (*Crassostrea margaritacea*), white mussels (*Donax serra*), redbait (*Pyura stolonifera*), seabird guano gathered from islands and artificial platforms and four different types of seaweed.

SA has not done any whaling since 1976 but remains a member of the International Whaling Commission.

The international sealskin market has collapsed, so that in 1989 only 3 100 pups and 671 bulls (much less than the allocated quotas) were culled at Kleinsee, on the West Coast where the largest Cape colony of *Arctocephalus pusillus* can be found.

News items: 1990

The timber industry earned close on R2 billion in export revenue during 1988/89.

The Lesotho Highlands Water Project got under way in January 1991 with the commencement of construction of the Katse Dam. When the first phase is completed in 1997 the dam will feed South Africa's PWV area with about 16 cubic metres of water per second.

The governments of SA and Botswana have agreed to undertake a joint study of the Limpopo River system above the confluence of the Limpopo and Sashe rivers. A group of consulting engineers will evaluate present utilisation and availability of water in the river. The Limpopo forms the border between Botswana and SA.

A total of 136 604 tons of hake, 4 955 tons of monk, 1 650 tons of kingklip and 8 945 tons of ribbon fish were landed in the 1989 fishing season.

The new Sea Fishery Act came into effect on 1 July and the Sea Fishery Amendment Act on 19 October. In terms of the latter, the maximum fine for foreign vessels illegally catching in South African waters was increased from R100 000 to R1 million, with a minimum of R250 000 and compulsory confiscation of boat, cargo and equipment. The fine for transhipping at sea was raised to R500 000 to discourage circumvention of South Africa's anti-gill-net fishing regulations. No permits had been granted for catching tuna with gill-nets in South African fishing waters. However, the gill-net controversy flamed up when, at the request of the Taiwanese Squid Fishery Association, some 100 squid fishers from the Falkland Islands, carrying tuna gill-nets on board, were allowed into Table Bay harbour for supplies and fuel and to disembark some 500 South African labourers. It was later announced that this had been a once-only concession and that no further permits for entering South African ports would be issued to gill-netters.

The new legislation changed the licensing procedure for commercial and semi-commercial fishing vessels. All such craft now had to be licensed by 30 June, licence fees depending on vessel length. In addition, a permit is needed for each fishery sector, the fee being R15 per sector payable before the commencement of the season for each fishery. The legislation further provides for the establishment of a Quota Board (which has been appointed) to allocate individual quotas within the overall quota for each fishery regulated by quota.

The present seal population along the South African coast is estimated at 1,2 million seals, making the Cape fur seal one of the most common in the world, but local concessionaries had difficulties because of increasing resistance to the use of feral mammals in the fur trade. A concession was therefore granted to a Taiwanese company in 1989 to harvest seal pups and bulls at the Kleinsee colony. Approved methods of harvesting were to be used under supervision and a factory was to be built at Port Nolloth for the full utilisation of the carcasses. Only a small fraction of the allocated quotas was harvested in 1989 and utilisation was poor. There was widespread reaction to these developments, ranging from unqualified support for even greater harvests because of the impact of large seal numbers on other members of the ecosystem and man, to qualified support for the principle of rational harvesting, to criticism of the harvesting methods on humanitarian grounds, to misgivings about the details of the particular concession, to outright condemnation of all harvesting on moral grounds. The outcome was the appointment of an 11-member committee of inquiry into the scientific aspects of seal utilisation.

The committee, consisting of eminent South African environmental scientists with expertise in various fields, was to report by 30 September. To date, the report has not been made public.

Longline fishing for kingklip and hake was banned from the end of 1990. As a phasing-out measure the kingklip quota was reduced from 2 500 tons to 1 000 tons and the closed season on the South African coast extended from 15 September to 15 October to 15 July to 15 October.

The Trees for Africa Foundation launched a project in April to plant at least 5 million trees in South Africa over the next five years.

For the first time in the RSA's history, heavily mineralised ground water from boreholes was desalinated. Bitterfontein and Nuwerus in southern Namaqualand were the first to receive this 'sweet' water in May 1990. In the past, potable water had to be transported to this area.

World Meteorological Day was celebrated on 23 March, World Environment Day on 5 June, National Arbor Day on the second Friday of August, and National Marine Day on the first Friday of December.

Acknowledgements:

Department of Water Affairs and Forestry
Sea Fisheries Research Institute

Mining, minerals and energy 12

It is the policy of the South African government to leave the exploitation of the country's mineral resources to private enterprise. Mining laws are designed to encourage private entrepreneurs by providing them with security of title to prospecting and mining rights and by allowing them a fair and attractive return on capital. Mining laws do not differentiate between South African nationals and foreigners in the acquisition of prospecting and mining rights.

South Africa's mineral wealth is found in diverse geological formations, some of which are unique and very extensive by world standards. In terms of mining production, the most important of these is the Witwatersrand basin, which yields some 98 per cent of South Africa's gold output. Another is the Bushveld Complex, a sill-like geological feature occupying about 50 000 km^2 of the central, eastern and western Transvaal. A large part of the world's reserves of a number of important minerals is found in and around the Bushveld Complex — platinum and platinum-group metals (PGMs), chromium, vanadium, nickel, fluorspar and andalusite.

According to recent official estimates, South Africa has 56 per cent of the world's discovered chrome ore reserves and the largest known reserves of vanadium and andalusite. The combined total of South Africa's reserves of platinum, chromite and vanadium ore constitute an important mineral province in the world. The deposits of manganese ore in the north-western Cape are the largest proven reserve base in the world — about 3 990 million tons of unmined metal.

South Africa also has substantial reserves of other industrially-important metals and minerals, including antimony, asbestos, diamonds, coal, fluorspar, iron ore, nickel, lead, zinc, phosphates, uranium, titanium, vermiculite and zirconium.

Mineral sales were worth R37 365 million in 1990. In 1989 mining contributed about 12 per cent to the gross domestic product (GDP) (at current prices), while mineral export sales accounted for 51 per cent of total export revenue.

No less than 77 per cent of all mineral production is exported to more than 80 countries. Export earnings from more than 60 different minerals were R28 998 million in 1990.

Gold has been the main source of foreign currency for years and currently accounts for almost 65 per cent of the value of mineral export sales to foreign countries. South Africa is the world's largest producer of gold, providing an annual production of about 600 tons.

Among the most important commodities traded in the non-gold sector were coal, the PGMs, diamonds, iron ore, copper, manganese ore, zirconium, zinc, asbestos, chrome ore and vanadium. South Africa has become one of the world's leading exporters of bituminous (steam) coal. In 1990 coal exports totalled 46 million tons (valued at more than R3,6 billion), as against local sales of 137,8 million tons to meet both domestic and industrial power requirements and to feed the oil-from-coal industry. About 30 per cent of chrome ore production is exported, and the balance is used to produce ferrochromium, of which the Republic is the world's largest producer. Most of the manganese ore is exported in the raw state, the remainder being used to produce ferromanganese and manganese metal. South Africa is the world's largest exporter of vanadium and in 1988 accounted for about 99 per cent of the western world's requirements.

The Minerals Bureau, a branch of the Department of Mineral and Energy Affairs, was established to promote the optimum use of South Africa's mineral resources. It monitors and analyses all mineral commodities with regard to South African and world supply and demand, marketing and market trends. (The National Energy Council, Mintek and Geological Survey are discussed later in the chapter.)

Mining industry

The six most important mining corporations are Anglo American, Rand Mines (Mining and Services), Gold Fields of South Africa, Johannesburg Consolidated Investment Company, Genmin and Anglovaal. These six corporations, together with the mining companies they manage, account for nearly all the gold, uranium, coal, zinc, PGMs, lead, diamonds and silver produced in South Africa and a substantial amount of the output of the other minerals.

In 1990, more than 1 000 mines and quarries employed some 737 000 people, many from neighbouring countries. More than R9,5 billion was paid out in wages. In the gold-mining industry alone, more than 340 000 workers go underground each working day.

Some 4 500 apprentices are trained every year at 17 training centres at gold, coal and other mines. Prospective gold miners are trained at seven colleges with a total enrolment of about 650 at any one time.

The mining industry houses about a million people, including the families of many miners and is the largest supplier of housing after the state itself. In recent years some 8 000 houses and new single quarters for 40 000 miners were built annually.

Through the Rand Mutual Assurance Company, the mining industry provides care and compensation in the case of accidents. Specialist medical care is provided by the Rand Mutual Hospital in Johannesburg. The comprehensive medical infrastructure of the industry includes group hospitals in the mining areas, as well as clinics and stations on mines for emergency treatment.

Miners enjoy comprehensive sporting and recreational facilities at no cost to themselves. There are more than 100 soccer fields, including 17 floodlit stadiums for about 7 000 players and 500 mine teams. The mines also provide equipment, facilities and coaches for various other sports activities.

Chamber of Mines

The Chamber of Mines of South Africa is a volunteer organisation consisting of independent mining finance corporations and individual mines and mining companies. Together they account for over 85 per cent of South Africa's mineral output.

The Chamber of Mines provides an extensive advisory and service function to its members and the industry on a co-operative basis, in such areas as industrial relations, education and training and security and health care, as well as technical, legal and public affairs, environmental conservation, rescue and statistical services.

The 'family' of the Chamber of Mines includes the Employment Bureau of Africa (Teba) which serves most of the nearly 500 000 unskilled and semi-skilled workers at member mines, Comro, the mining research organisation, Rand Refinery and the Nuclear Fuels Corporation of South Africa (Nufcor).

The Chamber, through its Employee Assistance Programme, has a comprehensive range of rehabilitation and social services for all its employees.

The Chamber runs a Rescue Training Service with branches in Carletonville, Dundee, Evander and Welkom and a rescue drilling system for use on coal mines.

Mineral wealth

South Africa's mineral wealth can be divided into:

Precious metals
Gold
Gold is synonymous with South Africa. About 47 per cent of the world's gold has been mined in the country over the past century. Today the goldfields form a discontinuous arc, 430 km long, stretching across the Transvaal and the OFS. In 1989 there were 37 large gold mines in operation, 20 small mines and 13 tailings retreatment concerns.

Most gold-mining companies exploit more than one reef in the Witwatersrand Supergroup. The extensive areas at present being prospected, promise to add significantly to the country's unmined gold reserves.

The average grade of gold ore milled in 1989 was a mere 4,99 g of gold per ton of ore. Stopes are usually about one metre in height and in general cannot accommodate large machines. Hence most gold mines remain labour intensive. There is an increasing tendency, however, towards mechanised mining methods where the width of reefs allows this. To date, several gold mines have adopted these mechanised techniques based on trackless transportation of ore.

The gold bars produced by the mines weigh slightly more than 31,1 kg each and contain about 84 per cent gold, 11 per cent silver and 5 per cent base metals. This gold is refined and the silver separated at the Rand Refinery in Germiston.

The bars are refined initially to a fineness of at least 99,5 parts in 1 000 (the standard grade) which is adequate for most purposes. For special purposes, some gold is refined electrolytically to a fineness of 9 999 parts in 10 000.

The bulk of the refined gold production is sold by the South African Reserve Bank in 400-ounce bars at the price ruling on the London bullion market to dealers, banks, institutions, large private buyers, and others who together constitute the world bullion market. Small amounts of the Reserve Bank's purchases are channelled to the South African Mint, which supplies local manufacturers.

The platinum-group metals (PGMs)

Six related noble metals, all with a silvery appearance, constitute the platinum group of metals (PGMs). They are platinum, palladium, rhodium, ruthenium, iridium and osmium, and generally occur together in varying proportions.

In South Africa platinum, palladium, rhodium and ruthenium are mainly found in the Bushveld Complex, while osmium and iridium are found in the Witwatersrand Conglomerates. At the current rate of mining the ore will last for several generations.

The approximate recovery grades of PGMs from the various reefs of the Bushveld Complex are: Merensky Reef 5,31, UG2-reef 5,97 and on the Platreef 2,89 g/ton.

Platinum, a precious noble metal, enjoys limited demand as an investment medium in the form of coins and bars and in the manufacture of jewellery. Its most important role, however, is its use in the reduction of toxic exhaust fumes of cars. In 1990 this consumer sector accounted for 49,2 per cent of total western world demand. Platinum also plays a significant role as a catalyst in the manufacture of petrol from crude oil and in the production of nitrogenous fertilisers. The other metals of the group are used mainly in the chemical and electrical industries. Some are

Table 1 South Africa's* role in world mineral production, 1988

Commodity	Unit	Production	World		Market economies	
			%	Rank	%	Rank
Alumino-silicates	kt	260	46	1	56	1
Antimony [a]	t	5 917	9	4	21	2
Asbestos	kt	146	3	7	8	5
Chrome ore	t	3 708	32	1	48	1
Coal [b]	kt	181 000	5	6	11	3
Copper [c]	kt	168	2	14	3	11
Diamonds [d]	k car	8 506	9	5	11	4
Ferrochromium	kt	994	29	1	38	1
Ferromanganese	kt	695	10	2	16	1
Ferrosilicon	kt	87	3	9	4	7
Fluorspar	kt	328	6	5	14	2
Gold	t	618	33	1	40	1
Iron ore	Mt	25	3	8	5	6
Lead [c]	kt	90	3	11	4	7
Manganese metal [e]	kt	37	53	1	66	1
Manganese ore	kt	4 793	17	2	33	1
Platinum-group metals	kt	***	21	3	37	2
Phosphate rock	kt	***	2	9	3	7
Silicon metal	kt	39	6	7	7	5
Silver [c]	t	200	1	15	2	12
Titanium minerals [f]	kt	***	21	2	23	2
Uranium [cj]	t	3 799	na	na	9	7
Vanadium [gh]	t	31	44	1	69	1
Vermiculite	kt	209	40	2	40	2
Zinc [c]	kt	90	1	15	2	11
Zirconium minerals [j]	t	***	16	2	18	2

*   Excludes Bophuthatswana, Ciskei, Transkei and Venda
**   Excluding centrally planned economies comprising Albania, Bulgaria, China, Cuba, Czechoslovakia, Germany, Hungary, Kampuchea, Korea DPR,
     Laos, Mongolia, Poland, Rumania, the USSR and Vietnam
*** Classified
a = metal in concentrate; b = bituminous and anthracite; c = contained metal; d = gem and industrial, rough; e = electrolytic; f = metal content of minerals,
excluding slag; g = contained V_2O_5; h = includes Bophuthatswana; j = concentrate; na = not available
Source: Minerals Bureau of South Africa, October 1990

used in combination with platinum to enhance or modify its properties.

Gemstones

Diamonds

South Africa is currently the world's fifth largest producer of natural diamonds. A high percentage is of gem quality.

Diamonds occur in pipes and fissures of kimberlite, as well as alluvial and marine deposits. Pipes of kimberlite are commonly circular in shape, and become smaller with increasing depth where diamonds of lesser value are found. The well-known Premierpipe, the largest in South Africa, covers an area of 54 ha.

Approximately one out of every 100 pipes can be economically mined and contains diamond concentrations varying from one part in 5 million to one part in 100 million parts rock. As the elements erode diamond-bearing pipes, the stones are liberated from the kimberlite and can then be transported over long distances. Such diamonds can be transported in rivers and can be concentrated as alluvial deposits in riverbeds. This kind of deposit is mainly found in the western to south-western Transvaal, the northern OFS and the northern Cape.

Alluvial diamonds transported by rivers enter the sea and are distributed along the shore by wave action to form alluvial diamond fields. Diamond deposits are restricted to the west coast, in particular the coast line north and south of the Orange River mouth at Alexander Bay. Due to weathering of alluvial and marine diamonds, most of these diamonds are gemstones.

Diamond-mining operations in South Africa are dominated by De Beers Consolidated Mines, a company originally formed through the consolidation of the old Kimberley mines. The former Kimberley mine, the 'Big Hole', has been declared a national monument, and a museum depicting the history of diamond mining in the country has been established near the site.

Table 2 South Africa's* role in world mineral supply, Reserve Base**, November 1990

Commodity	Unit	RSA	World		Market Economies***	
			%	Rank	%	Rank
Alumino-silicates [a]	kt	50 800	37	1	47	1
Antimony [b]	t	120 000	3	6	6	4
Asbestos [c]	kt	8 200	6	4	11	2
Chromium [a]	Mt	2 400	56	1	58	1
Coal [d]	Mt	58 404	10	4	20	2
Diamonds [e]	M car	360	24	2	27	2
Fluorspar [f]	kt	32 000	11	3	30	1
Gold [b]	t	20 000	44	1	53	1
Iron [b]	Mt	6 000	6	6	9	5
Lead [b]	kt	5 000	4	4	6	4
Manganese [b]	Mt	3 992	82	1	91	1
Nickel [b]	kt	10 690	9	6	12	5
Platinum-group metals [b]	t	26 700	69	1	82	1
Phosphate rock [g]	Mt	2 310	6	3	7	3
Titanium minerals [b]	kt	31 100	10	5	11	5
Uranium [bh]	t	317 000	na	na	19	2
Vanadium [b]	kt	5 400	33	1	51	1
Vermiculite [a]	kt	73 000	na	na	40	2
Zinc [b]	kt	1500	5	4	6	4
Zirconium minerals [b]	kt	6 900	14	2	16	2

*   Excludes Bophuthatswana, Ciskei, Transkei and Venda
**   Reserve Base (as at 30 June 1990); The Reserve Base is the in situ demonstrated resource from which reserves are estimated. It includes resources that are currently economic (demonstrated reserves) and marginally economic
***   Excluding centrally planned economies comprising Albania, Bulgaria, China, Cuba, Czechoslovakia, Germany, Hungary, Kampuchea, Korea DPR, Laos, Mongolia, Poland, Rumania, the USSR and Vietnam
a = ore, in situ; b = contained metal; c = contained fibre; d = bituminous and anthracite proved recoverable reserves; e = gem and industrial; f = contained CaF_2; g = contained concentrate (38% P_2O_5); h = recoverable at a cost of less than US $80/kg U; na = not available
Source: Minerals Bureau of South Africa, November 1990

South Africa has an established diamond cutting industry. It produces cut and polished gems of high quality which are eventually used in jewellery. According to policy, local production is processed where possible. Low-quality stones and synthetics are channelled to the industrial sectors worldwide.

Other gemstones
Various semi-precious stones, including emeralds, have been produced in the past, but tiger's-eye has been the only one of significance in recent years. Tiger's-eye is a hard, silicified alteration product of crocidolite asbestos sporadically found in the Griqualand West area of the Cape Province. Typical colours are yellow, golden-brown, blue and red. Total sales realised some R944 000 in 1990.

Ferrous metals
Chromium
This metal imparts certain valuable characteristics to ferrous and nonferrous alloys. The steel industry absorbs about 76 per cent of total chromium production, mainly in production of stainless steel and steel which has to withstand high temperatures. Approximately 11 per cent is used in the production of chemicals, mainly paints, colourants for metals and tanning agents.

Some 13 per cent of all chrome ore mined is used in the production of refractory materials such as bricks for lining furnaces. Well-graded concentrates are also applied as a refractory lining in foundry moulds. Mineable chrome ores consist exclusively of the mineral chromite.

No less than 74 per cent of the world's discovered reserves occur in the RSA and Bophuthatswana as layers within the Bushveld Complex. There is a consistency of grade and seam thickness over strike distances of up to 200 km and to vertical depths in excess of 1 000 metres.

In 1990, production declined marginally from 4,27 million tons in 1989 to 4,22 million tons, a decrease of 1,2 per cent. Most of the chrome ore sold in the RSA is used in the production of ferrochromium by six smelters, all located in the Transvaal. In 1989 output of chromium ferro-alloys totalled 938 000 tons of which 831 000 tons were exported.

Iron
In 1990 some 8 742 000 tons of crude steel were produced. South Africa's iron ore resources are estimated to be 9 400 million tons, more than adequate for domestic requirements for many generations and for substantial exports. More

than 4 000 million tons of high-grade hematite ore occur in the Postmasburg-Sishen region of the northern Cape.

The iron content of 85 per cent of these reserves is between 66 and 69,9 per cent iron, while a further 11 per cent contains from 63 to 65,9 per cent iron and the remainder from 60 to 62,9 per cent iron. There is also a large quantity of ore with less than 60 per cent iron.

These deposits supply a large proportion of domestic demand and the entire export trade. Exports increased by 23,9 per cent in 1990, earning R815 million in foreign exchange.

Manganese
South Africa holds the largest known deposits of metallurgical-grade manganese ore in the world that can be mined profitably according to current techniques. The reserves occur in a 90-km belt from Postmasburg in the northern Cape northwards to Hotazel. Deposits of chemical-grade ore are scattered across the south-western Transvaal.

Some 95 per cent of the manganese ore as well as ferro-manganese alloys are used in the steel industry. Manganese oxide is used to manufacture torch batteries and as an oxidation agent in the reduction of zinc and uranium ore.

South Africa is the western world's second largest producer of ferromanganese, and the largest producer of silicomanganese and electrolytic manganese metal. In 1990 3,8 million tons of manganese ore were produced in South Africa, of which 2,2 million tons were exported.

Vanadium
South Africa holds the world's largest known reserves of vanadium in the Bushveld Complex of the central Transvaal. These reserves, estimated at about 5,4 million tons of metal, are believed to be about 33 per cent of the known world total.

Vanadium-bearing ore is mined at three mines in the Transvaal and one in Bophuthatswana. The ore is processed by four companies in South Africa and one in Bophuthatswana to produce high-grade vanadium pentoxide, and also further processed for production of the master alloys ferrovanadium and nitrovan and certain additives used in the chemical and petroleum industries. The main use, however, (90 per cent) is in the steel industry for hardening steel.

Nonferrous metals
Antimony
Consolidated Murchison's Mine, located at Gravelotte in the north-eastern Transvaal, is the

Table 3   Mineral production and sales, 1990 (preliminary)

Commodity		Production	Local sales		Exports		Total sales	
		Quantity	Quantity	Value (R)	Quantity	Value (R)	Quantity	Value (R)
PRECIOUS								
Diamonds	car	8 681 589	**	**	**	**	**	**
Gold	kg	596 787	**	**	**	18 821 995 962	**	18 821 995 962
Platinum-group metals	kg	**	**	**	**	**	**	**
Silver	kg	162 933	16 113	6 797 122	158 556	53 654 029	174 669	60 451 151
METALLIC								
Antimony##		**	**	**	**	**	**	**
Chrome ore		4 223 445	2 406 411	218 789 573	1 059 880	190 897 432	3 466 291	409 687 005
Cobalt	kg	**	**	**	**	**	**	**
Copper#		181 227	75 776	553 267 257	93 951	607 467 123	169 727	1 140 734 380
Iron ore:		30 970 104	11 017 591	294 257 510	18 059 761	814 703 108	29 077 352	1 108 960 618
Hematite		25 320 565	8 663 274	233 364 634	18 059 761	814 703 108	26 723 035	1 048 067 742
Magnetite§		5 649 539	2 354 317	60 892 876	*	*	2 354 317	60 892 876
Lead##		69 425	2 746	6 470 012	87 717	131 384 942	90 463	137 854 954
Manganese ore		3 820 961	1 647 384	222 027 816	2 167 931	575 190 035	3 815 315	797 217 851
Monazite		**	**	**	**	**	**	**
Nickel#		**	**	98 135 811	**	171 356 729	**	269 492 540
Tantalite/colombite	kg	6	*	*	*	*	*	*
Tin#	kg	1 155 642	850 066	15 217 099	311 234	4 173 941	1 161 300	19 391 040
Titanium minerals		**	**	**	**	**	**	**
Uranium oxide	kg	3 020 022	**	**	**	**	**	**
Zinc##		75 548	56 902	163 293 163	8 823	18 158 675	65 725	181 451 838
Zirconium minerals		**	**	**	**	**	**	**
NON-METALLIC								
Andalusite		297 778	124 279	33 091 714	139 745	49 795 582	264 024	82 887 296
Asbestos		144 008	6 062	4 291 234	172 122	172 228 241	178 184	176 519 475
Barytes		2 714	2 742	901 845	*	*	2 742	901 845
Beryl	kg	1 000	*	*	*	*	*	*
Calsite		*	*	*	*	*	*	*
Coal:		175 574 967	137 830 886	4 114 046 163	46 122 237	3 610 625 609	183 953 123	7 724 671 772
Anthracite		3 911 857	606 741	55 428 113	3 092 802	269 344 952	3 699 543	324 773 065
Bituminous		171 663 110	137 224 145	4 058 618 050	43 029 435	3 341 280 657	180 253 580	7 399 898 707
Corondum		*	*	*	*	*	*	*
Feldspar		56 819	54 403	10 468 377	6 362	2 005 406	60 765	12 473 783
Fluorspar		338 047	37 598	9 003 519	234 416	79 759 769	275 014	88 763 288
Gypsum		387 158	394 398	10 878 721	78	2 340	394 476	10 781 061
Kieselguhr		125	151	58 807	*	*	151	58 807
Limestone and dolomite		20 235 045	16 606 071	410 537 997	75 437	9 261 759	16 681 508	419 799 756
Magnesite		110 874	139 049	10 509 053	*	*	139 049	10 509 053
Mica		1 795	*	**	*	**	*	**
Mineral pigments		3 016	1 239	235 812	*	*	1 239	235 812
Nepheline syenite		145	145	7 020	*	*	145	7 020
Phosphate concentrate		**	**	**	**	**	**	**
Pyrophyllite		2 935	**	1 218 901	**	2 635 726	**	3 854 627
Salt		728 868	739 859	76 161 227	87 312	7 906 522	827 171	84 067 749

Table 3 (Continued)

Semi-precious stones	kg	530 309	292 959	655 569	178 423	287 954	471 382	943 523
Silcrete		*	1 244	65 378	*	*	1 244	65 378
Silica		2 003 009	1 996 280	64 434 407	142	21 651	1 996 422	64 456 058
Sillimanite		256	133	35 336	406	161 134	539	196 470
Sodium sulphate		*	*	*	*	*	*	*
Sulpur (all forms)		678 947	673 219	131 118 955	*	*	673 219	131 118 955
Talc		11 758	8 477	1 972 437	*	*	8 477	1 972 437
Vermiculite		223 747	12 156	912 838	145 749	35 809 503	157 905	36 722 341
DIMENSION AND BUILDING STONE Granite and/or norite		+	20 071	5 803 466	398 649	160 332 375	418 720	166 135 841
Marble	m^3	4 345	2 197	1 004 999	502	364 499	2 699	1 369 498
Quartzite		+	124	100 898	*	*	124	100 898
Schist		+	*	*	*	*	*	*
Shale		392 228	389 610	2 421 518	*	*	389 610	2 421 518
Siltstone		+	458	65 889	*	*	458	65 889
Slate		+	20 394	5 999 562	10 242	6 648 403	30 636	12 647 965
CLAY Attapulgite		7 440	7 401	217 833	*	*	7 401	217 833
Bentonite		64 787	36 089	8 248 142	515	48 878	36 604	8 297 020
Fire clay		245 093	207 385	3 726 881	*	*	207 385	3 726 881
Flint (raw and calcined)		134 060	107 797	10 870 355	5 511	802 954	113 308	11 673 309
Kaolin		131 724	124 039	19 463 219	39	1 989	124 078	19 465 208
Aggregate and sand		+	40 094 095	493 833 798	*	*	40 094 095	493 833 798
Miscellaneous		—	—	1 369 340 305	—	3 470 427 535	—	4 839 767 840
TOTAL		—	—	8 367 062 557	—	28 998 109 805	—	37 365 172 362

All quantities in metric tons, unless otherwise specified
+   Not available
*   Nil
** Classified; where applicable earnings are included under Miscellaneous
#   Metal and metal-in-concentrate
Metal-in-concentrate
§   Including vanadiferous magnetite
—   Not applicable
Source: Minerals Bureau of South Africa. Based on returns up to 31 October 1990

only producer of antimony ore in South Africa. It is the world's largest single producer and accounts for about 10 per cent of world output (excluding US production). Both concentrates and antimony trioxide are exported.

Copper
South Africa is believed to have 1 per cent of the world's known reserves of copper and accounts for 2 per cent of world production.

Exploitation of the huge carbonatite complex at Phalaborwa is the country's most significant copper mining venture. Ore mined here contains about 0,5 per cent copper. Copper, with other minerals like apatite (phosphate ore) magnetite, vermiculite, phlogopite mica, baddeleyite (zirconium dioxide), uranothorianite and minerals containing the rare earth elements are mined by Palabora Mining Company (PMC) and Foskor.

Both companies treat ore from parts of the same ore body. In 1990 181 230 tons of copper were produced, 52 per cent of which was exported to earn R607 million.

Nickel
Nickel is produced as a by-product of platinum mining in South Africa. Total South African sales amounted to R269,5 million in 1990.

Lead
Primary lead production is confined to the Broken Hill Mine (Black Mountain Mineral Development Company) in the north-western Cape and Pering Mine in the northern Cape.

Tin
Tin is produced from two different geological units, the Pretoria Group and the Bushveld

Complex, both in the Transvaal. In 1990 1 156 tons of tin were produced. This represents more refined tin metal than is required for the local market and the surplus is exported. About 50 per cent of local consumption is used for tinplate and the balance in solders, bronze and white metals.

Titanium

The titanium minerals ilmenite and rutile are recovered from beach sand deposits and exported as titanium slag and natural rutile. The only producer in the country, Richards Bay Minerals, is in the process of expanding its titaniferous slag capacity from 750 000 tons per annum to one million tons per annum, with effect from 1991.

The demand for South Africa's slag for the manufacture of titanium dioxide pigment remains strong. The pigment industry accounts for about 95 per cent of titanium mineral consumption.

Zinc

Primarily zinc concentrate production comes from three mines in the northern Cape. In 1990 their output amounted to 75 548 tons of metal in concentrate. Sales realised R 181 million, of which 10 per cent was derived from exports.

The Black Mountain Mineral Development Company produces zinc concentrate together with lead and copper concentrates, from which silver is also recovered.

The zinc deposit at Gamsberg, some 15 km east of Black Mountain's Broken Hill Mine, has reserves of 143 million tons averaging 7,41 per cent zinc and 0,5 per cent lead. The Pering zinc-lead mine near Reivilo in the northern Cape attained full production in 1987.

Most of South Africa's zinc production, together with concentrates from the Rosh Pinah Mine in Namibia, is refined by the Zinc Corporation of South Africa at Springs in the Transvaal. Extensions to this refinery have increased capacity from 82 000 to 102 000 tons a year, sufficient for South Africa's requirements for the immediate future.

Zirconium

Zirconium minerals are produced from two sources. The beach sand deposits at Richards Bay yield large quantities of zircon (zirconium silicate), and the mineral baddeleyite (natural zirconium dioxide) is produced at Phalaborwa in the north-eastern Transvaal as a by-product of open-pit copper and phosphate· mining. South Africa is the world's second largest producer of zirconium-containing products.

Nonmetallic minerals

Alumino-silicates

The minerals andalusite, kyanite and sillimanite are used to make high-grade refractory materials. All three are composed of aluminium silicate and differ only in their basic crystalline structure. South Africa has deposits of all three minerals but particularly andalusite.

The Transvaal has the world's largest known reserves of alumino-silicates estimated at about 50,8 million tons, 37 per cent of world reserves. Sales of andalusite increased by 2,7 per cent from 257 194 tons in 1989 to 264 024 tons, valued at R82,9 million in 1990. Sillimanite is produced near Pofadder in the north-western Cape. Production in 1990 was 256 tons of which most was exported. South Africa's production of alumino-silicates represents about 46 per cent of the world output.

Asbestos

South Africa is the only producer of all three types of asbestos known, namely amosite, crocidolite and chrysotile. It is also the world's only large producer of amosite and crocidolite. The latter is found largely in the Kuruman region of the northern Cape, while amosite is mined only at Penge in the north-eastern Transvaal. The country produced 3,2 per cent of world requirements in 1988, which makes it the seventh largest asbestos producer. The USSR and Canada dominate the market with about 74 per cent of total production.

In 1990 crocidolite accounted for 10,1 per cent of production, chrysotile for 71,9 per cent and amosite for 18,0 per cent. Revenue from sales was R176,5 million, 97,5 per cent in exports.

Fluorspar

South Africa has the world's third largest known reserves of fluorspar. These are located mainly in the Transvaal and are exploited at the Buffalo and Vergenoeg Mines in the Bushveld Complex and in dolomitic terrain in the western Transvaal. Total production was 338 047 tons in 1990.

South Africa occupies fifth place in the world after Mongolia, Mexico, China and the Soviet Union, and contributed 6,4 per cent of world production during 1988.

Dimension stone

A particularly attractive, dark-coloured gabbro, commercially known as black granite, is mined in the Bushveld Complex in the Rustenburg and Belfast areas.

Much of the material leaves the country in the

form of large, rough blocks to be cut and polished in the destination countries.

Marble is produced from large deposits in the Vanrhynsdorp district about 300 km north of Cape Town. Total sales in 1990 came to R1,4 million of which 73,4 per cent was sold locally.

Slate is mainly produced in the western Transvaal. Production amounted to 30 636 tons in 1990. Total sales were R12,4 million.

Phosphate

From early 1977 South Africa became a major exporter of phosphoric acid, which is produced by two large plants at Phalaborwa and Richards Bay. They have a combined capacity of 635 000 tons of phosphorus pentoxide and export through the loading terminal at Richards Bay.

Most phosphate raw material, from which Fosfor recovers phosphate rock containing up to 40,3 per cent P_2O_5, is produced by the mine of PMC at Phalaborwa. The reserve base is about 2 310 million tons of phosphate concentrate, the third largest presently known in the world. At Phalaborwa each 100 m in depth can yield 300 million tons of concentrate.

Silica and silicon

Production of silica decreased from 2 181 682 tons in 1989 to 2 003 009 tons in 1990. Total sales, mainly to the domestic market, amounted to R64,4 million.

A very large, exceptionally pure deposit of quartz (SiO_2) is mined on the outskirts of Pietersburg in the northern Transvaal. The silicon dioxide content exceeds 99,9 per cent and most impurities are present in trace amounts. Glass sand is mined extensively on the Cape Flats as well as at Delmas and in the Magaliesberg in the Transvaal. A large quarry near Bronkhorstspruit supplies foundry sand to the steel industry on the Witwatersrand.

Vermiculite

Vermiculite is produced from a pipe-like body in the Phalaborwa Complex by PMC, which accounted for 39,8 per cent of the western world's production in 1988. Sales decreased from a total of 210 616 tons in 1989 to 157 905 tons in 1990, of which 145 749 tons valued at R35,8 million were exported.

South Africa's identified resources of vermiculite are estimated at 73 million tons, second only to those of the US.

Other minerals

In 1990, 2 714 tons of **barytes** were mined and used entirely by the local market.

Table 4 Gold production

Year	Production kg	Value R'000
1985*	670 755	15 291 076
1986*	638 047	17 283 295
1987*	602 172	17 494 502
1988*	617 719	19 686 977
1989*§	605 452	19 284 204
1990*§	600 500	18 641 700

* Excluding Bophuthatswana
§ Preliminary
Source: Chamber of Mines of South Africa and the Minerals Bureau of South Africa

Table 5 Gold* supply and demand by market economy countries (ME), 1989

Supply	Tons	Per cent
RSA production**	605	22,2
Other production	1 048	38,5
Total ME mine production	1 653	60,7
Total ME scrap	303	11,1
Net deliveries from centrally planned economies	296	10,9
Net official sales	225	8,3
Net disinvestment in Europe and North America (by difference)	246	9,0
TOTAL	2 723	100,0
Demand		
Carat jewellery	1 811	66,5
Electronics	138	5,1
Official coins	127	4,7
Dentistry	49	1,8
Medals, imitation coins	19	0,7
Other industrial/decorative applications	63	2,3
Total fabrication	2 207	81,1
Identified bar hoarding	516	18,9
TOTAL	2 723	100,0

* Including scrap
** Minerals Bureau of South Africa
Source: Gold Fields Mineral Services Ltd, 1990 Gold 1990, pp 13, 31, 36

Table 6 Production of South African diamonds, 1987—90

Year	Carats
1987	9 050 992
1988	8 504 563
1989	9 115 880
1990	8 681 589

Source: Minerals Bureau of South Africa

The value of **bentonite** sold was R8,3 million in 1990, while 515 tons worth R48 878 were exported.

Corundum deposits are generally small and sporadic and only suitable for exploitation by the small miner. At present there is only one producer with an annual output of five tons of high-grade crystal corundum which is consumed locally. Corundum is the second hardest natural mineral.

Some 60 000 tons of **feldspar** are produced annually for local consumption. In 1990 sales were worth R12,5 million.

One of South Africa's important industrial mineral exports is high-grade **flint clay**. In 1990 some 134 060 tons of flint clay were produced of which 15 per cent was exported. Flint clay is added to mixes of other clays and raw materials to make refractories. It shrinks only slightly on being fired and is therefore added to inferior clays to counteract shrinkage.

In 1990, 394 476 tons **gypsum** were sold to realise R10,9 million.

Kaolin occurs in many areas, but economically the most significant deposits are in the Cape Peninsula and in the Grahamstown and Riversdale areas. Total kaolin sales in 1990 were 131 724 tons worth R19,5 million.

A small quantity of **kieselguhr** is produced for local consumption. The quality is poor and cannot compete with imported diatomaceous earth.

The sales of **lime** and **limestone** grew from R371 million in 1989 to R419,8 million in 1990. In the same period, annual exports increased to R9,3 million.

Magnesite is mined in the Barberton district. Local sales of 139 049 tons in 1990 realised R10,5 million.

Raw materials suitable for use as **mineral pigments** are also mined. In 1990, only ochres and oxides were produced, of which about 1 239 tons were sold locally, realising R235 812.

Salt is produced from inland and coastal pans which are formed by solar evaporation, and from sea water near Port Elizabeth and other sites along the coast. Total sales of salt in 1990 amounted to 827 171 tons, valued at R84 million.

Mica production totalled 1 795 tons in 1990, of which about 40 per cent was exported.

Huge deposits of **sulphur** occur as iron pyrites and nonferrous metal sulphides. Sulphur in the form of pyrite and sulphuric acid is recovered from various mineral, mining and processing operations.

Talc has been produced on a small scale for many years from mines in the Barberton and Piet Retief districts in the Transvaal.

An unusual rock known as **wonderstone** consists mainly of the mineral pyrophyllite. It is produced near Ottosdal, west of Klerksdorp in the Transvaal. Sales were valued at R3,8 million in 1990.

Interesting facts about mining

An ochre mine near Mossel Bay, dating back to about 2500 BC, is the oldest known mine in South Africa.

The world's deepest open pit is the Kimberley Open Mine with a depth of nearly 366 metres and a diameter of about 457,2 m.

The world's deepest mine is Western Deep Levels at Carletonville, with a depth of 3 466m.

The largest gold-mining complex is Free State Consolidated Gold Fields with a mining area of 32 918 ha excluding prospecting areas.

The world's two largest platinum mines are found near Rustenburg in the Transvaal.

Production of one fine ounce of gold requires on average 6,22 tons of ore, 39 man-hours, 5 441 litres of water, 572 kilowatt-hours of power (sufficient to run an average household for ten days), 12 m^3 of compressed air, varying amounts of explosives, stores and chemicals, and the use of capital equipment worth hundreds of millions of rand.

The world's largest diamond, the Cullinan, was found in South Africa in 1905. Uncut, it weighed 3 025 carats. In 1986 the second largest uncut diamond, the 599 carat Centenary, was found at De Beer's Premier Mine near Pretoria.

South Africa experienced its worst mining disaster at the Coalbrook north shaft of Clydesdale Collieries in 1960 when 432 miners were trapped underground. All rescue attempts failed.

Energy

The **National Energy Council** (NEC) was established to take overall responsibility for the energy policy of South Africa. It is a statutory body and, in terms of the Energy Act , 1987, the aims of the NEC are to direct, promote and co-ordinate the energy interests of the country in co-operation with the private and public sectors.

South Africa has extensive energy resources. Of these coal and uranium are the most important non-renewable sources. They form the cornerstone of the country's energy supply for the future.

Although coal is the dominant feedstock for conversion to electricity, South Africa's first nuclear power station is in operation. It is foreseen that there will be a gradual shift to nuclear energy as the coal reserves are depleted in the first half of the 21st century. Current dependence on imported crude oil is countered by production of synthetic liquid fuel from coal, a continuing search for crude oil and a strategic oil stockpiling programme. Research into the appropriate application of renewable energy sources which holds great potential for the country, also receives attention.

Coal

Coal, of which the country has abundant deposits, is the predominant energy carrier, providing about 83 per cent of primary energy needs. Most electricity is generated in coal-fired power stations and coal is also the basic raw material for the Sasol synfuel plants.

In situ mineable coal resources have been estimated at 121 200 million tons, of which 55 300 million tons are recoverable.

In 1990 coal sales totalled approximately 184 million tons of which 138 million tons were used locally. More than 55 per cent of local coal consumption is used to generate electricity, mostly at large power stations (some of which have an installed capacity in excess of 3 600 MW) which use about 12 million tons of coal each per year. A further 33 per cent was sold to commerce and industry (including the production of synthetic liquid fuels and other chemicals), 5 per cent for metallurgy, 6 per cent to merchants and households and 1 per cent to mining and transport.

The country is a major exporter of energy, especially in the form of coal and electricity. Coal exports were worth approximately R3 610 million in 1990. This made coal the largest earner of foreign exchange after gold.

Uranium

Nearly all South African uranium is processed and marketed by the **Nuclear Fuels Corporation of South Africa** (Nufcor), a private company closely associated with the Chamber of Mines. Each gold mine producing uranium has a share in the company.

In terms of uranium reserves South Africa, with 13,6 per cent of the western world's resources, ranks third. Total reserves that can be recovered at less than 80 dollars per kg were estimated at 305 000 tons of uranium in 1989.

These reserves are scattered throughout the country, but uranium is largely mined as a by-product of gold and, to a lesser extent, of copper. In 1989 gold mines accounted for 97 per cent of total production (a total of 3 472 tons of uranium oxide).

The **Atomic Energy Corporation** (AEC) operates all the facilities associated with production of nuclear fuel. These include plants for uranium conversion and uranium enrichment and fabrication of nuclear fuel elements. These plants can meet the country's nuclear fuel needs and the first reload of nuclear fuel, which consists of 56 fuel-elements for use at one of the Koeberg reactors, was completed in 1989 and handed over to Eskom.

The AEC also operates the facility for the disposal of radio-active waste at Vaalputs, some 100 km south-east of Springbok in the north-western Cape. This facility handles all Koeberg's medium and low level waste.

In keeping with the marketing strategy of the AEC the products of organisation, services and technology are put at the disposal of the industry according to commercial principles.

The technology development programmes of the AEC are aimed at the nuclear sciences and are conducted to support the aims of both the organisation and the Republic in this industry.

Electricity

Although South Africa geographically covers less than 4 per cent of the continent and has just over 6 per cent of its population, the country supplies more than half of all electricity generated in Africa.

Electricity accounts for more than 27 per cent of total net energy consumption. In 1990 about 147 000 million kWh were sent out in the Republic. Of this, **Eskom** supplied 93 per cent at an average selling price of 7,9c/kWh. The rest is generated by mines, industries and a few municipalities which operate their own power stations. The growth rate in Eskom's electricity sales has been 3,9 per cent a year over the past five years. Commerce and industry are the biggest electricity consumers in South Africa.

Eskom supplies electricity to about 3 900 large users (mines, heavy industry, Spoornet and municipalities) and about 238 000 users who demand less than 100 kW (urban domestic users, farms and light industries). Sales to major users amounted to about R10 billion in 1990, while small users bought electricity worth more than R700 million.

Coal remains the main source of generation. In 1989 some 89,4 per cent of Eskom's electricity was supplied by its coal-fired power stations. Eskom distributes its electricity through a national grid or transmission system comprising more than 220 000 km of lines and cables.

Because South African rivers are dependent on seasonal rain, it is impossible to generate hydro-electricity in significant quantities without water being stored. The size of the required dams is such that hydro-electric power stations are only economical if built in conjunction with the Department of Water Affairs and Forestry.

Synthetic fuels
Manufacture of fuels and chemicals from coal is the main activity of **Sasol**, a world leader in conversion of coal to oil and gas. It operates the only economically viable oil-from-coal plant in the world.

Sasol also refines imported crude oil at the Natref refinery at Sasolburg. The company manufactures chemicals, ammonia-based explosives and fertilisers and produces ethylene and polypropylene for the plastics industry. The group now employs more than 33 000 people. Its

mines include the largest underground collieries in the world, producing in excess of 35 million tons of coal a year.

Crude oil and natural gas
The government approved the development of the gasfields off the south coast at Mossel Bay and Mossgas will probably produce the first liquid fuel from gas in 1992. The reserves are estimated to be enough to keep Mossgas in production for the next 30 years.

The search for oil continued during 1990.

Petroleum refining industry
Four refineries process imported crude oil. Three are situated at the coast and one inland.

The country's total liquid fuel requirements are supplied by the crude oil refineries and the Sasol synthetic fuels plants. The crude oil refineries have been adapted to produce those

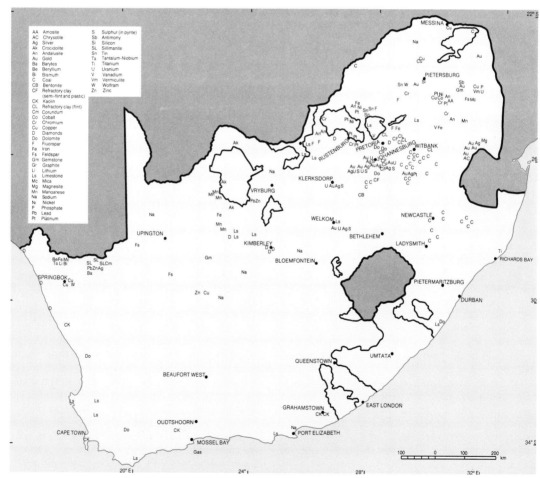

Distribution of actively mined mineral resources in South Africa

products that cannot be supplied by the synthetic fuels plants. South Africa exports refined petroleum products to neighbouring countries.

Renewable energy

South Africa is well endowed with most forms of energy and its coal reserves in particular will ensure adequate energy until well into the next century. Although the role of renewable energy is as yet small in comparison with coal, renewables will in future become more important in supply of energy for the basic needs of developing communities in remote regions.

Supply of electricity to consumers in remote areas by means of photovoltaic (PV) systems and wind turbines, often in hybrid combinations with diesel generators, is cost-effective compared with the capital needed for electricity network extension over long distances. The demand for small PV systems for radio/TV and lighting is growing steadily and the local PV market is currently estimated at 700 kWp per annum.

Solar and wind energy data bases are being compiled, and research is under way to evaluate the potential of these and other forms of renewable energy such as hydro, biomass and energy from municipal waste.

Fuel wood is still the largest source of household heat energy in the remote rural — and mostly developing — sectors of the community. Local shortages are being experienced and the negative impact of this on the environment is growing steadily.

An extensive biomass programme which includes reafforestation and agro-forestry, is being planned.

News items: 1990

The first reload of locally manufactured nuclear fuel elements was supplied to Eskom's Koeberg reactor during the year.

The world's first commercial corex (coal reduction) plant for the production of liquid steel was commissioned by Iscor.

Several gold mines were threatened with closure when the dollar price of gold fell to its lowest level in four years. The Melamet Commission of Inquiry was appointed to investigate the viability of the East Rand Proprietary Mines (ERPM) in order to decide whether further state assistance to the mine was justified. Because of falling profits, due to the low gold price, and rising costs, almost 30 000 workers were retrenched at gold mines in the Transvaal and the Orange Free State.

Locally produced nuclear fuel was recently used, for the first time ever, to reload one of the reactors at the Koeberg nuclear power station.

A wollastonite concentrating reclaiming plant — the first in the country to process the mineral commercially — was commissioned near Garies in Namaqualand.

The first international symposium on nuclear technology in Southern Africa organised by the SA Branch of the Institution of Nuclear Engineers was held at Eskom's Megawatt Park in June.

Up to the end of June, 238 lives were lost on mines and 3 929 miners injured (according to NUM).

The De Beers Group's overseas diamond-selling organisation sealed a five-year, R13 billion sales agreement with the Soviet Union's diamond industry. The deal, which will give the Soviets marketing access through the Central Selling Organisation, includes holding the Soviet stockpile of rough diamonds in London as collateral for a R2,6 billion advance.

An oil discovery, reportedly the best ever in South African waters, was made near Stilbaai in the Cape Province.

Fuel prices increased sharply during the year. On 4 September and 20 October 1990 the National Energy Council announced increases of up to 22 per cent in the price of all fuel products. Three weeks later the fuel price was decreased. A further decrease became effective towards the end of December.

All the Xhosa miners at Hlobane Colliery, near Vryheid in Natal, opted to return to Transkei following bloody clashes with Zulu mineworkers which killed 10 people and injured 52.

The jacket of Mossgas first production platform was placed in the sea, 85 km from Mossel Bay, in October.

At least 1 800 Iscor workers in Pretoria will be retrenched or transferred as part of a rationalisation programme to take place over three years.

About 2 000 power station and 1 500 colliery workers faced retrenchment after Eskom's announcement that it was closing three of its eastern Transvaal stations — a move which was expected to lead to the closure of two collieries.

Sabine Severin (18) is the first woman in South Africa to opt for mining as a career. She has completed her first year of training in the Rand Mines training centre on surface. She has also done training in several service departments on surface. She will do her underground training later.

In an attempt to recover more than R70 million in electricity arrears from 30 Black residential areas, Eskom instituted legal action against six of them. Three of the townships were ordered to pay more than R4,5 million owed to Eskom.

Altogether some 52 000 workers have lost jobs on South African gold mines since 1987.

The National Union of Mineworkers (NUM) and Iscor reached agreement on moves aimed at ending violence on Natal mines which claimed 11 lives.

The Anglo American Corporation's Free State Consolidated Gold Mines and the National Union of Mineworkers concluded a R1 million labour relations agreement to assist retrenched workers.

Anglovaal announced the closure of its copper mine at Prieska in December.

Acknowledgements:

Atomic Energy Corporation of South Africa
Chamber of Mines
Department of Mineral and Energy Affairs (including the Minerals Bureau of South Africa)
Eskom
Mintek
Sasol

Transport

The co-ordination of transport is the responsibility of the Department of Transport. Transnet, which is regarded as the national carrier, consists of five business divisions — a railway system (Spoornet), a comprehensive road transport service (Autonet), harbour support services (Portnet), South African Airways (SAA) and pipelines (Petronet) for the conveyance of petroleum products.

Taking into account Transnet's functions as well as its total employee complement of 168 419 in March 1990 and capital assets exceeding R65 000 million (land excluded), the company is one of the largest business undertakings in the country. As a purchaser of goods and stores and as one of the major employers in the country, Transnet makes an important contribution to the national economy. The employees are distributed as follows: Spoornet 138 947, Portnet 14 407, Autonet 4 125, SA Airways 10 325 and Petronet 615. Group headquarters, technical, financial and manpower services account for 25 551 employees.

Road transport

Responsibility for road planning, construction and maintenance as well as urban transport is shared by three tiers of government, viz central government through the South African Roads Board (SARB), the four provincial administrations and local authorities.

By 1990 the provincial and national road network consisted of 55 383 km of surfaced and 130 368 km of unsurfaced roads. It is estimated that streets under the control of municipal authorities comprised 37 000 km of surfaced and 9 000 km of unsurfaced roads. The total network thus covers about 232 000 km.

National roads

The SARB is responsible for planning, designing and construction of national roads.

The National Road system is a system of high standard roads which connect all the major centres of the country to each other, and to neighbouring countries.

These roads consist of some 1 275 km of dual carriageway freeway, 1 237 km single carriageway freeway and 3 527 km of unlimited access single carriageway main road.

A total of 545,7 km of these roads are operated as toll roads in the various provinces. Alternative toll-free routes must always be available.

Provincial roads

Planning, construction and maintenance of numbered roads and bridges, other than those falling under the SARB or local authorities, are the responsibility of the provincial administrations of the four provinces. In the Cape Province, 34 divisional councils and two regional services councils are responsible for certain classes of roads and receive extensive financial and technical assistance from the Cape Provincial Administration.

According to calculations for the period 1986/87 to 1989/90 by the Division of Roads and Transport Technology of the CSIR, about 58 per cent of total expenditure on provincial and national roads goes towards the construction of new roads and bridges, 30 per cent towards maintenance of existing roads and 12 per cent towards general administration.

Municipal roads

The construction and maintenance of most roads and streets falling within the municipal boundaries of cities and towns are the responsibility of the local authority concerned.

The municipal road and street network in 1990 comprised about 46 000 km, of which 80 per cent was surfaced. Expenditure on roads by local authorities amounted to an estimated R691 million for 1988/89.

Road expenditure

Expenditure on provincial and national roads totalled R1 812 million during the 1989/90 financial year. This amount includes the expenditure on toll roads.

Urban transport

Urban areas declared metropolitan transport areas (MTAs) have a Metropolitan Transport Advisory Board (MTAB) at their disposal. Both short and long-term programmes for adequate transportation development are drawn up by the core city of each MTA and are revised and adjusted annually, taking progress and changing circumstances into account. Eight such core areas already exist, namely Johannesburg, Cape Town, Pretoria, Durban, Pietermaritzburg, Port Elizabeth, the East Rand and Bloemfontein.

Motor cars

Private motor cars are the most important mode of personal travel by road, both intra-city and intercity. In 1989 there were more than 5 million motor vehicles, more than 3 million of which were motor cars. This means that nearly 184 of every 1 000 persons in the country owns a vehicle.

Taxis

Since the 1970s the microbus or combi has, apart from private use, been operated more like a bus than a taxi. Since 1985 it has become popular in metropolitan areas, especially on the Witwatersrand. The vast majority of taxi permits are issued to Black owners or operators of combi taxis.

The Southern Africa Black Taxi Association (Sabta) aims to enhance and maintain the standard of taxi drivers with a view to promote road safety in the interests of the public. This is done in co-operation with the National Road Safety Council and a number of sponsors.

The taxi industry continues to grow and now also concentrates on long-distance transport.

Passenger transport

In urban areas passenger road transport services are undertaken by local authorities as well as private bus companies which operate scheduled bus services between peripheral areas and central points. Luxury intercity bus services are well patronised.

Table 1 Motor vehicles (licenced and exempted from licensing), 1988-89

	1988	1989
Motor cars	3 170 552	3 274 955
Minibuses	151 845	174 445
Buses	29 095	28 221
Commercial vehicles	1 190 525	1 227 645
Motor cycles	320 363	316 531
Tractors	237 051	180 832
Trailers	453 050	466 175
Caravans	140 367	142 902
Other	62 221	73 352
TOTAL	10 297 086	5 885 058

Source: National Road Safety Council

In a new transport era bus operators in particular are obliged to make economic adjustments. Unrenumerative low-demand services are rationalised while high-demand routes are more intensively served. In areas where bus services have been discontinued, passengers are conveyed by other modes of transport, notably combi taxis.

Goods transport

Road transport accounts for roughly one third of all freight transported by land in South Africa.

Local deliveries are made by Autonet — the road transport unit of Transnet — or by private companies on contract to Transnet to and from stations, depots and harbours. A system involving a special cartage plant for conveyance of containers was introduced with the advent of containerisation in 1977.

The Road Transportation Act, 1977, distinguishes between two categories of hauliers — professional cartage contractors who convey goods by public road for reward and ancillary hauliers, i.e. businesses which transport goods for their customers in the normal course of their trade or industry. Authorisation to undertake such transport is granted by a local transportation board or the NTC in the form of a public or a private road carrier permit, as the case may be. There are two forms of exemption and the system of economic control has recently been considerably relaxed in respect of road freight.

Normally professional hauliers may provide their services within 40 km and auxiliary hauliers within 80 km of their place of business or within prescribed exempted areas without a permit. Both may, however, be authorised by permit to convey specific classes of goods over longer distances.

Private sector hauliers (professional and ancillary) have formed national associations. Together these bodies represent an estimated 50 per cent of all privately-owned road freight vehicles.

The provinces have a uniform policy for conveyance of abnormal loads. This policy relates the axle masses of freight vehicles to the damage caused to road pavements, bridges and culverts. It also determines the maximum dimensions of abnormal loads, power-mass ratios and mass distribution required, as well as permit fees and general operating conditions in this regard.

Road safety

South Africa's road vehicle collision and fatality rates compare unfavourably with those of most other countries. In 1989, 435 000 road collisions were recorded in which 11 000 people were

Table 2 Road vehicle collisions and casualties

	1989	1990*
Number of collisions	434 089	360 108
Number of persons injured	116 508	95 862
Number of persons killed	10 877	9 166

* Summary of road traffic collisions in the RSA, Jan - Oct 1990
Source: National Road Safety Council

killed and 117 000 injured. Nearly half of those killed were pedestrians. The total cost of these collisions to the country in 1989 were estimated at R7 154 688 000 (based on 1988 cost factors projected on 1989). The number of vehicles involved in all types of collisions in 1988 totalled nearly 742 000 as against 647 000 the previous year.

South Africa's road fatality rate is one of the highest in the world. However, the number of persons killed in road vehicle collisions for every 100 million km travelled has remained relatively constant over the past three years. This is very encouraging in view of the increase in the population, the number of vehicles and the number of vehicle kilometres travelled.

Promotion of road safety is primarily the responsibility of the **National Road Safety Council** (NRSC). The NRSC derives its funds from a levy on fuel. The country has been divided into 10 regions to promote road safety on a national basis.

Accident insurance

The Multilateral Motor Vehicle Accidents Fund Act, 1989, provides cover to owners or drivers of all motor vehicles in respect of claims by third parties for bodily injury to themselves or the death of any persons caused by or arising from negligent driving of motor vehicles.

Payment to third parties is guaranteed by the Multilateral Motor Vehicle Accidents Fund (MMF), which is financed by means of a levy on fuel used by motor vehicles. The MMF may also compensate third parties for loss or damage caused by negligent driving of unidentified motor vehicles.

Railways

The local railway network, under the control of Spoornet, is divided into 10 geographical areas or regions, each under the control of a regional manager. Headquarters are in Johannesburg, Pretoria, Cape Town, Port Elizabeth, East London, Durban, Bloemfontein, Kimberley, Empangeni and Saldanha.

To facilitate operation of unit trains, a special zoning system has been introduced. The country has been divided into areas or zones, each with its own identification symbols, so that trucks, suitably labelled, can be marshalled into trains that will by-pass certain nominated yards en route to their destinations. This system ensures shorter transit time, less shunting and therefore less danger of accidents or damage, quicker turn-around time of trucks, more speedy delivery of goods and greater efficiency.

It has become more economical to use electric energy for traction and today more than 82 per cent of all traffic is hauled by electric locomotives. Most intercity passenger and goods services are operated by electric locomotives, while the intensive suburban passenger train services of the SA Rail Commuter Service in the Witwatersrand, Pretoria, Durban and Cape Town areas are operated by multiple-unit electric train sets. About 18 455 km of track are electrified.

Centralised traffic control (CTC) has been installed on all important main lines. At present some 6 100 route km of CTC is in operation. Increased traffic capacity is obtained by computer-optimised signal spacing and computer aids to train control.

A new system enables vacuum-braked goods trains to pass intermediate inspection depots up to 500 km. Longer air-braked trains are being used to an ever-increasing extent. Cast-iron brake blocks on goods trucks are being replaced by composition brake blocks. Freight cars designed to transport certain specific commodities are being introduced in ever growing numbers.

The Scheffel bogie, invented by a Transnet engineer, is a high-stability diagonal suspension system which permits higher speeds with greater safety, gives better riding qualities and reduces rail and wheel wear, produces less rolling resistance and facilitates heavier wagon loads.

Transnet had 41 class 10E1 3 kV DC chopper controlled locomotives and 50 class 10E 3 kV DC locomotives in service in 1989. These locomotives are used to haul coal traffic over the DC-lines to Ermelo from where the class 11E locomotives haul the loads to Richards Bay. Due to the development of a holding air brake system, class 11E locomotives haul trains comprising 200 coal trucks — 20 800 tons — over the Ermelo-Richards Bay line.

Currently there are 2 365 electric locomotives in service of which 100 are shunting locomotives, as well as 1 434 diesel locomotives of which 78 are shunting locomotives and 40 narrow-gauge locomotives.

On 31 March 1988 there were 7 684 passenger coaches in service. During 1988/89 eight modules of the 8-M type commuter train were put into service. Three modules, each comprising four coaches, make up a train set. The 8-M trains are to be used in the Cape western region (Khayelitsha line). The two prototypes, 6-M and 7-M, the forerunners of the 8-M train set, are already in service in that region. A total of 36 class 8-M modules are to be delivered under the new contract. The suburban train service (Metro) is under the control of the SA Rail Commuter Service, a separate legal entity from Transnet.

The Blue Train, South Africa's world-renowned luxury train, runs regularly from Pretoria to Cape Town (1 599 km). Other well-known trains are the Trans-Oranje which runs between Cape Town and Durban (2 088 km), the Trans-Natal which runs between Johannesburg and Durban (721 km), the Trans-Karoo which runs between Cape Town and Johannesburg (1 530 km), the Amatola which runs between Johannesburg and East London (1 023 km), the Algoa which runs between Johannesburg and Port Elizabeth (1 112 km), the Bosvelder which runs between Johannesburg and Louis Trichard (503 km) and the Komati which runs between Johannesburg and Komatipoort (532 km). The Trans Karoo and the Blue Train have facilities for carrying passengers' cars.

Spoornet operates an extensive door-to-door container service to and from stations within the country and Namibia and also conveys containers to a number of neighbouring states. Container terminals have been established at City Deep (Johannesburg), Bayhead (Durban) and Belcon (Cape Town).

In October 1987 there were 4 853 flat bed trucks for conveyance of containers. Spoornet's fleet of containers (Sartainers) comprises 14 453 units, including 6 939-m units with a capacity of eight tons, nearly 1 000 tanker containers for the door-to-door delivery of chemicals, oil, wine and other liquids and 21 250 mini-containers. In 1988/89 more than 270 000 container loads were conveyed.

In terms of the policy of deregulation, the first narrow-gauge branch line was privatised in 1987 when the then SATS sold the right to operate the 122-km line between Port Shepstone and Harding in Natal to the Port Shepstone and Alfred County Railway Company.

The main training centre for Spoornet staff is at Esselen Park near Johannesburg, and the major maintenance and repair facility, the largest in Africa, is located at Koedoespoort, Pretoria. In March 1990 a new management school was opened at Esselen Park for middle and top management training.

Aviation

Airports

The Chief Directorate of Civil Aviation is responsible for the planning, construction and operation of state airports. Nine state airports within the borders of the RSA are operated by the directorate: J B M Hertzog (Bloemfontein), D F Malan (Cape Town), Louis Botha (Durban), Ben Schoeman (East London), Jan Smuts (Johannesburg), B J Vorster (Kimberley), H F Verwoerd (Port Elizabeth), P W Botha (George) and Pierre van Ryneveld (Upington).

South Africa's first international airport, Jan Smuts in Kempton Park, was opened in 1953 and has since become the country's principal airport. The airports at Durban (Louis Botha) and Cape Town (D F Malan), originally acquired by the government as national airports, are now classified as international airports.

The customs aerodromes (ports of entry) are D F Malan (Cape Town), Jan Smuts (Johannesburg), Louis Botha (Durban), Rand Airport (Germiston), Komatipoort, Messina, Lanseria (Krugersdorp), Wonderboom (Pretoria), and Grand Central (Johannesburg).

Table 3 Total number of passengers on domestic flights handled by all airlines at South African state airports during 1989/90

Airports	Total number of passengers	Increase/decrease compared with previous financial years (%)
Jan Smuts	5 811 100	+ 8,29
D F Malan	2 409 200	+ 9,91
Louis Botha	1 978 500	+ 7,18
H F Verwoerd	761 800	+ 9,06
Ben Schoeman	365 900	+ 5,78
J B M Hertzog	246 100	+ 0,49
B J Vorster	116 900	+ 4,47
Pierre van Ryneveld	39 900	+ 4,45
P W Botha	215 200	+ 17,02
TOTAL	11 944 600	+ 8,31

Source: Department of Transport

South African Airways

South African Airways (SAA) provides an extensive network of air services between all major centres within the RSA, between Johannesburg and some neighbouring countries and between the RSA and several cities in Europe, South America, Israel and the Far East.

SAA operates a fleet of 42 aircraft consisting of two Boeing 747-344s, six Boeing 747-244s, five Boeing 747 SPs, one Boeing 747-406, 17 Boeing 737-244s, nine Airbus A300s, one JU 52/3M and one Harvard. Seven Airbus A320s and three Boeing 747-400s are on order.

As a founder member of the International Air Transport Association (IATA), SAA operates many of its services in pool with other IATA and non-IATA members to offer air travellers an integrated air network.

SAA is the principal operator of domestic air services. By January 1991, SAA operated 644 services a week.

Civil aviation

The control of civil aviation is vested in the Minister of Transport and of Public Works and Land Affairs. The Chief Directorate of Civil Aviation assesses the design and construction of aircraft and the control of maintenance necessary to ensure continued airworthiness. Certificates of airworthiness are granted for each aircraft, maintenance schedules and flight manuals are approved and personnel and organisations building, modifying or maintaining aircraft are licensed or approved.

The types of aircraft on the South African register vary from Boeing 747s to microlight aircraft. The total number of registered aircraft exceeds 5 000.

In terms of the Air Services Act, 1949, no person may provide an air service for reward except in terms of a licence granted by the National Transport Commission. Foreign air carriers operating to South Africa under bilateral and commercial air agreements are exempt from the licence requirement.

Licences are issued for four classes of air services, viz scheduled, non-scheduled, flying training and aerial work. More than 80 organisations are licensed to provide flying training at about 75 aerodromes. Aerial work includes aerial spraying, crop-spraying, provisioning of ships and off-shore oil rigs, banner-towing, and so on. Some 90 operators are licensed to undertake photographic and geophysical surveys, crop-spraying and allied agricultural services.

The Chief Directorate of Civil Aviation provides air traffic services throughout the

Table 4 Total number of passengers on international flights handled by all airlines at South African state airports during 1989/90

Airports	Total number of passengers	Increase/decrease compared with previous financial years (%)
Jan Smuts	1 895 900	+ 16,60
Louis Botha	85 500	+ 25,55
D F Malan	103 000	+ 13,46
J B M Hertzog	1 600	— 75,00
TOTAL	2 086 000	+ 19,80

Source: Department of Transport

country and, together with the South African Air Force, is engaged in a joint expansion programme of air traffic services. The directorate also examines those who wish to obtain licences as pilots, navigators and flight engineers.

Air traffic control is available at about 20 important airports. Air traffic controllers are trained and licensed by the directorate and rated in four categories — aerodrome control, approach control, area control and radar. Aerodrome flight information service is supplied at aerodromes where traffic density does not warrant a full air traffic control service.

All accidents and incidents in which civil aircraft are involved must be reported to the Chief Directorate of Civil Aviation. The directorate conducts investigations to determine probable causes and all factors involved so that steps can be taken to prevent recurrences.

In March 1990 there were 261 licensed aerodromes, of which 154 were public and 107 private aerodromes. There were also 76 approved heliports.

Some 30 feeder airlines operate about 300 routes. They link more than 85 smaller towns to the major centres served by SAA. Charter air services are available in all the larger cities and towns and in many smaller centres. About 150 operators are licensed to provide this class of air service from and to about 300 airfields scattered throughout the country.

Aerospace industry

The South African aerospace industry, with Atlas Aircraft Corporation as the focal point, encompasses a full range of activities, from research through design and development, manufacture, maintenance and repair of a wide range of aerospace equipment, from fixed and rotary-wing aircraft and missiles to sophisticated ancillary and ground support systems.

Using the latest technologies Atlas, in conjunction with a network of private sector suppliers and subcontractors, has produced modern jet trainer aircraft, turbo-jet engines, a full range of highly effective missiles and communications and electro-optical systems over the past two decades (see the chapter on National security). Today the country has the technological capability and capacity to design and develop a comprehensive range of modern aerospace products to meet all its own requirements. Recent local developments include the CSH-2 Rooivalk combat support helicopter as well as the Celstar GA-1 glider, specially developed for aerobatic competitions and manufactured completely from composite materials.

The technological spin-off of these and other developments has benefited the country's manufacturing industry as a whole. A notable example is the establishment of facilities which produce aerospace quality precision castings and forgings. Composite materials are increasingly used in new products. All new products are tested against stringent international specifications and standards.

In aircraft per capita of the population, South Africa ranks among the first 10 countries in the world. Lanseria Airport near Johannesburg has more aircraft movements a month than any other airport in Africa. These aircraft range from ultra-light machines through large airliners to supersonic military aircraft, from light piston-engined helicopters to turbo-engined rotary wing aircraft and remotely piloted vehicles. Comprehensive facilities have been developed to maintain and repair all these aircraft. The manufacture, operations and maintenance facilities are supported by a logistics system which includes up-to-date computerised resource planning and project scheduling.

Harbours

Some 12 694 vessels with an aggregate tonnage of more than 330 million called at South African ports in 1987/88. In 1988/89 cargo totalling 100 591 468 tons (petroleum products excluded) were handled in South African harbours. These harbours are constantly being improved to provide first-class facilities and services at reasonable tariffs. Facilities and services are comprehensive, including navigational aids along the entire coast. There are no fewer than 55 lighthouses of which 36 are automatic and 19 manned.

Portnet provides all harbour services except stevedoring and cartage of breakbulk cargo at Durban and Walvis Bay. The services provided include pilotage, tugs, berthing, shore labour for shipping and discharging, tally clerks and checkers. All large tugs are fitted with salvage and fire-fighting equipment. Portnet also operates port grain elevators at Durban and East London.

The ports of Durban, Port Elizabeth and Table Bay have been expanded to provide large container terminals for deep-sea and coastal container traffic while East London has a smaller terminal to handle conventional and coaster feeder vessels carrying containers.

Durban harbour is South Africa's foremost and busiest port in terms of general cargo handled. The bay has an area of 893 ha and a depth in the harbour entrance channel of 12,8 m at low water ordinary spring tide. Quayage available for commercial shipping is 15 195 m. Durban harbour can accommodate deep-sea ro-ro vessels and has five deep-sea and two coastal container berths as well as repair facilities. Privately owned bulk storage and handling facilities for various products are provided in the port.

The Ben Schoeman dock in Table Bay has a water area of 112,7 ha with five additional berths for container handling as well as a pier for coastal ro-ro traffic. Ship-repair facilities are comprehensive. The bulk of South Africa's fruit exports is handled here.

Port Elizabeth harbour has an enclosed water area of about 115 ha and more than 3 400 m of quayage alongside for commercial shipping with depths of up to 12,2 m at chart datum. In addition, anchorage is available for vessels of any draught in a partly sheltered roadstead.

East London, the only river port in South Africa, has nearly 2 600 m of commercial quayage with low-water depths alongside varying from 8,5 m to 10,7 m. Tankers with an overall length of 204,2 m and a maximum loaded draught of 9,9 m can be accommodated at the tanker berth, which is 259 m long.

Saldanha Bay, 110 km north-west of Cape Town, was developed primarily for export of high-grade iron ore from Sishen in the northern Cape Province. A railway line of 861 km was built from Sishen to the ore terminal. Saldanha Bay is the largest port on the west coast of Africa. The port area, nearly 5 200 ha, is about four times larger than the combined areas of the ports of Durban, Cape Town, Port Elizabeth and East London. It is one of the best natural harbours in the world and the only breakwater which had to be constructed was a 1 700-m spending beach type. Anchorage is provided in the lee of the breakwater where the minimum water depth is

4,6 m at chart datum. Other facilities include a general purpose quay with a depth alongside of 2 m at chart datum, a tug harbour and many navigational aids.

Richards Bay was primarily developed to handle bulk cargoes such as bituminous coal and anthracite. This deepwater port, 193 km north of Durban, was commissioned on 1 April 1976. It can accommodate vessels of up to 90 000 tons but the quay walls and other facilities have been so constructed that it will be possible by further dredging to take vessels of up to 250 000 tons.

Commercial shipping

The South African ships' register is kept by the Department of Transport. Ships on this register operate as foreign-going ships, coasters, fishing vessels and harbour craft.

South African Marine Corporation (Safmarine) and Unicorn are the country's largest shipping lines. Their fleet of container, general cargo and bulk cargo vessels provides regular services between South African ports and all the major harbours of the world.

Training

The South African Merchant Navy Academy General Botha at Granger Bay has been totally integrated with the Cape Technikon. Deck and engineering officers complete their academic training at the Cape and Natal technikons. Lower classes of certificates are completed at the Training Centre for Seamen. The latter institution also caters for deck, engine room and catering department ratings together with fishermen of all grades. The former Antarctic research ship, RSA, is used for practical on board training.

Pipelines

The first petroleum products pipeline was completed in October 1965 and the first consignment from Durban to Johannesburg was delivered on 26 November 1965. Petronet renders this service.

Search and rescue services

The South African Search and Rescue Organisation (Sasar) is the authoritative and co-ordinating body in South Africa, Transkei, Bophuthatswana, Venda, Ciskei, the BLS countries and Namibia for all aviation and sea rescue services. Sasar's Executive Committee includes members of the SA Defence Force, the SA Police, the Department of Transport, the

Department of Posts and Telecommunications, Portnet, SAA and Safair (Pty) Ltd.

The National Sea Rescue Institute (NSRI) provides facilities and services that are supplementary to those provided by government departments. At present the NSRI has 20 service stations along the South African coastline.

News items: 1990

The Black taxi association, Sabta, opened a driving training school to increase safety standards of combi taxi drivers.

The number of applications for permits to operate combi taxis was 3 781 for the period 1 April 1985 to 31 March 1986. An indication of how this particular mode of transport has grown is obtained by comparing that figure with more than 38 300 permits actually issued during the period 1 April 1989 to 31 March 1990.

The Road Traffic Act, 1989, came into effect on 1 June. It includes stiffer fines and new legislation as part of the standardisation of separate provincial road legislation.

Total new car sales for 1990 were 209 600, a 5,3 per cent decrease compared to 1989.

The number of road collisions increased by 0,2 per cent from 322 477 in 1989 to 323 010 in 1990 during the period January to September.

The number of motor vehicles licensed in the Republic had risen to 5 004 206 by 1989/90.

An milestone was reached on 4 September when the Memorandum of Understanding on Road Transportation in the Common Customs Area Pursuant to the Customs Union Agreement between the governments of Botswana, Lesotho, South Africa and Swaziland was signed for facilitation of cross-boarder transport.

A standardised national driver's test K53 was introduced on 1 September. The K53 test emphasises defensive driving tactics and vehicle maintenance.

South African Transport Services (SATS) increased its fares by an average of 13,2 per cent from 1 February.

SATS became a public company, Transnet Limited, on 1 April.

The South African Rail Commuter Corporation Ltd (Metro) was launched in April. Metro, a separate legal entity from Transnet, would function in close collaboration with the Department of Transport.

Spoornet broke the world record for hauling the longest and heaviest freight train over the longest distance and will appear in 1991's Guinness Book of Records. Spoornet bettered the previous record on 26 and 27 Augustus 1989 on the Sishen-Saldanha line with a 7,3 km-long train consisting of 660 fully loaded iron ore wagons, 16 locomotives and three other wagons. The train weighed 71 208 tonnes and was hauled at an average running speed of 40,01 km/h over a distance of 861,5 km.

Spoornet introduced a R22 million stainless-steel train on test runs between Cape Town, Kraaifontein and Wellington.

The first of three multipurpose locomotive prototypes (class-14E dual voltage) with maximum speeds of 160 km/h was handed over to Spoornet.

Bellville introduced the country's first privatised station complex, the Bellstar Junction.

Magnum Airlines, Citi Airline and Border Airlines merged in June to create South Africa's biggest private commuter airline, Link Airways.

The Margo Commission's report into the Helderberg air disaster (1987) ruled out sabotage.

South Africa's first Civil Aviation Museum came into being in Kempton Park.

South African Airways (SAA) launched a conservation programme, the African Wildlife Heritage Trust. The SA Nature Foundation and the International Wilderness Foundation will be its main beneficiaries.

In June the South African shipping company Safmarine launched a new passenger service between Cape Town and Southampton on four container cargo ships.

Parliament accepted the Air Services Licensing Bill which provides for establishment of a neutral air services licensing council which will receive, adjudicate and grant applications for air services licences, as well as establishment of a carrier neutral licensing system aimed at safe and reliable air services.

Thirty-two students enrolled for the first National Diploma in Aviation Engineering: Avionics which started at the Pretoria Technikon in July.

SAA resumed flights to the Belgian capital Brussels, on 1 August. This service was terminated in 1988. A new air service to Madagascar and Nairobi was introduced while landing rights were granted to SAA in Rwanda.

Domestic air fares on SAA increased by 52 per cent from April 1989 to November 1990. This excludes a 6,7 per cent reduction effective on December. SAA's international fares increased by 29 per cent from January 1989 to November 1990. The increase in the price of aviation fuel from August to November 1990 was 129 per cent.

A passenger service charge of R3.00 for all domestic departing passengers and R10.00 for all international departing passengers respectively was introduced with effect from 8 October 1990 and 1 January 1991.

Air Zaire's new service to South Africa was officially inaugurated in August. South African Airways' weekly flight to Lubumbashi, Zaire was cancelled in October.

SAA was voted Best Carrier to Africa for the third consecutive year. It also won the 1990 Gold Award for Top Middle East/African Airline.

Johannesburg and Pretoria municipal and Putco buses were opened to all races during the year.

An average increase of 9 per cent in commuter train fares throughout the country was announced in October.

In terms of the Road Traffic Amendment Bill published in Cape Town, drivers of motor vehicles will in future have to carry their licences with them while driving.

In December, Trek Airways became the first applicant to be granted a licence to carry passengers and cargo on main domestic routes. Safair was granted an air transport licence to run daily scheduled freight flights in competition with SAA.

A regular multipurpose liner service was introduced between Durban and South East Asia by a Madagascar shipping group *Société Nationale Malgache des Transports Maritimes* (SMTM).

Acknowledgements:
Atlas Aircraft Corporation of South Africa
CSIR
Department of Transport
National Road Safety Council
Transnet

The Post Office provides the nation with telecommunications, postal savings and money-transfer services and performs certain agency services on behalf of the government.

On 1 April 1968 the finances of the Post Office were separated from the national exchequer and it has been run as an independent state business since then. The Post Office has a permanent capital of R199 million on which interest of 6 per cent a year is paid to the Treasury, but the Post Office is also empowered to raise internal and foreign loans to finance capital expenditure. The aim is to finance about 50 per cent of capital expenditure from revenue and the balance from loans.

In 1988/89 capital expenditure totalled R1 612,6 million, of which R1 339,4 million was spent on the expansion of telecommunications services, R155,3 million on buildings and land and R117,9 million on motor vehicles and office equipment, electronic data processing, mail handling and stock. Revenue exceeded expenditure by R894,5 million.

Financial services

Current savings account: There are more than 1 700 post offices in South Africa where savings bank business can be conducted. The income earned from an interest rate of 6 per cent was tax-free up to 28 February 1990. The tax benefits on income thus earned have been reduced by an increasing 20 percentage points a year as from 1 March 1990 and will continue until this benefit has been completely phased out at the end of five years.

Telebank: This is a computerised savings account. It allows cash to be deposited or withdrawn at counter terminals in post offices, as well as at automatic teller machines (ATMs). In total 287 of the larger post offices have been equipped with on line computer terminals, while 139 Telebank ATMs are in use at strategically situated offices. Combined with the MultiNet and Saswitch national networks created to link the ATMs of various financial institutions, Telebank clients have access to more than 3 900 ATMs countrywide. As in the case of post office savings accounts the income derived from 6 per cent interest was only completely tax-free up to 28 February 1990 and the tax benefits are also subject to the same phasing out conditions.

Savings Bank certificates: Investments in Savings Bank certificates are for an indefinite period. Certificates are available in multiples of R50, with no limit on the amount. There is a minimum investment period of six months. Interest on investments of up to R70 000 has been tax-free up to 28 February 1990 and is paid six-monthly from the date of issue. The tax benefits on the income from interest on this investment have also been reduced by an increasing 20 percentage points a year as from 1 March 1990 and will continue until this benefit will have been completely phased out. Further Savings Bank certificates are issued on the same conditions applicable during the phasing-out period. Interest at the rate of 11,5 per cent on daily balance is paid six-monthly. An investment package deal known as Senior Citizen Deposits — for people of 65 years and older — was marketed for a short period by the Post Office at the beginning of the year. The interest rate of 15 per cent per year on this 12-month fixed deposit is guaranteed. Interest is payable monthly and is fully taxable.

Money orders: There are 1 779 money-order offices in the country, in addition to many postal agencies. Money orders are valid for 12 months. During 1989/90, 2 806 027 money orders to the value of R468 678 915 were issued, while 2 576 838 to the value of R403 561 395 were paid.

Postal orders: Postal orders are not negotiable and are valid for three months. During 1989/90, 23 684 479 postal orders were issued and 24 694 784 paid.

Postal services

There are 1 779 post offices and 402 postal agencies in South Africa providing the following services in addition to the usual letter and parcel services: Registered service, certified mail service, cash on delivery (COD) service, insured parcel service, express delivery service, priority mail service and a freepost service. Only limited services are rendered at postal agencies.

The following services are available to foreign countries: Ordinary and registered services, ordinary, insured and COD parcel services, express delivery service and international priority service. Only the ordinary and registered services are available to all countries. In addition, a 'small packet' service is provided to facilitate transmission through the post of goods of small quantity or mass, whether dutiable or not, at lower rates than those for parcels.

Postal communications

South Africa has a network of postal routes over which mail is conveyed to and from cities, towns, villages and hamlets. All available modes of transport are used: Aircraft, trains and the road motor services of Transnet, departmental transport, vehicles of private mail contractors — even cycles. Domestic mail meeting the requirements of standardised mail is automatically conveyed by air.

Direct surface mail dispatches are forwarded to 74 countries and received from 66 and direct airmail dispatches are forwarded to 48 countries and received from 62. Of the surface and airmail dispatches, 52 and 44 respectively are exchanged on a reciprocal basis.

Mail for other destinations is forwarded via one or more of these countries. South African Airways (SAA) operates numerous flights to all the principal cities of South Africa and airmail is exchanged daily between the larger centres. Other domestic airlines are also used, especially to serve country districts.

All available air services are used to and from countries abroad. Twenty-five foreign airlines convey mail on behalf of the Post Office but the bulk of the outward airmail is carried by SAA. Urgent airmail articles for overseas countries (except parcels, express and registered articles) which are too late for the normal airmail connections are accepted at the Jan Smuts Airport post office up to two hours, forty-five minutes before the departure of the aircraft on which they are to be conveyed.

Table 1 Postal articles handled by the Post Office, 1 April to 31 March

| | 1988/89 | 1989/90 |
	(in thousands)	
Posted in South Africa for internal delivery	1 982 480	2 169 438
Posted in South Africa for delivery in other countries	128 543	136 156
Received from other countries	149 032	157 860
TOTAL	2 260 055	2 463 454

Table 2 Telegraph traffic

	1989/90*	1990/91**
Inland telegrams accepted	6 432 714	4 523 092
International telegrams accepted	755 081	511 644

* 1 April to 31 March
** 1 April to 31 December 1990

The Post Office depends largely on public transport, particularly Transnet's rail and road transport services, for the conveyance of domestic surface mail. Where public transport is inadequate, mail is conveyed by private contractors or departmental vehicles.

Departmental transport is used extensively to carry mail between main and branch post offices in cities and between post offices and railway stations in country areas. Sea mail is carried to all parts of the globe as and when ships are available.

Mail is delivered by postmen on foot, on pedal and power cycles, or in panel vans where this is justified by the volume of mail. To facilitate delivery, receptacles for postmen's excess mail are provided at strategic places in the large centres. Mail is also delivered into more than 800 500 private mail boxes.

Mail is sorted mechanically at the main post offices in Cape Town, Johannesburg, Pretoria and Durban. To facilitate this action a four-digit postcode was introduced in 1973. The first two digits refer to the applicable sorting route and province, while the last two identify the specific post office within the relative sorting route.

Philatelic services

The Division of Philatelic Services of the Post Office serves stamp collectors and dealers throughout the world. Apart from counter sales and cash mail orders, the division also operates a deposit account system whereby new issues are automatically mailed to collectors anywhere in the world. The number of deposit accounts exceeds 23 000. The Post Office also assists neighbouring states in the field of philately.

Telecommunications services

The Post Office's telegraph service handles about 23 000 telegrams daily. In December 1990 there were 883 teleprinter-equipped telegraph offices which could dial each other direct.

At the end of December 1990 there were eight

lectronic telex exchanges serving 14 698 sub-
cribers throughout South Africa. Automatic
ervices were available to subscribers at 198 in-
ernational destinations, while the international
nanual exchange in Johannesburg serves
nother four. On this date 1 110 international
elex circuits were in operation. PC-Telex was
leveloped locally and introduced to the market
luring 1990. It consists of a software package, a
ledicated printer and an interface and intercon-
ections which can be linked to a personal com-
outer (PC). PC-Telex thus allows an easy means
of connection between a PC and the internation-
.l telex network.

The national and international teletex service
offers the user office-to-office typewriter com-
nunication at a transmission speed 40 times
aster than that of a regular telex. The terminals,
vhich are supplied and maintained by the Post
Office, can also be used as electronic
ypewriters, memory typewriters with editing
unctions and as telex terminals.

In March 1990 the automatic exchanges
otalled 1 035 and the main services in use
.mounted to 3 080 333 of which about 96,0 per
ent were connected to automatic exchanges. All
.utomatic exchanges are connected to the na-
ional dialling system and all subscribers con-
ected to such exchanges can dial direct. These
.ubscribers also have access to 412 manual ex-
hanges for connection to the required sub-
.cribers. The Post Office also provides a
elephone conference facility for a maximum of
.ix participants from various centres. The Post
Office has a nationwide network of microwave
ystem channels to link the South African Broad-
asting Corporation (SABC) and M-Net TV
.tudios and transmitters. These include
nicrowave links to the satellite earth station at
Iartebeesthoek to enable them to receive and
ransmit TV programmes to and from other
ountries. Optical-fibre networks carrying voice
.nd data have been established in and between
.ll major centres.

The international telephone service has
leveloped-into a communications network com-
orising more than 6 721 circuits over which more
han 214 countries can be reached. Telephone
ircuits are routed via open-wire landline,
oaxial cable and microwave systems to neigh-
ouring countries, while those to other countries
.re provided via a 360-channel sub-marine cable
Sat-1) and the Intelsat Atlantic and Indian
)cean communications satellite systems. Cir-
uits in the Sat-1 cable, commissioned to link
South Africa with Portugal, are extended to
everal other countries in Europe and North

Table 3 Telex traffic

	1989/90*	1990/91**
Inland telex calls (metered units)	119 779 831	73 445 834
International telex calls (paid minutes)	6 426 390	3 733 341

* 1 April to 31 March
** 1 April to 31 December 1990

America through other sub-marine cable sys-
tems. A satellite earth station for operation in the
Intelsat global system has been established at
Hartebeesthoek near Pretoria.

The automatic international telephone exchange in Johannesburg links up with the sub-
marine cable and the satellite earth station at
Hartebeesthoek. Manually operated international calls are handled by the Cape Town international manual service centre. Operators at
that centre can dial direct to numbers in most
countries, while direct subscriber dialling is
available to 176 other countries. During 1990 the
analogue manual switchboards were replaced by
50 digital switchboards.

The time division multiple access (TDMA)
system is a digital system over which coded
telecommunications information is transmitted
via satellite at very high speeds. The frequency
band used for this system is allocated to participating earth stations, including South Africa,
for a short period in turn which depends on the
number of circuits required by respective participants. This short period of access is repeated
every two milliseconds. The RSA had three
TDMA systems operational by the end of 1990
rendering the capability to provide digital connections to correspondents with similar systems
covered by both the Intelsat Indian and Atlantic
Ocean satellites.

The Post Office supplies various telephone
instruments all of which are locally designed and
manufactured. These include the Erica
telephone, the Disa telephone, the Disa Plan
System (DPS) and the Business Telephone System (BTS).

Videotex, or Beltel as it is known in South
Africa, is a communication medium by means of
which information stored in a central computer
can be retrieved via a telephone line for display
on a dedicated videotex terminal or on a personal computer equipped with the necessary
modem and software. Software packages for
personal computers are available for Beltel users
(PC-Bel) and Beltel information/service
providers (IP-Bel, EC-Bel and TS-Bel). Beltel
offers the user information on a variety of subjects, transactional and calculatory facilities and

an electronic message service. At the end of December 1990, Beltel had a growth rate of 70 per cent per year and a total of 17 645 registered users. Data may be conveyed on dedicated point-to-point analogue leased lines or digital leased lines. The latter service is referred to as Diginet and provides high-speed transmission up to 1 920 kilobits per second. Data may also be conveyed through Saponet-P, a public packet-switched network of the Post Office. At the end of December 1990 a total of 3 978 was using Saponet-P. Three international connections offer access to more than 70 packet-switched networks in 34 countries. Triple-X access to Saponet-P is also possible.

The provision of modems for data transmission services was totally deregulated by 1 April 1985, thereby permitting the use of approved privately-owned modems supplied under licence by the private sector. However, the department is still supplying certain types of modems for rented services while stocks last.

At the end of December 1990 there were 49 490 Post Office modems in use working at speeds ranging from 200 to 64 000 bps (bits per second).

The Post Office's Telecommunication Development Institute studies and develops new telecommunication terminals and services for public use as well as systems for internal use. The work is undertaken in close co-operation with the CSIR, universities and industry to ensure the best results and to eliminate duplication and waste of resources. The Post Office laboratory at Derdepoort, Pretoria, undertakes research and development in various areas and also designs and modifies equipment.

Maritime services

Communications with ships at sea are maintained through Post Office radio stations at Cape Town, Durban, Port Elizabeth and Walvis Bay.

Table 4 Telephone services as at 31 March

	1989	1990
Exchanges (automatical and manual)	1 664	1 702
Exchange connections: Business servies	832 883	921 090
Residence	1 927 455	2 056 490
Public coin and card phones	40 968	40 759
Farm lines	64 718	61 994
TOTAL: Main service	2 866 024	3 080 333

Several remote-controlled very high frequency (VHF) receiving and transmitting stations provide full coastal coverage. Long-range telegraph and telephone services, a short-range VHF telephone service, a radio telex service between ships at sea and South Africa as well as international telex subscribers exist. Telephone and telex services to ships are also available via the International Maritime Satellite organisation (Inmarsat) (Inmarsat C terminals).

Amateur radio

Amateur radio station licences are issued to persons who comply with the Postmaster-General's requirements and one of these requirements is to pass a prescribed examination. The RSA has reciprocal agreements with several oversea countries regarding recognition of amateur radio station licences. A visitor's amateur radio station licence is also available to qualified visiting radio amateurs from abroad. Even if there is no reciprocal agreement between the RSA and the country of origin, a tourist can be issued with a guest licence. A novice licence (for persons over 12 years of age who have passed the appropriate examinations) was introduced in 1990.

Citizen band

A citizen band radio communication service exists over nine channels. A licence may be issued to any person at the age of 18. The service may not be used to communicate for business purposes between fixed points, nor for publicity or public and political campaigns.

Motorphone service

A motorphone service enabling a person to make telephone calls worldwide from the inside of a motor vehicle is available in the Pretoria-Witwatersrand-Vereeniging complex as well as in the Durban-Pietermaritzburg areas and Cape Town and vicinity. The systems in the latter two areas can accommodate up to 3 000 motorphone clients each. About 5 900 clients currently use this facility.

Toll-free service

Toll-free service 080 was taken into service on 1 March 1990. The experimental toll-free 0100

A collection of special stamps issued in 1990 and a 21c denomination stamp from the fifth definitive series

service was withdrawn from the market at the end of September 1990. The new service offers the user an extensive range of sophisticated service options. So, for instance, a client who has more than one office in the Republic and who has been allocated only one toll-free number can have calls routed simultaneously at a particular time to more than one destination. The specific destinations can be changed independently according to the time of the day and the day of the week or public holidays.

The new toll-free service was well received in the market place as was proved by the fact that at the end of December 1990 nearly 1 000 of these services were in operation.

News items: 1990

The Post Office earned a record operating surplus of R894 million in the 1988/89 financial year. In 1989/90 an operating surplus of R693 million was realised.

The Fifth Fixed Stamp Series: Succulents, which was introduced on 1 September 1988, is still in use. Special series introduced during 1990 are Co-operation in Southern Africa, additional (R5 and 21c) stamps in the Fixed Series, National Stamp Day, South African Birds, Tourism (for the first time in history foreign languages are used) and National Orders of South Africa.

Botswana, Cyprus, Lesotho and Mozambique were included in the international priority-mail service. This post office service is available to 27 countries worldwide.

The Post Office received a merit award for conservation from the Transvaal Institute of Architects for the redevelopment of the Main Post Office on Church Square.

The Post Office handled up to 7,9 million postal articles per day in 1990.

A record R8,1 billion Post Office budget raised tariffs by an average 4,3 per cent.

The Post Office's two main functions — postal services and telecommunications — were separated. The telecommunications undertaking would be called Telkom and the postal undertaking Postal Operations.

South African Posts and Telecommunications (SAPT) gave the go-ahead to the private sector to market cordless telephones.

Grant Dalziel (12) of Alberton became the youngest radio amateur in the country when he received his licence on 8 December.

Acknowledgements:
Department of Posts and Telecommunications

The media

15

Because of its diverse population South Africa has an abundance of newspapers, magazines, radio stations and TV channels. Distribution of news and information is very professional and South Africa has Africa's most advanced media.

Advertising revenue and news are the lifeblood of the printed and electronic media. The year 1990 will go down in history as one of the most newsworthy years ever and one which greatly benefited the media. Record sales of newspapers and magazines were registered when the African National Congress (ANC) and other political groups were unbanned and Mr Nelson Mandela was released from prison. Scrapping of regulations imposed under the state of emergency meant that the media were able to serve the community more effectively on the news scene.

Although 1990 saw an economic recession in the country, media and advertising stood their ground with television doing better than in previous years. The subscription channel M-Net increased its adincome by almost 70 per cent.

The printed media's income and circulation figures dropped slightly, but other than the demise of a new daily in Johannesburg, nothing dramatic took place in this industry. Publications catering for the Black reader market showed healthy growth.

As usual the advertising front was volatile with some agency mergers and a definite increase in retrenchment of staff. While some smaller agencies did remarkably well, the outlook for 1991 was not promising. The dissolution of U-5, one of the larger advertising agencies, came as a shock to the industry.

Radio and television

The first radio broadcast in South Africa was made on 29 December 1923 while a one-channel television service was introduced on 5 January 1976. Broadcasting Centre, situated on a 15 ha site west of Johannesburg, is the headquarters of the South African Broadcasting Corporation (SABC). There are broadcasting centres in all major cities and studios and offices in other centres, including two offices abroad.

The SABC broadcasts 24 sound services in 16 languages. Twenty-three of these services are internal — of these seven are nationwide, six are community services, nine are for the Nguni and Sotho-speaking peoples, and one is for Indian listeners. There is also an external radio service broadcasting outside South Africa. Audience research shows that some 12 million listeners tune in daily to the various internal sound services.

Radio RSA, the Voice of South Africa, is the SABC's short wave external service broadcasting from Johannesburg to Africa and the Indian Ocean islands in seven languages.

The SABC radio news department compiles more than 300 bulletins for the 24 radio services each weekday. For internal news coverage the service relies on its 30 editorial offices, a country-wide network of about 1 300 correspondents and more than 2 000 news contacts, as well as on the South African Press Association (Sapa). World news is provided by international agencies, 20 strategically located foreign correspondents, a news monitoring section and the SABC's own representatives in London and Washington.

The SABC offers its viewers four television services in seven languages. TV1 transmits in English and Afrikaans, TV2 in Zulu and Xhosa, TV3 in South Sotho, North Sotho and Tswana and TV4 in English and Afrikaans.

There are more than two million licensed television viewers in South Africa. At peak hours more than six million people watch TV1, more than three million TV2 and TV3 and more than three million TV4. This makes South Africa by far the largest television audience in Africa. Eight per cent of broadcast time on all services is allocated to advertising.

Approximately 50 per cent of all programmes transmitted are produced in South Africa. They are augmented by programmes purchased overseas and by co-productions undertaken with other television programming organisations. South Africa uses the PAL colour system.

The television audience of M-Net, the subscription television service launched in October 1986, has grown to 407 366 subscribers. This represents the most extensive pay television network in the southern hemisphere.

Television news is fed by news teams reporting from all parts of the country using modern portable electronic cameras and line-feed equipment. Ad hoc satellite feeds are arranged from wherever major news events occur.

The Press

The printed media had a humble beginning in the 19th century when the first edition of a government newspaper, the *Cape Town and AfricanAdvertiser,* was published. The first independent publication, *The South African Commercial Advertiser,* was published in 1824 by Thomas Pringle and John Fairbairn. Eighteen editions later the paper was banned. It reappeared only after various representations to the authorities in London.

Technical and editorial handling of the printed media in South Africa are considered to be the best in Africa. More than 5 000 newspapers, magazines and journals are registered locally — more than in the remainder of Africa. In 1990 a total of 63 new publications were registered and approved by the Department of Home Affairs.

South African newspapers and magazines are well organised into press groups which have burgeoned over the years because of take-overs. The major press groups are the Argus Printing and Publishing Company, Nasionale Media (which in 1990 celebrated its 75th year as a company), Perskor and Times Media. At the end of 1990 there was heavy bargaining for Perskor shares which were offered on the Johannesburg Stock Exchange. Nasionale Media bought 25 per cent of these and became a co-owner of the group with the controlling body remaining Dagbreek Trust. The Rembrandt Group is the other major

Table 1 Main newspapers

Name	City of publication and address	Frequency	Price*	Language	Audited circulation July—Dec. 1990
Beeld	PO Box 5425, 2000 Johannesburg	MD	70c	A	99 909
Business Day	PO Box 1138, 2000 Johannesburg	MD	R1,00	E	32 287
City Press	PO Box 3413, 2000 Johannesburg	Sun.	R1,20	E	134 732
Daily Dispatch	PO Box 131, 5200 East London	MD	60c	E	35 050
Diamond Fields Advertiser	PO Box 610, 8300 Kimberley	MD	50c	E	8 071
Die Burger	PO Box 692, 8000 Cape Town	MD	80c	A	74 555
Die Transvaler	PO Box 845, 2000 Johannesburg	MD	60c	A	46 867
Die Volksblad	PO Box 267, 9300 Bloemfontein	AD	70c	A	24 780
EP Herald	PO Box 1117, 6000 Port Elizabeth	MD	60c	E	29 900
Evening Post	PO Box 1121, 6000 Port Elizabeth	AD	50c	E	23 166
Ilanga	PO Box 2159, 4000 Durban	Bi-W	60c	Z&E	124 552
Imvo Zabantsundu	PO Box 190, 56000 King Williams's Town	Sat.	30c	X&E	36 561
Oosterlig	PO Box 525, 6000 Port Elizabeth	MD	50c	A	9 280
New Nation	PO Box 10674, 2000 Johannesburg	W/E	70c	E	70 223
Post (Natal)	PO Box 1491, 4000 Durban	Sun.	50c	E	48 906
Pretoria News	PO Box 439, 0001 Pretoria	AD	70c	E	25 751
Rapport	PO Box 8422, 2000 Johannesburg	Sun.	R2,20	A	362 272
Sowetan	PO Box 6663, 2000 Johannesburg	MD	50c	E	184 401
Sunday Star	PO Box 1014, 2000 Johannesburg	Sun.	R2,20	E	92 603
Sunday Times	PO Box 1090, 2000 Johannesburg	Sun.	R2,20	E	520 844
Sunday Tribune	PO Box 1491, 4000 Durban	Sun.	R2,00	E	126 565
The Argus	PO Box 56, 8000 Cape Town	AD	70c	E	103 368
The Cape Times	PO Box 11, 8000 Cape Town	MD	R1,00	E	59 421
The Citizen	PO Box 7712, 2000 Johannesburg	MD	70c	E	134 931
The Daily News	PO Box 1491, 4000 Durban	AD	70c	E	98 467
The Natal Mercury	PO Box 950, 4000 Durban	MD	70c	E	63 109
The Natal Witness	PO Box 362, 3200 Pietermaritzburg	MD	70c	E	28 218
The Star	PO Box 1014, 2000 Johannesburg	24 hr	70c	E	221 256
Weekly Mail	PO Box 260425, 2023 Excom	W/E	R1,80	E	30 968 (Jan—June)

The abbreviations used are the following:
MD (morning daily), AD (afternoon daily), Sun. (Sunday), Sat. (Saturday), W (weekly), W/E (weekend edition), Bi-W (bi-weekly), 24 hr (24 hours), Z (Zulu), X (Xhosa), E (English), A (Afrikaans)
* Prices given for second half of 1990
Source: Audit Bureau of Circulation (ABC)

partner in Perskor. Other important publishers include Caxtons, Thompsons Publications, Republikeinse Pers, Publico and Penrose, while many others are registered on the Johannesburg Stock Exchange.

In terms of the Newspaper and Imprint Registration Act, 1971, any person intending to print and publish a newspaper at intervals not exceeding one month, must apply to the Director-General of Home Affairs, Pretoria, for registration of such a paper.

South African newspapers are based mainly on the British model and the powers of management and editorial are separate.

There is a clear difference in political views, with almost all Afrikaans-language papers supporting the National Party.

Both English and Afrikaans newspapers have a proud tradition of helping to shape the fortunes and policies of political parties. Moreover, several have made a substantial contribution to the current process of political change by helping to prepare the public for essential reforms. Afrikaans newspapers have done much to inform their traditionally conservative readers about pending changes and movement towards a more open society.

As in most nations endorsing Western values of democracy and freedom of expression, there has always been some tension between the Press and South African government. This relationship is usually under severe strain at a time of national crisis when the government and the media differ on the nature and extent of the threat to national security.

In addition to the usual common law checks on the Press there are statutory restraints on freedom of the Press in certain fields. Publication of certain information and photographs having a bearing on the defence of the country, or information regarding prisons and prisoners are, for instance, prohibited.

Relevant acts are the Internal Security Act, the Publications Act, the Prisons Act, the Defence Act, the Police Act, the Criminal Procedure Act, the Nuclear Energy Act, the Public Safety Act, the National Supplies Procurement Act and the Petroleum Products Act.

While the South African Press is one of the few collective mass media in Africa to be regarded as 'free' (in the Western sense), the question of freedom of speech has been a bone of contention between the government and the press for a long time. When strict temporary restrictions were imposed by the government after declaration of a state of emergency on 12 June 1986, the media voiced its disapproval in unequivocal terms. The state of emergency imposed the most severe restrictions on the media since the emergency regulations enforced during World War II. Both local and foreign media were forbidden to publish anything deemed 'subversive' or 'inciting'. However, with the opening of Parliament on 2 February 1990 the media emergency regulations were abolished, a step widely welcomed locally and abroad. In June the state of emergency was partially lifted.

The Media Council, which succeeded the Press Council in 1984 as a voluntary self-disciplinary tribunal for all media, adjudicates on complaints that press reports or photographs are factually incorrect, contain unfair comment, could endanger state security or law and order, are harmful to race relations, are obscene and lascivious, or violate an individual's privacy. The Media Council is empowered to reprimand respondents or to direct that a correction and/or its finding be published. In 1990 the Media Council adjudicated 86 cases of which 42 were settled. The chairman is Prof J van Rooyen.

All Newspaper Press Union (NPU) member publications subscribe to the Media Council's Code of Conduct and non-NPU publications may also do so. The NPU actively encourages this to ward off threats of legislation from government.

In 1990 most dailies held their circulation figures. Not one showed any remarkable growth. *The Citizen* (134 931) and *The Sowetan* (184 401) managed to do only marginally better than their counterparts compared with their figures in the latter half of 1989. From July to December 1990, only 12 of the newspapers monitored (see Table 1) showed increased circulation. The largest daily, *The Star* (Johannesburg), sold an average of 221 256 newspapers in the last six months of

Table 2 Winners of three major annual press trophies

	FREWIN*	McCALL**	CRONWRIGHT***
1988	Cape Times	Natal Witness	South Coast Herald
1989	Natal Mercury	Pretoria News	Paarl Post
1990	The Argus	Natal Witness	District Mail

*   Best Daily
**   Best daily with circulation under 50 000
*** Best country newspaper
Source: Audit Bureau of Circulation (ABC)

1990. *Beeld* is the largest Afrikaans daily (99 909) and *The Sunday Times* (520 844) is the largest Sunday newspaper.

Market surveys show a far higher percentage of Afrikaans readers of English-language newspapers than vice versa and English-language newspapers generally also have a higher percentage of Coloured and Black readers as is the case with *The Star* (60 per cent) and *The Citizen* (53 per cent). Because of the language situation, there is a system of quasi-monopoly over large areas of the newspaper press, especially in the Afrikaans market. *The Star* became the first 24-hour newspaper when it started its morning edition in 1990.

The size of the country — 1 800 km separating the main centres of Cape Town and Johannesburg — still precludes national dailies in the true sense of the word. The only really national newspapers are the two Sundays, *Sunday Times* and *Rapport,* both published simultaneously in various cities, using the printing facilities of related dailies.

There are about 100 provincial or country newspapers in South Africa. Of this number, 14 are published for Black readers, three for Coloureds and three for Indians. A few appear daily and some bi-weekly, but most are weekly tabloid papers serving particular towns or districts by covering local affairs and carrying local advertising. Most are bilingual and avoid national politics. The most popular publication day is Friday.

Newspapers appearing only in certain neighbourhoods, known as *knock-and-drops* or *freebies* and distributed free of charge, have a guaranteed readership with advertising their only source of income. The Audit Bureau of Circulation in 1989 listed 58 such papers. They are distributed mainly in the PWV area, but are often found in other urban areas.

Since the 1970s magazines have done well in a competitive market. According to the Media Yearbook of SARAD (SA Rates and Data) there are about 300 consumer magazines and more than 500 trade, technical and professional publications. In 1990 *Huisgenoot* was still the magazine with the largest circulation (516 819). Its English counterpart, *You,* had a 16,5 per cent increase in circulation, pushing it to 199 207. Two other magazines that showed strong growth in the latter half of 1990, were *Sarie* (11,1 per cent) and *Femina* (9,2 per cent). The most popular business magazine is the *Financial Mail* (circulation 32 440).

The past few years have heralded a new approach to covering political and social news by a section of the Press referred to as the 'alternative Press', whose publications are not NPU members and are not part of the 'mainstream', sometimes referred to as the 'establishment' Press. The latter refers to publications produced by major press groups or publishing houses and affiliated to the NPU. The fact that some of the alternative media are financed from abroad endorses the view that these publications form a separate section on South Africa's media scene.

Outspoken and hypercritical of the political, social and economic situation in South Africa, these papers (both to left and right of the political spectrum) were among the first to be affected by the emergency regulations. One of them, *The Weekly Mail,* started a daily called *Daily Mail* in June. It closed down on 4 September 1990 due to lack of advertising and readership support.

Distribution

In cities, newspapers rely heavily on street sales and house-to-house delivery, but café's and general dealers' stores provide additional selling points with postal delivery declining in importance.

Outside the cities newspapers are distributed by railway and special truck services, often covering hundreds of kilometres on a single run. The cost of bulk transport by air is very high.

Much of the distribution of newspapers is undertaken by the Allied Publishing Company, run by a consortium of some media owners, and commanding a nationwide distribution network. It distributes mainly English-language papers. The Afrikaans press groups, Nasionale Media (Nasionale Nuusdistribueerders — NND) and Perskor (Republikeinse Pers — RP), handle most of their distribution themselves.

Press organisations

The Newspaper Press Union (NPU) is an association of newspaper publishers and proprietors established in 1882. It is an employers' organisation registered in terms of the Labour Relations Act, 1956. With the South African Printing and Allied Industries Federation and the South African Typographical Union (Satu), it is the oldest industrial council in the country. Membership of the NPU includes all major urban daily, weekly and Sunday newspapers (excluding *Die Afrikaner* and *Die Patriot*) 93 provincial or local newspapers and 54 magazines.

Other press organisations are: the Specialist Press Association of South Africa (SPA), the Conference of Editors, the SA Association of Industrial Editors, the Audit Bureau of Circulation (ABC), the South African Union of Journalists (SAUJ), the Media Workers' Association of South Africa (MWASA) and the Foreign Correspondents' Association of South Africa.

News agencies

The South African Press Association (Sapa), a national news agency, is a co-operative, non-profit news-gathering and distributing organisation conducted in the interests of the public and its own members. Foreign news is received from Reuters, Associated Press and its own representatives in London. The main foreign news agencies operating in South Africa are Agènce-France Presse, Associated Press, Deutsche Presse Agentur, Reuters and United Press International.

Advertising

The advertising industry in South Africa is dynamic, growing and highly competitive. With sanctions on the way out and given that the laws of free enterprise will still prevail in the country and that production costs of advertisements can be kept down, the industry is certain to flourish even more.

It started more than 64 years ago with the founding of the first advertising agency, Lindsay Smithers-FCB. By 1988 there were more than 400 agencies. According to the Media Shop, there have been no more than the usual number of mergers or break-aways during the past three years. The agencies with the biggest billing are Ogilvy & Mather, Rightford Searle-Tripp & Makin.

The industry is served by various organisations like the Association of Advertising Agencies (AAA), the Association of Marketers (ASOM), the Advertising Standards Authority (ASA), the SA Advertising Research Foundation (SAARF)

and SA Market Research Association (SAMRA).

The ASA came under fire in 1990 when it banned a BMW advertisement of Hunt Lascaris that suggested BMW's were better roadholders when negotiating sharp bends on mountain roads. This advertisement was a play of words and on scenes in the award-winning Chapman's Peak advertisement of D'Arcy, Masius Benton and Bowles in which a Mercedes-Benz went over a cliff. The BMW advertisement had to be withdrawn.

Although South Africa was experiencing an economic recession in 1990, the advertising industry still managed to grow. The electronic media especially contributed to a growth rate in total adspend of almost 20 per cent, as compared with the 1989 amount.

Total adspend in 1990 was R1 844,7 million against the 1989 total of R1 548,9 million, according to Adindex. A feature of the latest statistics was that TV adspend rose to give the medium a 33 per cent share of all advertising expenditure. M-Net showed a 68 per cent growth. This trend contradicted expectations that adspend on TV had plateaued in 1989.

Radio grew by 32,1 per cent in 1990 and increased its market share to 11,5 per cent from 11,1 per cent.

Printed media have over the years lost more than 20 per cent of the market share going to 51,3 per cent in 1990 from R35 million in 1989. The total adspend on print in 1990 was R946,9 million.

Afrikaans magazines were hardest hit with an 8 per cent decline in ad revenue. Growth was registered in trade, technical and financial journals and Black, Coloured and Asian magazines. Advertising in the specialist press section was R110 million in 1989.

The outdoor advertising market showed a

Table 3 Loerie award winners* (prestige awards in advertising industry)

Agency	Grand Prix	Loerie	Special mention
D'Arcy, Masius Benton & Bowles	3	10	13
Ogilvy & Mather, RST & M	1	11	22
Meridian	1	3	5
Bernstein, Loxton	—	5	8
Hunt Lascaris TBWA	—	6	1
Bates Wells	—	2	1
Lindsay Smithers-FCB	—	2	—
Klerck & White	—	1	—
Jupiter Drawing Room	—	1	—
Partnership in Advertising	—	1	—
Tholet, Sievers & Associates	—	1	—

* All figures according to Adindex

steep growth rate of 46 per cent to R51,1 million in 1990 from R35 million in 1989.

Advertisements that were well received by the market in 1990 included ISM'S Elephant ad, Continental Tyres' rooftop ad, SAA's frequent flyer, Woolworths' footwear ad and Toyota's cage break-out. Of these some won awards in competitions abroad.

Top ten news events

The 10 events South Africans will probably remember as the most important on the local scene in 1990 were:

1. On 2 February State President F W de Klerk, in his opening speech in Parliament, announced the unbanning of 33 organisations, including the African National Congress, the South African Communist Party and the Pan Africanist Congress. Persons serving prison sentences merely on grounds of being members of these organisations, were released. Some emergency regulations, among others those on the media, were lifted. The unconditional release of Mr Nelson Mandela after 27 years as political prisoner, was also announced. Regarding the death penalty, Mr de Klerk said that, pending the final decision of Parliament on certain recommendations, all executions would be postponed. He announced that the Reservation of Separate Amenities Act, 1953, would be repealed by the Discriminatory Legislation regarding Public Amenities Act.

2. Unrest and violence was rampant throughout the year. Most of the violence occurred between ANC (Xhosa) and Inkatha (Zulu) supporters. In the Orange Free State it occurred mainly in the Gold Fields and neighbouring towns, and in the Cape Province mainly in Black residential areas around Cape Town and in the eastern Cape. Worst hit was Natal, where faction fighting had claimed 2 500 lives since 1986. In the Transvaal violence occurred mainly in the PWV area and by August the lives of more people than during the 1976 unrest had been claimed in Reef towns. The violence took various forms — people using AK47 machine guns or hand made weapons of any sort. By August violence had cost the country more than R3 billion. In September, for instance, commuters were attacked by panga-wielding gangs on Reef trains, leaving some 60 people dead and nearly 400 injured. Mr Nelson Mandela's appeal for violence between various groups to stop had no effect. According to the Institute for Race Relations (SAIRR), 3 038 people were killed in political violence during the period January to October 1990.

The unrest was discussed by Mr Mandela, two senior members of the ANC, the State President and the ministers of Justice and Law and Order on 16 August. On 11 September delegates of the ANC, UDF, Cosatu and Saco met with President de Klerk in the Union Buildings — Mr de Klerk expressed his concern over the unrest in Natal. The two leaders discussed the unrest situation, this time on the Witwaters-rand, on 14 September. On 8 October discussions on the violence were held in Tuynhuys between President de Klerk, Minister Adriaan Vlok, Minister Gerrit Viljoen, Mr Joe Slovo, Mr Alfred Nzo and other officials. The continuing violence in Black residential areas was again discussed by Mr de Klerk and Mr Mandela on 8 December.

Despite progress made with the talks, Mr Chris Hani, military leader of *Umkhonto we Sizwe,* said in December the armed struggle

Table 4 Magazines with the largest circulation

Name	Frequency	Price	Language	Audited circulation* July to December 1990
Bona	M	R1,75	E	291 154
Car	M	R2,80	E	135 178
Cosmopolitan	M	R3,95	E	115 462
Fair Lady	F/N	R2,50	E	172 747
Huisgenoot	W	R1,95	A	516 819
Landbouweekblad	W	R2,20	A	62 237
Living and Loving	M	R2,75	E	111 766
Rooi Rose	F/N	R2,25	A	154 462
Sarie	F/N	R2,70	A	231 849
You	W	R1,95	E	199 207
Your Family	M	R2,80	E	229 528

The abbreviations used are the following: W (weekly); F/N (fortnightly); M (monthly); E (English); A (Afrikaans)
* Source: Audit Bureau of Circulation (ABC)

should be increased. In the eight days up to 11 December the death toll in Black residential areas on the East and West Rand rose to 100.

SAP measures to combat violence included cordoning off of some hostels in Black residential areas with razor wire to control entry, roadblocks, a curfew in Black residential areas on the Reef and a reward for information regarding possession of illegal firearms. Police not only became the target of attacks while trying to keep factions apart, but became targets themselves. By August 42 policemen had been killed and 403 injured in unrest-related incidents. From 1 October to 22 November alone 19 members of the SAP died in unrest-related incidents. The SAP introduced stringent measures to end the unrest on the Witwatersrand — Operation Iron Fist was deployed as well as a curfew in Black residential areas worst hit by violence. Accusations against the SAP took a turn in December when the ANC claimed that the SAP was supporting Inkatha and released a video showing an Inkatha member disembarking from a Casspir during peace talks in strife-torn Natal. The SAP produced photographs showing that both Inkatha and ANC representatives were transported in Casspirs to the talks organised by the SAP. Police action was, however, criticised by Mr Justice Goldstone, who led a commission of inquiry into the killing of 12 people and the injuring of 287 at Sebokeng when 50 000 people demonstrated and police opened fire on the crowd. In a bid to restore peace in Tokoza and Phola Park, the ANC and the Inkatha Freedom Party agreed to try to put an end to the violence, and a delegation of political and church leaders visited the areas. Mr Mandela was, however, forbidden to set foot in a Tokoza hostel and was warned that a war would break out should he do so.

3. Following President de Klerk's speech, there was renewed contact with foreign countries, resulting in three trips abroad by the State President to 10 European countries, major African countries and the first-ever official visit by a South African State President to the United States. Increased contact with foreign countries, including Eastern European countries, and the major changes taking place within the country, gave rise to the establishment of trade missions in new countries and lifting of certain bans and restrictions, such as Britain's ban on new investment in SA. In December the General Assembly of the United Nations, for the first time in history, recognised the changes taking place in SA.

4. After his release on 11 February from the Victor Verster Prison, Mr Mandela was appointed deputy president of the ANC. He be-

came the ANC's spokesman and enjoyed extensive press exposure. He affirmed the ANC's aim to nationalise mines and industries. During the course of the year this statement varied from full-scale nationalisation to exception of key sectors of the economy. Eventually Mr Mandela stated that only some sectors would be included in such a step. He undertook to redistribute wealth by using the money invested in some of the large insurance companies. Mr Mandela undertook extensive trips abroad, including to Malaysia, Australia, Europe, the USA, Africa, Indonesia and the Far East. American reaction to his visit varied, as was the case with pleas for financial assistance in Japan. His support of sanctions against SA drew increasing criticism.

5. The disappearance of six schoolgirls, aged 11 to 14, during the past two years reached a climax on 15 January when paedophile Cornelius Gerhardus (Gert) van Rooyen (52) and his lover Francina Johanna Hermiena (Joey) Haarhoff (48), suspected of abducting the girls, were tracked down by the police. They committed suicide before they could be taken into custody. Although Van Rooyen's house was thoroughly searched by the Police, no clue to the girls' whereabouts was found.

6. At least 25 babies died in Johannesburg's Park Lane and Morningside clinics, either from Klebsiella bacterial infection or because of contaminated material used in drips. The Adcock Ingram company admitted that two batches of a paediatric potassium admixture supplied to the clinics were contaminated.

7. Two commissions of inquiry were appointed during the year to investigate alleged irregularities in the SA Police and in the Johannesburg City Council. Mr Justice L T C Harms was appointed as a one-man judicial commission of inquiry into alleged police hit squads and the Civil Co-operation Bureau (CCB). The commission concluded in November that no police hit squad had existed and that there was no evidence that the CCB had murdered activist Dr David Webster. The CCB was operationally disbanded in the latter half of 1990. The Hiemstra Commission of Inquiry was appointed to conduct a survey on alleged spy activities in the Johannesburg City Council. The spy ring allegedly supplied information to Military Intelligence and the Security Police. The commission found that an estimated amount of R1,8 million of ratepayers' money had been paid over five years to more than 100 individuals and 20 organisations. The commission's report was published in September, finding that former management committee chairman Mr Danie van Zyl had set up the spy

ring with four senior council officials and that he had not informed the council of the spying operation.

8. Mr Piet (Skiet) Rudolph, deputy leader of the Boerestaat Party, was connected to the theft of arms worth R600 000 from Air Force headquarters in Pretoria and went underground for several months. In June, while still in hiding, he sent a video recording to *Beeld,* an Afrikaans newspaper, giving details of the stolen weapons and how he had planned a 'bloody and violent' overthrow of the government. Police offered a R50 000 reward for information which would lead to his arrest. After 185 days on the run, Mr Rudolph and an associate, Mr Chris Beetge, were arrested by the Security Police in Pretoria. The Orde Boerevolk then offered a R100 000 reward for information which would lead to the person who had betrayed Mr Rudolph. Mr Rudolph appeared in court for the first time on 1 November on charges related to the arms theft and six bomb explosions. He pleaded guilty, was denied bail and the case was postponed to January 1991. While awaiting trail, Mr Rudolph went on a 25-day hunger strike. In March 1991 he became the first right-wing activist to be granted unconditional indemnity.

9. In the course of the year high-level contact between the government and the ANC was maintained and President F W de Klerk and Mr Nelson Mandela met several times. Most important were the discussions held between President de Klerk and Mr Mandela on 9 February, two days before the latter's release from prison, the meeting in Tuynhuys from 2-4 May following which the Groote Schuur Minute was published, the meeting in the Union Buildings to avert the pending crisis in the negotiation process, the Pretoria talks on 6 August culminating in the Pretoria Minute, in which the ANC vowed to stop the armed struggle from that date.

10. Rent boycotts and water and power cut-offs, mainly in the Transvaal and the Orange Free State, made headlines throughout the year. Estimates showed that only about 37 per cent of Black residents in the OFS paid service charges to local authorities. Meanwhile the Transvaal councils started cutting off services to defaulting Black residential areas. In June residents of Black residential areas throughout the country said they would consider resuming payment of service charges only if the government wrote off the rent arrears owed by 82 Black local authorities in the Transvaal. The City Councils of Soweto, Dobsonville and Daveyton and the Transvaal Provincial Administration signed the Greater Soweto Accord on 24 September, estab-

lishing the Central Witwatersrand Metropolitan Chamber and thereby sealing the agreement to end the 5-year Soweto rent boycott. This ratified an agreement to write off R516 million owed in rent and services charges.

On 16 October essential services, including electricity, water and sewerage were cut off in several Black residential areas in the eastern Transvaal which were in arrears for amounts up to R1 million. On the following day all civic associations in Transvaal Black residential areas hit by rent boycotts were negotiating or planning negotiations with local town councils and the Transvaal Provincial Administration. Meanwhile, political activists in Black residential areas urged people to withhold bond repayments and to destroy every second new house. The Pretoria Regional Services Council approved a loan of over R17 million to the Atteridgeville, Mamelodi and Zithobeno Township Councils to meet arrears on electricity, sewage and water payments to the end of October. By 31 December Black residents owed local authorities more than R762 million for rent, services and other levies. Three Black residential areas were ordered by the Rand Supreme Court in December to pay Eskom more than R4,5 million for electricity arrears — Tembisa (East Rand) had to pay R3 628 266, Kagiso (West Rand) R949 760 and Katlehong on the East Rand R10 292.

Other stories
Other events which made headlines were: A diamond contract between De Beers of South Africa and the Soviet Union; Dr Allan Boesak's resignation as president of the World Alliance of Reformed Churches after disclosure of his relationship with TV personality Elna Botha; a tornado which hit Welkom and caused extensive damage; 24 Sasol workers were exposed to deadly gamma beams; the biggest car bomb yet found in South Africa; Dr Wynand Malan's resignation as one of the leaders of the Democratic Party; at least seven farmers were murdered by gangs of roving killers in the southern Natal Midlands; the bank robbery believed to be the largest in SA history; the rescue of an East London family held captive in Mozambique; a spread of satanism and related crimes; a Piper Seneca aircraft which disappeared en route from Richard's Bay to the Grand Central Airport near Johannesburg; 700 Sasolburg High School children who sustained burns during a torch-light procession; tense relations between South Africa and Transkei; Mrs Winnie Mandela charged with four counts of kidnapping and four of assault with intent to

commit grievous bodily harm; an ANC activist, Mr Bhekumusa Jabulani Ximba, took refuge in the American Consulate in July; the drought in the northern Transvaal, believed to be the worst in living memory; Odile Harington, a South African convicted of spying against the ANC in Zimbabwe, who was released from prison after four years; cutbacks in military spending; public outrage at the government's announcement that seals were to be clubbed by a Taiwanese company; the possible closure of 18 gold mines due to the low gold price; increases in the fuel price; the crisis in education (see chapter on Education); a NG Church confession that apartheid was a sin; at least 352 people slightly injured when two passenger trains en route to Johannesburg crashed between the Phomolong and Mzinhlope stations in Soweto in December; PAC rejection of the government's invitation to hold talks; David Frost won the Million Dollar Golf Challenge at Sun City in December; Mr Donald Woods, former editor of East London newspaper *Daily Dispatch,* arrived in December with his wife and five children for a 5-week visit — they fled the country in 1977 after the death of Black Consciousness leader Steve Biko; the Civic Association of Southern Transvaal's call for a Black Christmas in certain Transvaal towns was backed by the United Democratic Front and the South African Communist Party; Remo Benetti (47), bass guitar player of the band *Hit and run,* shot dead five people on 12 December before turning the gun on himself; the Republic of China's government agreed to pay R2 000 compensation to each of the 42 South African fishermen injured on Chinese fishing boats; proposed divorce action between Afrikaans singer Bles Bridges and his wife Leonie; death of Fransie Geringer, well-known progeria sufferer; announcement by General Magnus Malan, Minister of Defence, that assassinated senior Swapo official, Mr Anton Lubowski, was an agent for South Africa's Military Intelligence; the first Afrikaans rock festival called 'Houtstok'; the NP opened membership to all races; Mr Oliver Tambo, president of the ANC, returned to South Africa after 30 years in self-exile; the Natal rugby team shocked rugby enthusiasts by beating Northern Transvaal in the Curry Cup final; protest marches and stay-aways which were the order of the day.

News items: 1990

A number of restrictions on the media were lifted in February. Restrictions which remained in force included certain security emergency regulations. By June one of the few remaining restrictions was that dealing with televising of scenes of unrest.

The Radio Amendment Bill, providing for the licensing of all earth stations and extending power to the Postmaster General, was published in February.

Paul Weaver and Gareth Furby, two British journalists covering the Gatting rebel cricket tour, were expelled by the government in February — Weaver for misrepresentation of facts and Furby for entering South Africa on false pretences.

Christian Television (CTV) was formed in March by seven Christian organisations.

In March the board of the SABC was expanded to include six new members and eight re-appointments.

Afrikaans broadcasts on Radio RSA, the SABC's foreign service, were terminated in March. A survey by the *Voice of America* showed that English broadcasts of Radio RSA on shortwave were ninth on the popularity list of international broadcasting stations in the USA.

In March M-Net introduced *K-TV,* a channel for children aged from 3 to 12. In July the SABC introduced *Junior Sport,* aimed at viewers under 21.

In April M-Net financed four new Afrikaans films, the *Pluimpie* Award for the best Afrikaans advertising slogan as well as SA's biggest literary prize — R50 000 each for two newly published works.

Mr Joe Latakgomo, senior assistant editor of *The Star,* was awarded the 1990 Nieman Fellowship in April.

Iscor spent R8,6 million on TV advertisements and R4,5 million on printed advertisements when it became a public company in April.

A number of accounting firms advertised in the press after the profession decided to allow advertising from April. The legal profession followed suit.

A world record was set in May when an SABC radio broadcast was made from Western Deep Levels gold mine near Carletonville — the world's deepest mine shaft.

Mr Max du Preez, editor of the alternative newspaper *Vrye Weekblad* and Mr Harvey Tyson, retiring editor of *The Star,* received the Pringle Award for press freedom from the Southern African Union of Journalists in May.

Radio 702 celebrated its 10th anniversary in May and increased its listeners from 286 000 in 1989 to 344 000 in 1990. In August the station won an award from the American National Association of Broadcasters for the finest radio promotional video of 1990.

Mr K E Masinga (86), the SABC's first Black announcer, died in June.

In June the SABC obtained exclusive rights to broadcast segments of CNN International's 24 hour news service.

The Mercedes-Benz *Chapman's Peak* TV commercial won a Golden Lion award at the Cannes International Advertising Awards Festival in June.

The first edition of *The Daily Mail* was distributed in Johannesburg in June.

At the annual presentation of the Loerie Awards in June, the top prize, the Grand Prix for a campaign, went to the D'Arcy agency for the Mercedes-Benz campaign. It was also awarded the Grand Prix in the television and cinema advertisements category.

Umsebenzi (The Worker), the newspaper of the South African Communist Party, appeared in Johannesburg on 14 July for the first time in 40 years.

The news service of the SABC celebrated its 40th anniversary on 17 July.

Mr Sam Mabe, assistant editor of *Sowetan* and prominent Black media union organiser, was assassinated in Soweto in July. Although this incident was not directly linked to the harassment of Black jounalists to 'support the struggle', these journalists complained throughout the year that they were intimidated and threatened by certain individuals and organisations when they reported objectively on political issues. The Argus company established a R20 000 Sam Mabe memorial scholarship for journalism.

By July it was estimated that 1 367 000 adult Blacks watched TV1 daily.

The alternative newspaper *Weekly Mail* found several international backers while R4 million was raised through shares, mostly held by South Africans.

Mr Thami Mazwai of *Sowetan* was awarded the 1990 Rosholt Fellowship in Journalism in August.

In October television licence fees increased by 50 per cent from R80 to R120 a year.

In accordance with an agreement reached with a Moscow library the State Library in Pretoria receives the *Moscow News* in exchange for *The Star: International Airmail Weekly*.

In November Mr Nikolai Reshetniak of the Moscow *New Times* became the first Soviet journalist to settle in South Africa as a correspondent.

Mr John Featherstone was nominated chairman of Sapa in November.

Mr Tertius Myburgh (55), former editor of *Sunday Times* and South Africa's roving ambassador designate, died on 2 December.

M-Net was granted permission in December to broadcast television news, breaking the SABC's 15-year monopoly of television news.

Mr Roelf Jacobs (49), manager of the English and Afrikaans Radio Service of the SABC, died on 11 December.

M-Net acquired Information Trust Corporation (ITC) for R21 million in December.

The government approved increased Christian broadcasting on television in December.

Prof Kobus van Rooyen, former chairman of the Publications Appeal Board, was elected chairman of the Media Council in December.

For the 10 months January to October adspend amounted to R1,484 billion, representing a 19,5 per cent increase over the corresponding period last year. From January to October television accounted for 32,8 per cent of adspend, followed by the daily press (17,7 per cent), consumer magazines (12,4 per cent), radio (11,4 per cent), other press (7,7 per cent), trade and technical (7,3 per cent), the weekend press (6,5 per cent) outdoor (3,0 per cent) and cinema (1,2 per cent).

Acknowledgements:
Mr P Diedericks, School for Communications Sciences, Pretoria Technikon
South African Broadcasting Corporation (SABC)

Manpower and industrial relations

16

The Department of Manpower represents the state in the tripartite system of industrial relations. A scientific structure based on the six fundamental human rights which underlie the collective relationship between employers and employees has been devised for the manpower and industrial relations systems in South Africa. These are the right to work, the right to associate, the right to negotiate collectively, the right to withhold labour, the right to protection and the right to development.

Right to work

The right to work implies an obligation to provide work and the question of whether the state or society — or both — are responsible for providing work has been central to discussions in South Africa during the past few years. The government supports the free-market economic system in which maximum freedom is allowed for the private sector to stimulate economic growth to create employment opportunities. But South Africa has a mixed economic system — partly socialist and partly free market — and the responsibility to create job opportunities rests on both the state and the private sector.

The state does accept responsibility in this regard and in the financial year 1989/90 all state departments and administrations spent some R80,08 million on job creation. During this financial year 780 698 unemployed persons were employed under the job creation programme. A total of about 13,3 million man-days were worked during the year.

The private sector also made a contribution and a number of projects were launched by various organisations. 'Job Creation South Africa', a combined effort by the National African Federated Chamber of Commerce (Nafcoc) and Barlow Rand Foundation, spent some R2,5 million on the first contract to establish a considerable number of Black entrepreneurs.

The right to work should be restricted as little as possible by the state and employers. Work permits, closed-shop provisions, allocation of residential group areas and several other measures are examples of restrictions in the South African labour market and system of industrial relations. These restrictions are firstly the result of legislation by central, provincial and municipal authorities and, secondly, of collective agreements between employers and trade unions. Since lifting of restrictions in 1987 people of all race groups can move freely, thus increasing their usefulness and exercising their entrepreneurial rights in a wider area.

Closed-shop practices are seen to place restrictions on a person's right to work because membership of a trade union is a condition of employment. Employees on their part undertake to work only for employers who have signed such an agreement. The object is to strengthen the position of the union in its dealings with the employer and to strengthen the union's control over the work force.

Trade unions favour closed-shop agreements because of their advantages for the union movement. The opponents of closed-shop agreements hold that, apart from negating a worker's right to disassociate, these agreements also impair his right to work because he may not work for the employer of his choice if that employer has a closed-shop agreement with a union of which he is not a member.

By the end of 1990 closed-shop arrangements were included in some 30 Industrial Council agreements covering about 230 000 workers. Apart from these closed-shop agreements in the private sector, the employment market is now relatively free from restrictions on the right to work.

Restrictive monetary and fiscal measures introduced by the state, followed by the announcement of the state of emergency, the imposition of sanctions by some major trading partners and disinvestment by multinational corporations, outflow of foreign capital and the moratorium on foreign debt repayments had a detrimental effect on the labour market.

Real gross domestic product (GDP) decreased by about one per cent during 1990. Total employment in the non-agricultural sectors of the economy, however, decreased by 0,5 per cent during the period June 1989 to June 1990. If mining is excluded, employment increased by about 0,1 per cent in the same period. The biggest concentration of workers in June 1990 were to be found in the manufacturing industry (1 461 308) followed by the government and services sector (1 266 771), trade and accommodation (813 808), the mining industry (676 621), transport and communication (361 268), construction (417 500) finance and insurance (186 280) and electricity (50 900).

In 1989 some 328 000 workers (about 5,4 per cent of the employed labour force) were artisans and apprentices, while the occupational category of professional, semi-professional and technical workers account for about 675 000 workers or more than 11 per cent of the employed labour force.

It is the state's policy not to place immigrants in employment if local workers are available for such work.

In terms of interstate arrangements with neighbouring states many foreign workers are employed in South Africa. However, owing to the difficulty of patrolling the country's borders it is not easy to determine with any degree of accuracy how many illegal immigrant workers are employed in South Africa. Most legal contract workers are employed in the mining industry.

The state does not compete with the private sector in providing employment and only employs public servants to serve a basically private enterprise economy.

The state, through the Department of Manpower does, however, provide work for physically disabled persons in its sheltered employment schemes. The department has 13 factories in which handicapped workers manufacture a wide range of products. Vacancies are filled by handicapped persons only.

Registered unemployment of all population groups generally increased during 1990, with unemployment in the service capacities, operator, clerk and unskilled occupations being relatively high.

According to the Current Population Survey, unemployment decreased markedly amongst Blacks, Coloureds and Asians while the rate for women was much higher than that for men. In June 1989 (June 1988 = 18,9 per cent) the rate for Black women was 16,3 per cent and that for Black men 8,3 per cent (June 1988 = 10,6 per cent). In June 1989 57 and 69 per cent of Black and Coloured unemployed persons respectively were under 30 years of age.

Unemployed workers who contribute to the Unemployment Insurance Fund while employed, are entitled to certain benefits from the fund.

Table 1   Number and membership of registered trade unions, 1989 and 1990

| Membership | Trade unions | | Membership | | | | | | | | | |
| | | | Whites | | Coloureds and Asians | | Black people | | Unspecified | | TOTAL | |
	1989	1990	1989	1990	1989	1990	1989	1990	1989	1990	1989	1990
Whites	32	29	238 883	232 087	—	—	—	—	—	—	238 883	232 087
Coloureds	14	16	—	—	20 836	49 655	—	—	—	—	20 836	49 655
Black people	25	20	—	—	—	—	233 113	418 602	—	—	233 113	418 602
Whites and Coloureds	4	6	5 267	5 546	427	2 150	—	—	—	—	5 694	7 696
Coloureds, Black people	28	18	—	—	25 116	25 016	310 466	307 844	—	—	335 582	332 860
All population groups	69	58	165 633	151 469	121 885	244 068	201 932	236 731	—	—	489 450	632 268
Whites, Black people	4	4	20 988	19 281	—	—	1 121	4 442	—	—	22 109	23 723
Membership composition unspecified	36	47	—	—	—	—	—	—	—	—	822 900	739 347
TOTAL	212	198	430 771	408 383	168 264	320 889	746 632	967 619	822 900	739 347	2 168 567	2 436 238
Increase			—	—	—	152 625	121 847	220 987			84 244	267 671
Decrease			8 908	22 388	94 349		—				-	83 553
Percentage Increase			—	—	—	90,7	14,6	29,6			4,0	12,3
Percentage Decrease			2,0	5,2	35,9		—				-10,2	-

Right to associate

The right or freedom to associate manifests itself through employers' organisations and trade unions.

Voluntary registration of employers' organisations and trade unions takes place with the Department of Manpower after an applicant organisation has applied in a prescribed manner. Registration permits the organisation to apply for membership of an industrial council, an organisation in which formal negotiations are conducted between registered employers' organisations and registered trade unions in a particular industry, on either a national or a regional basis.

These negotiations cover the entire fabric of relationships, including salaries, wages and conditions of service. The 91 industrial councils are autonomous bodies which seek to prevent or settle disputes by negotiation between employers or employers' organisations and employees or trade unions.

There are 198 registered trade unions whose membership is increasing. It is estimated that about 62,2 per cent of all members of registered trade unions are Black. At the end of 1990 there were 105 multiracial unions with 1 371 615 members. Total membership of all trade unions (registered and unregistered) accounts for about 25,7 per cent of the economically active population.

Unregistered unions are legally obliged to furnish membership particulars to the Department of Manpower. About 40 unregistered trade unions with a fluctuating estimated paid-up membership of 293 000 operate in the industrial relations system.

Trade unions may join in federations or confederations, which may be registered with the Department of Manpower in terms of the Labour Relations Act. The number of trade union federations now stands at ten.

Although the public sector is excluded from the formal system of industrial relations in terms of the Labour Relations Act, 1956, many trade unions have been formed in this sector.

Municipal workers have strong trade unions such as the South African Association of Municipal Employees, which negotiate on their behalf with municipal employers in industrial councils for municipalities. During 1990 Black municipal workers extended their union's activities to many more municipalities.

The most important trade union groups or federations are the South African Confederation of Labour (Sacla), National Council of Trade Unions (Nactu) and the Congress of South African Trade Unions (Cosatu).

Employers also have the right to associate in employers' organisations and register their organisations with the Department of Manpower. At present there are 238 registered employers' organisations and 11 federations of employers' organisations on the books of the department.

Right to bargain collectively

The purpose of employers' organisations and trade unions is to protect and promote the interests of their respective members in the relationship that exists between them. This is done by negotiation or collective bargaining between representatives.

There is both a formal and an informal system of collective bargaining. The formal system is provided for in legislation, while the latter operates outside the parameters of any statutory structure.

Informal collective bargaining is that between employers and trade unions or worker organisations outside any legislative structure. This is commonly known as shop-floor or factory-level bargaining. Such collective bargaining has dominated the industrial scene during the past few years and appears to be on the increase. Unregistered trade unions cannot negotiate in the industrial council system and are confined to this type of bargaining. Many registered trade unions do informal collective bargaining because of the informality of proceedings, rapid results, high degree of flexibility and wider range of negotiable items. Informal bargaining also tends to be conducive to better and closer relations between management and workers. It is impossible to determine with any degree of accuracy how many informal agreements are concluded every year since most are private arrangements between management and a particular trade union. It has, however, been estimated that during 1990 about 650 of these agreements were concluded and that their terms cover some 800 000 workers in the private sector.

It is estimated that current industrial council agreements covered about one million workers. Industrial councils collectively administer 132 agreements, 72 of which provided for, inter alia, pension, provident, sick and holiday benefits, and medical and training facilities.

Negotiation remains the most important method of preventing and resolving labour disputes. The new labour dispensation introduced in 1979 has in fact developed negotiation as the most important means of power sharing between employers and trade unions.

The Wage Board determines wages and conditions of service for hundreds of thousands of employees in the unorganised section of the economy. The number of such wage determinations does not vary much from year to year. Trade unions increasingly come to informal wage agreements with employers in the industry or other trades where wage determinations are applicable. A number of wage determinations have already been suspended or their suspensation is being considered due to a lack of justification for their upkeep. Indications are that this tendency will last. The state, in terms of the provisions of the Basic Conditions of Employment Act, 1983, protects workers in their relationship with employers by laying down maximum hours of work, minimum periods of leave, minimum periods of sick leave and many other basic conditions of service.

Right to strike

The South African system recognises a fundamental labour right, namely the right to withhold work or labour. The employer has the right to withhold the opportunity to work from his employee(s) ('lock-out') and the worker has the right to withhold his labour from his employer. The Labour Relations Act lays down certain procedures to be followed before a party can legally lock-out or strike.

Several mechanisms are available for settlement of industrial disputes, namely negotiation, mediation, arbitration, conciliation boards and adjudication by the courts.

Negotiation: In 1990, 3 657 disputes were referred to industrial councils. Of these, 1 108 were settled by these councils while 719 were referred for settlement by other measures. In 203 cases the disputes referred to industrial councils were settled between the disputing parties. Only 193 disputes ended in deadlock. Some 1 047 disputes were carried over into 1991 for settlement by industrial council negotiation.

Mediation: In 1990 industrial councils applied for the appointment of 49 mediators to settle disputes. Mediation is also used in the informal system of industrial relations. In 1989 mediation was resorted to in 15 disputes, mostly between management and workers at factory level.

Arbitration: Often parties differ so drastically that the deadlock cannot be resolved by negotiation. Such an agreement provides for the appointment of an arbiter (arbitrator) and an exact definition of his tasks. Arbitration frequently takes place outside the provisions of the Labour Relations Act. As far as labour is concerned, private arbitration and the media facilities provided by private institutions are being used increasingly. In the period June 1989 to 31 October 1989 a total of 205 arbitrations were handled by private institutions.

Conciliation boards: Establishment of a conciliation board is voluntary. Conciliation boards have a very good track record in conflict resolution. In 1990, 8 752 applications for establishment of conciliation boards were received, compared with the 5 767 in 1989. Of these applications, 48 were withdrawn before they could

Table 2 Cases referred to the Industrial Court, 1990

Nature of function	Carried forward from 1989	Received during 1990	Total for 1990	Completed	Partly heard	In other stages of progress
Court of Law Functions (section 17 (11) (a)) (until 31.8.1990)	—	—	—	—	—	—
Urgent interim relief	21	333	354	320	—	34
Reinstatement orders	329	1 179	1 508	1 095	—	413
Arbitrations (sections 45, 46 and 49)	7	35	42	11	—	31
Unfair labour practices (section 46 (9))	1 546	5 108	6 654	3 726	—	2 928
Demarcations (section 76)	3	6	9	4	—	5
Appeals (section 21A)	—	2	2	1	—	1
Appeals (section 13(3) of Act 115 of 1984)	—	—	—	—	—	—
Appeals (section 26 of Act of 1983)	—	—	—	—	—	—
Investigations (section 46(7)(c))	—	—	—	—	—	—
Referrals (section 77)	—	—	—	—	—	—
TOTAL	1 906	6 663	8 569	5 157	—	3 412
TOTAL: 1989	1 295	4 575	5 870	3 964	65	1 841

be considered, 6 367 were granted and 2 211 were refused on the grounds of shortcomings or for other reasons. By the end of 1990, 126 applications were still being processed for consideration. In 1 148 cases the parties settled their dispute before the conciliation boards began their activities.

Adjudication by the courts: In 1990, 1 179 applications for reinstatement were received and 329 were carried over from the previous year. Of these, 786 were either withdrawn by the applicants before hearing or not proceeded with and 105 were withdrawn during hearing. The court granted or refused 199 reinstatement orders and postponed 38 indefinitely. During the year 35 disputes submitted for arbitration were added to seven carried over from the previous year. In all, 5 108 new cases of alleged unfair labour practices were referred to the court, while 1 546 were carried over from the previous year. Of these, 1 906 were withdrawn before hearing, 731 were settled by the parties before hearing and 456 during hearing. The court made 527 determinations and 163 cases were indefinitely postponed.

In 1990 there were 885 strikes, as against 942 in 1989. Many of these strikes were illegal in terms of the provisions of the Labour Relations Act. About 341 000 workers were involved in these strikes, which involved a loss of 2 729 844 man-days.

The average duration of strikes in 1990 was almost eight days in terms of man-days lost. Disputes about wages were the most important causes (51,6 per cent), while 13,9 per cent stemmed from wages with other related issues. Most strikes occurred in the Pretoria, Witwatersrand, Durban and eastern Cape regions.

Right to protection

The employee's right to protection implies an obligation on both the state and the employer to provide adequate health and security standards. The right implies, among other things, restrictions on the number of working hours, age restrictions, casualty insurance, provisions for protective clothing, security in working conditions and health protection. In most cases the right to protection is imposed upon employers by legislation.

Underlying the right to protection is the right that employer and employee have to maintain their relationship in accordance with reasonable standards. Unreasonable labour relations implying unreasonable discharge, victimisation, discrimination, selective discharge of groups of employees and one-sided change of conditions of service.

The Basic Conditions of Employment Act, 1983, determines the measures within which the employer and employee have to arrange their relationship with regard to minimum working conditions. The Act stipulates aspects such as working hours, leave, sick leave, and prohibit work on certain days (such as Sundays). The Act only provides minimum standards and it is up to each party to campaign for more favourable conditions of service.

Employees are protected against dangers in their working place by various other legal conditions. In most cases protective measures are exercised by statutory bodies established in accordance with the particular law. Often these security measures also apply to the general public.

The Workmen's Compensation Act, 1941, provides for financial compensation for workmen who in the course of their employment sustain injuries or contract industrial diseases which result in medical expenses and/or temporary or permanent disablement. In cases of fatal accidents or death caused by an occupational disease, compensation is paid to the workman's dependents. Compensation and medical expenses are covered by the Accident Fund. Contributions to the fund are made by employers in respect of employees earning not more than R36 000 a year. The state and certain local authorities are exempted from these contributions although their workers are covered under the Act.

The National Occupational Safety Association (Nosa) was established in 1951 by the country's largest employers' organisations in conjunction with the Workmen's Compensation Commissioner. Its objective is to foster among workers and management alike an awareness of the need for safety in all work operations in order to prevent industrial accidents and occupational diseases.

The extent of the problem of industrial accidents is alarming and may be gauged from the fact that more than 230 000 occupational accidents which cause either injury or disease are reported every year. Nearly 1 900 fatalities and more than 18 000 cases of permanent disablement occur each year. The annual cost of all these injuries has been estimated at R250 million, excluding damage to buildings, materials, plants and equipment.

The Machinery and Occupational Safety Act, 1983, vests the Department of Manpower with

extensive statutory powers to safeguard employees against hazards inherent in their work situation. Inspectors operating from 12 centres
throughout the country apply the provisions of
the Act, which seeks to ensure the safety of
persons in the normal course of their employment or while using machinery. Every incident in
the workplace must be reported to an inspector
if such an incident causes death or the likelihood
of death, unconciousness, loss of a limb, or an
injury or illness that can lead to a permanent
physical defect or absence from work for at least
14 days. During 1990 a total of 8 861 incidents
were reported in terms of section 17 of the Act.
These incidents resulted in 8 044 people being
injured or killed. The records show that, of the
above number, 435 people were fatally injured
and that 117 of the fatalities occurred in the
building and construction industries. As a result
of contraventions of the regulations, 727
prosecutions were recommended by inspectors
during the year under review.

The Mines and Works Act, 1956, administered
by the Department of Mineral and Energy Affairs, provides for the protection of mineworkers
in their work situation, while the Explosives Act,
1956, contains provisions to protect workers
handling explosives. The latter Act is administered by the South African Police.

The Unemployment Insurance Act, 1966,
protects contributors against the risk of loss of
earnings through unemployment, illness or
maternity, and in the case of women contributing
to the fund, adoption of children under the age
of two years. The Act provides for lump sum
payments to dependents of deceased contributors. Employers, employees and the state contribute to the fund and it earns interest on
investments. Contributions by employers and
employees registered with the fund were increased from 0,7 per cent to 0,9 per cent of wages
and salaries on 1 January 1987. On 1 May 1990
the income ceiling for members was raised from
R38 532 to R40 248 a year. The Minister of
Manpower has approved a further raise in the
minimum earnings ceiling from R40 248 to
R46 332 with effect from 1 January 1991.

These steps to boost the revenue of the fund
were taken to counteract the substantial increase
in disbursements in recent years and to get members who passed the income limit to contribute
to the fund again so as to share in its benefits.
These increases follow the downswing in the
economy and the sharp increase in the number
of unemployed. The reserves of the fund reached
the R1 billion mark in 1990. The financial position of the fund is therefore healthy and any
further increase in the rate of contributions is not
envisaged for the near future. About R562 million was paid out in benefits in 1989.

Right to development

Every employee has the right to develop through
education and training in order to equip himself
for his job. This right has been incorporated in
conventions and recommendations of the International Labour Organisation and decisions and
policies of the International Employers' Organisation. The governments and employers of
the industrialised nations, including SA, subscribe to this right, which is reflected in various
laws relating to the education and training of
workers.

The Manpower Training Act, 1981, established the legislative framework for the Department of Manpower's training policy whereby the
Department of Manpower practices its policy
regarding training. It provides for a National
Training Board, training boards for the industries, registration of training centres, training
of unemployed persons, appointment of training
advisers and certain other related matters.

The 33 training committees and 56 subcom-
mittees including 10 subject testing committees
which managed apprenticeship matters in
various industries during 1989, are to be replaced by training boards for each of the industries, which will be established by the
industries themselves.

These training boards will, apart from the administration of the training of apprentices,
promote and set standards for all training in their
respective industries. At the end of 1990 six such
training boards had already been accredited and

Table 3 Strikes and work stoppages, 1988-90

Year	Strikes and stop-pages	Working days lost				Estimated wages lost				Employees involved			
		Whites	Col-oureds	Indians	Black people	Whites	Col-oureds	Indians	Black people	Whites	Col-oureds	Indians	Black people
1989	942	6 049	165 204	33 787	1 306 459	619 287	6 361 282	1 390 500	44 898 532	1 446	25 696	6 605	163 757
1990	855	17 214	275 027	63 368	2 374 236	1 151 968	11 517 979	2 398 905	86 045 591	2 989	36 530	9 098	292 480

accepted full responsibility for training in their industries.

During 1990, 9 054 new contracts of apprenticeship were registered. At the Central Organisation for Trade Testing at Olifantsfontein, 12 885 trade tests were conducted in almost 300 designated trades, and 931 citizens of the TBVC states (Transkei, Bophuthatswana, Venda and Ciskei) as well as the self-governing states of South Africa were tested. Accredited training boards will also be able to establish their own trade test centres and conduct their own trade testing.

The Manpower Training Act also provides for registration of regional training centres, private training centres and industrial training centres. Regional training centres have been established in certain regions by groups or associations of employers. Employers who have their workers trained at these centres receive a cash rebate on their course fees for certain approved courses. During 1990 the nine regional training centres, covering almost the whole of South Africa with satellite and mobile training centres offering 433 approved courses, trained 31 650 workers.

A private training centre may be established by any employer or person for training its own employees as well as those of other employers. During 1990 a total of 251 094 employees were trained at 1 457 registered private training centres offering in excess of 24 000 approved courses.

Industrial training centres are established by training boards for training of employees for the benefit of their respective industries. As this is a new provision in the Act, no such centres had as yet been registered by the end of 1990. All these training centres will in due course apply to the various training boards for accreditation in order to obtain recognition in the respective industries and to qualify for possible financial assistance from the training boards.

Two other types of training schemes are in operation throughout the country. The first group comprises training schemes under industrial council agreements. In 1990, 17 640 persons were trained in seven industries under such schemes. The second group of training schemes fall outside industrial council control and are established by groups or associations of employers and are normally administered by a training board. In 1990 19 686 persons were trained under 13 such schemes. In addition, the department administers a scheme for training of unemployed persons aimed at alleviating unemployment. The scheme has three prime objectives, namely to equip unemployed persons with

Table 4 Reasons for strikes and work stoppages

	1989		1990*	
	Strikes and work stoppages	Percentage of total	Strikes and work stoppages	Percentage of total
Wages	306	32,5	317	35,8
Wages and other matters	123	13,1	100	11,0
Trade union matters	28	3,0	22	2,5
Working conditions	184	19,5	109	12,0
Disciplinary measures	118	12,5	118	14,0
Other or unknown	183	19,4	219	24,7
TOTAL	942	100,0	885	100,0

* Figures for 1990 is for the period 1 Nov 1989 to 31 Oct 1990

(a) marketable work skills, thereby facilitating their entry into the labour market; (b) work skills which will enable them to enter the informal sector; and (c) work skills which will enable them to identify and utilise income-generating opportunities and to function as individual entrepreneurs in the informal sector.

Since the inception of the scheme in June 1985 until 31 October 1990, a total of 1 122 533 unemployed persons received training of whom more than 30 per cent were placed in employment after completing their training.

The training can broadly be divided into the following sectors:

Training for the formal sector
Many unemployed persons have problems obtaining suitable employment, probably because they have never worked or have not worked for a long time and consequently lack the necessary experience or training. Great emphasis is placed on structuring the courses to provide the unemployed with market-directed training.

Training for the informal sector
In the light of the phenomenon of structural unemployment the development of the informal sector is increasingly receiving attention. The training courses developed for this particular sector are planned to enhance the employability of the unemployed or to assist them in working individually and to identify and utilise income-generating opportunities.

Training in building skills
The huge shortage of housing in the country, low-cost housing in particular, creates job opportunities. To present marketable training, the department, in conjunction with the Building Industry Training Board, has developed a

scheme in terms of which unemployed persons are trained in building skills that link up with the modular training system of the building industry.

Training of the disabled
To afford the disabled person an opportunity to make a contribution towards the country's economy, thereby ensuring his own independence, the training given these unemployed persons extends from secretarial and business administration to handskills such as knitting. The training courses are generally longer than usual.

Training of entry-level computer programmers
This training was launched to accommodate returning national servicemen and includes completion of a 16 week intensive training course in COBOL.

Training of entrepreneurs
Due to the decline in the creation of new job opportunities in the formal sector of the economy, more emphasis is being placed on the informal sector as a source of job creation. The department, in conjunction with the private sector, developed a scheme in terms of which trainees will be allowed to develop their business skills during training in order to enter the small business sector and create new job opportunities.

The department also administers a scheme for training of artisans in certain trades in conjunction with the various education departments. It involves persons who are not apprentices or minors, except minors who have completed a first period of military service, in intensive training at one of five approved technical colleges, and in in-service training with approved employers for a prescribed period. During 1990 a total of 359 trainees started their intensive

Table 6 Persons trained under various programmes, 1988-90

Type of training	1988	1989	1990*
Apprentices in training	23 416	26 941	24 448
Trainees in training (section 30)	629	499	665
Regional training centres (section 31)	39 661	54 674	31 650
Private training centres (section 32)	259 805	319 649	251 094
Industry training centres (section 34)	-	-	-
Training schemes (section 39)	13 680	22 552	19 686
Unemployed persons (section 36)	242 893	198 915	169 415
Training schemes (section 48 of the Labour Relations Act)	4 879	8 518	17 640
TOTAL	584 963	631 848	514 598

* Information for the period 1 Nov 1989 to 31 Oct 1990

training, while 276 received in-service training with approved employers.

The state also provides various other financial incentives for training of workers. Apart from tax concessions, there are allowances for industrialists who train workers in any one of the decentralised development points in the new regional development programme which includes the self-governing Black territories. In 1989 about R3,624 million was paid to 31 industrialists for this purpose.

Provision is also made for grants-in-aid for registered trade unions, employers' organisations and federations for training schemes.

During 1990 a total of 239 persons were registered as certificated engineers and 1 198 persons were registered as installation electricians under the Machinery and Occupational Safety Act, 1983, with the Department of Manpower.

New amendments

The Manpower Training Amendment Act, 1990, through accreditation by the Registrar of Manpower Training of a training board for each industry, provides for devolution of power and control over training of apprentices to industries themselves. Such training boards have to promote training in the industry and liaise with other training boards, the government and educational institutions to enhance standards of training and the mobility of trained labour. The amendments also include establishment of a revolving fund to improve training of unemployed persons.

Table 5 Training of unemployed persons 1990*

Sector	Number of persons	
	Trained	Placed
Formal	80 176	17 768
Informal	59 940	18 446**
Building	28 188	2 098
Disabled	1 025	270
Entry-level computer programmers	86	57
Entrepreneurs***	0	0
TOTAL	169 415	38 639

* Information is for the period 1 Nov 1989 to 31 Oct 1990
** This figure includes persons who became self-employed
*** Training will commence early in 1991

Proposed amendments

Because to certain amendments, the Labour Relations Act, 1956 (LRA) became increasingly inaccessible, differences in opinion arose in respect of interpretation and legal certainty was forfeited in the process. In 1989 the Minister of Manpower requested the National Manpower Commission (NMC) to investigate the situation and to make recommendations concerning consolidation of the LRA. The NMC will submit its recommendations to the Minister early in 1991.

The so-called Saccola/Cosatu/Nactu accord which was reached on 7 May 1990 originated in the dissention caused by the 1988 amendments to the LRA. The accord contains legislative changes which the parties suggested be applied as interim measures while the consolidation investigation by the NMC will address actual long-term and structural changes. The matters addressed in the accord include redrafting of the definition of an unfair labour practice and deletion of strikes and lock-outs, relaxation of time limits for resolving disputes by conciliation

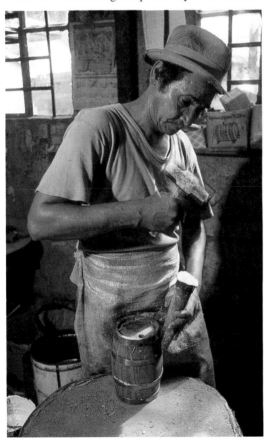

A cooper demonstrating a skill seldom seen today

boards and industrial councils, granting of interdicts with proper notice, omission of the presumption of trade union liability for illegal strikes and restructuring of the Labour Appeal Court.

After discussions between the government and the parties mentioned above, the so-called Labour Minute was signed on 13/14 September 1990 followed by an announcement that the Cabinet had accepted the S/C/N accord, as adapted by the NMC. An Amendment Bill was tabled during September 1990 and will probably be promulgated in 1991.

The government also committed itself, as a matter of priority, to launch investigations into the possibility of protecting farm and domestic workers in terms of labour legislation. The NMC is at present engaged in these investigations and recommendations have already been made in respect of the ways in which inclusion of farm workers could take place under the Unemployment Insurance Act, 1966, and the Basic Conditions of Employment Act, 1983. Interested parties have been given the opportunity to comment on these recommendations, whereafter the Department of Manpower will submit draft legislation to the government for approval.

Migrant workers and commuters

The main aim of all development programmes in South Africa is to create more jobs. Until now the economies of the self-governing territories, like most other developing countries, were incapable of providing sufficient jobs for all work-seekers, especially in the 'modern' sector.

At any given time of the year, about one third of all Black men are absent from the self-governing territories. They sell their labour on contract in the rest of South Africa as migrant workers for a set period of time, or as commuters. Approximately 1 500 000 of these migrant workers lived in the self-governing-territories in 1986, but sold their labour elsewhere, mostly in South Africa's metropolitan regions. More than half came from KwaZulu.

The huge difference between the gross domestic product (GDP) and the gross national product (GNP) of these regions reflects the absence of a large part of the labour force which earn wages and salaries outside the self-governing territories. In 1987 the GDP of the self-governing territories came to R430 per capita as against the average GNP of R1 159 per capita.

This indicates that the bulk of income is earned outside the borders of these territories. The major contributors to the GNP were commuters and migrant workers — 67,7 per cent of the total (38,8 per cent by migrant workers and 28,9 per cent by commuters). The largest contribution was made to the GNP of KwaNdebele (73,9 per cent), the self-governing territory situated nearest the Witwatersrand. The GNP per capita is highest in Qwaqwa (R1 873 in 1987) and lowest in Lebowa (R946). Of the total GDP of the self-governing territories agriculture contributed 12,8 per cent, construction 9,8 per cent, the manufacturing industry 12,6 per cent, mining 1,8 per cent and community services (health, education, etc) 44,7 per cent. These figures prove that the governments of the respective self-governing territories were until now the biggest employers.

According to the population census of 1985, some 4,1 million Black people or 76 per cent of all economically active Black people were employed in South Africa on a more or less permanent basis. Some were born in South Africa and have no relations with the self-governing territories.

Acknowledgements:
Department of Manpower

Until the discovery of the Kimberley diamond 'pipes' (1871) and the Witwatersrand gold reef (1886), the South African economy was based exclusively on agriculture, more or less self-sufficient but mainly at subsistence level.

The mining sector's vigorous development had an immediate and varied impact, changing agriculture from subsistence to market-orientated farming. The sudden influx of immigrants not only created a ready market for 'surplus' produce, but also provided new imported farming skills, know-how and technology. At the same time railway links between the main seaports and Kimberley — and later the Witwatersrand — created new export possibilities, including opportunities for agricultural products.

The city of Johannesburg soon became the focal point of economic activities other than mining, and a magnet for indigenous migrant labour. Today, economic activity in the region, which later became known as the PWV (Pretoria-Witwatersrand-Vereeniging) area, of which Johannesburg is the hub, accounts for about 40 per cent of gross domestic product (GDP). This economic predominance has been sustained despite several decentralisation programmes which have included restrictive measures as well as attractive incentives to locate in the less developed regions. The result is that economic development remains overconcentrated in a few geographical areas and this imbalance is in no small measure attributable to the discovery of gold on the Witwatersrand nearly a century ago.

In less than a century therefore, SA has advanced from a mainly agrarian economy to a modern, well-diversified economy in which agriculture, mining, secondary industry, commerce and a broad structure of service establishments contribute to the wealth of .the nation. More than 30 per cent of national production is derived from secondary industry and policy-makers are devoting particular attention to sound, accelerated development of this sector. South Africa manufactures a wide range of consumer goods, including food products, textiles, footwear and clothing, metal and chemical products, paper and paper products, while the volume of production of capital goods such as machinery and transport and electrical equipment has increased substantially since World War II. Part of the labour force is involved in the so-called 'informal sector'. Lately, the government has paid greater attention to this sector of the economy since it is an important source for creation of job opportunities.

Factors such as disinvestment, sanctions, the high rate of inflation and high interest rates underline the importance of gold in the South African economy. During 1990 the gold price dropped sharply to below $350, but by the end of the year it had recovered to an average level of about $377.

The high rate of inflation led to the issue of new coins as the nickel value of the existing coins exceeded its intrinsic value. The low financial rand attracted foreign buyers to purchase valuable property in the country. Such investments have not been a productive stimulus for the economy and have resulted in the loss to foreigners of a valuable and historical cultural heritage, particularly in the winelands of the western Cape. The Minister of Finance, Mr Barend du Plessis, has accordingly strictly limited investment by non-South African citizens.

Gross national product

The South African economy is one of the most 'open' economies in the world, i.e. foreign trade accounts for a much higher share of gross nation-

Table 1 Percentage contribution of various sectors to the gross domestic product, 1980-90, at current prices[1]

	1980	1985[4]	1990[4]
Agriculture, forestry and fisheries	6,8	5,8	5,1
Mining	21,1	14,8	10,7
Subtotal Primary	27,9	20,6	15,8
Secondary [2]	28,9	31,1	33,3
Tertiary [3]	43,2	48,3	50,9
TOTAL	100,0	100,0	100,0

1 Excluding Namibia
2 Secondary includes manufacturing, electricity, gas and water, and construction
3 Tertiary includes trade, catering, accommodation, transport, communication, finance, insurance, real estate and other community, social and personal services, including government
4 Information for the past four years is preliminary subject to change
Source: Central Statistical Service

al product than in the case of many other countries. This also means that the economy is highly susceptible to trends and developments in the economies of major trading partners.

In 1990, when GNP at market prices amounted to R252 630 million, exports of goods and services (including gold) were R69 487 million and imports R53 984 million. Foreign trade thus amounted to almost 48,9 per cent of GNP. Furthermore, the balance on the current account of the balance of payments is sharply anti-cyclical, swinging from a deficit of -4,8 per cent of GNP in 1982 to a surplus of 1,4 per cent in 1989.

Government consumption expenditure, which in recent years tended to account for a growing proportion of GDP, decreased slightly as a percentage of GDP in 1988, its share increasing to 19,2 per cent in 1990 from 13,5 per cent in 1980. This is largely attributable to increased spending on security and socio-economic services, such as education and health. Gross domestic fixed investment, as a percentage of GDP, declined for six consecutive years from 1982 onwards as a result of cyclical factors and a lack of confidence among entrepreneurs. In 1988, however, this ratio increased to 19,9 per cent from 19,1 per cent in 1987. It increased to 20,9 per cent in 1989.

In 1990, however, net personal savings declined and the proportion of personal savings to personal disposable income in 1990 amounted to only 1,3 per cent as against 3,1 per cent in 1988.

Since 1980 there has been a marginal decline in the proportion of the consumer rand spent on durable and semi-durable goods, balanced by a slight increase in the share spent on non-durable goods and services.

South Africa is better placed than most debtor countries to continue repaying its foreign debts. The ratio of foreign debt to total exports declined from 127,7 per cent in 1985 to about 92 per cent in 1987 and 79 per cent in 1989. Interest payments on foreign debt amounted to about 6,7 per cent of exports of goods and services in 1989.

An unacceptably high rate of inflation is one of the major current problems facing the

economy. The situation has steadily deteriorated since the beginning of the 1970s. During the period 1981-90 the average annual inflation rate, as measured by changes in the consumer price index, was 14,6 per cent. The growth rate of GDP in real terms was 5,4 per cent (1981), -0,4 per cent (1982), -1,8 per cent (1983), 5,1 per cent (1984), -1,2 per cent (1985), 0,0 per cent (1986), 2,1 per cent (1987), 4,1 per cent (1988), 2,1 per cent (1989) and -0,9 per cent (1990). (See Table 2).

The country's inflation rate is considerably higher than that of its major trading partners. In a country in which both imports and exports account for nearly 30 per cent of GDP, such a differential in inflation rates adversely effects the balance of payments. Because the price of South African exports continues to rise, these exports will become progressively less competitive on international markets if the rand does not depreciate accordingly.

The drop in the rand exchange value which is attributable to the sustained high inflation rate and outflow of capital since mid-1985 has raised the prices of imported goods — thus fuelling the rate of inflation even further. The effects of the prolonged drought, together with the higher rate of increase in unit labour costs, upward adjustments in a number of administered prices as well as an increase in the rate of general sales tax, caused the average consumer price index to rise by 18,6 per cent per month in 1986. It increased less sharply — by 12,9 per cent — in 1988. This increase could be attributed to a strengthening in the exchange rate of the rand, improved weather conditions for agricultural purposes, lower interest rates, smaller increases in administered prices, moderate wage agreements and optimistic inflationary expectations. The effect of various factors such as the exchange rate, interest and bond rates, administered prices, conditions in the labour market and inflationary expectations was, however, reversed and sharply increased the inflation rate to 14,7 per cent in 1989 and 14,4 per cent in 1990.

Seasonally adjusted and annualised rates of real economic growth amounted to -1,4 per cent, -0,8 per cent, -1,5 per cent and -0,3 per cent in 1990 respectively. For the year as a whole the growth rate amounted to -0,9 per cent.

After significant increases in the second and third quarter of 1990, the total real gross domestic expenditure declined sharply in the fourth quarter and for the year as a whole the decline amounted to -3,1 per cent. Steady advances continued to be recorded in real private consumption expenditure and for the calendar year 1990 it was 1,5 per cent higher than in 1989. Real gross

Table 2   Economic growth rates in real terms at 1985 prices, 1986-90*

	1986	1987	1988	1989	1990
GDP** at market prices	0,0	2,1	4,1	2,1	-0,9
GNP***	0,2	2,7	5,2	-0,7	-1,7
Terms of trade*** (1985 = 100) (gold included)	0,6	0,5	1,7	-7,6	-1,9

*   Excluding Namibia
**   Source: Central Statistical Service
***   Source: Department of Finance

omestic fixed investment decreased by about ,4 per cent in 1990.

Aggregate real inventories continued a ownward trend in the fourth quarter of 1990. 'he decline in commercial inventories could enerally be attributed to a significant decline in 1e physical extent of import goods as against an 1crease in merchandise export volumes in the ourth quarter of 1990. Aggregate real inven- 2ries declined significantly during 1990 as a vhole.

Real gross domestic product in 1990 was 0,9 er cent lower than in 1989. This may be com- ared with real growth rates of 2,1 per cent in 989 and of 3,7 per cent in 1988. The real growth ate of the gross national product amounted to 1,7 per cent in 1990.

Real gross domestic expenditure increased by ,2 per cent in 1988. In 1989 and 1990, however, eal gross domestic spending decreased by 0,8 er cent and 3,1 per cent respectively.

In 1988 growth fuelled by consumer demand nd private consumption expenditure reached a evel which prompted the authorities to intro- luce a number of measures to curb demand and low down the rate of growth generally. These neasures were designed to make credit more xpensive and included five increases in the bank ate from 9,5 to 18,0 per cent in the period etween March 1988 and October 1989, and a harp reduction in the assistance banks could xpect from the Reserve Bank. The effect of this olicy was evident during 1989 and 1990 when he real gross domestic expenditure declined by he above-mentioned percentages of 0,8 and 3,1 er cent respectively.

Economic planning

South Africa's economy is based on the prin- iples of the free-market economy, based on

private enterprise and ownership. However, the government is on occasion compelled to play the role of entrepreneur in the public interest.

Conferences between the government and businessmen were held in 1979 (Carlton Con- ference) and 1983 (Good Hope Conference) to lay the foundation for a partnership of co-opera- tion between the private and public sector.

The government, however, remains com- mitted to the philosophy that, in the final resort, it is private enterprise which has to combine all the elements of production most effectively to produce wealth. The state's function is to pro- vide the necessary infrastructural and socio- economic services and establish and maintain national and international order — a framework within which private enterprise can fulfil its primary function of producing goods and ser- vices unhampered.

Earlier the government frequently had to in- tervene when the private sector could not under- take essential projects including Sasol, Iscor and Eskom. The government has committed itself to a market-orientated system time and again over the past few years. Thus, the government's role in the economy has been scaled down by, among other things, the privatisation of Iscor.

In 1986 the State President's Economic Ad- visory Council (consisting of representatives from different spheres of the private sector) as- sisted by the Central Economic Advisory Service (CEAS) compiled and developed a strategy to improve long-term growth and the job creation potential of the economy. Another aim of the strategy is to reduce the inflation rate. This strategy is currently being revised.

The tenth Economic Development Programme (EDP), which is currently being compiled by the CEAS, will quantify economic objectives, and indicate measures to develop a practical framework to improve the long-term economic development potential of the South

Table 3 GDP by kind of economic activity at current prices and at factor incomes (R million), 1986-90*

eriod	Agriculture, forestry and fishing	Mining and quarrying	Manufacturing	Construction	Electricity, gas and water	Transport and communication	Trade	Other	TOTAL (GDP at factor cost)
986	7 242	20 214	30 277	4 507	5 632	11 448	15 228	34 939	129 487
987	9 430	19 379	35 752	4 915	6 827	13 217	18 995	41 416	149 931
988	11 760	21 903	44 105	5 822	8 231	15 535	22 521	48 400	178 277
989	12 539	23 582	52 289	6 556	9 232	16 825	26 829	58 952	206 804
990**	11 886	25 079	60 018	7 396	10 742	19 276	31 620	68 699	234 716

Excluding Namibia
* Provisional
ource: Central Statistical Service

African economy. It is anticipated that this document will be published during 1991.

Commercialisation

Commercialisation is an approach by which government activities are performed (within the framework of the public service) according to business principles by measuring the performance of a function or activity in financial terms.

The Commission for Administration is entrusted with the development of broad policies and guidelines for the commercialisation process, while the relevant departments/administrations are responsible for commercialisation actions. The commission will, however, monitor these actions and, at their request, advise the departments/administrations.

Commercialisation does not necessarily mean eventual privatisation of functions/activities, but there is a possibility of this occurring in future.

Privatisation

Privatisation means that the state is totally exempted from rendering a service to the community, including the financial obligations of such a service.

Privatisation is the field of operation of the Office for Privatisation which also manages those activities launched by public institutions and enterprises such as Transnet, the Department of Posts and Telecommunications, public corporations and local authorities.

Deregulation

Deregulation is related to privatisation and may in certain instances be a prerequisite for privatisation. It entails deliberate action to remove all unnecessary liabilities and impediments placed on economic activities by laws, regulations and prescriptions. Overall deregulation is the responsibility of the Competition Board, but individual institutions and the responsible political office-bearer are primarily reponsible for deregulation within their sphere of influence.

Decentralisation

Decentralisation involves establishment of industries and is the responsibility of the Department of Trade and Industry.

Through the years industrial development wa mainly concentrated in four metropolitan area — Pretoria-Witwatersrand-Vereeniging region Durban-Pinetown, Port Elizabeth-Uitenhage and the Cape Peninsula. These areas comprise : per cent of the country's surface area, but pro duce 80 per cent of all industrial products, while 73 per cent of all factories are situated here and 76 per cent of all factory workers work here.

In the past measures were taken from time to time to induce industrialists to erect factories in underdeveloped regions to distribute industria development more evenly over the whole

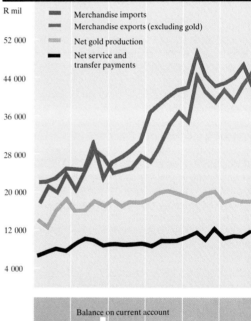

Balance of payments current account

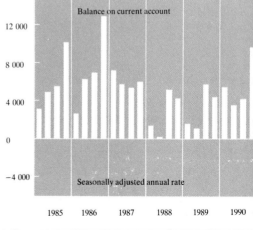

Table 4 Private and government consumption expenditure, and gross domestic fixed investment as percentage of the GDP, 1987-90

Period	Private consumption expenditure	Government consumption expenditure	Gross domestic fixed investment
1987	56,7	18,5	19,1
1988	56,2	17,8	19,9
1989	56,5	19,1	20,9
1990	58,1	19,2	20,3

Source: Department of Finance

country and to try to prevent work-seekers from flooding the cities. A decentralisation programme was launched on 1 April 1982 to accelerate development. The governments of South Africa and the independent Black States (Transkei, Bophuthatswana, Venda and Ciskei) introduced a package of incentives which was more advantageous than those of the previous 20 years.

South Africa and the four independent states have been divided into nine development regions, within which a number of 'deconcentration points' (near metropolitan areas) and new 'industrial development points' (where new job opportunities will alleviate pressure on metropolitan areas) have been identified.

During the scheme's first seven years of operation, 7 572 applications for assistance in new projects were approved, representing an investment of R10 205,3 million and creation of 513 152 jobs once all projects came on stream. Of the approved applications, 510 were from foreign investors whose projects would involve R1 652,6 million and create a potential 108 924 jobs.

Of all the development points, Port Elizabeth/Uitenhage, East London, Isithebe in KwaZulu, Phuthaditjhaba in Qwaqwa, and Botshabelo near Bloemfontein are the most popular among entrepreneurs. Applications approved for projects at these points during 1988/89 accounted for 43,5 per cent of all new jobs expected to be created.

Of the 1 042 applications approved during 1988/89, 14,5 per cent were for plants to manufacture metal products, 16,8 per cent for clothing and textile factories and 15,1 per cent for furniture and wood processing factories.

Small business development

The Small Business Development Corporation (SBDC) was launched in 1981 as a joint public

and private sector venture to help small entrepreneurs in both the formal and informal sectors to get their enterprises off the ground. SBDC equity is divided equally between the government and the private sector but the corporation is run on strict business principles.

During the first 10 years of operation (from 1981 to March 1991), the SBDC granted loans totalling R1 000 million to 29 000 entrepreneurs. During the same period property development projects of R256 million were completed. The 267 632 new jobs created and maintained by enterprises launched with the assistance of the SBDC cost an average of R3 116.

Apart from assistance to the SBDC, the government also financially assists 10 small business institutes which provide expert transfer service (training, advice, counselling, consultation and research) for the small business community.

The closed corporation as a form of enterprise was established in January 1985. It satisfies the requirements of the small entrepreneur. By 31 December 1990, 184 528 closed corporations

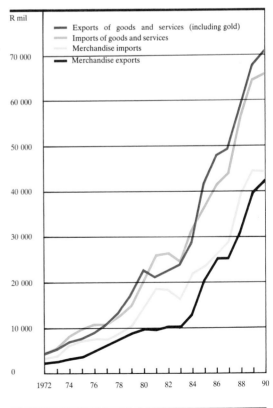

Imports and exports, 1972–90

had been incorporated, of which an estimated total of 30 739 had previously been companies. The law of closed corporations is developing into a full-fledged subsection of the South African legal system through judicial decisions.

Manufacturing

In 1990 the manufacturing industry was responsible for 23 per cent of the GDP (the largest single share) and employed 1,5 million people (about 13,2 per cent of the economically-active population). The industrial base has been widened and adapted to such an extent in recent years that South Africa could manufacture most, if not all, of its essential requirements should circumstances so demand.

The average size of manufacturing establishments has increased over the years. The company and closed corporation are the dominant forms of enterprise. In 1985, the latest year for which figures are available, companies and

Economic growth and price increases, 1965-90

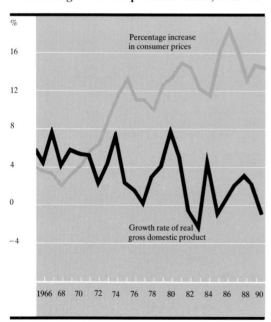

South Africa experienced conditions of fairly rapid growth and moderate price increases during the 1960s. Since the 1970s the country has been showing real signs of 'stagflation', i.e. continous increases in the rate of inflation coupled with lower real growth rates

closed corporations comprised 69 per cent of th total number of firms and accounted for 97 pe cent of net production output. Cartels, holdin companies and mergers, both horizontal and ci cular, are common.

Industrialists take an active part in a larg number of organisations to promote their inte ests. The most important national organisation are the South African Chamber of Busines (Sacob), the Steel and Engineering Industrie Federation of South Africa (Seifsa) and th Afrikaanse Handelsinstituut (AHI).

In 1989 the fixed capital stock of the manufac turing industry in 1985 prices amounted to a tot of R45 702 million. This represents an increas of 4,2 per cent a year between 1974 and 1989.

Shares and debentures are issued in the ope market and may be acquired by general buyer financial institutions such as insurance com panies and investment houses. In recent yea the mining houses have increasingly participate in this type of financing.

A second source of long-term funds is dire participation of financial institutions and in dividuals in the form of loans and securities. considerable proportion of the funds emanatin from mining houses is supplied in this way.

A recent study has indicated that between 4 and 50 per cent of long-term private industri financing is obtained from internal sources, i.e profits and depreciation allowances. It is inte esting to note that in 1989/90 taxes absorbed 26, per cent of industrial profits and 26,2 per cent c dividends whilst 47 per cent was retained. Al though the tax rate for companies amounts to 5 per cent, ample provision is made for deprecia tion and export allowances which in turn reduc the effective rate of taxation to the level indi cated above.

Most of the raw materials and semi-manufac tured goods required by industry are availabl from local sources. This applies particularly t raw materials derived from agriculture and th mining industry. SA has economically viabl deposits of more industrial minerals than mos countries, but special mention must be made c the large deposits of high-grade iron ore and th prices of basic iron and steel which are usuall marginally lower than in most Wester countries. Over the years dependence on foreig sources for industrial raw materials has gradual ly declined. Only some sectors, e.g. clothing an textiles, furniture (hardwoods), chemicals an transport equipment (components) still rely to greater or lesser extent on imports of ra materials or intermediate goods.

In 1989 total domestic demand for manufac

red goods amounted to more than R160 000
illion. The value of imported manufactured
roducts amounted to R33 379 million while the
alue of manufactured exports was R19 946 mil-
on in 1987.

The prices of manufactures increased by 14,1
er cent a year in the period 1980-90, as against
nly 2,1 per cent a year in the 1960s. The high
ate of increase during the decade is attributable
o a sustained rise in the cost of basic goods,
ntroduction of sales duties and general sales tax,
nd the decline in the value of the rand, which
ade imports of essential materials that much
ore expensive.

Commerce

outh Africa has the most sophisticated free-
nterprise commercial sector on the African
ontinent. It is government policy not to interfere
nduly with market mechanisms and state inter-
ention is limited to measures to protect the
onsumer against malpractices and exploitation.
or historical reasons the price of some primary
ommodities, agricultural produce especially,
re controlled and administered by control
oards in conjunction with the Ministry of
griculture.

The major consumer markets are the PWV
omplex, the Greater Cape Town metropolitan
rea, the Port Elizabeth, East London and
itenhage region in the eastern Cape, the Dur-
an, Pinetown and Pietermaritzburg region in
Natal, Bloemfontein and vicinity and the Free
tate gold fields region (Welkom-Virginia-
Odendaalsrus).

Trading licences, for retailers especially, are
ssued by local licensing authorities in terms of
rovincial ordinances. The system of trade licen-
es was drastically diminished by the
overnment's deregulation policy. In most in-
tances only registration of the businesses is re-
uired.

The retail sector is directly related to the broad
conomic function of satisfying man's needs. The
etailer is therefore at any time in history a uni-
ue window display of the needs of the contem-
orary consumer which result from his cultural
ackground, lifestyle, standard of living, tradi-
ion, external influence and preferences. Today
outh Africa can take pride in a network of retail
rade outlets which varies from the traditional
ural or corner shop to the most modern shop-
ing centres in the heart of cities, suburbs and
ven large towns.

The growth of modern giant retail concerns

The price of gold, the value and volume of gold produced

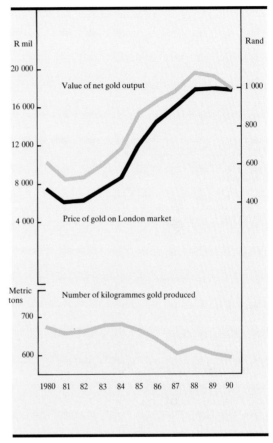

such as supermarkets and hypermarkets which
heralded a new period of one-stop marketing
and self-service methods, offers numerous
benefits to the modern consumer with limited
time for shopping.

An important outlet in rural areas is the
agricultural co-operative, a significant wholesale
and retail source of supply of a wide range of
commodities to farming communities. There
were more than 569 such co-operatives
countrywide with an annual turnover exceeding
R27,85 billion by December 1989. A significant
factor in the development of retail trade is the
rapid growth in the volume and sophistication of
the purchasing power of Black communities,
especially in urban areas. In 1985 Black people
accounted for 31,8 per cent of total disposable
income while the share of Whites was 55,5 per
cent. It has been estimated that at the current
rate of growth, Black people will command more

Table 5 Personal income and expenditure (R million), 1987-90

	1987	1988	1989	1990**
Remuneration of employees	85 108	99 196	117 047	136 650
Income from property*	20 095	24 741	30 467	34 646
Current transfers received from general government	4 809	5 365	5 032	5 983
Current transfers received from incorporated business enterprises	75	80	80	83
Transfers received from the rest of the world	358	363	461	399
Current income	110 445	129 745	153 086	179 757
Less direct taxes	12 354	14 497	19 412	22 147
Personal disposable income	98 091	115 248	133 674	157 610
Less private consumption expenditure	93 353	111 324	131 309	155 475
Less current transfers to general government	152	153	178	208
Less transfers to the rest of the world	163	162	133	132
Personal saving	4 423	3 609	2 054	2 073

*   Income from property consists of divident receipts: interest receipts less interest payments, rent receipts less maintenance cost, mortgage interest and
     provision for depreciation and the profits less losses of non-corporate business after provision for depreciation and after inventory valuation adjustment
** Provisional
Source: Department of Finance

Table 6 Capital account of the balance of payments (R million), 1987-90

Period	Capital movement*				Total capital movements (net inflow)	Balance of payments transactions	SDR allocations and valuation adjustments	Total change in gold and other foreign reserves
	Private sector		Central government and banking sector					
	Long term	Short term	Long term	Short term				
1987	-2 076	-1 118	375	-32	-2 851	1 885	330	2 215
1988	-160	-5 011	-1 013	-24	-6 208	-1 680	445	-1 235
1989	-955	-3 254	-275	139	-4 345	1 389	-1 190	199
1990*	-1 398	-898	-547	-31	-2 874	879	-520	359

*   A minus sign indicates an outflow
** Provisional figures
Source: Department of Finance

Table 7 Production and consumer price indices (1985 = 100), 1987-90

Period	Production prices of goods for domestic use			Consumer prices			Services	All items
	Goods produced in SA	Imported goods	All goods	Goods				
				Food	All goods			
1987	137,1	134,5	136,2	147,6	142,0		129,1	137,7
1988	156,5	149,3	154,1	170,9	162,6		142,0	155,4
1989	182,5	173,6	177,6	189,7	187,3		161,3	178,2
1990	205,0	191,3	199,4	220,1	216,3		181,1	203,8

Source: Central Statistical Service

ian half of total disposable income by the year 000.

Commerce is well organised into numerous odies representing various interests. They are ie Afrikaanse Handelsinstituut (AHI), Sacob, nd the National African Federated Chamber of 'ommerce (Nafcoc).

oreign trade

he importance of foreign trade to South .frica's economy is on the one hand evident om the relationship between its exports (goods nd non-factor services) and GDP and, on the ther, the relationship between imports (goods nd non-factor services) and gross domestic ex-enditure. The former relationship diminished) 28,5 per cent in 1989 from 36,5 per cent in 980. The former relationship decreased to 23,2 er cent in 1989 from 28,2 per cent in 1980. .lthough the foreign sector still contributes lar-ely to the South African economy, its relative nportance is declining. South Africa still ranks mong the 25 most important trading nations of ie West.

Merchandise exports (excluding gold) mounted to 70,4 per cent (R41 345 million) of outh Africa's total exports in 1989. Of this 8,6 er cent was agricultural products, 16,0 per cent iinerals, 13,1 per cent pearls, precious and emi-precious stones, precious metals and coins nd 22,0 per cent base metals. Regarding iinerals, South Africa is a major exporter of ranite, asbestos, iron, manganese, chrome and tanium ore as well as coal. Despite attempts to iversify its export base, South Africa is still irgely reliant on export of primary and inter-iediary commodities to earn foreign exchange.

Net gold exports are responsible for a large art of South Africa's foreign exchange earnings. .arnings from this source are directly linked to ie international gold price. The importance of et gold exports relative to total exports declined harply to 32,9 per cent in 1989 from 51,6 per cent i 1980. South Africa is still the world's largest old producer and was responsible for nearly 30 er cent of total production worldwide in 1989.

Imports mainly comprise capital goods, raw iaterials, semi-manufactured goods (80 per ent of total trade exports) and consumer com-iodities.

Expenditure by South African residents on ireign services is relatively large, comprising iainly cargo and insurance on goods, tourist affic and investment income.

Since 1985 South Africa has experienced a net outflow of capital abroad which amounted to a total of R4 908 million in 1990. This outflow is mainly countered by maintaining a certain balance on the current account of the balance of payment. Gold and foreign reserves are further applied for this purpose. South Africa is not the only country experiencing an outflow of foreign capital. According to the World Bank a change in structure has occurred in the availability of international liquidity. All developing countries (including South Africa) have therefore been experiencing an outflow of capital since the early 1980s.

The governments of South Africa, Botswana, Lesotho and Swaziland have a customs union agreement — the Southern Africa Customs Union (Sacu) — in terms of which there is a free interchange of goods between these countries, and they apply the same tariffs and regulations to goods imported from outside the common customs area. Similar agreements have been concluded between the governments of South Africa, Transkei, Bophuthatswana, Venda and Ciskei.

Excise duty is levied on certain locally produced goods, of which potable spirits, beer, cigarettes, tobacco, motor cars and certain petroleum products yield the highest revenue.

South Africa maintains formal trade relations with various other countries by means of treaties, trade agreements and membership of interna-tional institutions relating to trade. These rela-tions are managed by the Directorate of Foreign Trade Relations of the Department of Trade and Industry.

South Africa's participation in the activities of the General Agreement on Tariffs and Trade (Gatt) and the administration of international trade agreements are also handled by the direc-torate. It also deals with matters resulting from the activities of agencies of the United Nations that affect South Africa, e.g. the United Nations Conference on Trade and Development (UN-CTAD).

Other responsibilities include maintenance of trade relations with individual countries or groups of countries, where such relations are not governed by multilateral bodies. Thus the direc-torate administers South Africa's bilateral trade relations with countries or groups of countries, such as the European Community (EC).

Several organisations promote exports and ex-ternal trade relations in general. The major government agency involved in export promo-tion is the directorate of export promotion of the Department of Trade and Industry. The func-tions of the directorate are firstly to promote

Table 8 Growth of manufacturing industry

	1970	1985
Number of establishments	11 967	18 640
Employment	1 088 569	1 437 026
Employees per establishment[1]	91	77
Value added (Rm)[2]	16 267	27 596[3]
Value added per employee (R)[4]	6 889	9 250
Value of capital stock (Rm)[2]	9 585	27 396
Capital stock per employee	8 805	20 628

1 This figure gives some indication of the size of establishment
2 At constant 1985 prices
3 1990
4 This figure gives some indication of the productive capacity per employee
Source: Central Statistical Service

Table 9 Private consumption expenditure at current prices by type of expenditure (R million), 1988-90

	1988	1989	1990
Durable goods Furniture, household appliantes, etc	4 277	4 864	5 846
Personal transport equipment	4 860	5 427	5 800
Recreational, entertainment goods	1 722	2 138	2 598
Other durable goods[1]	619	734	894
Semi-durable goods Clothing and footwear	8 189	9 953	14 654
Household textiles, furnishings, glassware, etc	3 071	3 763	4 276
Motor-car tyres, parts,etc	3 129	3 546	4 210
Recreational, entertainment goods	1 620	2 084	2 591
Miscellaneous goods[2]	2 183	2 710	3 231
Non-durable goods Food, beverages and tobacco	40 489	46 761	55 200
Household fuel and power	2 937	3 394	3 887
Household consumer goods	2 528	2 879	3 410
Medical and pharmaceutical products	1 802	2 260	2 718
Petroleum products	3 667	4 820	5 526
Recreational, entertainment goods	1 129	1 491	1 705
Services Rent[3]	9 090	10 637	11 686
Household services, including domestic servants	2 253	2 339	2 441
Medical services	3 115	4 138	5 076
Transport, communication services	5 857	6 683	7 744
Recreational, entertainment and educational services	3 543	4 618	5 128
Miscellaneous services[4]	5 244	6 070	6 854
TOTAL	111 324	131 309	152 475

1 Jewellery, watches, therapeutic appliances, etc
2 Personal goods and writing and drawing equipment and supplies
3 Including imputed rent for owner-occupied dwllings
4 After adjustment for net expenditure of foreigners in the domestic market
Source: South African Reserve Bank

South Africa's export trade by developing th export market and assistance to South Africa exporters; formulation and maintenance of long-term plan aimed at promotion of foreig trade and technology, as well as the recruitmer of foreign industrial investments in South Afric managing the personnel and functions of office abroad and providing miscellaneous service organising trade fairs and exhibitions an providing advertising and publication service and identifying South African export products i order to assist companies to enter the expo market.

The directorate administers the General E> port Incentive Scheme (GEIS) and the Expo Marketing Aid Scheme (EMA) aimed at provic ing exporters with financial assistance.

The major private organisation engaged in e> port promotion is the South African Foreig Trade Organisation (Safto) established in 196 to assist South African companies to develo their export capability, to encourage long-tern commitment to exports by the private sector an to develop international marketing programme for specific South African products.

Various other organisations promote trade be tween SA and specific countries. Examples ar the South African-German Chamber of Trac and Industry, the Netherlands-South Africa Chamber of Commerce and Industry, the Sout African-British Trade Association and Sout African binational chambers of commerc abroad.

Factors favouring investment

The main fields of investment are mining an beneficiation of industrial products, physical ir frastructure, chemicals, metals, electronics, th automobile industry, textiles, paper and pulp.

Positive factors favouring investment includ a broad technological base which is continuall being expanded and refined, a highly traine managerial class, an enterprising population, a abundant supply of unskilled labour and an ir creasing supply of skilled and semi-skille labour. There are many specialised financial in stitutions to assist industrialists, including a wel developed money and capital market and sophisticated stock exchange.

The CSIR, the South African Bureau of Stanc ards (SABS) and the Council for Mineral Tecl nology (Mintek) provide research an development facilities for existing and prospec tive industrialists and mining houses.

No legal disabilities or restrictions of any cor

sequence attach to foreign investment as opposed to domestic. Foreign investment has never been expropriated or nationalised. Comprehensive provision has, however, been made for payment of compensation, should it become necessary to expropriate or temporarily utilise any asset belonging to non-residents.

The government does not itself invest in industrial enterprises launched by the private sector, but has established a number of organisations to provide financial and other assistance. Foremost among these is the Industrial Development Corporation (IDC), established to finance new industries and assist existing industries in expanding, modernising and generally improving their efficiency.

News items: 1990

The South African economy reached the upper turning point of the business cycle in the first half of 1989. Since the fourth quarter of 1989 the gross domestic product declined in each successive quarter up to the fourth quarter of 1990. The GDP declined by almost 1 per cent during 1990.

The South African Reserve Bank maintained a policy of monetary discipline through positive real interest rates which enabled it to bring the growth in the money supply to within the limits of between 11 per cent and 15 per cent set by it as a target for 1990. The aim of this tight monetary stance is to re-establish the stability of the rand both internally and externally by curbing the unacceptably high rate of inflation.

Inflation varied between 10,9 per cent (1978) and 18,6 per cent (1986) over the period 1976 to 1990 contributing to the decline in the value of the rand from $1 = R0,87 in 1976 to $1 = R2,53 in December 1990.

The consumer price index increased by 14,3 per cent on average during 1990. The monthly rate of inflation declined steadily from 15,1 per cent in January 1990 to 13,3 per cent in July 1990. An increase to 14,3 per cent occurred in September and 15,3 per cent in November as a result of oil price hikes caused by the Gulf crisis. The rate decreased to 14,6 per cent in December. Monetary authorities have expressed their resolve to maintain monetary discipline until such time as the inflation expectations have dissipated to the desired extent.

Since the debt standstill of August 1985 and financial sanctions South Africa has become a capital exporting country which has manifested in the repayment of foreign debt. The latter declined to $20,6 billion in December 1989 from an amount of $23,7 billion in 1985. This occurred at a time when the external value of the rand declined rapidly so that in terms of rand considerably larger amounts were remitted than those suggested by the dollar values. The amount remaining inside the net was reduced to $7,3 billion by the end of 1989 from $13,6 billion on 31 August 1985.

The price for this huge capital export was the lower growth potential of the South African economy with attendant lower employment creation possibilities. This resulted in large scale unemployment, of the Black population especially.

Private consumer spending continued to show a mild rise during the third quarter of 1990. This rise in consumer demand over the entire span of six quarters of the current downswing was a feature which largly softened its severity. The resilience in private consumption expenditure during the third quarter is largely the result of wage and salary increases granted by general government; relatively high settlements negotiated by trade unions in all sectors of the economy and the lowering of income tax announced in the 1990 budget.

The gold price had several up and down movements throughout the year. The highest average monthly gold price in 1990 was in February i.e. $417 per ounce. It declined steadily to $352 in June, whereupon it increased to $395 in August and then fell to $378 in December. A variety of factors influenced the price, the most prominent being the Gulf crisis.

The current account of the balance of payments recorded a surplus of R3,5 billion during the first three quarters of 1990, which was 75 per cent higher than the R2 billion for he same period of 1989 and even higher than the R3,1 billion recorded during the whole of 1989. Increase in the real merchandise exports was the main contributor to the larger surplus as it rose by 5,8 per cent in the first three quarters of 1990 compared to the increase of 3 per cent in imports. Merchandise imports on the other hand increased noticeably in the third quarter, mainly as a result of the high level of mineral imports. If these imports are excluded, the volume of imports declined by 8 per cent during the first three quarters of 1990.

The gold and foreign exchange reserves held by the South African Reserve Bank declined from R5,7 billion in January 1990 to R5,1 billion in June 1990. An increasing trend then occurred to R6,6 billion in November, but a decline occurred in December to R6,2 billion.

New car sales (an indication of economic growth) for the year 1990 (209 598 units) declined by 5,4 per cent compared with the corresponding period in 1989.

The South African Chamber of Business (Sacob) was established in March 1990 with the amalgamation of the Association of Chambers of Commerce (Assocom) mainly representative of the wholesale and retail sector and the Federated Chamber of Industries (FCI), which mainly voiced the opinions of the manufacturing sector. The amalgamation had the aim of uniting the business sector in its collective approaches to various issues it addresses.

The price of bread increased by 15 cents a loaf in November 1990 to finance an increase of 15,5 per cent in the wheat price, among other things. Price control on bread would be lifted in 1991.

A trade pact was signed between South Africa and Madagascar on 16 August 1990 after 15 years of strained relations. The pact consists of exchange of trade missions and granting of landing rights to South African Airways.

The first-ever trade agreement with Rumania which includes promotion of tourism, was signed on 26 October 1991.

Polish and South African businessmen signed a trade agreement in April whereby South Africa will export large quantities of iron ore to Poland and import chemicals in turn. A Polish South Arican chamber of trade and industry was established in June, allowing free trade between both countries.

Hungary lifted all official trade and financial sanctions against South Africa in August after an agreement was signed between the two countries.

On 1 August, Johannesburg became the first city in South Africa to deregulate street trading as part of a formal policy. The city council accepted that informal trading was an economic necessity and resolved to identify sites by means of special signs where street vendors can trade.

The European Community (EC) lifted the ban on new investment in South Africa on 15 December.

The gold index of the Johannesburg Exchange reached its lowest level in four years on 13 December 1990 when it closed on 1 141.

For the first time in 37 years, when figures first became available, individuals spent more than their after-tax income. Personal savings during the January to September 1990 period were minus R1,625 billion compared with a positive R2,060 billion during the same period in 1989.

Diamond sales of De Beers Centenary's Central Selling Organisation (CSO) dropped to 1,69 billion dollars during the last half of 1990 from 2,48 billion dollars during the first half of 1990.

Higher petrol and oil prices pushed the annual rate of increase in the producer price index (PPI) to 15,8 per cent in December, its highest level in more than a year.

The inflation rate for December 1990, as measured by the Consumer Price Index (CPI) was 14,6 per cent, which was 0,7 percentage points lower than the rate for November 1990 (15,3 per cent) and 0,7 percentage points lower than the rate for December 1989 (15,3 per cent).

Acknowledgements:
Central Economic Advisory Service
Central Statistical Service
Commission for Administration
Department of Trade and Industry
Small Business Development Corporation
South African Reserve Bank

Public finance

South Africa has a three-tier government system but final financial authority is vested in the central government, which also provides most of the funds of the four provincial administrations. Treasury subvention to the four provinces has increased to R8 719,7 million in 1989/90, or 12,2 per cent of the central government's budget.

Local authorities and Regional Services' Councils are financially independent of both central and provincial governments, but some aspects of their loan and revenue sources are subject to approval by the Treasury and the provincial administrations.

In 1989/90 the four independent states of Transkei, Bophuthatswana, Venda and Ciskei (TBVC states) derived between 14 and 37 per cent of their national budgets from their own sources, while the figure for the self-governing territories varied from 7 to 16 per cent. The remainder of the income of the TBVC states is financed by transfers, budget assistance and concessionary loans of the Development Bank of Southern Africa (DBSA) and the Commission for Economic and Development Co-operation in South Africa. The transfers mainly constitute their share in the Southern African Customs Union of which Swaziland, Botswana and Lesotho are also members, the Joint Regional Monetary Agreement and refunding of taxes paid by citizens of the TBVC states working in the Republic as migrant workers. The remainder of the budget of the self-governing territories derives from direct help, concessionary loans from the DBSA and tax remuneration.

It is a feature of the South African economy that a number of basic business enterprises are, or were until recently, owned by the state. The most important are the Post Office (with its network of postal and telecommunications services) and Transnet Limited (with its five components, namely Spoornet, Portnet, Petronet, Autonet and SAL). Commuter services were corporised in 1990 as the South African Commuter Service. The financial system of the Post Office is linked to that of central government, but its current revenues and expenditures do not pass through the Treasury. Parliament, however, approves the Post Office budget. Both organisations are in a process of reorganisation aimed at being self-sustaining and profitable. The South African Commuter Corporation will in future only receive a subsidy from the Treasury in remuneration for the uneconomical service it provides. Transnet itself will in future be managed as a self-sustaining public corporation.

A number of public corporations such as Foskor and the Aluminium Corporation of South Africa (Alusaf) are financed directly by central government or indirectly through the Industrial Development Corporation (IDC). Several of these corporations, such as Sasol and Eskom, though initially financed by the state, have become largely self-sufficient in terms of revenue for current and capital expenditure. In the private sector Iscor has now been wholly privatised while Sasol is partly privatised.

Revenue

The government's main sources of income are taxes, both direct and indirect, on companies and individuals, and various duties, such as customs and excise duties.

Income tax

Income tax is levied on income derived, or deemed to have been derived, from sources within South Africa. Liability is thus also incurred by any non-resident person or company receiving income from South African sources. The tax year runs from 1 March to the end of the following February, but the law provides for cer-

Exchange rate of the rand

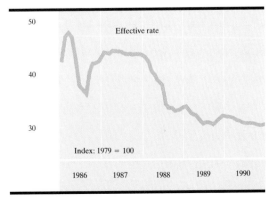

Index: 1979 = 100

tain classes of taxpayers to submit their returns on a date other than the end of February.

In the case of companies, tax is levied on taxable income which, briefly, consists of gross income (excluding accruals of capital nature) less all deductions (mainly expenditure incurred in the production of the income) authorised by the law. A distinction is drawn between four types of companies — gold-mining, diamond-mining, other mining and non-mining companies.

In the case of individuals, tax is levied on taxable income which is determined in the same manner as that of companies. The first R2 000 of interest and building society dividends received by individual taxpayers are exempt from tax. Dividends from all sources are excluded from taxes as from the 1990/91 tax year. Foreign dividends on shares acquired by the taxpayer before he became ordinarily resident in South Africa are also exempt from tax.

Persons who derive income from sources other than remuneration, e.g. a trade or profession or investments, and also companies, must make two payments of provisional tax during the course of the tax year. Provisional taxpayers may make a third topping-up payment six months after the end of their tax year.

Non-residents pay tax on dividends derived from SA. The non-resident shareholder's tax is 15 per cent and is payable on declaration of dividends distributed to companies which are not South African companies to individuals not resident nor carrying on business in South Africa and to holders of bearer scrip. The tax is levied upon the shareholder, but the company paying the dividend to the shareholder is required to withhold the amount payable.

Tax on royalties is levied at the rate of 50 per cent on 30 per cent royalties and similar payments to foreigners.

Tax on donations is payable by the donor on the value of the property which is donated by him. The rate of taxation is 15 per cent on the value of the property after deduction of an amount of R20 000.

Estate duty is payable at 15 per cent on the taxable value of the estate above R1 million.

Transfer duty is payable by purchasers of fixed property. For individuals the rate is 1 per cent on the first R30 000 of the value of the property and 3 per cent on the balance. For companies the rate is 5 per cent.

Customs duties are levied on a wide range of imports, while excise duties are collected on wine, beer, spirits, tobacco products, petrol and motor cars produced locally.

Table 1 Inland Revenue (R million)

	1989/90	1990/91 Estimates	1991/92* Estimates
Income tax			
Companies (other than mines)**	11 152 000	12 401 000	13 713 200
Individuals**	18 241 460	22 900 732	29 139 000
Gold mines	1 015 000	631 000	490 000
Other mines	1 320 000	1 619 000	1 225 000
Sales tax**	16 420 000	18 207 000	19 444 000 ***
Gold mining leases	326 000	181 000	140 000
Stamp duties and fees	630 000	700 000	655 000
Non-resident shareholder's tax	440 000	425 000	430 000
Transfer duty	650 000	755 000	675 000
Estate duty	80 000	82 000	75 000
Interest and dividends	370 912	60 789	55 000
Other	1 430 000	712 700	611 000
TOTAL: INLAND REVENUE	52 075 372	58 675 221	66 652 200
Central Energy Fund	0	0	0
TOTAL: ORDINARY INCOME	61 385,0	67 396,4	74 866,0
Direct taxes	32 822,8	46 688,7	53 532,2
Indirect taxes	26 738,4	19 917,0	20 949,0
Miscellaneous	1 823,8	790,7	384,8

* After tax proposals are taken into account
** Gross collections, that is before payments to self-governing territories
*** VAT from 30 September 1991
Source: Department of Finance

With the exception of certain basic foodstuffs, general sales tax (GST) of 13 per cent is payable by end-consumers on most goods and services. Value-added tax (VAT) is to be introduced at the rate of 12 per cent on 30 September 1991 and will replace GST. VAT will be levied on the supply of goods and services at all stages of the production and distribution chain, as well as on importation of goods and certain services. The change-over to VAT will address the two major shortcomings of GST, namely tax evasion and double taxation.

Agreements to avoid double taxation on the same income are in force between South Africa and a number of African and foreign countries.

In order to encourage foreign investment in industry, special deductions are allowed when taxable income is determined. These include special allowances for machinery and buildings used in manufacture, and an export market development allowance. Details are available from the Board for the Decentralisation of Industry and the Industrial Development Corporation.

Monetary policy

South African financial institutions may nowadays be divided into monetary (or money-creating) institutions and non-monetary institutions. Monetary institutions comprise the South African Reserve Bank, the Corporation for Public Deposits, the short-term business of the Land Bank, the Post Office Savings Bank, and private deposit-taking institutions and mutual building societies. In turn, private deposit-taking institutions comprise the former discount houses, commercial (clearing) banks, merchant banks, general banks and equity building societies. The non-monetary sector includes permanent building societies, participation

Table 2 Effect of personal income tax rates, 1991/92 (R)

| Taxable income | Unmarried | | | Married | | | | | |
| | Under 62 | 62-64 | Over 65 | No children | | | Under 65 | | |
				Under 62	62-64	Over 65	1 child	2 children	3 children
10 000	0	0	0	0	0	0	0	0	0
11 000	135	15	0	0	0	0	0	0	0
12 000	345	225	0	0	0	0	0	0	0
13 000	555	435	0	170	50	0	70	0	0
14 000	765	645	0	360	240	0	260	160	60
15 000	975	855	0	550	430	0	450	350	250
16 000	1 225	1 105	0	760	640	0	660	560	460
17 000	1 475	1 355	0	970	850	0	870	770	670
18 000	1 725	1 605	0	1 180	1 060	0	1 080	980	880
19 000	1 975	1 855	0	1 390	1 270	0	1 290	1 190	1 090
20 000	2 225	2 105	125	1 600	1 480	0	1 500	1 400	1 300
25 000	3 675	3 555	1 575	2 750	2 630	650	2 650	2 550	2 450
30 000	5 325	5 205	3 225	4 050	3 930	1 950	3 950	3 850	3 750
35 000	7 125	7 005	5 025	5 500	5 380	3 400	5 400	5 300	5 200
40 000	9 075	8 955	6 975	7 100	6 980	5 000	7 000	6 900	6 800
45 000	11 075	10 955	8 975	8 850	8 730	6 750	8 750	8 650	8 550
50 000	13 125	13 005	11 925	10 750	10 630	8 650	10 650	10 550	10 450
55 000	15 225	15 105	13 125	12 700	12 580	10 600	12 600	12 500	12 400
60 000	17 365	17 245	15 265	14 700	14 580	12 600	14 600	14 500	14 400
65 000	19 515	19 395	17 415	16 750	16 630	14 650	16 650	16 550	16 450
70 000	21 665	21 545	19 565	18 800	18 680	16 700	18 700	18 600	18 500
75 000	23 815	23 695	21 715	20 900	20 780	18 800	20 800	20 700	20 600
80 000	25 965	25 845	23 865	23 000	22 880	20 900	22 900	22 800	22 700
100 000	34 565	34 445	32 465	31 600	31 480	29 5000	31 500	31 400	31 300
150 000	56 065	55 945	53 965	53 100	52 980	51 000	53 000	52 900	52 800

Source: Department of Finance

Table 3 Assets of discount houses (R million), 1988-90

End of year	Negotiable certificates of deposit	Treasury bills	Land Bank bills	Trade bills, promissory and acceptances	Government stock	Land Bank debentures	Stocks of local authorities and public corporations	Bills of and loans to public corporations	Other assets	TOTAL ASSETS
1988	20	—	—	431	250	5	—	—	249	955
1989	53	—	34	390	685	—	35	4	228	1 429
1990	142	64	350	559	381	—	1	2	280	1 779

Source: South African Reserve Bank

Table 4 Liabilities of general banks (R million), 1989-90

End of year	Deposits							Foreign	TOTAL DEPOSITS
	Domestic						Total		
			Fixed and notice						
	Demand	Savings	Short term	Medium term	Long term	Total			
1989	7 913	1 007	4 752	8 004	3 148	15 904	24 824	275	25 099
1990	4 775	489	3 456	8 736	4 988	17 180	22 444	246	22 690

End of year	Other liabilities to the public				Total liabilities to the public	Capital and reserve			Other liabilities			TOTAL LIABILITIES
	Acceptances on behalf of customers	Loans and advances received	Other	Total		Domestic	Foreign	Total	Unearned finance charges	Other	Total	
1989	—	5 527	390	5 917	31 016	1 445	14	1 459	—	857	857	33 332
1990	—	5 886	977	6 863	29 553				—			

Source: South African Reserve Bank

Table 5 Selected items and transactions of unit trusts (R million), 1988-90

Year	Market value of security holdings[1]				Cash and deposits	Market value of net assets[3]	Transactions in units[4]			Transactions in securities[7]			TOTAL ASSETS[8]
	Securities of public sector[2]	Stock debentures and preference shares	Ordinary shares	Total			Gross sales[5]	Repurchases[6]	Net sales	Purchases	Sales	Net investment	
1988	249	67	3 363	3 679	749	4 458	777	400	377	2 303	1 988	315	3 243
1989	171	68	5 388	5 627	1 058	6 736	1 313	804	509	3 132	2 820	312	4 056
1990	262	52	5 492	5 806	1 817	7 649	2 068	1 000	1 068	3 524	2 919	605	5 233

1. At the end of the period
2. Approved securities comprise securities issued by the government, local authorities, the Land Bank, Eskom and the Rand Water Board, and other securities approved by the Registrar of Unit Trust Companies
3. Market value of security holdings, plus cash, deposits and accrued income, less current liabilities, as at the end of the period
4. By the management companies
5. At selling prices. Including the exchange of shares, at market value, for an equivalent amount of units, at selling prices
6. At repurchase prices
7. At actual transaction values
8. At book value, as at the end of the period
Source: South African Reserve Bank

mortgage bond schemes, long and short-term insurance companies, pension and provident funds, unit trusts and other financial institutions. The distinction between the different types of financial institutions has been blurred by gradual extension and overlapping of activities, as has happened with financial deregulation in many other parts of the world.

The **South African Reserve Bank** formulates and implements monetary policy, and regulates the supply (availability) of money by influencing its cost. Monetary policy is guided by the mission of the Reserve Bank, formulated in 1990, to protect the domestic and external value of the rand. Consistent combating of inflation is therefore the cornerstone of the bank's policies. The Reserve Bank assumes responsibility for:

— assisting the South African government, as well as other members of the Economic Community of Southern Africa (Ecosa), in the formulation and implementation of macro-economic policy;
— formulating and implementing monetary policy in such a way that the primary goal of the Reserve Bank will be achieved in the interest of the entire community it serves;
— ensuring that the South African money and banking system as a whole is sound, meets the requirements of the community and keeps abreast of developments in international finance; and
— informing the South African community and all interested parties abroad about monetary policy specifically, and the South African economic situation in general.

The Reserve Bank is managed by a board of 14 directors of whom seven represent commerce and finance, industry and agriculture. The remaining seven, including the governor and three deputy governors, are appointed by the government. The governor usually acts as chairman of the board but the minister may also appoint another director to act in this capacity.

The bank has various instruments at its disposal to implement monetary policy. These are changes in the bank or discount rate; open-market transactions, changes in requirements with regard to cash reserves and liquid assets of banks and building societies and managing of the 'float' of the exchange rate.

The Reserve Bank issues South Africa's banknotes (printed by the SA Bank Note Company, wholly-owned subsidiary of the bank) and controls the SA Mint Company, also a wholly-owned subsidiary of the bank. The bank undertakes national and international transactions on behalf of the state and acts for the government in trans-

actions with the International Monetary Fund (IMF). The bank also advises on floating of new government stock issues on the local and overseas money markets, and is actively involved in buying and selling government securities. The Reserve Bank is the custodian of the country's gold and other foreign exchange reserves. All gold produced is sold to the bank, which decides on marketing of the precious metal, as well as on currencies and institutions in which foreign exchange reserves are kept.

The bank is also banker to other banking institutions. It is the custodian of the statutory cash reserves which all registered banks are required to maintain with it. It also provides facilities for clearing and settlement of interbank claims. South Africa now has three automated clearing bureaux, which in 1990 processed 336 million cheques (about one million every working day).

In 1986 it was decided that the bank should set specific target growth rates for the broadly defined money supply, M3, to assist the monetary authorities in their efforts to control the money supply with a view to curbing inflation. In 1990 the guideline rates for the M3 money supply were set at 11 to 15 per cent, i.e. three percentage points lower than the 14 to 18 per cent targeted in 1989. Actual growth in the money supply in 1990 amounted to 12 per cent — well within the guidelines.

South Africa has a dual **exchange rate** system — the commercial rand, used for international payments, which was trading between $0,35 and $0,42 in 1989, and the financial rand, a form of exchange control and at the same time an instrument for foreign investment, which traded at between $0,23 and $0,28 in 1989.

The financial rand system can be used by non-residents to repatriate capital from South Africa. For every seller (an investor who wishes to repatriate his funds) there must be a foreign buyer, who benefits by the substantial premium between the commercial and financial rands.

This system has no influence on the state of the country's foreign exchange reserves. All non-resident investors can invest financial rands freely on the Johannesburg Stock Exchange (JSE) and in unlisted companies, but application has to be made for permission to invest in certain other assets such as real estate.

Dividends on investments are freely transferable in commercial rand, and there has never been any restriction on such remittances.

The **Corporation for Public Deposits** accepts call money from public bodies and invests these funds in approved securities.

The main activity of the **Public Investment**

Table 6 Long-term insurance business*-assets (R 000), 1986-89

End of year	Stock and loans of or guaranteed by						Assets in the Republic							GRAND TOTAL
	Money in hand and with banks, building societies, etc	Government of Republic, a provincial administration and administration of Namibia	Local authorities and administration boards	Rand Water Board, Eskom and Land Bank	Stock of approved institutions	Stock of approved foreign governments, local authorities and institutions	Loans against policies	Mortgage bonds	Other claims	Stock of companies	Corporeal property	Claims against approved companies outside the Republic	Foreign assets	
1986	2 579 786	8 135 273	1 112 318	4 180 524	2 167 929	215 691	581 166	500 202	5 501 807	24 683 338	4 066 157	—	2 966 389	56 690 572
1987	5 519 227	8 709 728	1 692 813	4 773 805	2 476 537	191 970	639 398	502 093	7 337 034	37 465 298	4 760 034	105	3 359 684	77 427 726
1988	9 419 345	11 943 557	2 076 862	4 980 264	2 552 921	176 521	755 674	502 845	9 319 796	35 166 733	5 685 778	—	3 444 474	86 024 770
1989	11 862 667	13 339 518	2 259 663	5 159 240	2 703 931	258 991	946 408	589 789	12 204 501	56 697 010	9 184 432	—	6 671 063	121 877 213

Including professional reinsurers
Source: Annual Report of the Registrar of Insurance

Table 7 Short-term insurance business*-assets (R 000), 1986-89

End of year	Stocks and loans of or guaranteed by						Assets in the Republic							GRAND TOTAL
	Money in hand or with banks, building societies, etc	Government of Republic, a provincial administration and administration of Namibia	Local authorities and administration boards	Rand Water Board, Eskom and Land Bank	Stocks of approved institutions	Stocks of approved foreign governments, local authorities and institutions	Outstanding premiums	Mortgage bonds	Other claims	Stocks of companies	Corporeal property	Claims against approved companies outside the Republic	Foreign assets	
1986	921 446	890 259	64 284	370 306	69 067	20 295	333 299	76 865	422 202	1 458 719	103 318	—	229 465	4 959 525
1987	1 028 643	1 350 689	91 918	426 449	89 758	24 815	234 206	82 102	512 070	2 249 446	124 220	1 101	228 521	6 443 938
1988	1 539 455	1 518 501	101 625	563 764	121 213	16 053	277 721	103 742	740 961	2 775 733	167 155	0	219 246	8 145 169
1989	2 533 308	1 248 287	81 913	494 957	112 817	16 204	303 191	117 081	1 129 355	4 479 183	243 732	0	247 787	11 007 815

* Including professional reinsurers
Source: Annual Report of Registrar of Insurance

Commissioners is to manage pension funds, which various public authorities are required to hold with them, and invest these funds (now mostly long-term funds) in government and other securities.

The **Local Authorities Loans Fund** provides capital funds for loans to local authorities. The capital employed by the fund was R703,8 million at 31 March 1989.

The **Land and Agricultural Bank of South Africa** (the Land Bank) mobilises and lends funds for assistance to the country's farming community, agricultural co-operations and agricultural boards of control.

The **Development Bank of Southern Africa** is a multilateral institution, established in 1983, to support economic development in Southern Africa through loans, technical assistance and training to both governmental and non-governmental development agencies. Membership of the bank is open to independent Southern African states or, through associate membership, to countries outside Southern Africa.

The bank seeks to address the unacceptably large difference in the quality of life, access to economic opportunities and control over economic resources — both in respect of earnings in the market place and in provision of public goods and services — between different regions and sections of the population.

The bank's mission involves providing support to a sustainable development process that involves community involvement and the use of resources.

It promotes these interventions in ways that can mobilise private sector resources rather than simply extend the role of the already overburdened public sector.

The bank is also structured to administer grants from any local or overseas, public or private source for a development fund earmarked for specific development projects.

Activities of the bank occur within the nine development regions demarcated in terms of the common regional development policy adopted in 1982 and in Lesotho and Mozambique.

Over the seven years since inception the bank has approved 1 213 loans or grants of just over R5 billion for more than 700 projects and programmes. By the end of December 1990 there were 1 729 projects in the project cycle. A total of 67 new loans to the value of R238 million were approved by DBSA in the nine months from April to December in the 1990/91 financial year.

The bank's financial resources are made up of the share capital contributions of its members, contributions to its Development Fund, loans obtained from the financial markets, recoveries for agency functions performed and servicing of loans it has been granted. By December 1990 it had successfully raised R520 million in private-sector funding for development finance on the country's capital market since its maiden entry into the market in May 1990.

Private banking sector

An important recent development in the banking sector has been passing of the law on deposit-taking institutions, the Deposit-Taking Institutions Act, 1990. The concept which is central to the Act is the definition of a 'deposit'. This definition is wide and encompasses virtually all forms of money borrowing and lending transactions. This definition embodies the economic concept of intermediation and is aimed at regulating the business of deposit-taking to promote the financial soundness of the banking sector, thereby ensuring smooth functioning of the payments system and stability of the financial system.

Although the Registrar of Deposit-Taking Institutions may investigate the activities of an institution, declare it a deposit-taking institution and compel it to register as such, up to early 1991 only former banks, discount houses and equity building societies have been registered as deposit-taking institutions. The regulations pertaining to them are aimed at effective risk management by the institutions themselves and adequate disclosure of relevant information to the Registrar and the general public. In order to maintain prudence and safeguard the deposits of the general public, all institutions must comply with certain requirements in respect of paid-up share capital and unimpaired reserve funds, and with certain liquid asset and cash reserve requirements.

The Usury Act also affects the functioning of deposit-taking institutions in that it prescribes the maximum interest rates that may be charged by financial institutions on loans to the public.

Although current legislation does not distinguish between different kinds of deposit-taking institutions, the main business of these institutions may be used to classify them. It should, however, be remembered that competitive forces, amalgamations and takeovers have caused demarcation lines between the business of the various classes of monetary institutions to fade.

At the end of 1990 **commercial banks** offered a network of more than 3 100 branches and agencies. They offer a complete range of financial and related services. Commercial banks have also entered the insurance field either by forming new companies or purchasing equity in established institutions. Recently there have also been a number of mergers between banks and building societies.

Merchant banks deal with a few large depositors. Apart from acceptance credit activities, substantial lending operations in the form of loans, discounts and advances are undertaken. They assist companies as well as individuals with equity and loan-participation schemes, medium-term loans and bridging finance. They are experts in banking techniques, the money, capital, forward and future markets, foreign exchange regulations and dealings, import and export finance and lending techniques. As financial advisers, they are also fully conversant with stock exchange procedures and rules, company law, tax law, accounting techniques, funding sources, techniques of merger and acquisition, techniques of new issues and other technical exercises.

General banks offer a variety of banking, financial and related services to individuals as well as corporate concerns but have no cheque account facilities. Their services are concerned with monetising assets for industrial develop-

ment purposes; participation in the development of new ventures; provision of special services to both local and foreign investors; and extending hire-purchase credit and leasing finance. Some general banks have extensive branch systems.

Four institutions concentrated on **discount house** business at the end of 1990. They mobilise call money, which is then channelled into short-term official and non-official paper. Their activities are controlled by certain understandings regarding their portfolios with the Reserve Bank. They have rediscount facilities with the Reserve Bank and there is often close co-operation with merchant banks.

Although the initial difference between banks and building societies is fading, **building societies** still have an important place in the South African bond market. Although some building societies merged with banks in 1989, the total assets of the seven remaining institutions registered as building societies amounted to more than R28 billion at the end of 1989.

There are two kinds of building societies. Mutual building societies (of which there were three at the end of 1989) operating under the renamed Mutual Building Societies Act and building societies operating under the Building Societies Act. The latter group, of which there were four at the end of 1989, were originally

Table 8 Liabilities of merchant banks, 1989-90

End of year	Deposits							Capital and reserves				TOTAL ACCEPTANCE FACILITIES	
	Domestic					Foreign	Total deposits	Domes-tic	Foreign	Other liabilities	Total* liabilities	Utilised	Granted
		Fixed and notice											
	Demand	Short term	Medium term	Long term	Total								
1989	2 376	940	809	424	2 172	287	4 835	619	—	2 279	7 734	3 274	5 343
1990	2 641	660	743	1 159	2 562	599	5 802					2 380	2 402

* Excluding liabilities under acceptances

Table 9 Selected transactions of permanent building societies (R million), 1988-90

End of year	Liabilities to public for purposes of:		Liquid assets			New advances and re-advances granted during period			Mortgage loans paid out during period	Advances granted but not yet paid out	Capital repayments on mortgage loans
	Liquid asset require-ments	Prescribed investment require-ments	Total hold-ings	Excess hold-ings	Other finan-cials assets	Gross		Net loans total			
						Total	Build-ing loans				
1988	33 824	—	2 479	166	1 060	10 096	3 286	9 434	9 670	2 529	6 353
1989	28 828	—	2 311	98	1 029	7 978	2 319	7 392	6 525	1 961	5 052
1990	34 056	—	2 053	93	970	9 647	2 224	8 956	8 011	2 699	5 787

Source: South African Reserve Bank

registered as permanent building societies but, in terms of the new Act, gained equity status and their shares are now quoted on the JSE.

Although the original purpose of building societies — to attract genuine savings from the small saver — has been retained, these societies are now allowed to accept limited amounts of time deposits of less than 12 months in addition to limited amounts of negotiable certificates of deposits. They may also accept wholesale deposits. At the same time building societies are subject to the same liquid asset requirements as banks.

Insurance companies. The Insurance Act, 1943, provides for registration of both long-term and short-term insurers, including professional reinsurers operating in both the long-term and short-term markets and who accept risks from other insurers and reinsurers only.

The Act stipulates that the assets of long-term insurance business must be kept separate from any other business conducted by the insurer. A total of 93 insurers were registered under the Act on 31 December 1990. Of these, 36 were registered for long-term business only, 45 for short-term business only and 12 for both long-term and short-term business. The total included eight insurers which no longer issue new policies and whose existing business is gradually being run off as well as five insurers which conduct business in Namibia only.

Apart from registered insurers, the Act provides for licensing of agents to act on behalf of brokers or underwriters at Lloyd's of London.

The Pension Funds Act, 1956, provides for registration of **pension and provident funds** and orderly management of their affairs so that assets will be sufficient to pay the promised benefits to members or their dependents. Apart from funds from the private sector, there are another nine official pension funds for employees of the state and certain government institutions.

At the end of 1988 12 937 funds were registered under the Act with 5 123 551 members, of whom 499 652 were pensioners. These figures are not a true reflection of the number of members and pensioners because some persons are members and pensioners of more than one fund.

The Friendly Societies Act, 1956, provides for the establishment, management and control of **friendly societies**. There is a total of 158 self-administered societies. Of these, two were registered provisionally and 156 finally.

Unit trusts are registered in terms of the Unit Trusts Control Act, 1981. In operation at present are 31 open-end unit trust schemes in stock exchange securities and 16 closed-end schemes in

property shares. In terms of the Act, management companies must be approved and registered by the Registrar of Unit Trust Companies. A management company must have a capital of at least R2 million available for its unit trust operations. It must also show its intention of administering the trust in the interest of its unit holders by having its own resources at all times invested in every unit portfolio of the trust

Contributions by main sources of revenue to total collections, 1980/81 and 1990/91

1979/80

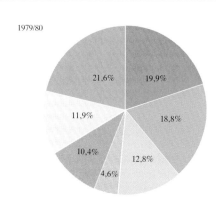

1990/91

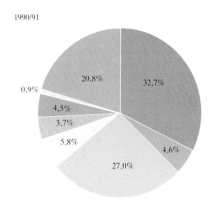

Income tax on individuals
Income tax on companies
Income tax on gold mines
Excise duty
Customs duty
Sales tax
Fuel levy
Other income

to an amount equal to at least 10 per cent of the underlying securities in such a unit portfolio.

The consent of the Registrar of Unit Trust Companies must be obtained to carry on participation bond business in terms of the Participation Bonds Act, 1981, which defines and secures the rights of those investing in **participation mortgage bonds**. The Act describes and defends the rights of people who have invested in participation mortgage bonds. By 31 December 1990, 38 participation mortgage schemes had been registered.

The **Johannesburg Stock Exchange** operates on the basis of a two-way auction market between brokers acting as agents for their clients. Stockbrokers can also deal for their own account and as arbitrageurs with foreign markets. The Stock Exchange is a member of the International Federation of Stock Exchanges.

The Financial Markets Control Act, 1989, came into effect on 10 August 1990. This Act provides for establishment of exchanges for trading of derivative instruments, such as futures and options contracts, and fixed interest-bearing instruments.

The South African Futures Exchange was licensed on the same day in terms of the same Act. At present this exchange trades futures contracts which are all cash-settled only. It plans to allow trading of option contracts soon. No formal exchange for trading of fixed interest-bearing instruments has yet been established.

News items: 1990

The self-governing territories were given far less budgetary assistance than had been requested. Allocations to the six states would be considerably less than the R3,5 billion of the 1989/90 financial year.

A total of 1,7 per cent of the total tax paying public paid 73 per cent of the country's tax in respect of the 1990 tax year.

The new Mint near Verwoerdburgstad will be one of the largest in the world on completion. I will produce approximately 2 000 million coins per year.

A new 5c coin was issued by the SA Mint in February, making it the second of nine new serie coins to be phased in over a two-year period. A new 1c coin was issued in September. A new 10c coin made of steel and plated with a mixture of copper and tin, came into circulation on 2 December.

The International Investment Bank of China opened for business in South Africa.

South Africa received R4 877 811 114 from the Customs Union Agreement, Transkei R548 915 000, Bophuthatswana R623 354 000, Venda R90 390 000, Ciskei R221 776 000, Botswana R467 548 000, Lesotho R263 643 000 and Swaziland R186 831 000.

Income tax totalling R30,46 million was written off as irrecoverable in the 1989/90 financial year.

After the first six months of the fiscal year the shortage before loans seemed about R1 000 million less in the current fiscal year than the R8 000 million budgeted for.

The big five wildlife animals will appear on the new series of banknotes instead of the portrait of Jan van Riebeeck, according to an announcement by the Minister of Finance in October.

Income from personal revenue in the 1990 tax year rose by 24,9 per cent.

Gold and foreign exchange holdings showed their biggest increase in years in December.

Acknowledgements:
Department of Finance
Development Bank of Southern Africa
South African Reserve Bank

South Africa with its diversity of animals and plants, its mineral resources and its kaleidoscope of socio-ethnic patterns is a natural laboratory offering scientists a unique opportunity for research. As the technological leaders in Africa, South African scientists have made important discoveries in widely diversified areas, the results of which have often also benefited other African countries and the rest of the world.

National research policy is the responsibility of the Minister of National Education, while the Minister of Trade, Industry and Tourism is responsible for technological policy.

They are assisted by the Scientific Advisory Council, the Chief Directorate of Science Planning in the Department of National Education, the Advisory Council for Technology and the Directorate for Technology Promotion in the Department of Trade and Industry.

The Associated Scientific and Technical Societies of South Africa (AS & TS) promote the interests of the various scientific, professional and technical disciplines and provide secretarial, liaison and club facilities for the constituent societies.

Surveys of resources (funds and manpower) devoted to research and development (R & D) are conducted biennially. The 15th report in this series — *Resources for R & D, 1987/88* — was released in 1989 and showed that total expenditure on R & D amounted to R1 329 million in 1987/88 (0,88 per cent of the gross domestic product — GDP). During the same year 39 237 people devoted about 52 per cent of their time to R & D.

The government sector supplied 38,3 per cent of R & D funds, the business sector (including state corporations) 41,3 per cent, the tertiary education sector 19,7 per cent and the non-profit and foreign sectors together about 0,8 per cent.

Of the R & D effort, 21,9 per cent was directed at the primary economic sectors, 31,8 per cent at the secondary sectors, 9,0 per cent at infrastructural services, 6,1 per cent at health services, 16,0 per cent at education and other community services and 15,2 per cent at the advancement of basic scientific knowledge.

There are various big research organisations in South Africa and research is done on nearly every possible area.

Scientific councils

Council for Scientific and Industrial Research (CSIR)

The CSIR is a market-orientated research, development and implementation organisation in the field of physical sciences and is a technology partner to its clients in the private and public sectors of the economy.

Its mission, as a leading source of multi-disciplinary and extensive scientific and technological expertise in South Africa, is to develop, transfer and apply new, improved or adapted scientific and technological expertise to strengthen industry, commerce and the supporting infrastructure. It also aims to protect the environment; to initiate and undertake fundamental research to develop innovative technologies of high potential market value and to provide extensive scientific and technical information services.

The CSIR also manages the SA Science and Technology offices in Washington, London, Bonn and Paris to promote exchange of scientific and technical information between South Africa and foreign scientists and scientific institutions.

The CSIR's research, development and implementation activities centre in 14 operational divisions namely: Building Technology; Aeronautical Systems Technology; Earth, Marine and Atmospheric Science and Technology; Energy Technology; Food Science and Technology; Forest Science and Technology; Information Services; Materials Science and Technology; Micro-electronics and Communications Technology; Textile Technology; Production Technology; Roads and Transport Technology; Water Technology; Advanced Computing and Decision Support.

Foundation for Research Development (FRD)

The FRD is an impartial statutory body responsible for promoting the provision of an appropriately skilled workforce for the scientific and technological sector to stimulate economic growth and socio-economic prosperity. This is achieved mainly through supporting individuals and programmes at universities, technikons and museums.

The FRD promotes national and international

science liaison and provides information to decision-makers on priorities and trends in science and technology.

Three national research facilities offering various opportunities for advanced scientific and technological training form part of the FRD. They are the National Accelerator Centre (NAC), the South African Astronomical Observatory (SAAO) and the Hartebeesthoek Radio Astronomy Observatory (HartRAO).

The FRD was established in 1984 as a part of the CSIR and became a separate entity in October 1990.

Council for Mineral Technology (Mintek)

Mintek is a research council, partly financed by the state. Its primary functions are to promote mineral technology by means of research, development and transferring of technology to industry and to foster establishment of new metallurgical ventures.

As a result of the Mineral Technology Act of 1989 Mintek is now an autonomous organisation, generating an increasing proportion of its income from contract research for South African and international companies. Its annual budget is around R70 million and it employs more than 900 people.

Mintek's important research stems from the need to increase earnings from mineral exports by turning them into products of higher value before they are exported. Mintek is closely involved in the identification and development of markets for minerals and beneficiated products.

Human Sciences Research Council (HSRC)

The HSRC is the national agency for research into the human sciences. It also advises the research community on research priorities to be undertaken in the national interest and on research methodologies, research co-ordination and implementation. Through its Centre for Science Development it financially assists research projects at universities, technikons and other research bodies.

In 1990 the HSRC was engaged in more than 800 research projects of which about 300 were completed. In addition a wide range of services and products were provided to a large number of private and public sector clients.

After an extensive organisation development programme during 1990, the HSRC consisted of five groups
—Human Resources (including human development, environmental management, human resources strategies and organisation development).

—Education (including educational assessment, learning and instructional design, psychology in education, and educational systems and strategies).
—Social Dynamics (including social security and care, political and constitutional matters, social development, and communication and contemporary culture).
—Information Dynamics (including the Centre for Research Methodology, Computer Centre, Mark Data, Centre for Statistics, product services and information network).
—Centre for Science Development (including funding, ecology of research, and research in science development).

During 1990 the HSRC completed a number of research projects, which included the following topics: Environmental management in a new democracy, squatters, training of Black managers, development of women in organisation, marketing of fresh produce, salary and wage surveys, training strategies, computer literacy, TV for education, literacy strategies, the results of victimisation, extension services, fighting in Natal/KwaZulu, group protection and violence on TV.

Medical Research Council (MRC)

The MRC is an independent statutory body which was established in terms of legislation in 1969. The council consists of 16 members, all of whom have distinguished themselves in a medical or other profession related to the MRC.

The MRC's main purpose is to promote the health of the South African population by means of research. This is done, among other things, by fulfilling a leading and co-ordinating role in the field of biomedical research, establishing research priorities and conducting or supporting fundamental and applied research on its own or in conjunction with experienced partners.

The MRC functions on a national basis and, in addition to international scientific contact, also maintains close contact with certain countries with whom it has concluded treaties of co-operation.

In 1990 the MRC realigned its research priorities under two groups. One focuses on community health research and the other on clinical and experimental research.

The MRC's research organisation reflects its dual action, through the institution of national programmes and through joint research. National programmes comprise medical research of national importance. For this purpose the MRC has its own institutes for research into nutritional illnesses, tuberculosis, illnesses in a tropical environment, environmental diseases, epidemiology and trauma. Research undertaken in conjunction with universities and other research institutions throughout the country includes research centres and units for diseases of the liver, hereditary deviations of the skeleton, organ transplants, Aids, circulation diseases, perinatal mortality and ischemic heart diseases.

South African Bureau of Standards (SABS)

The mission of the SABS is to contribute towards strengthening South Africa's economy and enhancing the quality of life of all its people by promoting quality and standardisation.

In carrying out its mission, the SABS, among other things, prepares and updates standards in collaboration with interest groups. It administers the Quality Mark Scheme in respect of products for which national standards exist, with the SABS Standardisation Marks serving as proof that the product meets the appropriate standard specification.

Organisations whose quality systems comply with the relevant standards are listed and audited. Consignments are inspected and tested on behalf of purchasers to verify conformance to agreed requirements. Goods are inspected, tested and analysed. Precision instruments, measuring and scientific apparatuses are tested and calibrated and certified reference materials are supplied (for test purposes).

In carrying out its functions, the SABS co-operates with government departments, local authorities, other public institutions and commerce and industry, as well as with the governments of other countries and international organisations.

General research areas

Energy

The National Energy Council (NEC) co-ordinates all policy-directed research in the field of energy. This includes transport energy, new and renewable energy and energy for developing areas, coal, electricity, energy efficiency, energy economy and forecasting, and energy communication.

Geological Survey

Geological Survey is a branch of the Department of Mineral and Energy Affairs in the Ministry of Mineral and Energy Affairs and Public Corporations. Its primary task is to create and maintain a geological knowledge infrastructure for South Africa as a basis for mineral exploration, mining

and construction activities, measures to promote optimal land use and minimising the detrimental effects of natural disasters such as floods and earthquakes.

For this purpose geological and geophysical engineering, geological, metallogenic and geochemical mapping, and research are carried out to document and unravel the geology of the subcontinent.

Other research organisations

The **Sasol** group of companies produce fuels, petrochemicals, fertilisers, explosives and tar and a variety of other products from coal. Research is undertaken by the R & D Department of Sasol Technology (Sastech), which has about 400 employees and a budget of more than R50 million (1990/91). Main research emphasis is on improvement of the Fischer-Tropsch synthesis, new processes, development of new products and improved raw material utilisation. Sasol also carries out research into synthetic fuels, catalysis, petrochemical product development, coal technology, gasification, biotechnology, environmental science and process development.

The Research and Process Development Department of **Iscor** has a total staff complement of 337, providing technical support for raw material provision and iron and steel production, as well as products. Recently indispensable contributions were made through provision of steel for the Mossgas project — for the offshore and onland (Mossref) structures — and the commissioning of Corex's direct reduction process.

Eskom's Engineering Investigations Division has laboratories for research into chemistry, process control, electrical engineering, mechanical engineering, materials and environmental sciences.

The **South African Institute for Medical Research** (SAIMR) was established to research prevention and treatment of human diseases. The Institute has approximately 2 400 employees and consists of four divisions: Research, diagnostic laboratory services, production (serum, vaccines and laboratory reagents) and teaching and training. Research is done on diseases and health dangers that are of specific importance to South Africa.

The **Bureau for Economic Research** (BER) at the University of Stellenbosch is an independent and objective economic research organisation rendering a service to organisations ranging from small one-man businesses to policy-makers at the highest level of government.

Agricultural research

Agricultural research is conducted by the Department of Agricultural Development, several universities and a variety of organisations in the private sector. Economic research related to agriculture is done by the Department of Agriculture.

The Department of Agricultural Development has a Chief Directorate: Agricultural Engineering and Water Supply consisting of three Directorates, namely Agricultural Mechanisation, Irrigation Engineering and Soil Conservation and Drilling Services.

The Directorate of Agricultural Mechanisation undertakes research, development, testing and technology transfer into agricultural implements, planning of mechanisation, agricultural structures, animal housing and agricultural energy sources.

The Directorate of Irrigation Engineering is responsible for research into irrigation engineering. This includes development and evaluation of irrigation equipment. In addition, it is responsible for technology transfer in irrigation, planning of state irrigation schemes, development of irrigation board projects and administration of the irrigation subsidy scheme for farmers.

The functions of the Directorate of Soil Conservation and Drilling Services include research, development and special investigations into soil conservation engineering; planning, design and construction of key soil conservation works; supplying engineering advice to regional soil conservation technicians, administration and technical control of subsidy schemes for soil conservation, bush control and flood assistance. The directorate carries out the department's countrywide state drilling programme by physical drilling work and related inspection services by 16 drilling inspectorates. This directorate administers financial aid programmes for state drilling as well as drilling by private drilling contractors for farmers.

The Directorate of Biometric and Datametric Services of the Department of Agricultural Development renders a biometric service to the research personnel of the department in planning experiments, analysis and interpretation of research results, as well as a datametric service of computerised support for the researchers and management of the department.

The **Citrus and Subtropical Fruit Research Institute** (Nelspruit, Transvaal) seeks to optimise the production and quality of citrus and subtropical crops, including coffee, tea, nuts and spices.

The **Tobacco and Cotton Research Institute** (Rustenburg, Transvaal) does fundamental research into aspects of quality in conjunction with the tobacco and cotton industry. Extensive applied research results in improved cultivation practices, cultivars and insect control programmes, enabling the farmer to produce a better quality of leaf tobacco and cotton fibre.

The **Vegetable and Ornamental Plant Research Institute** (Pretoria) aims to promote production of potatoes, vegetables and ornamental plants through research and business advice. Research on these crops is designed to develop improved cultivars through cultivation and selection. Because of increased public opposition to the use of chemicals greater attention is being devoted to development of disease-proof plants and studies on the biological control of diseases and plagues.

The **Fruit and Fruit Technology Research Institute** (FFTRI) at Stellenbosch is responsible on a national basis for all research regarding cultivation and after harvest technology of deciduous fruit and other appointed crops (berries, nuts, rooibos tea, dates, olives, kiwi fruit, figs and hops). The institute offers specialist advice to these associated industries, which market their products both locally and abroad.

The **Viticultural and Oenological Research Institute** (Stellenbosch) supports the wine, table and raisin grape industries through research and specialist advice. It also houses the national vinotheque, a collection of almost all the country's commercial wines.

The **Animal and Dairy Science Research Institute** (Pretoria) undertakes fundamental and applied research and provides auxiliary services to ensure an adequate supply of economically-produced animal protein and fibre through optimal production systems. Fields of research include various aspects of livestock production and quality, especially performance testing, nutrition, animal breeding, physiology, dairy science and meat science.

The **Grain Crops Research Institute** (Potchefstroom) researches summer grains (maize, grain sorghum, buckwheat, rice), small grains (wheat, oats, barley, rye, triticale) and oil and protein-rich seeds (groundnuts, sunflower, soy beans, dry beans, lupins and cowpeas).

The **Veterinary Research Institute** (Onderstepoort, Transvaal) conducts basic and applied research into diseases affecting all domesticated animals of economic importance to agriculture, as well as into public health risks arising from animal products. Vaccines are produced for most infectious animal diseases.

The **National Botanical Institute** (Pretoria), an amalgamation between the Botanical Research Institute and the National Botanical Gardens, is responsible for the collection, description and identification of South African plants and their preservation in the National Herbarium, along with research into taxonomy, anatomy and cytogenetics of indigenous plants. Studies are also undertaken on plant ecology and the economic potential of indigenous plants.

The **Soils and Irrigation Research Institute** (Pretoria) promotes optimal utilisation of natural agricultural resources, soil, water and climate, and contributes to protection of these resources. Specialised techniques are developed or adjusted to reach these goals. The institute also develops national agricultural resources information systems.

The **Plant Protection Research Institute** (Pretoria) undertakes fundamental and, in specific cases, applied research into the entomology, arachnology, nematology, acarology, plant pathology, plant bacteriology, plant virology and weeds. Apart from the research station at Rietondale (Pretoria), there are research units at Rosebank (Cape Town), Uitenhage, Stellenbosch, Saasveld, Cedara and Sabie.

The **Grassland Research Centre** (Pretoria) undertakes research on field and pasture plants to provide information for efficient utilisation.

The **Research Centre for Plant Biotechnology** (Pretoria) undertakes advanced biotechnological research into all agricultural crops to promote plant cultivation.

Water

Water research is co-ordinated by the Water Research Commission (WRC). The organisations most active in water research are various divisions of the CSIR, the Department of Water Affairs and the universities.

The main areas of research are the following: Surface hydrology; ground water; hydrometeorology; agricultural water utilisation; water pollution; municipal effluent; industrial water and effluent; drinking water; treatment technology; water ecosystems; transfer of information and technology.

The Division for Water Technology (DWT) of the CSIR specialises in research on water quality, including technology to meet effluent and water quality standards and to establish reclaimed water as an additional water source. The DWT is also a world leader in the biological monitoring of water to detect potentially toxic substances, as well as in research on activated sludge processes.

The Department of Environment Affairs is involved in water-related research activities through the Weather Bureau and the South African Forestry Research Institute. This institute is a world leader in the field of the effects of afforestation and veld management on quantity and quality of catchment water yield.

Fisheries

Research on South Africa's fish resources, their conservation and judicious exploitation is carried out by the Sea Fisheries Research Institute of the Department of Environment Affairs. Research is designed to provide parameters for estimates of stock sizes and optimal yields for the different fisheries.

Environmental research

The Chief Directorate: Environmental Conservation of the Department of Environment Affairs annually finances several research programmes covering a wide field. The programmes comprise subjects such as waste management and pollution, nature conservation, cultural conservation, rivers, the coastline and marine environment and the atmosphere. Some programmes are conducted in collaboration with the FRD and others are undertaken for the department by the CSIR. Research is also undertaken for the department by universities. Research on man-environment interaction sponsored by the department is co-ordinated within the Programme for Human Needs, Resources and the Environment by the HSRC.

The Weather Bureau functions under the Department of Environment Affairs, providing a weather service for South Africa. It issues weather forecasts and warnings for protection of life and property. A climatological service is provided for a wide range of users, including engineers, farmers, insurance companies, attorneys and researchers. A new monthly climatological report is published as soon as possible after the end of each month. The data is collected from selected stations and enables users to respond timeously to changing circumstances. Research and development work is carried out to improve the quality of these services but research of a more basic nature is also undertaken. Meteorologically aligned research and development work supporting and improving the above-mentioned services is of cardinal importance for the bureau.

A new satellite earth station has been installed and enables forecasters to monitor development of weather systems on a continuous basis.

Tourism

Research on tourism is co-ordinated through the research programme of the South African Tourism Board. Its research aim is to identify and utilise skilled resources that will serve the tourism industry on a continuing and long-term basis by collecting, processing, analysing, interpreting and making available relevant information, as well as by co-ordinating tourism research at national level so that the industry's decision and planning can be based on a sound foundation. The different research fields comprise domestic tourism, natural resources facilities and infrastructure, marketing and trade audit and financial and statistical analysis.

Private sector

Research on mining is carried out chiefly by the Chamber of Mines Research Organisation (Comro) and the large mining groups, while the Council for Mineral Technology (Mintek) conducts research into minerals.

Comro is an applied research and development organisation serving mainly member companies of the Chamber of Mines of South Africa. It is funded by the private sector.

South Africa's gold mining industry works on deeper levels and under more difficult circumstances than any other mining industry in the world. Comro's research on gold mining is primarily concerned with ensuring the health and safety of the workforce and covers the areas of rock engineering and the underground environment. In addition Comro conducts contract work with individual mining houses and mines on areas beyond its core programme of work.

Comro's coal mining research takes place on a smaller scale than that of gold mining, because the coal mining industry can make use of various overseas developments. Areas in which research is undertaken include strata control, mining, maximising extraction of coal and the underground environment.

Research is also carried out by a large number of industrial companies with facilities to meet their specific needs. Among the more important are the following:

Anglo American Corporation of South Africa (applied metallurgy, processing of precious metals, base metals and coal); Agricura (synthesis and testing of veterinary remedies, insecticides, herbicides; entomology); Cullinan Holdings (refractories and electrical porcelain); De Beers Industrial Diamond Division (manufacture and application of synthetic diamonds and other super-hard materials); Johannesburg Consolidated Investment Company (metallurgy, mineralogy, chemistry, chemical engineering); National Chemical Products (chemistry, microbiology and animal nutrition); Noristan (pharmacologically active compounds, pharmaceutical formulations); Metal Box Company of South Africa (corrosion mechanism, microbiology); Plessey (SA) (development of electronic instruments); Rembrandt Group (development and improvement of tobacco and liquor products); South African Pulp and Paper Industries (wood technology, paper manufacture, water treatment); Standard Telephones and Cables (SA) (long-distance transmission of information, lightning protection).

News items: 1990

Researchers of the department of microbiological pathology at Medunsa found a new cause for diarrhoea-related diseases in South Africa. They also developed a diagnostic technique to trace the germ more quickly.

In February a miniature horse received an artificial limb — a first in veterinary science for South Africa.

Also in February the HSRC announced development of a method of accurate population counting in Black residential areas by using aerial photographs.

The CSIR's external income rose from R166,9 million in 1988/89 to a budgeted R211,1 million in 1989/90. This was mainly due to the increase in research contracts — from about 2 500 in 1984 to the present more than 5 000.

An agreement to establish a research centre for improved breeding strains of racehorses was signed in Pretoria in February. The centre will be situated at the Faculty of Veterinary Science of the University of Pretoria at Onderstepoort.

During the year the HSRC started a study on the country's aged population. The survey will form the basis of a database which could be used for policy-making, planning and provision of services for the country's aged.

The South African research ship *RSA Africana* conducted a major research programme on Antarctic krill in the South Orkney/Elephant Island region of South Africa in February to evaluate the potential for the national exploitation of this food.

Armscor was declared company of the year in February by *Engineering Week,* an engineering magazine.

Prof Siegfried Petrick, head of the ophthalmology section of the Faculty of Veterinary Science of the University of Pretoria was one of two ophthalmologists from outside Europe who were invited to take part in a congress for veterinary surgeons held in Switzerland in March.

The international Coelacanth Trust was established in Johannesburg in March to save these 'living fossils' from extinction.

The HSRC was 21 years old in May.

Two Cape researchers were voted the best achievers in the national programme of the HSRC and the Scientific Advisory Council to determine which research projects can be applied most usefully in practice. Mr Ockert Augustyn of the oenology section of the Viticultural and Oenological Research Institute in Stellenbosch won first place, while Dr Johan van der Spuy of the Medical Research Council was second.

In May Mr Larry Leach, a researcher of the Department of Botany at the University of the North, became the first researcher in Africa to receive the Golden Cactus Prize from the International Association of Succulent Studies.

The University of Stellenbosch planned research on earth satellite systems after Grinaker Electronics (Grinel) announced a sponsorship for a chair in Earth Satellite Systems at the university in May.

In May Guinevere Kaufmann of the department of astronomy at the University of Cape Town became the first South African to receive the Zonta Amelia Earhart bursary.

In June the Overberg missile-testing range near De Hoop in the southern Cape won the Armscor Environmental Management Award for successfully preserving the nine sensitive ecological systems in the area.

A national code of ethics aimed at protecting animals against unnecessary abuse in experimental laboratories was announced by the Minister of Agriculture in August.

A Division of Forest Science and Technology was established at the CSIR in Pretoria in August after a government decision to rationalise research on timber.

From 1 September the Overberg and the coastal region up to Mossel Bay was given its own weather forecast. In the past this region's weather was incorporated with that of the Peninsula and the Boland.

In October the South African Bureau of Standards (SABS) and the equivalent German organisation (DQS) signed an agreement in terms of which each will accept the other's quality system certification.

Dr Brian Clark succeeded Dr Chris Garbers as president of the CSIR on 1 October.

Dr Brian Clark, President of the CSIR, said South Africa compared well internationally in five scientific fields: Ornithology, zoology, water resources, ecology and general and internal medicine.

The South African Bureau of Standards promoted greater awareness of quality during Standards Week from 8—14 October.

The FRD was established as an independent statutory research council, apart from the CSIR, on 1 October. Dr Reinhardt Arndt is the first president of the independent FRD and Dr Chris Garbers, former president of the CSIR, the first chairman of the FRD board.

The MRC celebrated 21 years of medical research in South Africa in September. The MRC's Gold Medal for Outstanding Achievement was awarded posthumously to Prof George Findlay for his work on dermatology and for furthering medical knowledge. Nine silver medals for excellent service were also awarded to researchers during the MRC's 21st celebrations.

Five South Africans visited the Republic of China in October to take part in a meeting on biomedical engineering.

In November researchers of the University of Stellenbosch used advanced space computer programmes to develop a wheelchair specifically for 'African circumstances'.

The MRC's Exploratorium, believed to be the first in the world to be dedicated to medicine, opened at the SA Museum in Cape Town in November.

In November Dr Walter Prozesky, Deputy President of the MRC, was elected a Fellow of the Royal Society of South Africa in recognition of his contribution to science. The society has 112 fellows.

A group of Aids specialists from African countries visited South Africa at the invitation of the MRC in November. The group came to find out more about the country's Aids research programmes and to assess the extent of Aids in Southern Africa.

A fossil, probably that of a Vjoesjkovia, an animal which lived about 210 million years ago, previously found only in the Soviet Union and

China, was found near Paul Roux in the eastern
Orange Free State in November.

A river research programme was started by the
FRD in the Kruger Park in November as the
future of five major rivers — the Crocodile,
Sabie, Olifants, Letaba and Luvuvhu — caused
concern.

In November the President's Award of the
Foundation for Research Development went to
Dr Ahmed Barwa, a lecturer in physics at the
University of Durban-Westville.

In December the CSIR announced a project
to undertake research into the disposal of
sewage via offshore pipelines at a cost of approximately R205 000.

Professor Margaret Smith and Dr Philip
Heemstra received the R20 000 Bill Venter
award for the most outstanding publication by
university personnel for their book *Smith's Sea
Fishes* in December.

South African medical history was made in
December when the eyes of an elderly Cape
Town woman who had suffered from retinitis
pigmentosa were removed for research purposes
after her death. One was sent to Britain and the
other kept at the University of Cape Town.

The Planetarium at the Witwatersrand
University in Johannesburg celebrated its 30th
anniversary in December.

Mr Cornel Engelbrecht invented a throw-away
cardboard shopping trolley which was patented
worldwide in December.

Acknowledgements:

Chamber of Mines
Council for Mineral Technology (Mintek)
Department of Agricultural Development
Department of Environment Affairs (including the Weather Bureau & Sea Fisheries Research
  Institute)
Department of Mineral and Energy Affairs (including the Minerals Bureau & Geological Survey)
Eskom
Human Sciences Research Council (HSRC)
Iscor
Medical Research Council (MRC)
Sasol
South African Bureau of Standards (SABS)
South African Institute for Medical Research (SAIMR)
South African Tourism Board (Satoer)
The CSIR
Foundation for Research Development (FRD)
Water Research Commission

In the RSA 'own' affair administrations are responsible for specific aspects of government, such as provision of education for Whites, Coloureds and Indians. At the same time there are separate departments of education for the self-governing Black territories (KwaZulu, Lebowa, Gazankulu, Qwaqwa, KwaNdebele and KaNgwane) and in the four Black independent states (Transkei, Bophuthatswana, Venda and Ciskei). In these territories and states the responsibility for education rests with the department of the state or territory concerned.

Central government controls provision of education for Blacks living in the RSA outside the self-governing territories and the independent states. The Department of Education and Training carries out this task.

In the past, each cultural community controlled its own education policy and segregation was enforced by law. Although primary and secondary education is still officially organised along racial lines, some state and many private schools have accepted pupils from different race groups. Of approximately 1 700 White schools, more than 200 opened their doors to all race groups in 1991. Almost all the approximately 200 private schools were already open. The 17 500 schools originally established for Blacks, Indians and Coloureds are, for all practical purposes, already open to children of all race groups.

South Africa's education system has to provide for 11 language groups. Two of these, Afrikaans and English, are official languages, which all have to learn to be able to enter the labour market.

The same basic content and subject matter are prescribed for all schools in the RSA although content and method are adapted to pupils' needs and abilities.

Expansion of primary education facilities is still a vital component of the overall programme for Black education, but because a large number of Blacks fail to register the birth of their children, planning is considerably impeded. Invariably, more children than expected arrive at school on the first day.

Education in all state-aided schools is at present provided free of charge up to the end of the senior secondary school phase. Private institutions are subsidised by the state.

Compulsory education

Except for Black children, school attendance is compulsory for all children between the ages of 7 and 16. Under normal circumstances this entails education in the junior primary, senior primary and junior secondary phases (each of three years' duration), and an additional one year of the three year senior secondary phase.

Differentiation in education

There is a variety of educational institutions to cater for the diversity of pupil and student needs, aptitudes and interests.

The medium of instruction varies from school to school to suit the needs of the particular community. As far as possible the child's mother tongue serves as the medium of instruction. There are state and state-aided schools with either Afrikaans or English as the medium of instruction. In some cases provision is made for both Afrikaans and English-speaking children in the same school, but they are taught in separate classes.

In most Black schools the initial medium of instruction is the child's home language (an indigenous language such as Zulu, Xhosa, Sotho, etc.). During the first few years (usually four) the Black child is taught one of the official languages, English or Afrikaans, to enable him to study mainly through the medium of English or Afrikaans from his fifth school year.

Facilities are provided for pupils to study in specific career-oriented directions. There are, for instance, agricultural, commercial and technical schools and colleges which pupils attend full-time after they have completed the primary phases of their education.

Special education is offered at schools for the handicapped such as the blind, partially-sighted, deaf, epileptic, cerebral palsied and autistic, those with learning disabilities or other physical handicaps. There are training centres for the mentally-handicapped while child-care, reform and industrial schools also train children.

Pupils with specific interests or needs may attend special schools or classes on a part-time basis to study, for example, music, art, ballet and drama. Special facilities are also provided for remedial education and for gifted pupils.

Education in the senior secondary school phase is differentiated horizontally (choice of subject and subject matter) as well as vertically (different levels of difficulty) to suit the individual student's needs, abilities and interests.

Pupils unable to make satisfactory progress in an ordinary school are referred to classes or schools for slow learners.

Auxiliary services

Numerous auxiliary and support services are available. Some have been tailored to meet the specific needs of a department while others accommodate the needs on a national level.

An example of a service catering for specific needs is one introduced for Black schools. Panels consisting of staff specially trained to handle children with behavioural or other problems are being formed at all schools. A mentor system has been introduced in conjunction with these panels, the mentors seeking to build a relationship of trust with all pupils in their groups.

In the field of research, complete braille systems have been standardised in five African languages and braille typewriters and other special equipment, including taped material, are used in schools for the blind.

Table 1 Number of educational institutions for 1990*

	Public ordinary school education	Special school education	Private ordinary school education	Technical college education	Teacher training	Technikons	Universities
House of Assembly Cape	970	28	62	21	6	2	4
Natal	369	11	59	9	3	1	1
OFS	278	5	4	5	1	1	1
Transvaal	1 707	45	129	35	6	4	5
Total	3 324	89	254	70	16	8	11
House of Delegates Cape	9	—	1	—	—	—	—
Natal	359	14	24	3	1	1	1
OFS	—	—	—	—	—	—	—
Transvaal	79	4	5	—	1	—	—
Total	438	18	30	3	2	1	1
House of Representatives Cape	1 793	52	13	12	11	1	1
Natal	65	4	1	1	1	—	—
OFS	47	—	—	—	—	—	—
Transvaal	105	4	3	1	1	—	—
TOTAL	2 010	60	17	14	13	1	1
Black people Cape	1 130	11	10	4	4	—	—
Natal	808	9	12	2	1	—	1
OFS	2 670	4	13	3	2	—	—
Transvaal	3 111	20	26	13	8	1	3
Gazankulu*	504	1	—	1	3	—	—
KaNgwane*	277	—	—	1	2	—	—
KwaZulu*	3 107	7	8	9	10	1	—
Lebowa*	1 888	2	14	6	8	—	—
Qwaqwa*	198	1	—	2	3	—	—
KwaNdebele	220	—	—	1	1	—	—
TOTAL	13 913	55	83	42	42	2	4
GRAND TOTAL	19 694	222	384	129	73	12	17

* Self-governing territories
** All figures are preliminary
Source: Department of National Education, Preliminary Education Statistics for 1990, NATED 02-214 (90/08)

A number of national services are provided

— The National Film Library provides video casettes, films and computer software for schools and other educational institutions. Educational software is used in teaching and training programmes.

— The Foundation for Education, Science and Technology (Fest) publishes a number of cultural and scientific magazines, some of which are designed to provide support for teachers in the classroom. It also administers an annual national Science Olympiad, while other bodies organise olympiads in a number of other fields.

— The Section for the Evaluation of Qualifications functions under the auspices of the Committee of Heads of Education and provides evaluation of qualifications on request to determine whether holders of qualifications may be employed in education in the RSA or not.

Pre-primary education

Facilities for free pre-primary education have been provided on a limited scale by most education departments. Classes and schools established by private initiative are subsidised by the state. Any person or organisation may start a pre-primary school without government aid, provided that such a school is registered and its activities are controlled by a state department of education.

Ordinary primary and secondary education

Pupils enrol for junior primary education at the beginning of the year in which they turn six or seven. The junior primary phase lasts for three years. Basic learning activities during this phase involve learning to read, write and calculate, broadening of the pupil's knowledge of the world in which he lives and development of his language proficiency. Basic living, thinking and behavioural skills are also taught. A start is made at learning one additional language.

After the junior primary phase he progresses to the three-year senior primary phase. During this time learning activities centre on reading and oral proficiency in the mother tongue and the second language, mathematics, history, geography, general science and a skill such as needlework, woodwork and/or handwork.

Table 2 Headcount of pupils/students for 1990*

Population group	Public ordinary school education	Special school education	Private ordinary school education	Technical college education	Teacher training	Technikons	Universities	TOTAL
Whites	971 587	14 969	52 801	48 852	9 467	53 795	153 807	1 305 278
Indians	242 323	5 580	5 904	5 976	734	5 864	18 854	285 235
Coloureds	847 647	6 558	7 865	4 625	7 636	6 942	18 112	899 385
Black people Self-governing territories	3 317 895	1 934	7 210	4 595	21 733	1 369	—	3 354 736
Rest of RSA	2 167 103	5 036	30 074	8 126	10 514	15 454	96 137	2 332 444
TOTAL	5 484 998	6 970	37 284	12 721	32 247	16 823	96 137	5 687 180
GRAND TOTAL	7 546 555	34 077	103 854	72 174	50 084	83 424	286 910	8 177 078

* All figures are preliminary
Source: Department of National Education, Preliminary Education Statistics for 1990, NATED 02-214 (90/08)

Table 3 Number of teaching personnel for 1990*

Population group	Public ordinary schools	Special schools	Private ordinary schools	Technical colleges	Teacher training colleges	Technikons	Universities	TOTAL
Whites	69 265	4 429	5 738	3 215	3 069	3 798	16 838	106 352
Indians	13 301	1 066	92	192	255	391	1 248	16 545
Coloureds	46 375	2 222	331	645	1 187	586	3 610	54 956
Black people	157 354	2 622	3 436	1 454	3 894	1 334	9 230	179 324
Self-governing territories	80 728	509	223	594	2 375	120	—	84 549
Rest of RSA	76 626	2 113	3 213	860	1 519	1 214	9 230	94 775

* All figures are preliminary
Source Department of National Education, Preliminary Education Statistics for 1990, NATED 02-214 (90/08)

At about 12 or 13 the pupil reaches the three-year junior secondary school phase. While his general knowledge of the common academic subject is broadening, he is also being prepared to make a career choice.

Pupils who have passed the junior secondary phase, enter the three-year senior secondary phase. They are allowed, however, to leave the school system when they turn 16. At the end of the senior secondary phase they write a public examination in six subjects. The examination in each subject is conducted on a maximum of three levels, e.g. Higher Grade, Standard Grade and Lower Grade.

Certificates are issued to successful students indicating the subjects and level on which they were taken, as well as the student's achievement in each subject.

Education for the gifted

Differentiated education within the internal school set-up enables gifted pupils countrywide to study more subjects on the higher, more comprehensive grade and to pass Std 10 with more than the required number of subjects. Pupils who complete one or more subjects before their final matric examination can start university courses.

Education for the gifted is not limited to the classroom but includes excursions, visits to museums, planetariums and the theatre. Special attention is devoted to creativity and the leadership characteristics commonly found among gifted children are encouraged.

Tertiary education

Post-school career oriented training is offered at several institutions:

Universities

Requirements for university entry are set by the Joint Matriculation Board (JMB). Departmental senior and school-leaving certificates are recognised for university entry if they meet certain criteria set by the JMB.

In South Africa (excluding the independent states) there are 17 universities, all of which accept undergraduate and post-graduate students of all population groups.

Unisa, which has developed into the largest teletuition university in the world, caters for students from all over the world.

All universities are autonomous institutions and their affairs are managed by their own coun-

cils and senates. They are subsidised by the state. Subsidies account for the greater part of the gross income of most universities.

Each university has its own Students' Representative Council (SRC) elected by the students to promote their interests.

The nature of the courses is highly professional and scientific and includes a sound degree of empirical and theoretical research.

Technikons

There are 12 technikons which offer training in a host of technical and other disciplines at the post-senior certificate level. (See table 3)

Technikon RSA instructs students by correspondence.

Courses are offered in commerce, industry,

Table 4 Teacher training colleges: Headcount for 1990*

Population group	Diplomas providing training up to a level of three years past std 10	Diplomas providing training up to a level of more than three years past Std 10	TOTAL
Whites	655	8 812	9 467
Indians	201	533	734
Coloureds	5 565	2 071	7 636
Black people Self-governing territories	21 733	—	21 733
Rest of RSA	10 319	195	10 514
TOTAL	32 052	195	32 247
GRAND TOTAL	38 473	11 611	50 084

* All figures are preliminary
Source: Department of National Education, Preliminary Education Statistics for 1990, NATED 02-214 (90/08)

Table 5 Technikons: Headcount of enrolled students for 1990*

Technikon	Male	Female	TOTAL
Cape	4 330	2 540	6 870
Northern Transvaal	1 910	890	2 800
Mangosuthu	995	374	1 369
ML Sultan	2 839	2 111	4 950
Natal	3 047	2 481	5 528
OFS	1 494	1 511	3 005
Peninsula	2 636	1 724	4 360
Port Elizabeth	2 529	1 446	3 975
Pretoria	5 648	4 216	9 864
RSA	22 675	5 475	28 150
Vaal Triangle	2 837	1 555	4 392
Witwatersrand	5 415	2 770	8 185

* All figures are preliminary
Source: Department of National Education, Preliminary Education Statistics for 1990, NATED 02-214 (90/08)

agriculture, health, engineering, art and design,
technology and the performing arts. The general
nature of the course is less practical than those
offered at the technical colleges but more prac-
ical than those of the universities. A fair amount
of theory, planning and design is included.

The levels of training, examination and certification extend from T1 to T6 (Laureatus).

Technical colleges and institutes

Technical colleges and institutes offer post-
school vocational education. The major
categories of students are school leavers requiring career-oriented training, adults who want to
improve their qualifications and persons seeking
retraining for another vocation, or training in
handicraft, commercial, social and community-
oriented courses. The courses at these institutions are usually, but not necessarily, followed by
students who have left ordinary school without
completing the senior secondary phase. The
courses offered include courses in all types of
commercial, industrial, agricultural and engineering skills. The courses are very practically
oriented and include theory and design. The
levels of training, examination and certification
extend from N1 to N6. National examinations are
conducted for all courses offered by the institutions.

These colleges are regarded as community
centres and offer a wide range of formal and
non-formal courses to prepare students for
employment in commerce and industry. Indentured apprentices receive their theoretical training at these colleges before they undergo the
standard trade tests to qualify for full artisan
status. Employers usually release apprentices
for a quarter each year to attend theory lectures
for a period of 13 weeks.

Teacher training

Most secondary school teachers and, to a lesser
extent, primary and pre-primary school teachers
are trained at universities. Universities also offer
courses for teachers in highly specialised areas,
for example in schools for the deaf, blind, mentally retarded, etc. Advanced training for
teachers, such as B.Ed, D.Ed and Ph.D degrees,
is also offered by the universities.

Departmental colleges of education offer
three to four-year diploma courses for primary
school teachers and, to a lesser extent, for secondary school teachers.

Practising teachers can also enrol for distance
education with Vista University, the University
of South Africa and several departmental colleges for further training.

Table 6 Technikons: Permanent appoint-
ments for 1990*

Technikon	Number of personnel		
	Male	Female	TOTAL
Cape	369	298	667
Northern Transvaal	189	155	344
Mangosuthu	165	94	259
ML Sultan	240	87	327
Natal	448	242	690
OFS	86	98	184
Peninsula	312	136	448
Port Elizabeth	207	148	355
Pretoria	611	492	1 103
RSA	120	260	380
Vaal Triangle	221	288	509
Witwatersrand	434	410	844

* All figures are preliminary
Source: Department of National Education, Preliminary Education Statistics, 1990 NATED 02-214 (90/08)

Table 7 Universities

University	Type	Enrolment 1989	Language medium	Personnel 1990*
Cape Town	Residential	13 322	English	2 932
Durban-Westville	Residential	7 308	English	1 018
Medunsa	Residential	1 806	English	1 099
Natal	Residential	12 158	English	2 819
North	Residential	9 207	English	1 258
Orange Free State	Residential	9 078	Afrikaans	1 768
Port Elizabeth	Residential	4 698	English/Afrikaans	729
Potchefstroom	Residential	8 717	Afrikaans	3 724
Pretoria	Residential	21 875	Afrikaans	3 724
Rand Afrikaans	Residential	8 569	Afrikaans	906
Rhodes	Residential	3 679	English	1 113
South Africa	Teletuition	113 204	English/Afrikaans	2 647
Stellenbosch	Residential	13 827	Afrikaans	2 981
Vista	Distance education	23 833	English	624
Western Cape	Residential	11 718	English/Afrikaans	1 574
Witwatersrand	Residential	17 923	English	3 159
Zululand	Residential	5 520	English	775

* All figures are preliminary
Source: Department of National Education, Preliminary Education Statistics for 1990, NATED 02-214 (90/08)

Adult education

The DET runs a comprehensive adult education programme to promote literacy and numeracy among adult Black people who have never attended school, or to give those with some schooling the opportunity to improve their qualifications.

A system of part-time classes has been introduced in many areas to promote literacy and numeracy among those Coloured adults who have never had any formal schooling or who attended school for only a short period. Formal primary and secondary education are also offered for those who wish to improve their educational qualifications.

Prevocational and vocational training

A number of institutions specialising in training of adults in specific vocational skills have been

Twelve technikons and 17 universities provide post-senior certificate education to students

established. Motor-mechanic, panel-beating, electrical, electronic, welding, building, commercial and engineering skills are involved.

A system of part-time classes has been introduced to promote literacy and numeracy among people who have never had any formal schooling or have attended school for only a short period. This system also provides for formal primary and secondary education for those who wish to improve their school education qualifications. There are also part-time classes for the benefit of people interested in learning useful skills, such as gardening, cookery, needlework and other home-making skills for women including skills for men such as woodwork and building.

Prevocational and vocational training is provided for the general public and for specific groups according to particular needs.

Correspondence colleges and private vocational schools make an important contribution to education in general. The Correspondence College Council in Johannesburg, a statutory body, exercises control over correspondence colleges and ensures acceptable standards. All private correspondence colleges must be registered with this council.

Foundation for Education, Science and Technology (FEST)

FEST resorts under the Department of National Education. Its main aim is promotion of knowledge and culture among all population groups in South Africa. FEST publishes journals including *Lantern, Spectrum, Archimedes, Klasgids, Crux* and *Our art I, II and III* and is involved in administration of the *Tydskrif vir Letterkunde.* FEST organises the annual National Youth Science Olympiad for pupils in the RSA and self-governing territories. The 100 top achievers attend the National Science Week in Johannesburg and Pretoria and about 26 top achievers attend the International Youth Science Fortnight in London. FEST annually organises two Afrikaans Olympiads, one of which is for pupils studying Afrikaans as a second language. Every second year a mathematics and science convention is held for teachers of all population groups.

News items: 1990

January
The National Education Crisis Committee (NECC) held talks with the government to evaluate the examination process in Black education. At the same meeting in January it was agreed to extend the deadline for the registration of pupils by another week.

About 72 000 pupils from schools of the Department of Education and Training were involved in stayaway actions from 24 January to 13 February. This implies that more than 15 per cent of all Black pupils in these schools received no education for three weeks.

February
Santam Insurance announced 10 bursaries of R2 000 each to art students at universities or technikons throughout South Africa.

Dr E P Ndaba was appointed regional chief director of the Natal Region of the Department of Education and Training, thus becoming the highest ranking Black official in the public service.

March
The top management of the Federal Teacher's Council undertook a study tour of America, Britain and several European countries.

According to Dr Boet Schoeman, deputy director-general of the Department of National Health and Population Development, about 55 per cent of all adult Blacks employed have five years or less education and about half of Black and Coloured children leave school before completing Std 2.

A centre for assisting dyslexia-sufferers of all ages was opened at the Technikon, Pretoria.

Pupils of the Afrikaanse Hoër Meisieskool, Pretoria, were the overall winners of a competition held by the South African Guild for Speech and Drama Education.

The government allocated R1 000 million to end high-priority backlogs of such facilities as classrooms among disadvantaged South Africans.

South Africa's first school of writing, known as the ATKV School for Writing, was opened in Potchefstroom.

A R5 million educational foundation, Mentor, was founded by the Institute of Chartered Secretaries and Administrators. It will provide business education for a wide spectrum of deserving students who would not otherwise have the funds to study.

Education at 820 of the 2 069 Black public schools of the Department of Education and Training was disrupted due to violence and strikes by teachers — a total of 11 646, or 20 per cent, of teachers took part in the schools boycott.

April

In April the total female illiteracy rate in South Africa was 28 per cent. Statistics for the various population groups were: Asian — 22 per cent; Blacks — 53 per cent; White — 1 per cent; Coloured — 35 per cent.

The International Year of Literacy was launched on 4 April.

Due to reduced quotas, a total of 3 565 fewer students were accepted at the teachers' colleges of the Department of Education and Culture.

The government allocated R184-million for the salary adjustment of female teachers.

May

In May classes at 29 Coloured schools around Johannesburg came to a standstill, as teachers demanded better working conditions.

The Gary Player Foundation, in partnership with a number of international companies, opened the first of an intended series of farm schools near Lanseria Airport, Johannesburg.

A draft syllabus for the physical education of mentally handicapped children was implemented in special schools in the Transvaal and by May the pupils' co-ordination and use of upper limbs had improved by 87 per cent.

According to an investigation carried out by the HSRC, the attitude of Black pupils to Afrikaans varied from neutral to positive.

The government embarked on a policy according to which empty White schools are sold for use by pupils of other race groups. A total of 26 empty or under-utilised schools were converted to Coloured, Black and Indian schools in June. Countrywide there were 177 225 fewer pupils in White primary and secondary schools.

June

Coloured teachers at schools in Eersterus went on strike from 7 June in sympathy with the Progressive Teachers Union (PTU), and this resulted in examinations having to be postponed indefinitely. Education in Soweto came to a standstill, thus affecting the future of 219 000 pupils. The largest recognised teacher organisation in the country, the National Teachers' Unity Forum (NTUF) broke ties with Mr Gene Louw, Minister of National Education. The NTUF was later joined by the Transvaalse Onderwysersvereniging and the Teachers' Federal Council.

According to the Department of Education and Training only 30 per cent of the syllabus is covered at Sowetan schools.

A record number of 2 835 entries were received for the Suid-Afrikaanse Akademie vir Wetenskap en Kuns/Trek Petroleum History Olympiad.

Ten high school pupils received bursaries of R2 000 each in Santam Insurance's art project for school leavers.

Prof Flip Smit was elected Vice-Chancellor and Rector of the University of Pretoria.

The HJM Retief Laboratory for Reading Science, the first of its kind in South Africa, was opened in Pretoria.

Sanlam donated R100 000 to the Urban Foundation for the advancement of science education among Black pupils in the Transvaal.

The College for Continued Education in Graaff-Reinet was handed over to the Police as an Academy for Tertiary Education with effect from January 1991. The first principal will be General Johan Coetzee, former Commissioner of Police.

July

Pupils in the Soweto and Alexandria areas returned to school on 10 July when Transvaal schools falling under the Department of Education and Training officially opened for the third term.

The government allocated a sum of R8 million to alleviate the problem of a textbook shortage in Black schools. Shortages arise because of the consistent failure of pupils over a number of years to return books lent to them.

A competition held by the Educational Opportunities Council and the American Information School resulted in a total of 117 Black students leaving for the US to study in education-related fields.

August

The Department of Education and Training approved a further 6 824 classrooms for Black pupils in the eastern and western Cape.

Professor Ephraim Mokgokong was elected new Vice-Principal of the Medical University of Southern Africa (Medunsa).

Parliament was informed in August that the pupil population of the Department of Education and Training had increased by about 80 000 in a year.

September

Dr Stoffel van der Merwe, Minister of Education and Training, agreed to postpone examinations for Black matrics by one week and announced that a larger group of candidates would be allowed to enter for supplementary examinations in a bid to accommodate demands for deferment.

The government announced three additional education models for White schools. Model A deals with private schools which will be established on the closure of state schools and which will be subsidised for 45 per cent of their running costs. This model has additional financial implications for parents and could become operative as from 1991. Model B deals with state schools wishing to change their requirements for admission within the stipulations of the Constitution. Model B will have no financial implications for parents and can be implemented from 1991. Model C deals with state aided schools which require legislation and can be implemented from a later stage.

By September about 90 000 non-matrics in Soweto had been taught only between 10 and 50 per cent of the year's curriculum because of school boycotts by teachers.

More than 2 000 Black mathematics and science teachers underwent supplementary training at the Northern Natal Learning Resource Centre (Siza) outside Newcastle.

October
Matric examinations of the DET began on 30 October and about 249 000 full-time candidates were expected to sit the exam at 1 725 centres. Those who did not pass, would be able to sit for the supplementary examinations in March and May/June 1991 on condition that they met with certain requirements.

Two vacant, former White, state-run primary schools in Johannesburg were offered to Black private schools.

The Transvaal Education Department announced that eight White schools in the Transvaal would close due to declining numbers.

By October a total of 177 225 places in White schools were empty.

November
The British government announced a scholarship scheme valued at R250 000 a year to honour former MP Mrs Helen Suzman. The scheme was established to help 20 Black women to study at the University of the Witwatersrand every year.

In an effort to correct the picture of SA presented in German schools, material provided by the Embassy in Bonn formed part of the curriculum in 350 German schools after November.

December
Coloured matrics achieved a record-breaking 79 per cent pass rate. The pass rate for students falling under the House of Delegates was 95 per cent.

Dr Mamphele Ramphele in December became the first Black woman to be appointed Vice-Chancellor of the University of Cape Town.

The Department of Education and Training returned the worst matric results in its history with a pass rate of 36,4 per cent.

General
Mr Gavin Relly, former chairman of Anglo American, was appointed Chancellor of the Rhodes University as from 1 December.

More than R58 million worth of damages was done to schools by pupils during the unrest of the past eight years.

According to the Department of Education and Training a total of 898 primary and secondary classrooms, which can accommodate 33 000 pupils, were built at Black schools in 1989.

Vista University is one of the fastest-growing universities in the country and has campuses in Mamelodi, Bloemfontein, Port Elizabeth, Soweto, the East Rand, Welkom and Kimberley, as well as a campus for correspondence tuition.

Altough there was a drop of 4 000 in the number of registration figures at the University of South Africa, it had the highest enrolment of students in the country, followed by the universities of Pretoria and the Witwatersrand.

Mr Sam Pellissier, principal of Sasolburg High School, was the first winner of the prestigious National Technotron Prize of R50 000 which will in future be awarded to the most innovative and inspiring teacher of mathematics and science.

Since schools falling under the jurisdiction of the House of Delegates were opened to all races at the beginning of the year, a total of 8 000 students other than Indians have registered at these schools.

St Alban's College, Pretoria, conducted classes called Matric Upgrade as part of its Outreach programme to bring education to disadvantaged communities. More than R1,5 million was budgeted for the programme's bursaries and projects.

The president of the CSIR, Dr Chris Garbers, was appointed Chancellor of Unisa.

A total of 457 families in six Southern African Black residential areas benefitted from the Israeli Home Instruction Programme for Pre-School Youngsters (Hippy) designed to equip mothers with the knowledge and skills to assist their childern's intellectual, emotional and social development.

The South African Institute for Library and Information Science (Sailis) proclaimed 1990 as the Year of the Reader.

More than 3 000 pupils of 280 schools country-wide took part in the annual English Olympiad.

Promat — Project Matric — which gives adult Blacks a chance to matriculate, has proved a success as an average of 78,7 per cent of the students at Promat's five colleges passed.

Professor James Leatt was appointed Principal and Vice-Chancellor of the University of Natal as from 1991.

For the first time the total number of pupils and students within the formal sector of education reached 8 million, of which 69,5 per cent were Black, 16 per cent White, 11 per cent Coloured and 3,5 per cent Indian.

Since the government's announcement of three additional models for White schools in September, 268 of the 2 500 White schools throughout the country applied to vote on the models. By the end of November the parents at 147 schools countrywide voted in favour of Model B. In November five Cape schools became the first public schools in the country to open their doors to pupils of all races. Several others soon followed suit.

Mr Louis Pienaar was appointed Minister of National Education in December.

Vandals caused damage of up to R1,4 million at Soshanguve central secondary schools with the result that the Department of Education and Training decided in December to close the hostels indefinitely.

Indian children can now start school at a younger age. Children born on or before 31 July 1985 can start school in 1991.

Acknowledgements:
Administration: House of Assembly
Administration: House of Delegates
Administration: House of Representatives
Department of Education and Training
Department of National Education
University of Durban-Westville

In terms of the Constitution, health services are both a 'general' and 'own' affair. This means that overall policy, standards and norms are laid down in legislation passed by all three Houses of Parliament, while each House is responsible for its own specific health matters. Health Policy is regulated by the National Policy for Health Act, 1990, which provides for control measures to promote the health of the inhabitants of the Republic and for that purpose to provide for the determination of a national policy of health, for the establishment of a Health Matters Committee, an Administrators' Health Council and a Health Policy Council, and for related matters. This Act came into effect on 1 November 1990.

The Department of National Health and Population Development, as the first-tier general affairs health authority, is responsible for formulation of national health policy and for co-ordination and overall planning of health care delivery at national level, as well as for monitoring health status and services.

All executive functions have been transferred to second and third-tier health authorities. The health service delivery system (hospitals, community health centres, clinics, etc) are controlled and managed by a number of authorities at various levels. The first level comprises the departments of Health Services and Welfare of the three Houses of Parliament, which are responsible for health and welfare services provided for each of the three population groups. The second comprises the four provincial administrations, which have retained the function of providing and managing curative services in hospitals, but are now also responsible for decentralised provision of other health services. These include promotive and preventive health services in areas where there are no local authorities, school health services for Black scholars (as the agent for the Department of Education and Training), oral health services, nutritional advisory services, community psychiatric services and family planning (as agent for the Department of National Health and Population Development). Provincial hospitals also manage hospital services on an agency basis for the health authorities of the administrations. The general practitioner plays an important role in providing these services for private patients.

The third level of the delivery system comprises the local authorities of all population groups. They run about 1 200 clinics to provide basic community health services (preventive and curative). These health authorities are all represented on the two central co-ordinating bodies — the Health Policy Council (HPC) and the Health Matters Committee (HMC). The four provincial administrators and Minister of Health and Population Development co-ordinate activities in the Administrators' Health Council.

The fourth branch of the delivery system comprises the autonomous departments of health of the independent Black states (Transkei, Bophuthatswana, Venda and Ciskei) and the six Black self-governing territories which are part of the RSA. These 10 ministries provide health services for about 16,8 million people — a major segment of the Third World component of the region. The approach followed in these territories is that recommended for developing countries by the World Health Organisation (WHO) — a comprehensive community-based and hospital-supportive service which encompasses all sections of the population.

The statutory bodies for the health service professions are the SA Medical and Dental Council (SAMDC), the SA Dental Technicians Council, the SA Nursing Council, the SA Pharmacy Board, the SA Associated Health Service Professions Board and the SA Council for Social Work.

The objective of the health authorities is to provide a balanced and comprehensive service within reach of the entire population by optimal use of available resources.

The National Policy for Health Act recognises that the socio-economic circumstances of a substantial proportion of the population reflect a typical Third World situation. It therefore embodies the health care philosophy of affordability, accessability, quality, equity and acceptability.

While the National Policy for Health Act provides for greater involvement on the part of all communities in health services at local level, it also provides for all communities to be represented at the apex of the decision-making system through co-ordinating bodies such as the HPC and the HMC.

Increasing need — the result of population growth and a shift towards state services due to costs in the private sector — and escalating health care costs have necessitated a shift in emphasis from curative to preventive services.

Because of this approach and a long tradition of excellence in medical services, the health status of all South Africa's peoples has improved significantly and compares favourably with similar developing countries. In the areas of highly specialised medical care, South African health services compare with those in the developed world.

The total national budget for health care amounted to R7 780 million in 1989/90. This amount included R808 million for the health departments of the six self-governing territories.

Health team
In 1988 the South African health team numbered 65,4 health workers per 10 000 of the population.

Physicians
In 1990, 23 139 medical practitioners were registered with the SAMDC. Of this total 6 337 (27 per cent) had specialist qualifications.

About 80 per cent of all doctors practise in urban areas where just over half of the total population resides. Doctors are trained at seven universities with medical schools. Medical students at these universities render health services to selected communities at clinics under the supervision of medical practitioners.

The Medical University of Southern Africa (Medunsa) caters for Black students who wish to be trained as doctors, dentists, supplementary health personnel and veterinary surgeons. Medunsa, which now has more than 1 000 registered students, receives applications for admission from all over Southern Africa.

Medunsa's own teaching hospital of 1 200 beds is under construction at a cost of more than R200 million. It is being built next to the 1 700 bed regional hospital at Garankuwa, near Pretoria, which is now used as training hospital. In both theoretical training at the university and practi-

cal training at the hospital, considerable attention is given to health care education and community medicine, for which the need is greatest among South Africa's Third World population.

Dentists
In 1990, 3 775 dentists, 297 dental and oral specialists, 628 oral hygienists and 139 dental therapists were registered with the SAMDC while 1 003 dental technicians were registered with the SA Dental Technicians Council. Dental assistants, who need not register with a council, form part of the dental team.

There are six oral and dental teaching hospitals connected to the universities of the Witwatersrand, Pretoria, Stellenbosch, the Western Cape, Durban-Westville and Medunsa. Dentists, excluding dental technicians and dental assistants, receive their clinical training at these hospitals, while dental technicians are trained at any of the following technikons: Natal, Peninsula, Pretoria and Witwatersrand.

All dental workers, excluding dental therapists, render services in both the private and public sectors. Dental technicians, on the other hand, work only in the public sector.

Pharmacists
In 1990, 8 930 pharmacists were registered with the South African Pharmacy Board. About 1 056 pharmacists were employed in provincial and state hospitals, while there were 3 570 pharmaceutical supply points in the country in 1989.

Nurses
The number of nurses (registered and enrolled) and nursing assistants was 148 558 in 1990. It gives South Africa a ratio of one nurse per 205 of the population. The nursing profession represents more than 50 per cent of the total professional manpower of health services.

The South African Nursing Council controls nursing education and the practice of nursing in South Africa. It prescribes the minimum requirements for the education and training of nurses and midwives, approves training schools and registers or enrols those persons who qualify in one or more of the basic professional or subprofessional categories.

Basic training for registration as a nurse and midwife and post-basic clinical and non-clinical courses for registered nurses are offered at universities, nursing colleges in association with universities, technikons and hospital schools, and for a nursing assistant at an approved school which may be a hospital, geriatric home or an institution for the disabled. The duration of the

Table 1 Registered medical interns, practitioners and dentists, 1989-90

	1989	1990
Medical interns	1 119	1 252
Medical practitioners	22 260	23 139
Dentists	3 693	3 775
TOTAL	27 072	28 166

Source: SA Medical and Dental Council (SAMDC)

basic course is four academic years. The minimum duration of post-basic courses for registration of an additional qualification is one academic year.

Supplementary health services
Most supplementary health personnel are trained at technikons at the cost of their prospective employers — either the state or a private institution — as is also the case with health workers in general.

Associated health service professions
In 1990, 402 qualified workers and 172 students were registered with the South African Associated Health Service Professions Board. Students are trained at the Natal Technikon in Durban.

Provincial administrations
The functions of the provincial administrations in the national health care programme are to provide and manage institutionalised curative services — hospitals especially — as well as to render comprehensive health care services by means of district surgeon and school health services, mobile and fixed clinics and community health centres. The functions of the district surgeon include medical examination of applicants for admission to the public labour market, recommendations regarding granting of disability allowances, international immunisations and issue of such certificates for travellers abroad, treatment of old-age pensioners, especially those in the rural regions, handling of rabies contacts, and medico-legal services which include giving expert evidence in the courts.

Hospitals
The Transvaal Provincial Administration (TPA) manages 77 hospitals which have a total of 21 909 beds with 1,15 million admissions and an average stay of six days. During the 1988/89 financial year more than 6 million casualty and out-patients reported for treatment.

In the Transvaal primary health care services are provided in accordance with the National Health Services Facility Plan from 56 community health centres, 11 community centre clinics and mobile clinics which visit about 16 000 service points to ensure treatment at an appropriate level.

The Natal Provincial Administration manages 30 hospitals, which have 12 937 beds and had a total of 470 000 admissions during the 1988/89 financial year. The average stay was 7 days. Out-patients and casualty cases total 2,8 million.

The Orange Free State Provincial Administration manages 29 hospitals. Five of these are managed on an agency basis on behalf of the Administration: House of Assembly and one for the South African Development Trust. These

Table 2 Practitioners registered as specialists, 1989-90

	1989	1990
Anaesthetics	731	754
Cardio-thoracic surgery	24	29
Cardiology	67	80
Community health	42	52
Dermatology	103	109
Diagnostic radiology	472	493
Ear, nose and throat (Otorhino-laryngology)	201	214
Internal medicine	767	798
Neurology	78	75
Neurosurgery	82	84
Nuclear medicine	13	16
Obstetrics, gynaecology	603	624
Ophthalmology	254	268
Orthopaedics	423	444
Paediatric surgery	16	17
Paediatrics	443	468
Pathology	101	100
Pathology (anatomical)	127	132
Pathology (chemical)	53	55
Pathology (clinical)	75	75
Pathology (forensic)	20	22
Pathology (haematological)	30	39
Pathology (medical microbiological)	4	3
Pathology (microbiological)	40	43
Pathology (virological)	6	7
Physical medicine	8	7
Plastic and maxillo-facial surgery	3	3
Plastic and reconstructive surgery	91	94
Plastic surgery	9	8
Preventive medicine	37	36
Psychiatry	309	322
Radiology	39	35
Radiology and electro-therapeutics	6	6
Surgery	554	567
Therapeutic radiology	69	71
Thoracic surgery	51	49
Urology	134	136
Venereology	2	2

Source: SAMDC

Table 3 Medical and dental students registered, 1990

University	Medicine	Dentistry
Cape Town	904	—
Medunsa	672	127
Natal	657	—
OFS	616	—
Pretoria	1 137	240
Stellenbosch	975	166
Western Cape	—	81
Witwatersrand	1 292	209
TOTAL	6 253	823

Source: SAMDC

Table 4 Dentists registered as specialists, 1989-90

Speciality	1989	1990
Community dentistry	18	18
Maxillo-facial and oral surgery	17	17
Maxillo-facial and oral surgery (dental)	54	62
Oral medicine and periodontics	27	30
Oral pathology	11	14
Orthodontics	91	91
Periodontics	5	5
Prosthodontics	57	60
TOTAL	280	297

Source: SAMDC

Table 5 Nurses on the registers and rolls of the SA Nursing Council, 1989-90

Category	1989	1990
A. Registers		
Basic nursing qualifications		
Registered in one capacity only	13 897	12 640
Registered in two capacities	49 194	51 478
Registered in three capacities	7 027	7 398
TOTAL	70 118	71 516
B. Rolls		
Enrolled nurses	27 521	29 059
Enrolled nursing assistants	46 844	47 983
TOTAL	74 365	77 042
GRAND TOTAL	144 483	148 558

Source: SA Nursing Council

institutions have a total of 3 732 beds where, during the 1989/90 financial year, 236 057 in-lying patients were treated for 1 394 179 patient days while 1 120 667 casualty and out-patients received attention.

Most large general hospitals, including the teaching hospitals of medical schools, are provincial institutions.

Provincial hospitals play a vital role in the training of physicians, nurses and supplementary health personnel. Physicians who have completed their studies are required to complete a year of internship in an approved provincial hospital before full registration.

Baragwanath, the largest hospital in the country (1 798 beds), serves primarily about 1,2 million Black people from Soweto and surrounding areas. More than 108 000 in-patients and 3 500 000 out-patients are treated every year. The other large provincial hospitals are the King Edward VIII in Durban, Tygerberg near Cape Town, Garankuwa near Pretoria, Groote Schuur in Cape Town and Pelonomi in Bloemfontein.

Ambulance services
The four provincial administrations are responsible for provision of ambulance services but local authorities also provide these. Ambulance service is mainly by road, although three provinces also provide an airborne intensive care service.

Fully-equipped private ambulances in which patients are accompanied by nursing staff are also supplied by the private sector.

There is a provincial ambulance training college in each of the four provinces, providing specialised emergency training courses. The colleges, in conjunction with technikons, offer a National Diploma in Ambulance and Emergency Care.

Local authorities
Some of the functions of local authorities are to supply their communities with pure water and other public health services such as sewage disposal and refuse removal systems. These sanitary and other environmental health services are regulated by health inspectors, who are local authority officials.

In areas outside the jurisdiction of local authorities the health inspection functions are performed by the Department of National Health and Population Development.

Privatisation
In total 88 private hospitals and 68 unattached operating theatres representing a total of 17 612 beds were registered with the Administration:

House of Assembly and 14 private hospitals with the Administration: House of Delegates. Many of these hospitals are owned and managed by consortiums of private physicians or by large business organisations.

Fees in private hospitals are generally higher than those for provincial hospitals and the facilities and staff are on a par with those available elsewhere. The mining industry also makes an important contribution to curative services as it has its own hospitals.

Ancillary resources

Various organisations also provide vital health services, most of which are managed on a voluntary basis.

The **South African Red Cross** renders emergency, health and community services as well as training in first aid and home nursing. It also operates an ambulance service, clinics, medical supply points, old-aged homes, an air ambulance and air rescue service as well as comprehensive youth programmes. In times of disaster the Red Cross provides essential services.

Medic Alert is a worldwide medical identification system. This organisation keeps a register of members' medical history such as allergies and medication. Members wear an identification emblem on which their medical problems and membership number are engraved. Health personnel have telephone access 24 hours a day to this register. Medic Alert also serves as register for donation of organs, tissue, bodies and pacemakers.

The **South African First Aid League** provides first-aid services at sport meetings and civil protection operations and training in first-aid. It also provides first-aid kits.

Poison centres are manned by experts 24 hours a day. They provide vital advice to doctors, pharmacists, hospitals as well as the public seeking advice on antidotes and treatment.

Life Line provides a 24 hour telephone emergency confidential counselling service to those in distress. Similar services are Child Line, Rape Crisis for rape victims, Suicide Anonymous, etc. The SA Police also has a child protection unit.

Hospices are centres established to improve the quality of life of the terminally ill through care, support and love. Nursing staff care for the physical, social, emotional and psychological needs of the patients and their relatives.

Costs

The general policy is that all patients, except for the indigent, should contribute towards their medical care according to their means. All pa-

tients admitted to provincial hospitals pay for examinations and treatment on a sliding scale in accordance with their income and number of dependents. If, in terms of the standard means test, a family seems to be unable to bear the costs, such a patient is classified as a hospital patient, in which case his treatment is financed partly or entirely by the provincial administrations or the health authorities of the administrations.

For instance, low-income out-patients pay between R5 ($2) and R20 ($8) for treatment at the Baragwanath Hospital. If the physician decides the patient is to be admitted, he either pays a one-time fee ranging from R5 to R15 per admission or R30 a day regardless of the diagnosis, treatment or length of stay in the hospital. This

Table 6   Qualified supplementary health personnel registered with the SAMDC, 1989-90

	1989	1990
Audiologists	1	2
Audiometricians	20	22
Clinical technologists	264	300
Dental therapists	115	139
Dieticians	530	595
Electro-encephalographic technicians	63	68
Food inspectors	38	38
Health inspectors	2 446	2 485
Masseurs	39	39
Medical physicists	65	71
Medical scientists	175	225
Medical technicians	555	593
Medical technologists (all categories)	3 644	3 717
Occupational therapists	1 297	1 383
Optical dispensers	108	113
Optometrists	1 035	1 107
Oral hygienists	582	628
Orthopaedic orthotists and prosthetists	260	264
Orthoptists	25	20
Physiotherapists	2 784	2 900
Podiatrists	139	148
Psycho-technicians	457	489
Psychologists	2 419	2 638
Radiographers: Diagnostic	3 156	3 304
Supplementary diagnostic	362	345
Remedial gymnasts	3	3
Speech therapists	39	40
Speech therapists and audiologists	781	812

Source: SAMDC

treatment may even include costly operations such as a coronary by-pass or heart valve surgery.

Most of the family and community health care services at the more than 1 600 clinics are provided free of charge by local and other authorities. In addition, certain basic dental health services are provided free of charge by about 300 full-time and 100 part-time dentists for certain categories of patients. Specialist services such as maxillo-facial and oral surgery and orthodontics are also available to indigent patients.

There is no national medical insurance programme as such. By the end of 1990, however, 200 private medical schemes had been registered in terms of the provisions of the Medical Schemes Act, 1967, providing health care cover for 5 331 850 beneficiaries. Some 41 industrial medical schemes operated under agreements in terms of the Labour Relations Act, 1956, providing health care cover for 743 462 beneficiaries.

Community health
Promotion of optimal use of resources regarding primary, secondary and tertiary health care is a function of the Department of National Health and Population Development. These services are mainly provided by local authorities, provincial administrations and private institutions.

Table 7   Persons registered with the Associated Health Service Professions Board (1990)

Profession/combination of professions	Number
Chiropractors	138
Chiropractors and homeopaths	1
Chiropractors, homeopaths and naturopaths	3
Chiropractors, homeopaths, naturopaths and osteopaths	2
Homeopaths	101
Homeopaths and herbalists	1
Homeopaths and naturopaths	57
Homeopaths, naturopaths and osteopaths	66
Homeopaths, naturopaths, osteopaths and herbalists	2
Homeopaths and osteopaths	6
Herbalists	1
Naturopaths	12
Naturopaths and herbalists	1
Naturopaths and osteopaths	9
Naturopaths, osteopaths and herbalists	1
Osteopaths	1
TOTAL	402

(Herbalists are not to be confused with traditional herbalists/healers)
Source: SA Associated Health Service Professions Board

The appropriate and timeous immunisation of children against infectious diseases is one of the most beneficial and cost-effective preventive measures known. In keeping with the WHO's expanded programme on immunisation, an immunisation campaign against tuberculosis, poliomyelitis, whooping cough, tetanus and measles was launched country-wide in 1990.

These services also include control of certain endemic diseases. Malaria is endemic in the northern and eastern Transvaal lowveld, and in the coastal regions of northern Natal. Control measures are aimed at counselling, vector control, tracing and treatment of cases.

From 1982 until 14 December 1990, 614 cases of Acquired Immune Deficiency Syndrome (Aids) were diagnosed in South Africa. Less than 6 per cent of these cases were infected because of blood transfusions and blood products. The Advisory Group on Aids was founded in 1985 and all blood used for transfusion has been tested since 1985.

A comprehensive Aids awareness campaign was launched in 1988 and intensified during 1989 to increase the level of public knowledge about HIV infection and Aids. Brochures were made freely available to the public, physicians, dentists and nursing staff. Since Aids is not only a medical problem but also a result of social behaviour, the programme concentrates on community participation to influence behaviour. Aids Training and Information Centres (ATICS) were founded in Bloemfontein, Cape Town, Durban, East London, Johannesburg, Pietersburg, Port Elizabeth, Pretoria and Richards Bay. The ATICS serve as a local source of Aids information and train trainers and counsellors. They also strive for community participation and involvement. An Interdepartmental Committee on Aids Prevention was established in 1990 and its first meeting took place in Cape Town on 23 January 1991. It is this Committee's responsibility to co-ordinate Aids Prevention activities in the public sector to ensure optimal efficiency, avoid duplication and allocate priorities.

An important part of the Aids Prevention initiative is for all sectors of the community, including non-governmental organisations, to co-ordinate and co-operate.

The most important **infectious diseases** in South Africa are tuberculosis, measles, malaria and typhoid. The latter two are endemic in certain parts of the country.

Ischaemic heart diseases is a serious problem in the RSA. The incidence of hyperlipidaemia, a major cause of heart disease, is among the highest in the world, yet the death rate for ischaemic heart disease among Whites has been declining steadily since 1968. The rate for Coloureds and Black people is rising slowly as urbanisation gathers momentum and Western lifestyles are emulated.

Preliminary evaluation results of Coris (a project jointly managed by the Department of Health Services and Welfare, Administration: House of Assembly, the Institute for Communication Research of the HSRC and the Heart Foundation of South Africa) show that the community has reacted to the information programmes with a positive change in behaviour.

In addition to brochures and pamphlets the Department of Health Services and Welfare, Administration: House of Assembly circulates a bi-monthly factual paper which highlights specific aspects of food and nutrition in an effort to promote healthy nutrition practices.

Promotion of **mental health** is one of the cornerstones of the health policy. The Department of National Health and Population Development is responsible for the development of national policy guidelines regarding the delivery of mental health services.

Mental health services are provided by the different provincial administrations and the departments of Health Services and Welfare of the three Houses of Parliament as well as the private sector. Patients with emotional psychiatric conditions are primarily treated in community psychiatric clinics, as well as in- and out-patient facilities of general hospitals. The minority of patients who are suffering from more serious conditions and requiring admission, are admitted under the Mental Health Act.

There are 19 state psychiatric hospitals with a total of 13 700 beds. Of these the provincial administrations administer 14. Altogether 9 780 beds are for psychiatric patients and 4 230 for mentally handicapped individuals.

The Department of Health Services and Welfare of the House of Assembly administers three hospitals (141 beds for acute psychiatric treatment patients and 1 060 beds for the mentally handicapped). The Department of Health Services and Welfare of the House of Representatives administers a total of 1 555 beds (659 for psychiatric patients and 896 for mentally handicapped patients).

Nine private psychiatric hospitals with a total of 473 beds, 24 general hospitals with 234 beds and one detached operating theatre with three beds are licensed by the Department of Health Services and Welfare of the House of Assembly to admit patients for intensive voluntary in-patient treatment.

There are also 8 978 beds for patients suffering from long-term psychiatric disorders or severe mental handicaps in 10 private psychiatric facilities. Of these beds, 2 990 are situated in the self-governing territories.

The administrations of the Houses of Assem-

Table 8 Reported deaths of specific notifiable conditions* in the RSA, 1988-90

Disease	1988	1989	1990**
Acute rheumatic fever*	—	—	0
Anthrax*	0	0	0
Brucellosis*	0	0	0
Cholera*	0	0	0
Diphtheria*	4	0	1
Encephalitis*	—	—	10
Haemorrhagic fevers in Africa*	1	0	0
Legionellosis*	—	—	0
Leprosy*	2	0	0
Leptospirosis	0	0	—
Malaria*	45	22	27
Measles*	288	150	51
Meningococcal infection*	98	110	72
Paratyphoid fever*	0	0	0
Plague*	0	0	0
Poisoning (agricultural or stock remedy)*	8	7	7
Poisoning (food)*	—	—	0
Poisoning (lead)*	0	0	0
Poliomyelitis*	4	0	0
Primary malignancy of bronchus	486	433	—
Primary malignancy of lung	555	507	—
Primary malignancy of pleura	5	1	—
Psittacosis	0	0	—
Rabies*	26	10	8
Rheumatic heart disease*	—	—	1
Smallpox*	0	0	0
Tetanus*	88	35	36
Toxoplasmosis	0	0	—
Trachoma*	0	0	0
Trypanosomiasis	0	0	—
Tuberculosis (all forms)*	2 264	2 064	1 771
Typhoid*	38	29	27
Typhus fever*	0	0	0
Viral hepatitis*	53	62	52
Yellow fever*	0	0	0

* New list of notifiable medical conditions —15 December 1989
** Provisional figures as on 29 January 1991, still subject to changes
Source: Department of National Health and Population Development

bly, Representatives and Delegates subsidise 22 licensed homes where 1 550 severely mentally retarded persons are treated. The Administration: House of Assembly has 20 halfway houses for 423 patients in this department alone and is responsible for 16 licensed homes which can accommodate 1 159 patients. Altogether 549 day care places are available in 24 day care facilities, for both psychiatric and mentally handicapped patients in this department.

There are also 13 halfway houses for psychiatrically handicapped persons. These homes are largely financed and managed by registered voluntary organisations. Some 946 other patients with severe mental handicaps attend 31 special care or stimulation centres on a daily basis.

In keeping with government policy to promote the care of the mentally handicapped persons in the community, 2 160 such persons are placed in subsidised so-called 'single care', usually with their parents.

A comprehensive **psychiatric community service** is managed country-wide by the health authorities of the administrations and provincial authorities. About 750 000 consultations are undertaken by these authorities by means of multidisciplinary teams comprising psychiatric nursing staff, psychiatrists, physicians, psychologists, pharmacists, social workers and occupational therapists.

Another function of the Department of National Health and Population Development is to prevent, control or reduce possible sources of hazards to public health, such as harmful foods, cosmetics, disinfectants, medicines, abuse of hazardous substances and various forms of pollution in conjunction with local and other authorities.

Food is controlled to safeguard the consumer against any harmful, injurious or adulterated products and representation regarding their nature, as well as unhygienic manufacturing practices, premises and equipment.

The Medicine Control Board requires registration of all medicine intended for human or veterinary use, before it is made available for public use.

Social welfare

In terms of the Constitution, welfare services are both a general and own affair. The Department of National Health and Population Development lays down the overall national policy, norms and standards. The departments of Health Services and Welfare of the administra-

tions of the three Houses of Parliament are responsible for the welfare services of the respective population groups. The Department of Planning, Provincial Affairs and National Housing formulates overall policy, norms and standards for social welfare services for Black communities, while the four provincial administrations are responsible for the executive functions. The Department of Development Aid is responsible for provision of welfare services in the trust areas and stimulation of services in the self-governing territories.

SA's social welfare services comprise a partnership between the private and public sector. As far as possible, welfare services are rendered by private welfare organisations, which are subsidised by the state. There are more than 1 600 private welfare organisations, some of which are organised on a national basis. They provide for social care of the aged, the handicapped, children, families and others in need of treatment, such as alcoholics and drug addicts.

Social workers play a vital role in the field of welfare. They identify social pressures and needs, use existing resources or establish those that might be lacking. They are involved in handling of social problems such as alcohol abuse, drug dependence, unemployment, family breakdown, neglect and maltreatment of children and work closely with members of other auxiliary professions. They also provide statutory services over a broad spectrum of service fields such as whether consent should be given for marriages of minors, pre-sentence investigations for the criminal courts to assist in the passing of a suitable sentence, supervision and community services; and children's and juvenile court inquiries to help protect children and young people. In 1990, 7 079 social workers were registered with the South African Council for Social Work.

Most churches in South Africa are involved one way or another in various facets of social care, that is to say charity work. Areas in which the church functions include child care, care of the aged, marriage counselling, family care, care of the disabled, the sick, alcoholics and criminals. A wide variety of professional people are available to serve the church and social welfare, inter alia ministers, pastoral psychologists, social workers and teaching staff.

Child care

Boys' Towns South Africa is a series of children's homes providing a total residential child-care programme for boys aged from 6-18, ranging from the under-privileged and neglected to the problematical. The essence of the programmes is self-realisation by means of the self-government system, education and spiritual development. Boys' Town receives a monthly state subsidy for every boy and its facilities accommodate all population groups. It is a registered welfare organisation controlled by a Board of Management whose members are individuals from within the South African community.

In divorce cases reports on the suitability of the respective spouses to have control or custody of the children are submitted. Professional services are available to the parents as well as the children before, during and after a divorce. The establishment of a family court is an important objective for more effective services to families. The first family advocate and a family counsellor were appointed in 1990. This new service was introduced in Pretoria and is intended to extend to the rest of the RSA as soon as possible.

The national child welfare policy is based on the principle that the child is best cared for within the family circle. Thus the state and private initiative are directed to the preservation and strengthening of family life. Referral to children's homes and places of safety is resorted to only when the family's problems are such that the temporary removal of the child from the family is the only recourse. On returning to the family he is usually placed under the supervision of a social worker who guides them through their new period of adjustment.

Foster care is one of the most common forms of substitute care, especially in the case of young children. In such cases a grant is paid to foster parents. Children's homes are state-subsidised.

Substance dependence

The Department of National Health and Population Development and the other welfare departments regularly launch information and educational programmes aimed at making the public more aware of the detrimental effect of alcohol abuse and drug dependence. South Africa's biggest problem is alcohol abuse, followed by drug abuse such as dagga smoking and other substance dependence. The National Plan for the Prevention and Control of Alcohol and Drug Abuse in SA is mainly aimed at prevention. Self-help community groups seem to be very successful in combating dependency problems. The state also manages and subsidises treatment facilities for alcoholics and drug addicts.

Care of the disabled

About 3,5 million people, or 12,7 per cent of the South African population, are disabled in some

or other way. Only those whose handicap is so severe that they cannot be assisted to live independently in the community are admitted to institutional care. Disabled people who do not need institutional care but cannot be employed in the open labour market can work in sheltered workshops. The Department of Manpower, in accordance with a programme to create employment for the disabled, runs 13 factories employing more than 2 000 handicapped people. There are several associations and information centres concerned with, inter alia, the rehabilitation of handicapped persons, their training, the creation and providing for job creation and establishing sports meetings to encourage and enable them to live an independent life. The new tendency is to integrate them with the community.

At present the TPA subsidises 13 protected workshops which make provision for 800 workers. One new workshop for the mentally handicapped will come into operation during 1991 and will make provision for 150 mentally handicapped persons. The TPA also subsidises six day care centres for uneducable mentally

Table 9 The main causes of death (based on the International Classification of Diseases) in 1990

Asians	
Diseases of the circulatory system	1 798
Accidents, poisoning and violence (external causes)	709
Diseases of the respiratory system	551
Endocrine, nutritional and metabolic diseases	533
Neoplasms	464
Whites	
Diseases of the circulatory system	13 075
Neoplasms	6 287
Diseases of the respiratory system	4 385
Accidents, poisoning and violence (external causes)	3 938
Symptoms, signs and ill-defined conditions	2 642
Coloureds	
Diseases of the circulatory system	5 492
Accidents, poisoning and violence (external causes)	4 349
Neoplasms	3 008
Diseases of the respiratory system	2 752
Infectious and parasitic diseases	2 454
Blacks*	
Symptoms, signs and ill-defined conditions	26 027
Accidents, poisoning and violence (external causes)	25 614
Diseases of the circulatory system	13 976
Infectious and parasitic diseases	13 081
Diseases of the respiratory system	10 148

* Registered deaths in 1989
Source: Central Statistical Service

handicapped children. Some 109 children receives care and stimulation at these centres.

An important component of care for the disabled is services rendered to psychiatric patients in psychiatric hospitals and care and rehabilitation centres for the mentally handicapped.

Care of senior citizens
Most services for senior citizens are provided by private welfare organisations and are state-subsidised. Accommodation for the aged includes fully-equipped housing units for self-sufficient people and care in conventional old-age homes, many having frail care facilities. Service centres that provide for the needs of the aged living in the community are also subsidised.

There are six homes for the aged in the Transvaal where 326 aged persons are cared for. A total of 370 frail and chronically-ill aged persons are cared for in two homes for chronically-ill persons. A third home for 250 chronically aged persons is expected to come into operation during 1991. Service centres are considered as a service which will enable aged people to remain in the community for as long as possible. At present there are 17 subsidised service centres in the Transvaal where 1 520 aged persons receive a hot meal twice a week and enjoy companionship, social interaction, cultural enrichment, etc.

Meals on Wheels for the Aged is a private welfare organisation that does not only provide food for the aged, but has 23 service centres countrywide where the aged may enjoy companionship, social interaction and cultural enrichment. Special Christmas functions are held and various other services are also offered to the needy aged. This body also runs nine old-aged homes.

Financial support
Social relief is given to individuals and families who are unable to provide in their primary existence needs. It is a temporary measure and every attempt is made to help these people until they have reached financial independence.

The Child Care Act, 1983, makes provision for a maintenance allowance for children to be granted to a widow, divorcee, single mother or married woman whose husband is unfit for work or detained in a state institution.

Social allowances are made payable by the different health authorities of the administrations and the provincial administrations. The awarding of all social pensions is subject to a means test. Occupational disease sufferers are compensated on differing grounds in terms of the relevant Act.

News items: 1990
Although motor vehicle accidents claimed more lives than heart disease in the below-40 age group, heart disease remained the greatest cause of death in all age groups according to payouts by insurance companies for death claims in 1989.

Researchers at Medunsa discovered a new cause of diarrhoea diseases in SA. A diagnostic technique to trace the organism has also been developed.

Professor Queenie Mokhuane has been appointed head of Medunsa's department of clinical psychology, making her the first Black woman in the country to hold such a position.

The Department of National Health and Population Development launched an intensive preventive health campaign against measles in March. Next to tuberculosis, measles has the highest fatality rate of notifiable infectious diseases in South Africa.

The first confirmed case of Congo fever in the eastern Transvaal was diagnosed in February.

About 55 000 people in SA carried the HIV-virus at the end of 1989 according to research findings of the SAMRC.

Aids has claimed the lives of 270 people in SA since it was diagnosed in this country in 1982, according to the Department of National Health and Population Development.

The Guest House Project — a community project aiming to ensure the dignity, confidentiality and practical care of people with Aids — opened its first home for people suffering from the disease in Kensington, Johannesburg.

Penalties for drug dealers and users, such as mandatory imprisonment for dealers, and scrapping of maximum fines to allow courts to impose whatever fines they like, were contained in new legislation tabled in Parliament in March.

The PWV area has a new source of emergency assistance — the Medical Rescue International Bell long-ranger helicopter based at the Johannesburg Hospital.

Birth to Ten, a ten-year study of the health and well-being of 4 000 children born in Johannesburg and Soweto during April 1990, was initiated by the MRC and launched at the University of the Witwatersrand Medical School.

A service to detect the presence of legionella bacteria — the cause of Legionnaires' Disease — in air-conditioning systems has been set up by the Health Programme of the CSIR's division of water technology.

About 10 000 people are killed on SA's roads annually. In an attempt to reduce the road death toll, the Medical Services Plan introduced a rescue service to give emergency assistance to people injured in motor accidents.

Registration procedures for doctors from foreign countries were relaxed in an attempt to alleviate a crisis situation at public hospitals. Previously, only doctors who qualified in Britain and Belgium were exempted from writing a test, as their qualifications were recognised in SA.

Study results showed the price of medicine in South Africa was higher than in most Western European countries. The first phase of the study, undertaken in 1988, showed South African medicine prices were in rand terms 20 per cent higher than in Britain, 70 per cent higher than in Australia but 41 per cent lower than in the USA.

The loss of radiographers through emigration to Canada has led to closing down of cancer machines and curtailment of services.

Provincial hospitals have been officially opened to all population groups during the year.

Medical practitioners', dentists' and specialists' contribution to the settlement of medical aid claims decreased from 55,3 to 47,5 per cent over the past seven years while claims for medicine and hospitalisation increased from 39,4 to 46,1 per cent over the same period.

A divorce help line was established in Pretoria.

A help line for runaway children who wish to send messages to their parents through third persons was also established.

Nurses received a salary increase from 24,2 per cent to 33,4 per cent on 1 July.

Rotary, Lions and Round Table clubs in South Africa clubbed together to offer terminally-ill children an opportunity to live out their dreams before they die, the 'Reach for a Dream' project.

Mr David Steele, a lecturer in Medunsa's department of microbiological pathology spent 18 months researching the Rotavirus at the National Institute of Health's Laboratory of Infectious Diseases in Washington DC after the WHO declared discovery of a vaccine for the virus a priority.

A R1 million terminal-care centre for cancer patients was given to the National Cancer Association of the Northern Transvaal by residents of Pretoria's Soetdoring retirement resort.

Violence in Black residential areas in Natal contributed to an increase in the incidence of rabies in the province because vets were not able to enter strife-torn areas to inoculate pets.

In future the University of the Western Cape will be solely responsible for training of pharmacists in the western Cape, while the combined training provided by the University of Stellenbosch, the University of Cape Town and the Cape Technikon will gradually be phased out.

Research results of two paediatricians at the University of Cape Town which could decrease the incidence of death due to measles by more than 50 per cent, was published in one of the world's most authoritative medical journals.

The Marais Clinic in Westlake, Cape, was reopened after 26 years because of the sharp increase in TB cases.

The government made R12 million available to put 26 community health centres, closed due to lack of funds, into commission.

The Junior Doctors' Association of South Africa was formed in Pretoria to campaign for better pay and improved working conditions.

The Chief Director of Hospital and Health Services in the Cape Province, Dr Hannah-Reeve Sanders, was the first woman elected to the SAMDC.

Apart from gastro-enteritis, respiratory illness is the major cause of death in South African children under the age of five, according to the MRC.

The first conference in South Africa on breast cancer was held in Johannesburg.

The first resource centre to aid South Africa's blind people was opened in Pretoria.

About 26 500 calls have been received since the inception of the child help line of the Department of Health Services and Welfare in the House of Assembly in 1989. The toll-free number is 0-8001-23321.

About 101 of the 73 000 babies born in South Africa every year are born with cleft face deformities. Some 1,38 of 1 000 White babies suffer from this genetic disorder at birth, while the number for Black babies is only 0,42 per 1 000.

A new type of TB which is resistant to TB treatment, highly contagious and considered as dangerous as Aids was identified in South Africa during the year.

The State President, Mr F W de Klerk, announced a boost of R50 million for health services in Natal/KwaZulu.

The Robyn Strong Clinic, for patients with brain injuries, was commissioned in Johannesburg on 1 September.

New equipment to the value of R1,3 million was installed in the cancer unit at the Groote Schuur Hospital.

A emergency number for ambulance services — 10177 (without an area code) — was introduced for large parts of the Cape and Natal.

The Theunis Fichardt Hospice in Pretoria opened its doors to patients on 5 July.

There were an estimated 2 055 street children in South Africa on 1 January 1990.

Altogether R3 231 466 was raised for SA's

needy children as people nationwide pledged their support for M-Net and the Kids Comic Relief Project on Red Nose Day in March.

Prof Francis Bosman was appointed the first family advocate to protect the interests of children in matters affecting family life.

The new child care amendment law determined that children of 14 (previously 18 years) could consent to medical treatment.

In December the eyes of an elderly woman who had suffered from retinitis pigmentosa were removed after her death in order to start research on the condition for the first time in SA.

Due to a lack of volunteers Suicide Anonymous were unable to operate 24 hours a day during the Christmas holidays.

By 15 December Groote Schuur Hospital had performed its 33rd heart transplant.

During the year health services and hospitals countrywide experienced a crisis due to strikes, the shortage of nurses and the resignation of academic personnel at training hospitals. A total of 33 strikes took place at Transvaal provincial hospitals from the beginning of May up to 22 August, compared with only four during the first four months of the year. More than 500 general workers at the Kalafong Hospital near Atteridgeville went on strike on 14 August to protest about wage increases as a result of the TPA's refusal to meet their demands. The Cillié Commission investigated the causes and consequences of the Garankuwa Hospital strike as a result of which 23 premature babies are alleged to have died. The strike at Garankuwa was the first where workers demanded the removal of hospital officials.

Acknowledgements:
Administration: House of Assembly
Administration: House of Delegates
Administration: House of Representatives
Cape Provincial Administration
Central Statistical Service
Department of National Health and Population Development
Department of Planning, Provincial Affairs and National Housing
Natal Provincial Administration
Provincial Administration of the Orange Free State
SA Associated Health Service Professions Board
SA Medical and Dental Council
SA Nursing Council
SA Pharmacy Board
Transvaal Provincial Administration

At the current rate of 2,0 per cent a year, rapid population growth is one of the Republic of South Africa's most pressing problems. At present fertility levels, Black women in the Pretoria-Witwatersrand-Vereeniging (PWV) area produce 2,6 children on average and those in the rural areas 5,4. It is estimated that the country's Black population will reach 49,0 million by the year 2010 — and that the population could double in slightly more than 30 years. Of this number, 26,5 million will be living in the three major urban areas of the PWV, Durban and Cape Town.

Authorities worldwide have known for some time of the existence of a direct relation between population growth and development. The higher the quality of life the lower the growth rate. It was also found that population growth in urban communities was lower than in the rural areas. To address the problems in a co-ordinated manner the government launched the National Population Development Programme (PDP) in 1984.

The primary goal of this programme is to establish a balance between the size of the population and subsistence resources (natural resources and socio-economic means). According to research and practice such a balance can only be achieved worldwide by improving the quality of life of all peoples and accelerating development with specific emphasis on changing fertility perceptions in favour of a small family norm. The integration of family planning in development programmes must be ensured, as must the involvement of communities in actions of the PDP, with particular reference to the areas of education, primary health care (including family planning), manpower training, the economy and housing.

Development programmes in the above fields are launched in co-operation with government departments and other government institutions as well as with the help of the private sector.

After thorough research it was decided that the following indicators would serve as PDP monitoring-instruments: total fertility rate (TFR); teenage pregnancies; contraceptive usage; infant mortality rate (IMR) and literacy.

A Council for Population Development, composed mainly of developmental experts from the private sector, was established to function as an advisory body for the PDP.

Community development

In terms of the Constitution, community development is an 'own' affair to be promoted and managed separately for the three communities represented in Parliament by their own administrations and institutions.

The Department of Planning, Provincial Affairs and National Housing is responsible for planning and policy-formulation for the development of Black communities outside the self-governing territories, while the provincial administrations are responsible for their implementation. The Department of Development Aid assists the self-governing territories and trust areas in South Africa. Housing is funded from revolving funds administered by the respective housing departments. These funds are annually replenished from public funds as

Table 1 Success of the National Population Development Programme in the RSA*

Indicator	Position according to PDP Monitoring Reports released			
	1986	1987	1988	1989
Total fertitility rate*	4,30	4,30	3,90	3,80
Teenage birth %	13,90	13,20	13,90	12,60
Contraceptive prevalence %	—	—	—	66,90
Infant mortality rate **	—	53,10	51,70	49,30
Literacy %	66,00	64,80	67,40	69,50

* Average number of children born alive to woman during her child-bearing years (15 - 49) assuming that the prevailing rates remain unchanged
** The number of live-born children who die under the age of one years per 1 000 births
Source: Department of National Health and Population Development

required, and can also be supplemented with funds borrowed on the open capital market.

Residential development for the four population groups is regulated to proceed separately in accordance with the custom and lifestyles of each population group on land designated in terms of existing legislation. On 1 February 1991 the government, however, announced its intention of repealing the Group Areas Act, subject to generally acceptable measures to ensure maintenance of civilised standards.

Community development in SA is a comprehensive concept. Any state housing pro-gramme includes provision of essential amenities such as schools, clinics, community centres, parks and recreation facilities, shopping complexes and adequate transport facilities. The object is to develop full-fledged and self-sufficient communities with the full participation of the people concerned themselves. People themselves are then responsible for their development because they are involved in decision-making processes.

While the main thrust of Black community development by the state is focused on urban areas outside the self-governing territories, the general development strategy for these territories includes all-embracing community development programmes, many of which are carried out with the assistance of the Department of Development Aid.

The state has announced that billions will be spent to bring an end to high-priority backlogs among disadvantaged South Africans. This will mean improved housing for disadvantaged people, particularly where inadequate housing exists. More land will be bought for new Black residential areas.

Housing

The change in the name of the Department of Planning, Provincial Affairs and National Housing to include 'National Housing', emphasises the importance the government attaches to housing. Its existing housing policy is based on the following principles:

— The individual is primarily responsible for his own housing;

— the state should play a direct role only in cases in which the individual is not in the position to satisfy his own housing needs;

— the primary task of the state is to create the necessary environment in which the private sector and the individual can undertake the provision of housing.

One of the main reasons for adopting these principles is that the government realises that it cannot meet the acute shortage of housing on its own and that the involvement of the private sector is necessary to make any meaningful inroads into the housing backlog. In the context of housing for lower-income groups, affordability is regarded as the crucial starting point. The adoption of appropriate standards is therefore also regarded as the single most important approach

Table 2 Demographic features

		Whites	Coloureds	Asians	Black people	TOTAL
Population composition (1990) %		116,30	10,40	3,10	70,20	100,00
Annual growth rate of the Population (1980-1990) %		1,05	1,78	1,72	2,39	2,07
Population increase (1980-1990) %		11,02	19,35	18,61	26,65	22,79
Sex — males (1990) %		15,80	10,00	3,00	71,20	100,00
Average age (1985) years		31,20	24,30	25,30	24,30	25,70
The aged — 65 years and older (1985) %		8,40	3,50	2,80	2,70	3,80
Children — under 15 years (1985) %		25,00	35,70	33,10	40,70	37,20
— under 16 years (1985) %		26,90	38,10	35,30	42,90	39,40
— under 18 years (1985) %		30,50	42,80	39,60	47,10	43,50
— under 21 years (1985) %		35,70	49,60	45,70	53,20	49,50
Urban population (1985) %		89,60	77,80	93,40	39,60	55,90
Non-urban population (1985) %		10,40	22,20	6,60	60,40	44,10
Life expectancy at birth (1984-86) years	Male	68,37	57,92	64,12	59,75*	—
	Female	75,84	65,52	70,74	64,73*	—

* (1985-1990) Mostert W P, Van Tonder J L, 1987. Projections of the South African population, Pretoria: Human Sciences Research Council, Report 5-158
Source: Central Statistical Service

towards coping with the desires and aspirations of the nation in a new SA. In order to grant all distressed citizens equal access to affordable shelter and to ensure utilisation of the available funds to its maximum advantage, the government has instructed the South African Housing Advisory Council (SAHAC) to review the present housing policy and to advise the government on the formulation of a national housing policy and a strategy to implement such policy. The national housing policy will have to ensure greater involvement by the private sector with regard to lower income groups. The proposals by SAHAC on a national housing policy will eventually form the basis of a White Paper on Housing and it is expected that this task will be completed by the end of 1991.

The Committee of Housing Ministers has also granted approval in principle for the implementation of a proposed capital subsidy scheme. The scheme will mean that a one-time subsidy will be granted to enable a person to acquire a serviced site with a view to building his own home. An income limit to qualify for participation in such a scheme will be determined.

SAHAC is continuously involved in research projects to find solutions to the housing problem. One such a project investigated the possibility of high density housing. In collaboration with consultants, a committee of SAHAC recently completed such a study and submitted its report to the council, which will consider it in the formulation of a national housing policy.

It is government policy to promote home ownership and every effort is being made to enable all population groups to own their own homes. Because every citizen is expected, as far as possible, to provide for his own housing needs with assistance from private sources of finance, the South African building society movement is among the best developed and most sophisticated in the western world.

The state assumes responsibility in two important respects. Firstly, it is concerned with identification and purchase of land which can be developed as close as possible to employment opportunities. Secondly, it concerns itself with making available land for development by the private sector or development of adequate available lots by the state for allocation to individuals and the private sector, i.e. with providing housing for the low income groups.

The state is responsible for about 70 per cent of the housing needs of Black people. Depending on circumstances, the state, through local authorities, provides serviced erven on which people can build their own houses either with their own money or finance from the National Housing Fund or private sources, such as building societies, financial institutions or their employers.

Since the government started selling its stock to private individuals, 37,07 per cent of the total number of houses available to Blacks were sold. During the same period a total of 44,74 per cent, 79,5 per cent and 36,69 per cent of houses available for Coloureds, Indians and Whites were sold to members of these groups. After that the government ceased building new houses and individuals have become responsible for building their own homes with the aid of loans.

Loans of up to R8 500 are granted for houses self-built by the members of the lower income group. In addition, the first-time home-buyers' subsidy scheme for Black people proved so popular that the funds allocated by the Department of Planning, Provincial Affairs and National Housing had been exhausted by July 1990. Approximately 21 500 Black home-owners had benefitted by September 1990.

For members of the Coloured, Indian and White population groups a total of 13 300, 8 600 and 20 500 homes were built in 1990 through the first-time home-buyers' subsidy scheme.

During 1990 a total amount of R1,096 billion was allocated by the state for provision of housing for the various population groups.

In recent years housing utility companies have emerged as an important agency for private sector involvement in housing for all population groups. More than 30 such companies have been registered. They are valuable sources of finance for those whose income precludes them from state assistance but is nevertheless too low to qualify for assistance by financial institutions such as building societies or commercial banks.

It has been accepted that the state alone cannot provide housing for all South Africans, even those in the low income groups. Thus the private sector is being involved to an ever increasing extent in building houses and upgrading the existing housing stock, especially in the Black residential areas.

The largest joint housing initiative by the state and the private sector is the South African Housing Trust (SAHT) which is managed by a board of directors drawn from the private sector. The SAHT focuses its efforts on self-build programmes in areas where unemployment is highest. Most homes are core houses which can be extended later.

The SAHT has established that to keep up with the population boom among Black people, SA needs to build 312 600 homes a year over the next decade. That equals 40 new cities with costs running at an astounding R6 billion a year.

Urban planning

About 15 million, or between 56 and 57 per cent of Blacks, are urbanised.

This figure is expected to reach 74 per cent by the turn of the century. This will mean that up to 26 million Blacks will then live in and around the large cities.

Urban planning is the function of provincial and local authorities in conjunction with central government.

In the case of a rapidly developing urban complex, the structure of the city-to-be is determined and a basic plan provided for land use and road and transportation systems. The plans are not static, but are continually amended to suit changing circumstances and incorporate new information and policy directives.

Free settlement areas

From March 1989 to December 1990 the Free Settlement Board, which was established on 1 March 1989, received 63 applications. Of these, 15 areas totalling 6 714,33 ha have been declared free settlement areas.

The free settlement areas that have been developed are mostly occupied by Indians, Coloureds and Whites except in the case of Hillbrow and vicinity (Johannesburg) where a vast percentage of Blacks are located.

Squatting is a serious problem in South Africa

Squatters

Squatting is a by-product of urbanisation and occurs countrywide. According to an estimate by the Urban Foundation, there are 7 million metropolitan squatters in South Africa. The Reef, that is, the 'inner' PWV area, has between 1,5 and 2,4 million squatters.

The increasing number of squatters places severe pressure on the country's resources. A major aspect in dealing with the squatter situation is the question of suitable and adequate land. In certain areas suitable and well-situated land is scarce.

However, good progress has been made with the acquisition of land in many areas. In order to accommodate the need of the low income group, a process has been established whereby land is acquired speedily. Such land is planned, demarcated into sites and provided with rudimentary services. Sites are allocated to persons on which they can erect any structure of their choice. Through a process of upgrading, the area can develop into a conventional town.

The government has repeatedly stated that in principle it is against forced removals in consideration of the settlement of people. However, cognisance must be taken of all factors. People's living space must offer the opportunity for improvement of their quality of life and for establishing economically viable and stable communities. In this process a short-term view cannot be adopted. Where it is necessary to relocate people due consideration is therefore taken of all aspects and the approach is to conduct the process through negotiation.

News items: 1990

SA's population doubles every 30 years. A new baby is born in SA every 26 seconds.

New home-financing schemes based on co-operation with pension and/or provident funds have been approved by the Government Committee for Financial Policy and Strategy. Were a small percentage of pension and life assurance assets to be used for the new scheme, R10 billion could be made available to finance new homes immediately, with a further 2 billion annually.

The government made a further R24 million available to purchase land where Black buyers could not afford the properties.

Eight major private sector home builders withdrew from the Black housing market because of unrest and bond repayment boycotts.

Backyard squatters in the PWV area number more than 1,1 million living in 66 539 shacks.

The SAHT is the largest supplier of affordable houses in the country. The total amount approved since the inception of the trust is R1,3 billion, with the total number of houses built with the aid of the trust being 20 877 by the end of September 1990. A further amount of R500 million was approved for projects. It is estimated that this amount will result in a further 62 681 houses and 54 831 erven.

A housing project worth R25 million, which will accommodate an estimated 5 000 Black people in Daveyton on the East Rand, was launched in October. A total of 1 000 houses priced at R12 500 and R27 800 will be built. With the use of a sliding form in concrete construction, a home at the project called Emaphupheni — Place of Dreams — can be built to roof height in two days.

The National Union of Metalworkers of South Africa has proposed a R4 billion plan to replace urban single-sex hostels with housing units, integrated into surrounding communities.

In 1990 the government spent R69 million to buy 9 152 hectares of land for low income groups. An amount of R40 million was allocated to fund the first-time home-buyers subsidy scheme for Black persons for the 1990/91 financial year.

The Central Witwatersrand Regional Services Council approved grants of more than R164 million for improvement projects in Black areas. Preference was accorded to Alexandra, Deepmeadow, Dobsonville and Soweto.

The House of Representatives embarked on a

Population growth, 1960–85

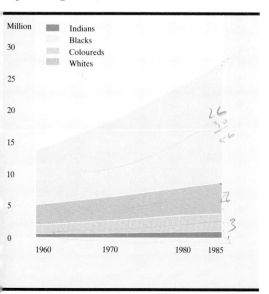

Million			
30	■	Indians	
		Blacks	
25		Coloureds	
		Whites	
20			
15			
10			
5			
0			
	1960	1970	1980 1985

self-build housing programme which led to building of 2 859 houses. A further 1 972 are still under construction.

In June 1990 Sasria, an organisation providing high risk insurance, announced that it would in future refund financial institutions which had incurred losses on low income housing because bondholders had refrained from or were prevented from paying bond repayments due to specific political circumstances.

The Urban Foundation introduced its Loans Guarantee Fund of R20 million, aimed at supplementing financing available at building societies for those in the lower income groups.

The Hans Seidel Foundation of West Germany donated R3,6 million to the Urban Foundation for housing loans for people in the lower income groups.

The Benoni City Council decided to make land demarcated as White residential areas available to squatters of the neighbouring Black area of Wattville. Some 3 000 squatters will be housed there.

In December 27 huts which had been erected by squatters in Dobsonville, Soweto, under the auspices of the Soweto Civic Association, were pulled down by the Dobsonville City Council.

According to the Transvaal Provincial Administration (TPA) more than 36 per cent or 84 743 of the total number of houses available to Blacks in the Transvaal have already been sold while almost 37 per cent or 123 212 of the houses available in the rest of the country have also been sold.

The President's Council's Committee of Economic Affairs is investigating the government's urbanisation strategy at the request of the State President, Mr F W de Klerk. Persons and bodies are invited to submit memoranda to this council by 15 March 1991.

Low-cost houses averaging about R 4 000 are being exported to Zaire, Mozambique, Botswana and Lesotho. These houses consist of four panels of fibreglass reinforced concrete, have a roof, floor and windows, are movable and can be bolted onto a platform.

Acknowledgements:
Central Statistical Service
Department of National Health and Population Development
Department of Planning, Provincial Affairs and National Housing

Cultural activities

South African cultural life consists of a kaleido-scopic variety of cultural forms and expressions. These reflect the great diversity of the popula-tion — old and new civilisations, developing and developed societies, indigenous and immigrant communities, all representing many different languages.

In terms of the present Constitution, culture is an 'own' affair. Government departments within this framework are the departments of Educa-tion and Culture in the administrations of the Houses of Assembly (Whites), Representatives (Coloureds) and Delegates (Indians) and the Department of Education and Training (Blacks).

The Department of National Education (DNE) is involved on national level. Its cultural division promotes cultural activities and oppor-tunities for all population groups and is respon-sible for fostering of educational and cultural relations with other countries.

The Culture Promotion Act provides for the establishment of councils for the promotion of cultural activities for the various population groups. These councils co-operate with — and support the activities of — a host of societies, associations and organisations, which foster cul-tural activities over a broad front. In this process the multi-faceted culture of South Africans is well considered.

The Cultural Institutions Act, 1969, provides that institutions of national significance may be declared cultural institutions to qualify for finan-cial and other assistance from the state.

To date, the following have been declared statutory cultural institutions and are ad-ministered by the Department of Education and Culture (DEC), House of Assembly: The South African Cultural History Museum, Cape Town; the National Cultural History and Open-air Museum, Pretoria; the Voortrekker Museum, Pietermaritzburg; the War Museum of the Boer Republics, Bloemfontein; the Michaelis Collec-tion, Cape Town; the William Fehr Collection, Cape Town and the Engelenburg Art Collection, Pretoria.

The following declared statutory cultural in-stitutions are administered by the DNE: The South African Museum, Pretoria; the Transvaal Museum, Pretoria; the Natal Museum, Pieter-maritzburg; the National Museum, Bloemfon-tein, the South African National Museum of Military History, Johannesburg; the Afrikaans Language Museum, Paarl; the National English Literary Museum, Grahamstown; the South African National Gallery, Cape Town; the Wil-liam Humphreys Art Gallery, Kimberley; the South African Library for the Blind, Grahamstown; the J L B Smith Institute of Ich-thyology, Grahamstown; the Science Founda-tion for Education, Science and Technology, Pretoria and the National Zoological Gardens of South Africa, Pretoria.

The following national monuments are also under the auspices of the DEC: The Voortrek-ker Monument, Pretoria; the 1820 Settlers Na-tional Monument, Grahamstown; the Louis Trichardt Garden of Remembrance, Maputo and the Huguenot Monument, Franschhoek. The department also gives financial assistance to two major cultural organisations — the *Suid-Afrikaanse Akademie vir Wetenskap en Kuns* and the 1820 Settlers Foundation, Grahamstown.

Cultural organisations

The main object of the *Suid-Afrikaanse Akademie vir Wetenskap en Kuns* (South African Academy for Science and Art) is the promotion of the Afrikaans language and literature, art and science. In March 1990 the organisation had 12 honorary members, 392 full-time members, 1 062 associate members and 12 correspondent mem-bers.

The major objectives of the *Federasie van Afrikaanse Kultuurvereniginge* (Federation of Afrikaans Cultural Societies) is to promote the Afrikaans language and the culture of Afrikaans-speaking citizens. The FAK has about 28 000 individual members while more than 3 700 cultural organisations are affiliated.

The main aim of the *Afrikaanse Taal- en Kul-tuurvereniging* (ATKV) is promotion of Afrikaans culture. The organisation administers 30 national projects aimed at promotion of Afrikaans music and drama and fosters Afrikaans culture.

The **English Academy of Southern Africa** promotes the interests of the English language and English language-based culture in Southern Africa.

The **South African Music Rights Organisation** (Samro) registers the works of serious composers of South African descent. Copies of some of the works are available in Samro's library.

From the accrued interest of the **Hendrik Verwoerd Trust Fund** the board of trustees makes awards of merit to any South African for outstanding service to the country and its people.

The *Boeresportgilde* is a recently established organisation with its own handbook stipulating the rules, scoring and clothing of nine different kinds of *boeresport*.

A cultural organisation which promotes traditional songs and dances of the Afrikaner is the *Afrikaanse Volksang- en Volkspelebeweging*

The **Federated Union of Black Artists** (Fuba) promotes the interests of Black artists.

Pamda (Pretoria Arts, Music and Drama Association) is a cultural organisation established to unite culturally the communities of Pretoria, Mabopane, Eersterus, Mamelodi, Atteridgeville, Garankuwa and Soshanguve. Pamda has 160 members.

Youth cultural organisations

The **Voortrekkers** is a cultural organisation for young Afrikaners. The **Boy Scouts** caters mainly for young English-speaking boys while English-speaking girls belong to the **Girl Guides**.

The **Children of Soweto Action Centre** (Cosac) is a non-profitable organisation which not only acquaints children with the mystery of the theatre, but also organises promotions on behalf of sponsors. These promotions extend as far as the independent states and self-governing territories.

Performing arts

South African Airways (SAA) is the largest sponsor of performing arts in the country. It sponsors the world series of opera worth R1,4 million and spread over four years.

Performing arts councils

Sacpac (South African Co-ordinating Performing Arts Council) is an encompassing organisation established to promote the interests of the four councils for performing arts. The functions of Sacpac rotate every three years to a different arts council.

The functions of the performing arts councils are decentralised on a provincial basis: The Performing Arts Council of the Transvaal (Pact), the Cape Performing Arts Board (Capab), the Performing Arts Council of the Orange Free State (Pacofs) and the Natal Performing Arts Council (Napac). Each of these councils is an autonomous registered, non profit-making company and each operates from its own modern theatre complex as a permanent home. Pact is headquartered in the State Theatre, Pretoria, Pacofs in the Sand du Plessis theatre complex in Bloemfontein, Capab in the Nico Malan Theatre centre in Cape Town and Napac in the Natal Playhouse in Durban.

These councils stage theatre, opera, ballet and music performances on a professional basis nationwide for adult and youth audiences in both official languages.

The councils are funded under a subsidy formula and receive their grant-in-aid via the Provincial Council of each province.

Among them, the councils annually stage more than 5 000 performances — not only in their home theatres but in others throughout their respective provinces. Audiences countrywide are now in the region of two million a year. The annual turnover (subsidies, grants and box-office receipts) is about R85 million a year.

Theatre

Apart from theatrical productions which are mounted by the four performing arts councils, most cities and towns still have amateur theatrical organisations, presenting plays in either English or Afrikaans.

Many foreign communities present amateur theatricals in their mother tongue. Productions are arranged by schools, cultural institutions, student groups, church and other organisations. Amateur societies receive grants from the DEC.

Ballet

Both Capab and Pact have established ballet companies capable of full-scale productions of classical ballets. Pact and Napac have also established smaller dance companies concentrating almost exclusively on 20th century works. Classical ballet productions and modern dance productions are presented by the various sister councils for Pacofs.

Opera

Each Performing Arts Council produces its own opera productions in the four provinces. South African Airways' World of Opera Sponsorship provides for one opera production in each province per year. An operatic theme is chosen annually by the four councils whereby Mozart operas will be presented one year, Verdi the next, and so forth.

Music

In music, the performing arts councils work closely with local music societies and groups. All four councils arrange performances by singers, instrumentalists, choirs, chamber orchestras and ensembles.

Members of the Association of the South African Phonographic Industry who market and distribute records are EMI (South Africa), Gallo (Africa), Teal Record Company, Gramophone Record Company, Trutone, RPM Record Company, WEA Records, Music for Pleasure and the CCP Record Company. Music, literary, dramatic and other artistic rights are protected by the Copyright Act as amended.

Professional orchestras

The major professional orchestra is The National Orchestra with 136 players. Other orchestras are the Cape Town Symphony Orchestra (72 members); the Capab Orchestra (45 members); the Natal Philharmonic Orchestra and the OFS Symphony Orchestra.

Other than military duties, performances are also presented by the South African Defence Force, South African Police, South African Navy and South African Air Force bands.

Many amateur and semi-professional orchestras also make a large contribution. In Soweto, the largest Black city in the country, young musicians are being trained in their own symphony ensemble.

Operation Outreach organises a project according to which members of the Pretoria Youth String Orchestra and the Northern Transvaal Youth Symphony Orchestra teach Black children of their own age to play musical instruments. This project is such a success that these pupils even sit for the examinations of the Royal School of Music.

The Cape Malay Choir Council annually presents the Top Eight competition for singing in which 31 choirs with 65 members each, compete for the Silver Fez and Koefija trophies. In 1989 the Breakaways of Silverton, Athlone won. These choir performances are very popular and in 1989 approximately 70 000 people attended.

Visual arts

One of Southern Africa's oldest and greatest art treasures is its rock art and more than 3 000 rock art sites have been recorded in the country. These are protected under the National Monuments Act, 1969, as amended.

Santam Insurance's project for child art is one of the largest in the country. Selected works are exhibited in South Africa and abroad.

Important museums include the SA National Gallery and Michaelis Collection in Cape Town; the Pretoria Art Museum; the Johannesburg Art Gallery; the Durban Art Museum; the King George VI Art Gallery, Port Elizabeth; the William Humphreys Art Gallery, Kimberley and the Tatham Art Gallery, Pietermaritzburg.

The art galleries of the universities of the Witwatersrand, South Africa and the Orange Free State and the Irma Stern Museum (University of Cape Town) have been accorded museum status.

The Pretoria Art Museum specialises in South African art while the SA National Gallery, Johannesburg Art Gallery, Durban Art Museum and Tatham Art Gallery concentrate on both European and South African art. The Johannesburg Art Gallery established the nucleus of an historical African art collection.

Literature

Literature is produced in the two official languages (English and Afrikaans) as well as in a number of African and Asian languages.

Apart from a few early, sporadic examples, the first **Afrikaans** texts date from the last quarter of the 19th century when the first determined effort was made to elevate Afrikaans, which at that stage had already been spoken at the Cape for more than a century, to a written language. Early Afrikaans literature was thematically restricted to close association with the fatherland in general and the Afrikaner in particular. Writers aimed at activating people to the struggle for their rights and at edifying, instructing or entertaining them. Comic and satiric verse was generally more successful than militant poetry, while in the area of prose and drama the first examples of historic-romantic, humorous-realistic and folklore-sociological narrative saw the light. The literacy products of this era were based mainly on a subculture, since writers were more or less isolated from any foreign influence.

After the Anglo-Boer War (1899-1902), during which practically no attention had been devoted to either the language struggle or the development of Afrikaans, Afrikaans literature was almost exclusively in the hands of a number of young writers. Through their work they were charged with the task of developing Afrikaans into a cultural language and shaping it into a sensitive instrument which would reflect the deepest emotions of both the nation and the individual, thus contributing to the official recognition of Afrikaans. The Anglo-Boer War and the South African nature, as in the work of C Louis Leipoldt (1880-1947) for example, were important stimuli for poetry immediately after 1900, although there were also examples of religious experience and poems dealing with the spiritual life and loneliness of the individual. In drama the emphasis shifted from historical romanticism and farce to man and his sociological problems, while the historical adventure story, romance, realism and didactics were perpetuated in prose and the animal world provided material for novels. The most important work in prose was in the less lengthy genres such as short stories, particularly those of Eugène N Marais (1871-1936), whose *Dwaalstories* (1927) were a highlight.

Poets writing around 1919 did not really attain the level of the previous generation, usually falling silent after a volume or two. They largely represented a transitionary phase. By the 1930s a new generation had appeared, displaying far greater professionalism in their work than their predecessors. This new breed, of whom N P van Wyk Louw (1906-1970), Uys Krige (1910-1987), W E G Louw (1913-1980) and Elisabeth Eybers (1915-) were the major figures, regarded poetry as a conscious task and strove to create verse in which every word and image were pure and artistically pleasing. In contrast to the local and typical portrayed by their predecessors, they demanded the right to explore all areas of human life and to give shape to them in their verse. Initially their poetry was directed at inner life and was self-analytical and confessional, but the danger of moralising and of becoming too isolated from the outside world was soon counteracted by a development towards poetry of portrayal and form. This development towards objectivity was most evident in the work of N P van Wyk Louw with his psychological ballads, dramatic monologues, epics *(Raka,* 1941; and *Tristia,* 1962), the latter being one of the most important volumes of Afrikaans poetry. Elisabeth Eybers explores the world of woman and her relationship to lover, husband and children, while her later work, produced in the Netherlands, displays a new, charged quality with verse stripped of all external ornament. Compared with the high flight of poetry, prose and drama were less impressive during this period and were mainly a continuation of former

trends, although realism was refined in the short stories and novels of J van Melle (1887-1953) and M E R (1875-1975).

The 1940s saw the debut of a further generation of poets who further expanded the work of those of the 1930s. From the outset the war, the city and a new social consciousness was more strongly evident among them and this susceptibility to contemporary and worldly stimuli led to stronger, sharper-edged verse, more compact poetry and an interest in the 'ugly' side of reality. The work of Ernst van Heerden (1916-) is striking in its portrayal of the struggle of a sensitive and defenceless man against the modern world and society, while compassion for the Jew, the Coloured and the socially disadvantaged is also evident in the work of this period. The most important poet of this generation was D J Opperman (1914-1985) who, in contrast to the conscious cultivation of individual emotions among the poets of the 1930s, explored every facet of reality in an almost mystical urge to identify with all earthly things. He wrote verse with concentrated economy of words expressed in forced metaphors and short-circuited images.

Since the middle of the 1950s a number of important poets have appeared. Among them are Peter Blum (1925-) whose poetry is striking in its rhythm, surprising imagery, neologisms and anti-sentimental, unmasking tonality. Adam Small (1936-) writes strong satirical, witty, derisive and often bitter political verse in which he uses the Cape Coloured dialect of Afrikaans. Ingrid Jonker (1933-1965) preferred free verse which tied up with the poetry of Eluard and that of the Dutch experimentalists of the 1950s.

The most important new talent is Breyten Breytenbach (1939-) whose originality, amazing power of imagery and exploitation of the face value of words illustrate his masterly command of the Afrikaans language in his love poetry, and protest and political poems about South Africa's racial conditions.

After Breytenbach the most important contemporary poet is Wilma Stockenström (1933-) with her meaningful exploration of Africa with its arid, harsh landscape and its early history of journeys of discovery, primitive life and palaeontological archaeology, written in terse and scaly language. Reaction to the overly amorphous structure is also evident among many poets who had their schooling in 'the art of verse' with Opperman (Ina Rousseau, Antjie Krog, Lina Spies, Fanie Olivier, Marlene van Niekerk) or perpetuate his tradition by playing with words and language (J C Steyn, Lucas Malan, Johann de Lange and Johann Lodewijk Marais), while

Sheila Cussons with her mystic, religious poetry is the foremost exponent of Roman Catholicism in Afrikaans.

In the mid-1950s a group of prose writers, later known as *Die Sestigers* appeared. In contrast to earlier Afrikaans prose *Die Sestigers* (among them Jan Rabie (1920-), Etienne Leroux (1922-1989), André P Brink (1935-), Chris Barnard (1939-), Abraham H de Vries (1937-) and Hennie Aucamp (1934-)) wanted to reflect in their novels and stories the complexity of life as such, with a predeliction for surrealism, the symbolic personality, anti-hero and outsider figure. The writers are more than ever outspoken about religion, sex and politics, linking up with contemporary West European and American trends in style.

In addition to *Die Sestigers* other prose writers also reflected a new idiom, with the renewal of the traditional novel set on a farm (Anna M Louw) and the portrayal of man in a hopeless struggle against inhuman laws (Elsa Joubert). One of the most important writers is Karel Schoeman (1939-) who in his best work provides the outsider figure with exceptional nuances through passive, indecisive main characters. Later writers tend more to the short story and among writers such as Etienne van Heerden, Koos Prinsloo and Alexander Strachan, the South African actuality of political violence and border war are dominant themes.

There has also been a measure of renewal in drama, although not as spectacular as that in prose. At this stage, however, Afrikaans drama is more than ever before reflecting the fertile influence of contemporary foreign literature (modern morality, the absurd, existentialist theatre and a new kind of epic drama). Some of the most important works have been written by Bartho Smit (1924-1986) and P G du Plessis (1934-), while Pieter-Dirk Uys (1945-) is particularly active in socio-political revue.

Not only White writers use this ethnic dimension to their own advantage. The works of Coloureds too display a wide variety and range: from *joie de vivre* to bitterness and irony and from the use of standard Afrikaans to the use of the crudish, cutting language of the Cape Flats.

With the exception of Arthur Fula, Afrikaans has up to now been unable to attract enthusiastic Black writers.

Afrikaans however succeeded in attracting writers from other White communities, like the Jewish poetess Olga Kirsch and Dutch, English and German-speaking writers such as Jan van Melle, the brothers Hobson, G H Franz, Peter Blum and Sheila Cussons, who is Irish by birth.

As a language Afrikaans is presently widely known and is increasingly enjoying the international recognition it deserves. Afrikaans literature has thus grown tremendously in a very short period and is broadening its horizons every day.

South African **literature in English** in the early years concerned itself mainly with farm life, South Africa's Black peoples and conditions in the mining towns of Johannesburg and Kimberley. The history of SA has proved a rich source of material for writers, but of even more abiding interest is the theme of racial interaction arising from the polygenesis of South Africa's peoples. This and other themes, including the diversity of the landscape itself, have proved a continuing inspiration to local and expatriot writers working in the areas of poetry, drama and fiction.

In all the genres there has been sustained development and in the last two decades the number of South African writers in English has greatly increased. This is attested to by the numerous anthologies of poetry and short stories that have appeared recently which give some insight into both past and present tendencies. The amount of indigenous drama being produced for both the stage and television has also greatly increased. South African 'protest drama' has aroused considerable interest at home and abroad and the work of Athol Fugard, in particular, has achieved worldwide recognition.

Turning to the novel one can observe a line of unbroken tradition from the fiction of Olive Schreiner through Sarah Gertrude Millin to Alan Paton. Though it may be individious to single out individuals in such a vast field as the contemporary South African novel in English, two names that stand out as international figures are Nadine Gordimer and J M Coetzee — both Booker Prize winners. However, there are many other perhaps equally talented novelists who are exploring the theme of a changing South Africa in both traditional and experimental prose fiction.

Literature for the **Indian** community in South Africa produced 15 prominent writers, including the poet Shabir Bhanoobhai and Brenda Kali, who wrote two novels.

Recent publications with **Coloureds** as subject without exception relates the social effect and psychological impact of the Group Areas Act on people. A more recent development in themes is crime among children who, due to circumstances, are homeless and become drug addicted.

The concept of **literature in African languages** entails two distinct components, oral art and written literature. Oral art goes back many centuries and was handed down from generation to generation by word of mouth. The central role of the oral tradition in the literary heritage of the Black peoples shows up in the fact that the first publications were in fact recordings of texts which were orally composed. In addition, numerous texts appearing in Xhosa, Southern Sotho and Zulu were first published in newspapers before being reissued in the form of anthologies and the like.

The past three decades have been marked by a considerable increase in the number of publications in Xhosa, Southern Sotho, Zulu, North-ern Sotho, Setswana, Xitsonga and Venda and has also seen the beginning of creative writing in Swati. This growth has been the result of both internal and external factors. While the foundation laid by previous generations acted as a stimulus for contemporary authors, the growth of Black literature was greatly advanced by the educational policies of central government and those of the independent states and the self-governing territories.

Generic diversity, comparable to those of the European languages, contributed to the rise of less-developed genres such as short stories,

Rock paintings of the early nomadic Bushmen are protected under the National Monuments Act

drama, essays and oral texts. While greatly benefiting the growth and diversification of the various literatures, the external stimulus has also had its disadvantages. On the one hand literature became too dependent on the school market, while on the other it led to a demand for genres in which authors had not yet been able to acquire the necessary skills. This has resulted in a situation which appears to be artificially stimulated rather than artistically realised.

The fundamental role of oral art shows up in its influence on written literatures. Novels, short stories and plays often repeat the didactic and moralistic objectives of folk tales. Themes are often signalled by means of proverbs, which are sometimes even used as titles of works. The episodic nature of some stories reminds one of the episodic and cyclic narratives of tradition. Characters often represent ideas, as in folk tales. Modern poetry too, shows influences of traditional poems, with formulaic compositional devices such as repetition and parallelism. Traditional metaphors abound.

Oral heritage continues to nourish written literatures with regard to aspects such as world view, subject-matter, theme, structure, style and devices for character delineation. Oral art coexists with the written literature and has opened new fields of interest, one of which may be called the oral-written interface.

Despite both internal and external disadvantages, however, the arrival of Black literature has become a fait accompli. Since 1960, when the South African Broadcasting Corporation established radio services in no less than nine languages, the various literatures have been enriched by regular broadcasts of dramas, serials, book readings and discussions and by the collection and recording of praise poems and a vast variety of folklore. The Educum Prize is awarded annually exclusively to Black writers who produce work of quality. De Jager-HAUM and various other publishers regularly launch competitions for writers.

Literature for children in African languages plays an important part in the education of South Africa's Black youth. Booksellers and publishers submit children's books in African languages to the Department of Education and Training's subdirectorate Media Centre Services for selection for the class library system. A panel of teachers drawn from the relevant language groups assists in evaluating the books, together with language experts from the ranks of the department and from outside. Preference is given to original works written in African languages rather than translations.

Libraries

South Africa's library and information services comprise two national libraries, four extensive provincial services, more than 670 public (municipal) libraries (most of which are affiliated to provincial services), 374 special libraries, 91 government libraries and 88 university and college libraries. These library services are staffed by 9 304 people, of whom 2 308 are qualified librarians. The book stock comprises about 47 million items and there are 1 570 service points.

The two national libraries are the State Library in Pretoria and the South African Library in Cape Town. The State Library serves as national lending library and clearing house for interlending between all local, Southern African and foreign libraries and compiles the national bibliography and union catalogue. The State Library compiles and publishes the South African National Bibliography (SANB), and two important bibliographical sources, viz Periodicals in Southern African Libraries and Index to South African Periodicals. The South African Library is the national archival and reference library and preserves the country's antiquarian treasures. In addition to this the library has a restoration service on national level. The South African Library for the Blind in Grahamstown is regarded by many librarians as the third 'national library' of the country.

There are five legal deposit libraries — the State Library, the South African Library, the Library of Parliament, the Bloemfontein Public Library and the Natal Society Library in Pietermaritzburg. One copy of every publication must be forwarded by publishers to each of these five libraries. In the case of a de luxe or very expensive edition, a copy need only be sent to the South African Library.

The four provincial library authorities develop and organise library services. In the Transvaal, Cape and Natal, some bigger cities are responsible for library services in their region. This means that Johannesburg, Pretoria, Roodepoort, Germiston, Cape Town, Port Elizabeth, East London, Durban and Pietermaritzburg have autonomous urban public libraries. The self-governing territories and independent states have their own national libraries and are responsible for their own library services.

There are more than 465 special libraries, which include the libraries of the two largest research organisations, the CSIR and the Human Sciences Research Council (HSRC). The subdirectorate Public Service Library Services of the Department of National Education co-or-dinates the library services of its government departments, divisions and institutions. Other special libraries are those of museums, public corporations, industries, other companies and research institutions in the private sector.

The South African Bibliographic and Informa-tion Network (SABINET), a computerised na-tional bibliographic network system, links libraries, information centres and the book trade via a telecommunications network to biblio-graphic data bases on a central computer facility.

The Conference of National Librarians of Southern Africa (CNLSA) facilitates relations and co-operation between national libraries on the subcontinent. The CNLSA therefore acts as a unique forum for common interests and counters isolation.

The South African Institute for Librarianship and Information Science (SAILIS) promotes the professional interests of all librarians and infor-mation scientists of all population groups. ALASA (the African Library Association of South Africa) is affiliated to SAILIS. It seeks to promote the reading habit among Black com-munities and the establishment of library ser-vices, especially in the Black self-governing territories.

Following UNESCO's International Year of Literacy, SAILIS declared 1990 the Year of the Reader. SA's entire library community was in-volved in different projects to promote literacy.

Historical records

The State Archives Service is a directorate of the Department of National Education and is ad-ministered in terms of the Archives Act, 1962. Archives are kept in different depots and inter-mediate depots — established in terms of the law — where they are accessible to the office of origin and the general public.

Each of the four provincial capitals has an archives depot to which archives, that are at least 30 years old, are transferred. Important and comprehensive private collections of documents are also kept.

The National Film, Video and Sound Archive specialises in tracing, obtaining, restoring, safeguarding, adaption, showing and distribu-tion of films, video tapes and sound recordings.

There are intermediate depots in Pretoria, Cape Town, Durban, Pietermaritzburg, Johan-nesburg and Port Elizabeth for archives not yet 30 years old but no longer required by the offices of origin.

The Cape archives depot contains the oldest archives of the country. The oldest original docu-ment bears the date 30 December 1651.

Archive documents covering the period up to 31 December 1960 are accessible to the public. Access to closed documents, including those after 1960, is allowed in exceptional circumstan-ces and only on the authority of the Minister of National Education.

Military archives are accommodated separately under the supervision of officers of the SADF, and access to these archives is subject to the approval of the Minister of Defence and the Minister of National Education.

The Institute for Contemporary History (INCH) of the University of the OFS is an im-portant depository for historical documents. It also has a research centre and an extensive com-puterised newspaper cutting system.

The institute houses more than 800 private document collections, which occupy more than 2 500 m of shelving space. These include the collections of all the State Presidents and Prime Ministers of South Africa since becoming a republic, as well as the collections of Cabinet Ministers, Members of Parliament, Provincial Administrators, newspaper editors and leaders in economic and cultural fields.

The institute also houses the official collec-tions of organisations such as the National Party, the South African Bureau of Racial Affairs (Sabra), the *Federasie van Afrikaanse Kultuur-verenigings* (FAK), the *Afrikaanse Taal en Kul-tuurbond* (ATKB), the *Afrikaanse Studentebond* (ASB) and the *OranjeVrouevereniging* (OVV).

Africana

The term Africana is used to describe the cul-tural objects of all the peoples of Africa, as well as historical objects pertaining to Africa.

The Africana Museum in Johannesburg is a municipal institution and limits its collection to south of the Zambesi River. The collections are among the most comprehensive in the country and include important collections of furniture, coins and medals, glass, ceramics, costumes, transport and items of archaeological (e.g. rock art), anthropological and ethnological interest. The history of Johannesburg is of prime impor-tance. The museum possesses the country's largest collection of pictorial Africana, i.e. originals, prints and drawings of Southern African interest. A new and much enlarged venue is at the planning stage.

A notable collection of printed Africana is that

of the Library of Parliament. Mr Harry Oppenheimer, a well-known businessman, owns an important private collection, some of which is open to the public.

Part of the William Fehr Collection is housed in the Castle of Good Hope in Cape Town while the prints, originals and maps are housed in an 18th century residence in Cape Town, *Rust en Vreugd.* In addition there is the Good Hope Collection at the Castle, where period rooms are being furnished.

The Mercedes-Benz collection is housed in the South African Cultural History Museum, Cape Town. This museum and its satellites, viz Bertram House, *Groot Constantia,* Koopmans de Wet House and the *Bo-Kaap Museum,* portray the cultural life of the early Cape and the cultures that influenced it.

The South African Cultural History Museum also controls both the *Stempastorie,* which deals largely with national symbols, and the South African Maritime Museum.

The National Cultural History Museum in Pretoria which recently experienced a disastrous flood, comprises prehistory, ethnology, archaeology, anthropology and cultural history. Part of its collection is housed in the other museums such as the Sammy Marks Museum, the Willem Prinsloo Agricultural Museum and the Pioneer Open-Air Museum at Silverton.

The Volkskas Museum claims to have the best coin collection and the Post Office Museum has a very fine collection of stamps.

Other important museums are the Killie Campbell Collection in Durban, the War Museum of the Boer Republics in Bloemfontein, the South African National Museum of Military History, Johannesburg, the Albany Museum, Grahamstown, the Alexander McGregor Memorial Museum, Kimberley, the Kaffrarian Museum, King Williams's Town and the *Oude Kerk Volksmuseum,* Tulbagh.

Cinema and films

Films and videos are distributed by Ster-Kinekor and Nu Metro. About 500 000 admission tickets, costing R7,50 on average, are sold every week at about 500 conventional theatres and 39 drive-ins. Ster-Kinekor, largest of the distribution and exhibition companies, operates a circuit of 170 four-wall cinemas and 39 drive-ins. Nu Metro theatres own 52 conventional theatres. About 250 feature films from the world's leading producers were screened during 1990, of which 78 were distributed by Ster-Kinekor. The film

Pretty Woman was voted top film for 1990 by both the Ster-Kinekor and Nu-Metro companies.

A film security bureau was established in 1981 in Johannesburg to combat illegal copying of films and videos.

Architecture

South Africa's African and western heritage, its climate and social structures have all made their mark on the history and character of its architecture.

The building methods of the indigenous people who used materials of their environment like grass, sticks, soil and stone formed the basis of South African vernacular. Typical South African architecture therefore varies from dwellings constructed of branches covered with vegetation to buildings of stone and daga with thatched roofs — a way of building based on traditional forms — whitewashed cottages with thatched roofs. This style was introduced to South Africa by settlers and developed into the well-known Cape-Dutch architecture.

Formal architecture (often based on pattern books) was introduced into South Africa during the two British occupations and continued through the Georgian and Victorian to the Edwardian era. Each South African region developed its own version of it.

South African architecture keeps track of the latest international trends and some fine examples of modern architecture are to be found in the country.

The Simon van der Stel Foundation, a national private cultural organisation founded in 1959, protects the country's architectural heritage by preserving and restoring buildings of architectural and/or historical significance. The foundation is a registered non-profitmaking company, governed by a National Council. The foundation has over 4 000 members and 18 branches in big centres countrywide to stimulate an interest in and awareness of conservation among members of the general public.

The main objectives of the National Monuments Council (NMC), are to preserve and protect our historical and cultural heritage, to encourage and promote conservation and protection of that heritage and to co-ordinate all activities related to monuments and cultural treasures so that they can be retained as tokens of the past and may serve as an inspiration for the future. A priority of the NMC is investigation of potential national monuments. To date, more than 4 000 buildings, sites or other properties have been declared national monuments. Archaeological and paleontological objects and terrains are automatically protected by law. This includes sites where rock art is found and fossils like those at Swartkrans and Makapansgat which are of international importance in the evolution of man. According to the Act as amended in 1986, provision is made for conservation areas and placing of items on the Register of Immovable Property, thus ensuring automatic protection for structures older than 50 years.

The council also cares for cemeteries and graves of those who died prior to 1914 in wars and rebellions in any area now included in the Republic, as well as those of Voortrekkers who died between 1835 and 1854. More than 60 000 graves, some 27 000 of which have already been attended to, are involved. The council is empowered to recommend establishment of national gardens of remembrance, of which about 25 have been created countrywide. Remains from many isolated graves which would be difficult to maintain properly, have been re-interred in these gardens of remembrance. The graves of South Africans who were killed in action in Britain and Europe are also maintained.

The council controls issue of permits for export of movable objects such as paintings and documents which have been in the Republic for more than 50 years and antiques more than 100 years old. The council also controls salvage of shipwrecks and salvaged goods older than 50.

Public holidays

The following days are public holidays in the RSA, Marion Island and Prince Edward Island: New Year's Day (1 January); Founders' Day (6 April); Good Friday; Family Day (Easter Monday); Workers' Day (1 May); Ascension Day; Republic Day (31 May); Kruger Day (10 October); Day of the Vow (16 December); Christmas Day (25 December) and Day of Goodwill (26 December).

News items: 1990

January

Listeners of the programme *Afrikaanse Treffers* voted Annalie van Rooyen's *Ek glo* most popular Afrikaans song of the year.

The Fifth Unisa International Piano Competition was held. The overall winner was Olivier Cazal of France. Ingrid Beute won both the

Oude Meester Travel Grant and the Adcock Ingram Award for the best performance by a South African.

South African Mbongeni Ngema was nominated for five Tony Awards and won best director awards in Los Angeles and Edinburgh. He was also nominated for a Grammy for his contribution to the New York *Sarafina!* album.

February

Britain ceased its cultural boycott of South Africa.

Unisa's Third International Song Competition was held and for the first time competitors from Eastern Bloc countries took part. Aleksandrina Pendatsjanska of Bulgaria was the overall winner.

The film *Cry Freedom* on the life and death in custody of Steve Biko was unbanned, nearly two years after it was seized by the Police.

To celebrate Elisabeth Eybers' 75th anniversary, two commemorative volumes were published; *Versamelde Gedigte* and a volume of essays titled *Uit liefde en ironie.*

Antjie Krog was awarded the Hertzog Prize for Poetry for *Lady Anne,* while T T Cloete received the W A Hofmeyr Prize for *Driepas* and Henriette Grové the CNA Literary Award for *In die Kamer was 'n Kas. Die Kind* by Jan van Tonder was awarded the ATKV Prize for Popular Literature. Breyten Breytenbach received the CNA Literary Award for English Literature for *Memory of Snow and of Dust.* The Ernst van Eerden Award for Creative Writing, issued by the University of the Witwatersrand, was taken by David Medalie for *The Shooting of the Christmas Cows.*

Whittle Productions of America requested permission to film extracts of Joyce Levinsohn's Children's Theatre production of *Songs and Tales from Africa* for inclusion in the Channel One series.

Wim Bosman's children's book *Dragtrunk of Addo* will be published by Maruzen Mates in Tokyo, Japan, as part of the *Smile* series.

March

Lakeside Majorettes, a Coloured drum majorette squad from Reiger Park, Boksburg, took part in the 23rd Annual Miss Dance Drill Team International Pageant in Los Angeles.

The ATKV started a project whereby sheet music of the 22 most popular Afrikaans songs of the previous year were identified and made available from the ATKV by means of a catalogue and order form.

The ban on the controversial film based on

André P Brink's novel, *A Dry White Season,* was lifted, as was the ban on Nelson Mandela's book, *The Struggle is My Life.*

April

*Feather,*the first literary agency dealing with film and television scripts, was established in Johannesburg.

Magda van Biljon's documentary film on the Bushmen was placed fifth out of 10 entries in the category for documentary films in the French Film Festival.

International Year of Literacy was celebrated in Johannesburg on 3 April, at a function organised by the READ Organisation.

The ATKV pledged an annual amount of R270 000 over five years to create a school for writers in co-operation with the University of Potchefstroom.

Isipingo Beach, a painting by Robert Gwelo Goodman, fetched a record price of R82 000.

Eight South African children visited New York to take part in the United Nations' World Children's Day festivities.

May

Fourteen Afrikaans singers participated in an Afrikaans music festival held in the amphitheatre of the Voortrekker Monument in Pretoria on Republic Day.

The first ever International Museum Day was held on 18 May.

The State Library last year received 22 502 serial publications and 24 730 papers under legal deposit and 5 657 other serials through subscription and exchange agreements.

Professors Eric Axelson and Andrew Pryor, both of the University of Cape Town, represented the SA branch of the international writers' organisation PEN (poets, essayists and novelists) at its 55th congress in Madeira.

South African director Louis Burke's first Broadway musical *Meet me in St Louis* was nominated for a Tony Award.

The Southern African Music Rights Organisation (Samro) awarded six bursaries of R3 000 each to young musicians.

South African filmmaker Anant Singh's company Videovision Enterprises signed a co-production deal with the British Broadcasting Corporation's Drama Department to produce a documentary on the musical *Township Fever.*

The Performing Arts Workers Equity (Pawe), a new body representing various categories of workers in the entertainment industry, was formally launched.

Rodney Phillips, former general director of Napac, was appointed deputy general manager of the Sydney Opera House in Australia.

South African musicians gathered at Le Chateau near Pretoria on Republic Day for the *Houtstok* Music festival.

Writer Breyten Breytenbach was appointed director of Taurus Publishers.

South African pianist Ingrid Beute won third prize in the 6th International Piano Competition in Marsala, Italy.

June

Mbuyiselwa (Jackie) Semela, dancer/-teacher/choreographer and a director of The Soweto Dance Theatre, was invited to participate in the prestigious American Dance Festival in North Carolina.

The Johannesburg Theatre Trust for Children was launched in Johannesburg.

Ladysmith Black Mambazo provided some of the background music in the *Storybook Classics* series starring actors such as Glenn Close and Robin Williams.

Record companies formed during the year were Creative Sound Recordings (CSR), Amor Music, Gallo Music Productions (GMP) within the CNA/Gallo organisation and Sun Music.

The Schweppes Company made available the largest single sponsorship in the form of 10 bursaries for aspiring dancers.

The Cape Town City Council won a bronze medal in the 32nd New York annual film and television festival for its video *Greening the city.*

The Johannesburg Public Library celebrated its centenary.

Fakes of famous sculptures by Anton van Wouw were sold as originals.

David Kramer, Paul Slabolepszy, David Goldblatt and Bobby Heaney teamed up for the production *The Eyes of their Whites* premiered at the Edinburgh Festival.

Wisselstroom, the first ever collection of homoerotic novels in Afrikaans was published by Human & Rousseau.

The first building in the Transvaal to be specifically designed for the State Archives Service officially opened its doors to the public.

The H J M Retief laboratory for reading science, the first of its kind in the country, was opened in Pretoria. The laboratory is used to train students in reading science and other practical aspects of library sciences.

July

Two Etienne Leroux collector's pieces were published; an edition of his uncompleted novel *Die suiwerste Hugenoot is Jan Schoeman* and a collection of documents relating to the ban on *Magersfontein! O Magersfontein!*

Santam's child art project drew 9 000 entries of which 100 were selected for itinerant exhibitions held at venues throughout the country. A further selection was made which will be exhibited in foreign countries.

According to his wishes Etienne Leroux's widow donated his books and documents to the University of the Orange Free State where they will become part of the Leroux Project.

Libraries countrywide were opened to all races.

Rosa Nepgen (80) finished the Afrikaans translation of Dante's *Divina Comedia.*

A South African documentary, *A Sahib in South Africa,* won an award at the Houston International Film Festival.

A record of 70 772 tickets were sold for the Standard Bank National Arts Festival in Grahamstown.

The ATKV and the SABC launched a competition to stimulate writing of original Afrikaans songs.

A Johannesburg record company, Eric Frisch Production, established a school to cater for composers, producers, musicians and technical staff at all levels in the recording, broadcasting and film industry.

The Library of Tape Aids for the Blind has a total of 15 857 titles mainly in English and Afrikaans, with small collections in other languages, and serves approximately 4 702 individual members and 135 mini libraries in schools, hospitals and old-age homes throughout Southern Africa.

August

An ensemble, *Theatre for Africa,* featured at the Edinburgh International Festival Fringe, while Michael Hunt and Lorraine Jaffit's production of Susan Pam's *Curl up and dye* won the Fringe First Award.

Clara Hooyberg, assistant cellist of the Pro Musica Orchestra, is one of only two South Africans who qualified for an international music course held in Interlochen, Michigan, America.

The Afrikaanse Taal- en Kultuurvereniging (ATKV) celebrated its 60th year.

The State Library in Pretoria receives the *Moscow News* and *The Star: international airmail* is sent to a Moscow library in accordance with an agreement reached.

The original Park Station is to be brought back to Johannesburg's central area as a museum as from 1991.

The South African Institute for Librarianship and Information Science declared 1990 the Year of the Reader.

The new version of the *Afrikaanse woordelys en spelreëls* was completed 25 years after the first edition.

Mrs Eulah Nissen of Bredasdorp was one of only seven florists worldwide who were invited to demonstrate flower arranging in Paris, France. She made a large arrangement of 3,5 m high and 2 m wide in only 15 minutes before 4 000 spectators in Europe's largest auditorium.

Excavations in Cape Town's dockland area have uncovered the remains of more than 40 wooden barrels of the type traditionally used to transport goods on sailing vessels.

The *Federasie van Afrikaanse Kultuurvereni- ginge* decided to open its doors to people of all races.

A record amount of R160 000 for a Pierneef painting was paid for *Plaas by Plumstead.*

The Post Office Museum in Pretoria celebrated its 10th anniversary on 7 August.

The sixth Roodepoort Eisteddfod was launched on 8 August.

The South African film industry's subsidy has been raised to a record amount of R50 million, according to an announcement by the Minister of Home Affairs and of National Education.

South Africa's first language route, one of the few in the world, was introduced and will be known as the Paarl Historical Language Route with eight different visiting points.

The National Orchestra was augmented by a quarter with the arrival of 30 international musicians between August and November.

The South African Association for Script Writers held a seminar in Johannesburg on writing of radio scripts.

Only three months after the formation of the multi-cultural Pretoria Youth Choir, it left for performances in Helsinki, Finland, at the invitation of an international educational music association.

September

National Literacy Week was celebrated during the first week of the month — 8 September was UNESCO's International Literacy Day.

Gallo Africa bought a major share in Nu Metro. The result will be 60 to 70 new cinemas in the country.

Two pupils of the Cape Province won the junior and senior sections respectively of the *Afrikaanse Taal- en Kultuurbond's (ATKB)* debating competition.

A Cape Town pupil, Morné van Rooyen, won

the gold medal in the history olympiad of the *Suid-Afrikaanse Akademie vir Wetenskap en Kuns* and Trek Petroleum.

A new concept was introduced at the HSRC's book festival. Parents send all particulars of their children to Create-a-Book and within 20 minutes a book exclusively for your child can be ready, complete with colour and hard cover and with room for the child's own photograph.

On a European tour the South African Youth Choir, with two British choirs, sang before the Pope and 8 000 people in the Nervi Centre in the Vatican City where they afterwards met the Pope and posed for a photograph with him.

Of the 1 500 new entries in the international Who's Who, 24 are South Africans.

The South African Chef's Association won second place in an international cooking contest held in Prague, Czechoslovakia. They prepared traditional South African fare and won 14 gold and six silver medals and a special prize salver.

Ster-Kinekor announced the establishment of 20 new cinemas in the Johannesburg area, bringing the total number of cinemas in this area to 91.

Drum majorettes of St Dominic's High in Boksburg won the South African championships.

November

The *Suid-Afrikaanse Taalbond* celebrated its centenary on 1 November.

Experiencing difficulty in selecting only 10 bursary winners in the Santam Insurance art competition, judges decided to award 11 bursaries instead.

Transvaal restaurants won top honours in the competition for restaurants held annually by Nedbank American Express Gold Card and *Style* magazine.

South African poet Mzwakhe Mbuli's debut song album, *Change is pain,* is being distributed in Germany by the Pirhana Record Company and in America by Rounder Records.

The standard of entries for the annual Sacpac Playwriting Competition was so low that no prize was awarded.

Furniture, a fifteenth-century grandfather clock, and a number of dresses from the Victorian era were damaged when a water pipe burst in the ceiling of the National Cultural History and Open-Air Museum in Pretoria.

Mbongeni Ngema and Gallo (Africa), formed the Committed Artists Records company.

A student from the University of the Witwatersrand, Basil Lawrence (20), became the youngest playwright to win the Amstel Playwright of the Year Award worth R15 000.

Anant Singh's locally made production *The Fever,* was screened by the BBC.

The records of Lt Col Courtenay Bourchier Vyvyan of the 217-day Siege of Mafeking in 1899-1900 were sold in London for R123 970.

The prize money for the 1991 Volkskas Bank Atelier Prize was doubled to R15 000.

South Africa's own walk of fame was opened at Starnet's cinema complex N1 City near Cape Town.

J M Coetzee won the British Sunday Express Book of the Year Award worth R100 000 for his novel *Age of iron.*

Prize money for the Cape Town Triennial was raised from R15 000 to R25 000, making it the top arts prize.

December

Contracts to publish a translation of Karel Schoeman's novel *'n Ander land (Another country)* in Britain and Germany were signed.

The South African Maritime Museum was opened at the Robinson dry dock in the Cape Town Harbour.

South Africa's first compact disc factory was opened at Midrand.

Artist Johann du Plessis won second place out of 3 000 entries for the Fifth International Miniature Exhibition in Toronto, Canada.

Starnet launched a new cinema chain. Seventeen new theatres were opened in Cape Town in less than two months.

Four theatres opened in The Mall in Rosebank, Johannesburg. The centre now has 10 theatres showing art films.

Total and the Urban Foundation held the first national farm choir competition in the Sand du Plessis Theatre, Bloemfontein.

The Tygerberg Children's Choir shared first place with two other choirs in an international choir competition held at the Musikhochschule in Graz, Austria.

In memoriam:
Poet Solomon Ignatius Mocke (77) — 5 January; writer Lize Swart — 8 January; cartoonist T O Honiball — 22 February; artist Anna Vorster (Schutte) — 15 April; film producer Albie Venter — 19 May; jazz pianist Chris McGregor — 26 May (in France); film and theatre personality Pierre de Wet (80) — 24 June; concert pianist Odette Ray — 30 June; South Africa's last concentration camp child — Paul Bosman (93); actor Richard Haines — 22 July; radio and TV-personality Marie Tromp — 16 August; actor Stuart Brown — 10 November; former editor of the *Sunday Times* and ambassador-

elect Tertius Myburgh (55) — 2 December; TV   9 December; newsreader and story teller Roelf
and film producer/director Daan Retief (64) —   Jacobs (49) — 11 December.

Acknowledgements:
Administration: House of Assembly
Administration: House of Delegates
Administration: House of Representatives
Africana Museum at the Public Library, Johannesburg
Department of National Education
Foundation Simon van der Stel
Human Sciences Research Council
Prof J C Kannemeyer, Division Sensal, HSRC
Prof S G Kossick, Department of English, Unisa
Prof C F Swanepoel, Department of African Languages, Unisa
Sacpac
State Library, Pretoria

In terms of religious affiliation South Africa is a plural community. Almost 80 per cent of the population professes the Christian faith although millions of Blacks still observe traditional African or tribal religions. Other major religious groupings are the Hindus, Muslims and Jews. A small minority of South Africa's population has no religious affiliation.

Generally speaking, South Africa's population is religiously orientated and religious beliefs play an important role in public affairs. Although freedom of religion is guaranteed by the Constitution, religious groups are often opposed to the government in certain contentious issues. Church-leaders have recently strongly resisted certain traditional policies.

The Christians

The largest grouping of Christian churches, the African Indigenous Churches (AICs), is almost exclusively Black while some smaller groupings are almost exclusively White (or Coloured). The large and influential Dutch Reformed Church (NGK), often seen as the prime author of apartheid, has more adherents among people of colour than among Whites.

There are many official and unofficial bilateral and multilateral ecumenical relations among the various churches. Among the most important of these is the South African Council of Churches (SACC) even though it is not representative of the entire spectrum of churches. The largest AICs, the Afrikaans churches and most of the Pentecostal and charismatic churches are not members of the SACC and usually have their own co-ordinating liaison bodies.

Church attendance in South Africa is good in both rural and urban areas and the church is well served by a large number of ministers and officials. On the whole, training for the ministry is thorough and intensive, based on a variety of models. The ministry patterns are greatly varied. The churches are increasingly broadening their leadership and ministry to include people of all ages and both sexes.

Apart from the work of the churches a number of Christian organisations operate in the RSA, doing important work in the mission field, giving aid, providing training and dealing with the media. (A comprehensive register appears in the South African Christian Handbook 1990. Florida: Christian Info.)

Extensive broadcasting of religious radio and television programmes underlines the importance of religion in South Africa. Virtually every newspaper carries a scriptural message of some kind every day. Various religious magazines and newspapers are distributed.

As in educational institutions, the SA Defence Force and the SA Police regard religious instruction as an intrinsic part of the training of recruits. In the SA Defence Force some 1 650 chaplains (of which the 130 full-time chaplains represent 37 denominations) attend to the spiritual needs of men and women. In the SA Police each of the 11 regions into which the Police is organised has a number of full-time chaplains additional to those ministering to the trainees in the colleges. Policemen and women can worship in their own congregations when not on duty. Thirty-three churches are represented by 28 chaplains and full-time religious workers in the Department of Correctional Services. In addition a further 1 741 part-time spiritual workers of some 56 churches and faiths are allowed official entry.

African Indigenous Churches (AIC)
One of the most dramatic aspects of Black religious affiliation has been the rise of the Black independent church movement. Although these churches originally resulted from a number of breakaways from White-controlled mission churches (the so-called Ethiopian churches) the movement has developed its own dynamics and momentum. Because it is so suited to the Black peoples' spiritual characteristics, its growth continues. The majority can therefore no longer be regarded as Ethiopian churches, but as Zionist or Apostolic churches.

It is estimated that about one in three of all the Black people belongs to the independent church movement. In other words, the 4 000 independent churches have a membership of more than seven million, making this movement the single most important religious grouping in the country.

The independent Black churches attract people from rural areas as well as from towns.

There are, for example, hundreds of separate churches in rural KwaZulu and about 900 from all ethnic groups in the urban complex of Soweto alone. In the northern Natal/KwaZulu and south-eastern Transvaal areas they number more than half the people as their members. In cities churches help people to adapt to the often harsh urban environment.

The Afrikaans churches

The English term 'Dutch Reformed' is not very helpful. The names of at least three Afrikaans churches could be translated in this way.

Until 1991 the Nederduitse Gereformeerde family of churches (NGK) in South Africa consisted of four independent churches which, according to the census, represent more than four million people.

At the last count the NG (mother) Church had 1 271 congregations with approximately 1,4 million members and 2 003 ordained ministers. It is divided into 11 regional synods under the control of the General Synod.

The NG Sendingkerk (NGSK) consists of 268 mostly Coloured congregations with 500 000 members, served by 262 ministers.

The NGK in Afrika (NGKA) was established when the Black churches in the different provinces and regions were affiliated as autonomous regional synods. The church now has some 472 congregations with more than 750 000 members, served by about 400 ministers.

The fourth member of this church family is the small Reformed Church in Africa, with approximately 2 500 (mostly) Indian members in ten congregations.

Recently the NGSK united with the NGKA to form the United Reformed Church in Southern Africa.

The Nederduitsch Hervormde Kerk (NHK) and the Gereformeerde Kerk (GK) are regarded as part of the Afrikaans church family. The NHK (Whites only) has nearly 130 000 members in approximately 300 congregations, served by 420 trained ministers. The smaller GK are divided into synods on an ethnic basis, but with one General Synod.

There are also several other churches with Afrikaans-speaking adherents. Some have very large memberships.

Roman Catholic Church

In recent years the Roman Catholic Church (RCC) has been growing strongly in numbers and influence, even though South Africa is predominantly Protestant. Its relationship with other churches is not tense and on the socio-political front especially the RCC and other churches work closely together.

Black people make up over 80 per cent of the membership of the Catholic Church in South Africa. According to the census there are nearly three million Catholics in South Africa.

Other Christian churches

Other established churches include the Methodist Church (2,7 million followers), the Church of the Province of Southern Africa (an Anglican Church with two million members), the various Lutheran churches (with approximately one million members), the Presbyterian Church and the Congregational Church (with nearly 500 000 followers). With others they form the nucleus of the South African Council of Churches.

The different Baptist groupings are not large, but they represent a strong church tradition.

The Pentecostal and Charismatic churches are a growing factor in South African Christianity and are joined in different groupings such as the International Fellowship of Christian Churches (IFCC) and the Church Alliance of Southern Africa.

The Full Gospel Church is an indigenous church with adherents in all sections of the population.

The Salvation Army started work in South Africa in 1883. It has an extensive network of community service welfare programmes.

Also active in South Africa are the Greek Orthodox and Seventh-day Adventist churches and other smaller groupings.

Black traditionalists

Nearly 5,5 million South Africans, i.e. 18 per cent of the total population, indicate that they are not affiliated to any religious organisation. The majority of these are African traditionalists, the second largest religious grouping in the country.

Because the traditional religion of the Black peoples has a strong cultural base it is understandable that the various tribes have different rituals, but there are certain common features. A Supreme Being is generally acknowledged but of far greater importance are the ancestors, the deceased elders of the tribe who are also known as the 'living dead'. They are regarded as part of the community, as indispensable links with the spirit world and the powers which control everyday affairs. These ancestors are not gods, but because they fulfil a key role in bringing either good or ill fortune, maintaining good relations with them is of the utmost importance and they must be propitiated by a variety of ritual offerings.

Magic is also important. Traditionalists believe the power of the spirits can be manipulated by certain professionals using elaborate procedures passed down by word of mouth.

While positive knowledge of herbs and other therapeutic techniques and the use of supernatural powers can work to the benefit of the individual and the community, some practitioners are able to work black magic, so they and their works are feared.

Because of the close contact with Christianity many Black people find themselves in transition somewhere between traditional African religion and Christianity.

Other religions

Most Indians retained their Hindu religion when they came to South Africa. Today nearly two-thirds of South Africa's Indians are Hindus, the rest being either Muslims (20 per cent) or Christians (12 per cent) with a sprinkling of other religions.

The Muslim community is small (approximately 500 000 followers, some 1,5 per cent of the population). The main components are the Cape Malays, officially part of the Coloured group, as well as 20 per cent of the Indians who are descended from North Indian immigrants. Islam also has a growing Black following.

The Jewish population was estimated at about 120 000 in 1990. Of these a small percentage are members of the United Progressive Jewish Community (the Reform Movement). The majority are Orthodox Jews.

Buddhism is rather disorganised in the RSA. The number of Parsees has decreased while a small group of Jains is concentrated in Durban. The Ba'hai faith is also establishing groups and temples in various parts of the country.

News items: 1990

Copies of the South African edition of a new English Bible translation — the Revised English Bible — became available in January.

An International Forum for Religion and Culture (IFRC) was established in Pretoria to make information on the influence of religion on different disciplines available on a co-ordinated basis.

A delegation from the Church Alliance of South Africa (Casa) — an umbrella body of

churches which claims to represent about 15 million Christians in South Africa — called on the State President in January and asked him to speed up reform and totally abolish apartheid in all its forms.

The Roman Catholic Sacramentary, used for celebration of the Eucharist, was published in Afrikaans after eight years of preparation.

Christian Television (CTV) was established in March 1990.

A special committee was appointed to investigate satanism and devil worship after the SA Police announced that at least 11 infants had been sacrificed and minors sexually molested in occult rituals in the Peninsula and towns in the Cape Province during the last three years.

Konteks, a family magazine of the Nederduitse Gereformeerde Kerk, was published for the first time in March 1990.

Dr Henry Ralph was the first South African to

Table 1 The religious affiliation of the SA population, mid 1990

Religious grouping	Number in thousand	Percentage
African indigenous churches	7 006	22,75
Nederduitse Gereformeerde Churches (NGK)	4 299	13,96
Roman Catholic Church	2 963	9,62
Methodist Church	2 747	8,92
Anglican Churches	2 026	6,58
Lutheran Churches	1 093	3,55
Presbyterian Churches	758	2,46
Congregational Churches	607	1,97
Nederduitse Hervormde Churches (NHK)	357	1,16
Apostolic Faith Mission	351	1,14
Baptist Churches	317	1,03
Gereformeerde Churches (GK)	243	0,79
Full Gospel Churches	228	0,74
Assemblies of God	179	0,58
Seventh Day Adventists	102	0,33
Other Christian Churches	773	2,51
TOTAL CHRISTIAN CHURCHES	24 052	78,09
Hindus	650	2,11
Muslims	434	1,41
Judaists	148	0,48
Other non-Christians	5 513	17,90
TOTAL NON-CHRISTIANS	6 748	21,91
TOTAL POPULATION	30 797	100,00

The religious percentages for the population groups were taken from the latest religious census of 1980 (Report no. 02-80-06) and are assumed not to have changed significantly
The total populations for the different groups are the mid-year estimates of the Central Statistical Service for 1990

complete the seven year daily study of the Talmud, known as the Shass.

Prof Johan Heyns, former chairman of the General Synod of the Nederduitse Gereformeerde Kerk, paid an unofficial visit to church leaders in Copenhagen, Budapest and Paris in May 1990.

The South African Council of Churches met in Bellville near Cape Town in June for its 22nd National Conference.

Pastor J T du Plessis, secretary of ecumenical affairs of the Apostolic Faith Mission, co-chaired the annual meeting of Roman Catholic and Pentecostal theologians in Switzerland in July.

A pulpit Bible donated by the Northern Transvaal military region, was sent to the Afrikaans community in Comodoro Rivadavia in Argentina in July.

Ds Nick Apollis was elected moderator of the NG Sendingkerk in September, succeeding Dr Allan Boesak.

All 70 000 Zulu Bibles printed in June were sold within three weeks.

The Methodist Church of Southern Africa's annual conference decided in October to resume payment of affiliation fees to the World Council of Churches from the beginning of 1991.

Professor Pieter Potgieter (50) became the youngest man ever to hold the position of Moderator of the Nederduitse Gereformeerde Kerk's (NGK) general synod.

The NGK general synod decided in October to allow women to become elders and be ordained.

Pastor Japie Lapoorta, principal of the Theological College Sarepta, was elected moderator of the Coloured section of the Apostolic Faith Mission in October.

It was announced in October that people of all race groups would in future be accepted at the Hugenot College in Wellington which falls under the General Synod of the NGK.

The NGK expressed itself in favour of a declaration of human rights in October.

Delegates of the NGK to the Church Conference at Rustenburg, Transvaal, in November confessed that apartheid was a sin. This gave rise to considerable controversy among ministers and members of the church in rural areas.

Acknowledgements:
Prof J J Kritzinger, Institute for Missiological Research, University of Pretoria

President F W de Klerk's speech at the opening of Parliament on 2 February 1990 had tremendous repercussions on the South African sporting scene. After years of increasing isolation the country was cautiously being welcomed back into world sport, provided that the reform changes initiated by Mr de Klerk were maintained, and also that the various sports in South Africa were each represented by a single governing body.

South Africa had been isolated by the international community on the sports field because of its political policies since the 1950s, although the Government scrapped discrimination in sport in the 1970s.

In 1979 the Government decided to depoliticise sport as far as possible. Various laws were amended to this effect.

During March 1985 virtually all the national sporting organisations endorsed a joint declaration in which they committed themselves to nonracial sports and games on all levels, to equal opportunities for all sportsmen and women, utilisation of existing facilities by all and improvement of inferior facilities.

By the middle of 1990, following President de Klerk's speech, many of the major sports which had previously been segregated along racial and ethnic grounds, were talking to one another. Apart from cricket, agreement in rugby, tennis, athletics, boxing, soccer and all other sports was well on the way.

South African and Black African sports leaders met in Harare in November 1990 and agreed to press ahead with a framework for South Africa's eventual return to the world sporting community.

By 10 December it was reported from Lillehammer, Norway, that the International Olympic Committee would visit South Africa in April 1991 for the first time in 20 years, and the chairman of its apartheid commission said South Africa could possibly be readmitted to the Games in 1992. South Africa was expelled from the Olympic movement in 1970.

In terms of the new Constitution (1984) each of the White, Coloured and Indian population groups regulate and manage its own educational schooling programmes, including official schools sports. The Constitution neither enforces multiracial competition, nor does it prohibit it. Sport is free of statutory control and sports clubs and organisations make their own rules. All teams or individual players are selected on merit, as are officials and members of controlling bodies. All 26 Olympic sports have a national controlling body representative of all participating communities.

Sport in the RSA is controlled by two major umbrella organisations: the South African National Olympic Committee (Sanoc) and the Confederation of South African Sport. Together they organise and stage national games and sports festivals, control the award of national colours and generally promote sport at national and international level. Other organisations concerned with sport are the Directorate of Sport and Recreation Advancement in the Department of National Education, the Sport Foundation of Southern Africa, the SA Association for Sport Science, Physical Education and Recreation (Saassper) and the SA Council on Sport (Sacos).

The Trimsa Federation promotes physical fitness and outdoor education, adventure, youth work and general health and recreational activities which are not usually recognised as sports.

The National Sport Congress (NSC), the sports wing of the African National Congress (ANC) was officially constituted as a sport organisation at a meeting on 20 May in Soweto with Dr George Mkhare as its first president.

One of the biggest sports events during 1990 was Mike Gatting's rebel cricket tour of South Africa. From the moment the English players set foot on South African soil the tour was plagued by protests. The position became untenable and the tour had to be curtailed. Later, the second leg of the tour was also discarded by the organisers.

Following the decision to curtail the tour, the rest of South African sport decided to agree to a moratorium on rebel or unofficial tours.

Apart from the Gatting tour a total of 1 628 sportsmen and women and coaches from 57 countries of 47 sports bodies visited South Africa during 1989, according to an announcement made in Parliament. A total of 829 South Africans of 40 sports bodies visited 24 overseas countries.

Sports events: 1990

Tvl = Transvaal; N-Tvl = Northern Transvaal; E-Tvl = Eastern Transvaal; S-Tvl = Southern Transvaal; OFS = Orange Free State; WP = Western Province; EP = Eastern Province; SS = Southern Suburbs; SN = Southern Natal; NN = Northern Natal; GW = Griqualand West

January

Athletics: Zola Pieterse wins her first race in SA after returning from the UK — the Dairy Belle Open 1 500 m, in 4'15"80 (Bloemfontein, 29/1).

Boxing: Dingaan Thobela wins his lightweight fight against Columbian Felipe Orozco on a 10th round TKO (Johannesburg, 22/1); Dingaan Thobela is voted South Africa's Boxer of the Year (Johannesburg, 23/1); Sugarboy Malinga outpoints American Tony Harrison over 10 rounds (Durban, 29/1).

Canoeing: Graeme Pope-Ellis and Tim Cornish win the Hansa Duzi canoe marathon in 8:43'39" (Durban, 20/1).

Cricket: The SA under 21 team (209/5) beats the SA Schools' XI (207/8) by two runs (Cape Town, 4/1); Mike Gatting's English team arrives in SA; Ewie Cronjé retires as president of the Free State Cricket Union (22/1); WP 507/9 declared (Gary Kirsten 175, Peter Kirsten 128; Rod Mc-Curdy 4/129, John Maguire 5/137) and 166/6 declared draws with EP 404 (Mark Rushmere 81, Kenny McEwan 101, Dave Rundle 3/96) and 18/2 (Currie Cup Final, Port Elizabeth, 26/1); English XI 305 (Mike Gatting 75) and 206 (Bill Athey 70; Hugo Lindenberg 3/57) beats Combined Bowl XI 152 (David Graveney 6/45, John Emburey 3/47) and 105 (Graveney 4/20, Emburey 5/36) by 254 runs (Kimberley); SA Universities XI 328 (Hansie Cronjé 104) and 160/9 declared draws with English XI 212 and 85/4 (Bloemfontein, 30/1).

Golf: Fulton Allem wins the Lexington PGA tournament with a score of 266 (Johannesburg, 20/1).

Power boating: Peter Lindenberg wins the SA Grand Prix Championships (Benoni, 7/1).

Rugby: Springbok centre Danie Gerber voted SA Rugby Player of the Decade for the 1980s by international BBC-TV commentator Ian Robertson (London, 2/1).

Soccer: Sundowns beat Moroka Swallows 1-0 in a R40 000 Challenge match (Pietersburg, 22/1).

Tennis: Wayne Ferreira wins the boys' under 18 title by beating Andrei Rybalko (USSR) 6-2, 5-7, 6-2; Ferreira and Grant Stafford win the boys' doubles title defeating Italians Andrea Gaudenzi and Fabio Beraldo 6-4, 6-4; Joanette Kruger wins the girls' under 16 title by beating Svetlana Komleva (USSR) 7-5, 6-4; and under 14 Neville Godwin beats Spaniard Gonzalo Corrales 6-4, 7-6 (15/13) (International Juniors' Tournament, Port Washington, 2/1), Michelle Anderson wins the girls' under 18 title by beating Joanette Kruger 6-3, 5-7, 6-1 (Puerto Rico); Gail Boon wins the Triumph SA women's single title by beating Robyn Field 6-2, 6-4 (Johannesburg, 19/1); Gail Boon beats Joanette Kruger 5-7, 7-5, 7-5 in the Triumph International's women's tournament (Pretoria, 26/1); Wayne Ferreira voted international doubles champion (London, 29/1).

February

Athletics: Jan Pienaar (N-Tvl) breaks his own SA shot put record with a shot of 20,47 m (Pretoria, 17/2).

Body-building: Hannes Coetzee (OFS) voted the overall winner at the SA senior championships (Port Elizabeth, 17/2).

Bowls: Rob Owsley (EP) beats team-mate Neil Burkett 21-20 in the SA Masters tournament (Durban, 1/2); Sylvia Phillips (E-Tvl) wins the SA Masters women's tournament by beating WP's Evelyn Chiat 20-18 (Johannesburg, 15/2).

Boxing: Jackie Gunguluzu retains his SA featherweight title by outpointing November Ntshingila over 12 rounds (East London, 19/2); Grant Mesias outpoints American junior welterweight Victor Mobley over 10 rounds (Pretoria, 20/2); Lybo Nkoko, SA bantamweight champion, beats Benito Rodriquez of Mexico with a TKO in the 5th round (Johannesburg, 27/2).

Cricket: SA Invitation XI 305/2 declared (Mark Rushmere 150 no, Daryll Cullinan 77 no) and 315/2 declared (Rushmere 151 no, Roy Pienaar 81). SA Invitation XI draws with the English XI 292/5 declared (Chris Broad 85; Omar Henry 3/115) and 198/5 (Henry 3/76) (Pietermaritzburg, 3/2); English XI 156 (Allan Donald 4/30, Richard Snell 4/38) and 122 (Donald 4/29) loses by 7 wickets inside three days to SA 203 (Roy Pienaar 84; Paul Jarvis 3/71, Richard Ellison 4/41) and 76/3 (First Test, Johannesburg, 8/2); English XI 217 loses by 5 wickets to SA 218/5 (One-Day International, Verwoerdburg, 16/2); SA 219/5 beats the English XI 205/7 by 14 runs (One-Day International, Durban, 18/2); SA 301/7 beats the English XI 94 by 207 runs (One-Day International, Bloemfontein, 20/2); English XI 296/8 (Kim Barnett 136) beats SA 162 (Mike Gatting 6/26) by 134 runs (One-Day International, Johannesburg, 22/2).

Golf: Phil Jonas wins the Goodyear Classic with a score of 287 (Port Elizabeth, 10/2).

Hockey: S-Tvl wins the Huletts Aluminium SA

under 21 indoors tournament by beating Natal Midlands 5-0 (Pietermaritzburg, 17/2).

Motor sport: Springbok Sarel van der Merwe and team-mate Bob Wollek (France) come third in the 24-hour Daytona Rally (Florida, 4/2).

Road running: Frith van der Merwe wins the 42,2 km SA women's marathon title in a record time of 2:27'36" and David Tsebe the men's title in 2:09'50" (Port Elizabeth, 24/2).

Snooker: Peter Francisco beats the world's fifth-ranked Terry Griffiths (Wales) 5-1 in the 4th round of the British Open tournament (London, 25/2).

Soccer: Kaizer Chiefs' Shane Macgregor is awarded the NSL-Sunday Times Footballer of the Year Award (Johannesburg, 1/2).

Swimming: Natal Springbok Lizelle Peacock betters her own SA 100 m breaststroke record with a time of 1'13"23 (Johannesburg, 26/2).

Tennis: Michelle Anderson ranked second to American Jennifer Capriati as the world's top junior girl's player (London); Jeff Coetzee becomes the first non-white South African under 12 Masters champion; Michelle Anderson and Marcos Ondruska win the under 18 titles (Johannesburg, 10/2); Dinky van Rensburg wins the Kansas City Classic by beating Nathalie Tauzlat (US) 2-6, 7-5, 6-2 (Wichita, Kansas, 11/2); Gary Muller beats first seed Stefan Edberg (Sweden) 6-1, 7-5 and Jimmy Arias (US) 4-6, 7-6 (7/4), 6-4.

Triathlon: Double Springbok Rockley Montgomery wins the SA Double Standard Championships in 5:13:41 (Lichtenburg, 3/2).

March

Athletics: Former American world champion Tom Petranoff hurls the javelin to a new SA and Africa record distance of 86,46 m (Port Elizabeth, 6/3); Karen Kruger sets a new Africa and SA women's long jump record of 6,85 m (Johannesburg, 24/3).

Bowls: Dave Poultney (OFS) beats former SA champion Dave Kempthorne 21-13 in the Metboard SA men's singles final (Cape Town, 31/3).

Boxing: Welcome Ncita becomes the new IBF junior featherweight champion by outpointing champion Fabrice Benichou over 12 rounds (Tel Aviv, 11/3); Brian Mitchell retains his WBA junior lightweight title by outpointing American Jackie Beard over 12 rounds (Grosseto, Italy, 14/3).

Cricket: Natal 202 loses by one wicket to EP 205/9 (B&H final, Durban, 30/3).

Golf: John Bland wins Dewar's tournament by one stroke on 274 (Durban, 3/3); Gary Player voted SA Sportsman of the Century (Johannesburg, 8/3); Trevor Dodds wins the Trust Bank

Champion of Champions Tournament with a score of 272 over 72 holes (Johannesburg, 10/3); Springbok Maeve Phipson wins the Ilovo Champion of Champions Tournament with a total of 147 over 36 holes (Durban); Springbok Gillian Tebbutt wins the Hong Kong Open women's tournament the second year in succession (Hong Kong); Gillian Tebbutt wins the Dewar's White Black Label South African amateur women's tournament (Cape Town, 23/3); David Frost honoured as Smirnoff and Topsport's 1989 Sports Star (Johannesburg, 26/3); Elrita Neethling (OFS) becomes the new president of the SA Women's Golf Union (Johannesburg, 28/30).

Road running: Frith van der Merwe wins a gold medal with her 10th overall place in an ultra-marathon with a time of 3:32'42" (Johannesburg, 17/3).

Rugby: The executive of the SA Rugby Board undergoes a shake-up at its 100th annual meeting when two Test Union representatives, Prof Koos Vermaak (EP) and Mr Steve Strydom (OFS), are outvoted, while Dr Louis Luyt (Tvl) resigns (Cape Town, 9/3).

Showjumping: Gonda Betrix is appointed Springbok captain (Johannesburg, 6/3).

Ironman competition: OFS's Gerrit Badenhorst wins the SA championships (Johannesburg, 3/3).

Swimming: Tvl wins the President's Cup (overall), Ellis Brown aggregate Swimming Cup; Heather Park (E-Tvl) and Darryl Cronjé (Natal) are the Best Women's and Men's Swimmmer respectively at the SA championships; E-Tvl wins waterpolo's Currie Cup (Johannesburg, 2/3).

Tennis: Amanda Coetzer ousts 6th seed Hana Mandlikova (Austria) 2-6, 6-2, 6-3 and Dinky van Rensburg beats Pam Shriver (US) in a women's tournament (Roca Raton, 8/3); Michele Anderson rated second to Jennifer Capriati (US) in the International Tennis Federation junior girls' list (London, 12/3).

April

Angling: The Springbok casting team wins the second test against Austria (Welkom, 11/4); a new African record of 250 kg registered for a swordfish at Club Mykonos's championships (Hout Bay, 26/4).

Archery: Stefan Erasmus (16) of Sasolburg wins the junior section of the world championships (Melbourne, 15/4).

Athletics: Marjorie van der Merwe wins the women's 1 500 m at the Topsport Prestige meeting in a time of 4:11'29" (Port Elizabeth, 2/4); Evette de Klerk, second in the 200 m (22'06), and Myrtle Bothma, second in the 400 m hurdles

(53'82), receive the annual Harry Beinart Medal, awarded to South African athletes who achieved the highest rankings on the 1989 world list (Johannesburg, 21/4); Evette de Klerk with a new Africa and SA record of 11,06 in the 100 m is voted best female athlete while Tom Petranoff is voted best male performer at Sanlam's SA senior championships (Germiston); Springbok Francois Fouché betters his own SA triple jump record with a jump of 8,19 m (Bloemfontein, 27/4).

Boxing: SA middleweight champion Charles Oosthuizen beats Australian Paul Toweel with a 2nd round TKO (Pretoria, 9/4); SA lightweight champion Abram Gumede beats Mexican Leonardo Valdez with a 10th round TKO (Durban, 16/4); Dingaan Thobela wins his lightweight non-title fight against Mexican Mauricio Aceves with a 8th round TKO (Biloxi, Missisippi, 29/4).

Clay-pigeon shooting: OFS's Hennie de Klerk and Prof Jack van der Linde are elected president and vice-president of the SA Clay Pigeon Shooting Association (Bloemfontein, 19/4).

Cricket: Jonty Rhodes (Natal — 208 runs for an average of 82,87) and Meyrick Pringle (WP — 17 wickets for an average of 4,79 wickets per 100 balls) are voted the best batsman and best bowler in the Benson & Hedges series (Johannesburg, 4/4); Wisden names Springbok captain and opener Jimmy Cook and Durban-born England batsman Robin Smith as two of its famed five cricketers of the year (London, 15/4).

Cycling: Willie Engelbrecht wins two events of the Auto X-tra Pretoria Grand Prix, taking second in a third (Pretoria, 14/4).

Golf: Gary Player (281) wins the 51st Professional Golfer's Association Seniors Championship (Palm Beach, 15/4); Mark McNulty's (280) wins the Cannes Open (Cannes, 16/4); Ernie Els with a score of 207 over 54 holes wins the Spoornet SA Classic (Kimberley, 21/4); André Cruse has a one-stroke victory in the R50 000 Kalahari Classic for a total of 211 over 54 holes (Sishen, 28/4).

Horse-racing: *Fancyful* wins the R250 000 Xerox Copier Challenge over 1 600 m (Gosforth-park, 7/4); *St Just* wins the 2 450 m SA Oaks and *Topa Inca* wins the 2 450 m SA Derby (Turffontein, 14/4); *Roland's Song* wins the R 500 000 Administrator's Champion Stakes (Turffontein, 28/4).

Jukskei: Jacques du Plessis (EP) is re-elected president of the South African Jukskei Board (Kroonstad, 2/4); The Springboks beat the Rest of SA 12,5-2,5 (Kroonstad, 5/4).

Road running: Willie Mtolo won the I&J Two Oceans marathon in 3:10'54" (Cape Town, 14/4);

Cornet Mathomane won the Jock Of The Bushveld 54 km ultra-marathon in 3:13'18" (Barberton).

Rugby: Ebrahim Patel is re-elected SA Rugby Union president for a third term (Port Elizabeth, 8/4); Tukkies beats Despatch 22-20 to win the SA Toyota Club tournament (Durban).

Squash: First seed Clair Nitch (Tvl) wins the SA under 21 women's singles title by beating Sjeanne Cawdry (Tvl) 9-1, 9-5, 9-2 (Johannesburg, 22/4); South African Stuart Hailstone beats world champion Jansher Kahn (Pakistan) 9-15, 15-11, 15-12, 15-13 in the European tournament (Karlsruhe, West Germany, 27/4).

Tennis: E-Tvl wins the SA junior interprovincial tournament beating N-Tvl 5-4 (Bloemfontein, 6/4); Springboks Danie Visser and Pieter Aldrich win the Standard Bank World Doubles Championship by beating Americans Rick Leach and Robert Van't Hof 6-7 (4/7), 6-4, 6-4, 7-6 (7/4) (Johannesburg, 7/4); Springbok Gary Muller beats Britain's Jeremy Bates 5-7, 6-1, 6-4 in the National Video and Camera Classic final (Cape Town, 14/4); Ros Fairbank-Nideffer is ranked 15th in the world by the Women's International Tennis Association (Miami, 24/4).

Water-skiing: Springboks Martin Daddy (WP) and Sheronne Zandberg (S-Tvl) become SA open champions (Kroonstad, 16/4); Evan Berger (Tvl) becomes SA barefoot water-skiing champion (Vereeniging, 22/4).

May

Athletics: Tom Petranoff hurls the javelin to a new world masters record of 84,74 m (Johannesburg, 12/5).

Billiards: Cys van Dijk (WP) becomes the new United SA champion when he defeats the holder Terry Riley by 1 002-850 (Vanderbijlpark, 13/5).

Bowls: Springbok Jo Peacock (WP) wins the SA women's singles title by beating Anne Pretorius (Tvl) 21-12; OFS's Dorothy Terblanche and Marian Herbst win the pair's title by beating Marge Chenery and Daphne Hoole from Millpark 21-7 (Port Elizabeth, 5/5).

Boxing: Pierre Coetzer scores a points win over American heavyweight fighter Everett Martin (Green Bay, Wisconsin, 5/5); Vuyani Bhungu outpoints South African junior featherweight champion Fransie Badenhorst to became the new champion (Johannesburg, 13/5); Howard Mpepesi beats SA lightweight champion Freddie Rafferty on a split decision in a 12 round fight (Johannesburg, 20/5); Super lightheavyweight Siza Makhathini wins the IBF's intercontinental title by outpointing Dave Garside of Britain (London, 22/5).

Cycling: Brig. Arno Combrinck is re-elected president of the South African Cycling Federation (Durban, 3/5); Willie Engelbrecht wins the South African track title the third year in succession (Durban, 5/5); Mark Wilkinson wins the 180 km South African Road title in 4:53'12" (Bethlehem, 26/5).

Full-bore-rifle-shooting: The Springboks win the Protea competition by beating the international Magpies 1 706-1 660 (Bloemfontein, 4/5); Pierre van Niekerk (Modder River) becomes the new SA champion (Bloemfontein, 5/5).

Golf: Gillian Tebbutt spearheads the Springboks to a 4-2 victory over the Rest of South Africa (Durban, 11/5); André Cruse wins the Trust Bank Classic with 203 (Kroonstad, 13/5); Des Terblanche wins the Caribbean Estates Pro-am with a score of 272 (Wild Coast, 17/5); Mervyn Galant wins the Marley Classic with a score of 213 over 54 holes (Johannesburg); Springbok Don Gammon wins the Philip Scrutton Trophy (London, 20/5); The WP Marlins retain their title at the Nomads under 23 teams tournament when they beat the Tvl Eagles 8,5-3,5 (Port Shepstone, 25/5); David Frost is ranked 13th in the world (Wentworth, 30/5).

Horse-racing: *Spook* and *Diesel* wins the R300 000 Smirnoff Futurity Handicap over 1 200 m (Pietermaritzburg, 19/5).

Netball: Northern and S-Tvl share the Oppenheimer Cup after they drew 15-15 in the interprovincial tournament (Odendaalsrus, 31/5).

Power-lifting OFS's Gerrit Badenhorst betters his own South African super-heavyweight dead weight record with 357,5 kg (Durban, 19/5).

Power-boating: Peter Lindenberg wins the penultimate Grand Prix of the 1989-90 South African Formula 1 series beating Patrick Lees into second place (Benoni, 12/5).

Road running: Bruce Fordyce wins the Comrades marathon from Durban to Pietermaritzburg a record ninth time in 5:40'25", with Nadine Harrison the women's winner in 7:02'42" (Pietermaritzburg, 31/5).

Show-jumping Bruce Dewar riding *Connecta Okinawa* wins the International A Grade Grand Prix (Pietermaritzburg, 25/5).

Snooker: Tvl Springbok Bill Smith wins the SA Amateur Championship by beating E-Tvl Springbok Terry Reilly 7-4 (Vanderbijlpark, 19/5).

Soccer: WP retains the Van Riebeeck championship beating EP 5-1 (Cape Town, 26/5); Iwisa Kaizer Chiefs' Lucas Radebe voted as Challenge Player of the Series (Johannesburg, 30/5); Sundowns and Blackpool draw 2-2 (NFL, 31/5).

Surfing: Durban surfer Carl Roux becomes the 25th SA senior champion and the first surfer from Defence to win the top title in the Reef Wetsuits SA championships (Victoria Bay, 27/5); Former Springboks and current world champions Martin Potter (7th) and Wendy Botha (6th) are both included in the top 10 placings of the international professional surfing championships (Port Elizabeth, 28/5).

Tennis: Ros Fairbank-Nideffer is ranked 17th women's singles player by the Women's International Tennis Association (Miami, 8/5); Wayne Ferreira wins the single's title by beating Brendon Walters 6-3, 6-4 and teams up with Pietie Norval to take the doubles title winning 7-6, 7-6 over Australians Carl Turich and Brett Richardson (Georgia, 13/5); Mariaan de Swardt beats Petra Horen 6-1, 6-4 to win the Majorie Sherman Challenge Tournament (Tel Aviv, 19/5); Elna Reinach and her Australian double's mate Nicole Provis win their second successive title when they beat Elizabeth Smylie (Australia) and Kathy Jordan (US) 6-1, 6-4 (Strassbourg, 27/5); Pieter Aldrich and Danie Visser win the Augusta doubles title by beating Steven Jung and Reid Rafter (US) 6-1, 6-4 in the final (Augusta, 29/5).

Volleyball: WP's A and B men's team and women's team win the South African championships (Port Elizabeth, 12/5).

Yachting: *SAL Voortrekker II* win the Diaz race (Durban, 18/5).

Waterski: Springbok Greg McEwan betters the South African barefoot-waterski record with a jump of 20,6 m (Middelburg, 2/5).

June

Boxing: Welcome Ncita successfully defends his IBF junior featherweight crown by thrashing Puerto Rican challenger Ramon Cruz in the 7th round (Rome, 2/6); Welterweight Nika Khumalo beats 9th ranked WBO American Robin Blake with a 5th round TKO and Dingaan Thobela wins his lightweight fight against Pasqual Arando with a 5th round TKO (Texas, 24/6).

Canoeing: Grahame Monteith (Tvl) wins the SA K1 championships on the Berg River between Herman and Gouda in a time of 2:00'04" (Cape Town, 17/6).

Golf: Roger Wessels retains his title in the Eastern Cape Classic by one shot over Ian Palmer for a total of 208 (Humansdorp, 2/6); Former Springbok Ian Hutchings wins the Maccauwvlei Masters with a total of 208 over 54 holes (Vereeniging, 9/7); André Cruse wins the Natal Classic (202) over 54 holes (Pietermaritzburg, 16/6).

Horse-racing: *JungleWarrior* wins the Schweppes Challenge of R400 000 over 1 600 m (Durban, 16/6); *Goldmark* with jockey Robbie Sham wins the R300 000 Gilbeys Stakes over 1 200 m (Durban, 30/6).

Motor sport: Ben Morgenrood wins both Wes-Bank Challenge races in his Mazda 323; Graham Duxbury in his Ford-Cosworth Sapphire sets a course record of 1:00'27" (Port Elizabeth, 16/6).

Netball: Northern and S-Tvl share the Oppenheimer Cup after they drew 15-15 in the interprovincial tournament (Odendaalsrus, 31/6).

Road running: Xolile Yawa retains his 21,1 km Ohlsson's Free State title in 64'52 (Bloemfontein); David Tsebe wins the Maize Power Phosphate half-marathon in 63'07 (Phalaborwa, 30/6).

Soccer: E-Tvl defeats SA Defence Force 4-0 to win the Reg Stringer South African Colts (under 19) interprovincial tournament.

Squash: First seed Liz Pratten (Tvl) wins the Fedlife SA Masters women's singles title by beating third seed Isobel Fyfe 9-4, 9-5, 4-9, 9-4 (Johannesburg, 30/6).

Table tennis: Springbok Steven Brown (WP) wins the Pickford's Removals SA championship by beating 10-times champion Alan Chiat 25-23 (Johannesburg, 25/6); B Roach and J Rudolph

Gary Player was voted SA Sportsman of the Century

win the men's and women's singles titles at the SA under 21 championships (Potchefstroom, 30/6).

Tennis: Ros Fairbank-Nideffer wins the Beckenham Grass Court singles title beating Gigi Fernandez (US) 7-5, 6-4 (London, 9/6); Mariaan de Swardt wins her third singles title in a row, when she wins the Women's Challenger Tournament beating Italian S Bonssignori 6-3, 6-7, 6-3 (Italy, 10/6); John-Lafnie de Jager (N-Tvl) is ranked fourth in the world's juniors doubles (London, 20/6).

Tug of war: False Bay wins the 720 kg and 680 kg sections at the SA club championships (Worcester, 7/6).

Yachting: *Allied Bank*, crewed by John Martin and his brother Ian, sets a record victory of 15 days 13 hours 40 minutes in the Monohull Division of the Prestige two-handed Trans-Atlantic race from Plymouth to Newport, Rhode Island (London, 29/6).

July

Athletics: Dries Vorster, the SA 400 m hurdles record-holder, and Evette de Klerk, the SA 100 m and 200 m record-holder, are crowned the 1990 Nedbank South African male and female Athletes of the Year (Pretoria, 27/7).

Badminton: Natal wins the A section and the Charles Bremner Trophy at the annual tournament by beating W-Tvl (6-1), N-Tvl (6-1) and S-Tvl (7-0) (Johannesburg, 3/7).

Baseball: Brian Lombard is re-elected president of the South African Baseball Federation (Cape Town, 21/7).

Boxing: Junior lightweight November Ntsingila scores a 7th round win over Frenchman Alindo Deabreu (Italy, 21/7); Francisco Reilly (W Tvl) becomes the first holder of the new South African amateur super-heavyweight title by knocking out Monty Botha (SAD) in the 1st round (Bloemfontein); Aladin Stevens recaptures his SA light-heavyweight title by beating champion Abraham Gumedi on a 10th round TKO (Johannesburg).

Canoeing: Springbok Mark Perrow wins the 230 km Berg River marathon in 13:34'42" (Cape Town, 14/7).

Golf: Wayne Player wins the Nevada Open scoring 203 over 54 holes (Nevada, 3/7); Laurette Maritz (275) beats Alison Nicholas of Britain to win the Laing Charity Classic (London, 9/7); Stephan Waltman (284) wins the SA Golf Foundation Matchplay title (Benoni); Gary Player wins the British Open Masters Tournament with a score of 280 over 72 holes (Scotland, 28/7); Derek James is declared winner of the SA

Winter Championships after play is suspended due to rain (Welkom, 29/7).

Hockey: Natal becomes the first winners of the Nedbank Champions Trophy men's title by beating S-Tvl 3-2 (Durban, 1/7); S-Tvl becomes the new boy's interprovincial champions by beating WP 2-1 (Pretoria, 13/7); Natal retains their Country Districts title when they beat SA Defence 2-0 (Durban, 28/7).

Horse-racing: Terence Millard's horses *Illustrador, Olympic Duel* and *JungleWarrior* take first, second and third place in the R1 million Rothmans July (Greyville, 7/7); *Face North* is the winner of the R500 000 Mainstay International over 1 800 m (Durban, 28/7).

Icehockey: SA beats Canada 7-4 (Johannesburg, 19/7).

Motor sport: Sarel van der Merwe in his Audi Quattro wins the WesBank Challenge Race (Johannesburg, 7/7).

Netball: WP wins the SA Open tournament by beating N-Tvl 35-30 (Durban, 7/7).

Power-boating Peter Lindenberg moves up to top spot in the international Grand Prix Series (Italy, 29/7).

Road running: Springboks Matthews Temane and Zithule Sinqe are rated the world's fastest and second fastest over the half-marathon by the International Association for Track and Field Statisticians (Johannesburg, 5/7); N- Tvl's Tsebe brothers, Springbok David (23) and Junior Bok Rammy (25), come first and second in the Ohlsson's SA half-marathon championships and Elana Meyer (WP) wins the women's section in a time of 70'20 (Durban, 21/7); Matthews Temane and Zola Pieterse win the 12 km men's (35'42) and the 6 km women's (19'44) section in the first Zola Budd Classic (Bloemfontein, 28/7); David Tsebe wins the 42,2 km Ford Marathon in 2:12'14" (Port Elizabeth).

Rugby: North beats South 38-12 in M-Net's annual match; OFS becomes the SA Unicorn Seven-A-Side champions when they beat Tvl 18-12 (Durban, 21/7); N- Tvl beats WP 25-12 (Lion's Cup final, 28/7).

Snooker: N-Tvl wins the Walker Cup SA title by defeating W-Tvl 17-1 (Pretoria, 22/7).

Squash: Top seeded Rodney Durbach (Pretoria Boys High) captures the SA School's under 19 title (Stellenbosch, 8/7).

Surfing: Professional Peter Lawson wins the Gotcha Tube Masters SA series (Durban, 29/7).

Swimming: Bloemfontein's Seals retains their overall and junior trophies at the SA interclub Winter Championships and newly formed East London club, Harlequins, takes the senior honours (Sasolburg, 14/7).

Tennis: John-Lafnie de Jager and Johan de Beer win one of the world's biggest junior's doubles title by beating South Americans Oliver Fernandez and Ernesto Minoz-Detote 6-4, 7-6 (England, 1/7); Unseeded Pieter Aldrich wins the Hall of Fame tournament by beating sixth seed Australian Darren Cahill 7-6 (12/10), 1-6, 6-1 (Newport, 15/7); Pieter Aldrich and Danie Visser regain their number 1 spot on the world doubles ranking after taking the title at the million dollar Mercedes Cup by beating Swedes Henricsson and Utgren 6-3, 6-4 (Stuttgart, 24/7).

Volleyball: Tvl wins the men's and women's section at the SA championships (Durban, 14/7).

Yachting: Brothers John and Ian Martin win the 3 000 miles race from Plymouth, England, to Newport, Rhode Island in a record time (Newport, 20/7).

August

Athletics: Myrtle Bothma is rated best female 400 m runner in the world by the British magazine *Athletics Today* (London, 15/8); Joe Stutzen is elected president of the SA Athletic's Union (Pretoria, 25/8).

Badminton: Johan Croucamp (S-Tvl) and Martie Mans (OFS) win the SA Masters men's and women's singles titles (Bloemfontein, 17/8).

Biathlon: N-Tvl Springbok and ultraman champion Nick Bester wins the Coral Reef interprovincial cyclo-run biathlon in 36'34 (Pretoria, 11/8); Nick Bester wins the Health World South African title covering the 10km run and the 40km cycle in 1:30'48" (Johannesburg, 25/8).

Bowls: The Senior Springboks win the Prestasi Senior Challenge against the Scottburgh side, who won the Prestasi/Aegis Senior Classic, beating them 21-15 (Margate, 4/8).

Boxing: Derrick Whiteboy beats Lybo Nkoko on a split decision to capture the South African bantamweight title in a 12 round clash (Eldorado Park, 5/8); SA fighters are recognised by the WBA after almost four years of isolation (Johannesburg, 11/8); Jaji Sibali retains his South African flyweight title when he beats Elijah Diphagwe on an 8th round TKO (East London).

Canoeing: Robbie Herreveld (18), SA junior title holder for four years, proves himself the Netherlands' Number One junior after paddling for the Dutch team in four international events in Switzerland, Northern Italy and France during a month-long tour (Johannesburg, 6/8).

Cricket: Hansie Cronjé is appointed OFS captain (Bloemfontein, 9/8); Geoff Dakin is re-elected president of the SA Cricket Union (SACU) (Kimberley, 25/8).

Cycling: Gary Beneke of the Southern Sun/M-Net team wins the 800 km Springbok Atlas Tour of the Winelands (Cape Town, 11/8); Willie Engelbrecht wins the 25th 100 km Il Campione in a time of 2:54'17" (Randburg, 18/8).

Golf: Wayne Westner (205) wins the Zwartkop Classic (Zwartkop, 3/8); David Frost is ranked 15th in the world (London, 6/8); Richard Kaplan breaks his own course record with a 9 under par 64 in the 2nd round on his way to winning the Nissan Challenge with a score of 202 over 54 holes (Benoni, 9/8); Justin Hobday wins the Caribbean Estates pro-am with a two under par 72-hole total of 278 (Wild Coast, 16/8); Mark McNulty (270) comes from two shots behind to win his third West German Open title (Düsseldorf, 26/8); Chris Davison (211) wins his first Sharp Winter Tour tournament in the Zululand Classic (Richards Bay).

Hockey: S-Tvl becomes the new SA champion by beating defending champion Natal 4-3 in the SA Nedbank men's interprovincial tournament (Johannesburg, 12/8).

Horse-racing: *Illustrador* wins the Gold Cup and puts his name in the record books after winning more than R1 million in stakes in only five starts over a period of less than three months (Greyville, 4/8); Three-year-old *Northern Guest* wins the R500 000 Chris Smith Bloodstock Super Series event over 1 400 m; six-year-old *Jungle Warrior* wins the R150 000 Champion Stakes over 2 100 m (Greyville, 11/8); *Sand* wins the R200 000 Clairwood Gold Vase race over 2 400 m (Clairwood, 25/8).

Motor sport: Tony Pond (Britain) and his navigator Geoff Mortimer win the Total Rally in their Cosworth Sapphire (Johannesburg, 4/8).

Netball: Bellville retain their SA Club championship title (Pretoria, 25/8).

Polo: The first British polo team to visit SA since 1983 arrives in Johannesburg (7/8); The British Isles beat SA 8-7 in the first test (Durban, 12/8); The Springboks defeat the British team 11-5 in the second test (Shongweni, 18/8); The British team wins the final BMW international series by defeating the Springboks 7-5 (Johannesburg, 26/8).

Road running: The Genmin team, with brothers David and Rammy Tsebe, wins the FNB company road relay for the second consec-utive year in a record time of 2:31'54" (Johannesburg, 12/8).

Soccer: By drawing 1-1 with Pirates in the second leg Double Action Sundowns lift the JPS Knockout Trophy on an 2-1 aggregate (NFL, 11/8).

Squash: Fourth-seeded Trevor Wilkinson captures the title in the Nedfin Open men's tournament defeating Gunner Way 6-9, 9-5, 9-1, 1-9, 9-6 (Johannesburg, 2/8).

Table tennis: The Pickford's Gazelles SA under 21 team goes down to the W-Tvl senior team, losing 8-5 (Johannesburg, 5/8); WP retains the SA women's interprovincial title beating EP 3-2 (Port Elizabeth, 21/8); Second seed Cheryl Sole (NN) beats Surita Odendaal (WP) 21-11, 21-15, 21-16 in the SA Women's championships final (Port Elizabeth, 24/8).

Tennis: SA junior tennis players feature prominently in the junior world rankings: Marcos Ondruska is ranked 11th in the singles and 19th in the doubles; Clinton Marsh 15th in the singles and 18th in the doubles; John-Lafnie de Jager 35th in the singles and 11th in the doubles; Michelle Anderson 41st in the girl's singles and 24th in the doubles; Joanette Kruger 63rd in the singles and 69th in the doubles.

Unity talks: The South African Cricket Union (SACU) sends a written invitation to the South African Cricket Board (SACB) to hold bridging discussions leading to SA's recall to the International Cricket Council (Johannesburg, 6/8); Delegations from the SA Road Running Association and the Natal Marathon Runners Association meet with the full executive of the Comrades Marathon Association (Botha's Hill, 7/8); History is made when the National Football League (NFL) and the Federation Professional League (FPL) agree to unite and form a single controlling professional body (Johannesburg, 27/8).

Wrestling: Danie Britz becomes the SA superheavyweight champion after defeating champion Danie Voges 2-1 (Port Elizabeth, 12/8).

September

Athletics: Chris Britz (Tvl) retains his 30km title in the SA road walking championships in a time of 2:26'16" (Durban, 15/9).

Badminton: Elana Fourie (GW) and Alan Phillips (WP) successfully defend their titles at the SA championships beating Vanessa van der Walt (S-Tvl) 11-7, 11-3 and Anton Kriel (S-Tvl) 15-6, 1-15, 18-14 (Durban, 12/9); WP wins the 48th SA championships and Anton Kriel (S-Tvl) and Elana Fourie (GW) are graded first in the men's and women's sections; Mr Harry Stavridis (N-Tvl) is elected president of the SA Badminton Union (Durban, 18/9).

Biathlon: Pascal Pau (Tvl) wins the SA ultra biathlon championships in a record time of 3:03'02" (Durban, 23/9).

Boxing: SA middleweight champion Charles Oosthuizen defeats Mexican Gonzales Montes on a 10th round TKO in a catchweight bout (Benoni, 2/9); Cape champion Linda Nondzaba wins the vacant SA welterweight title by beating Tvl's Frederick Siswana on a 5th round knockout (Johannesburg, 9/9); Freddie Rafferty recaptures his SA junior heavyweight title by beating defending champion Howard Mpepesi on a 10th round TKO (Durban, 16/9); Derrick Whiteboy retains his SA bantamweight title by beating Victor Sonaba on points (Johannesburg, 22/9); Dingaan Thobela wins the WBO lightweight title by a split decision over Mexican Mauricio Aceves (Texas, 23/9); WBA junior lightweight champion Brian Mitchell successfully defends his title a record-equalling 11th time with a unanimous 12-round points decision over American Frankie Mitchell; Welcome Ncita retains his IBF junior featherweight title with a knockout in the eight round over Panama's Geraldo Lopez; Jerry Ngobeni scores an eighth-round TKO win over American Jackie Beard in a ten rounder fight (Italy, 29/9); Welterweight champion Phumzile Madikane defeats Delroy Bryan of England on a TKO in the 7th round (Cape Town, 30/9).

Canoeing: The Springboks beat the Rest of South Africa (Bonnievale, 1/9); Tvl regains the SA K4 canoe interprovincial championships (Johannesburg, 23/9).

Cricket: OFS (179/7) wins the Pretoria Bank Challenge Trophy by beating N-Tvl (179/9) on a technical point (Pretoria, 29/9); King William's Town 233/5 (Lawson 81, Howell 82) beats the University of Port Elizabeth 231 (Kepler Wessels 95; Long 5/59) by 5 wickets (SA Club Championships, Johannesburg).

Cycling: Mark Beneke wins the *The Star* 110 km race in a time of 2:41'46" (Johannesburg, 2/9); Andrew McLean wins the 660km 1990 Hansom tour in a time of 17:26'49" (Graskop, 8/9); Willie Engelbrecht wins the Zoo Lake race (Johannesburg, 15/9); Willie Engelbrecht wins the Allied Cycle Tour of the Southern Cape over a distance of 517,8 km in a time of 10:57'14" (George, 29/9).

Equitation: EP beats the visiting American side scoring 46 points out of a possible 72 (Graaff-Reinet, 29/9).

Golf: André Cruse wins the Lombard Tyres Transvaal Classic with a score of 201 (Krugersdorp); S-Tvl wins the Rothmans Interprovincial championship for the 17th time in 29 attempts (Kempton Park, 13/9); Wayne Westner (200) wins the Brakecor Wool Festival Pro-am (Ermelo, 22/9); André Cruse becomes the first player in the history of the SA Winter Tour to earn more than R50 000 in one season (Johannesburg, 25/9); Wayne Westner and Justin Hobday (284) share the Sun City Classic first prize (Sun City, 27/9).

Gymkhana: Rustenburg wins the annual SA championships (Bloemfontein, 29/9).

Gymnastics: S-Tvl's Springbok Marie Thickett scores 9,60 on the beam; WP Springbok and SA champion Alan Daly scores 9,30 on the high bar at the Opel meeting (Bloemfontein, 7/9).

Hockey: Stellenbosch University retain their national women's Club Champion of Champions title when they beat 1989's runners-up, Wanderers, 3-2 (Pretoria, 8/9); Port Elizabeth's Walmer win the national men's Club Champion of Champions title when they beat Natal Technikon 2-0 (Cape Town).

Horse-racing: *Roland Song* wins the Computaform Champion Stakes over 1 800 m (Turffontein, 15/9).

Motor sport: Jannie Habig and Douglas Judd win the national championship Toyota Dealer Rally (Cape Town, 23/9).

Power-lifting: Bloemfontein's Gerrit Badenhorst betters his own world record with a total of 1 020 kg at the SA championships (Pretoria, 22/9).

Road running: Matthews 'Loop-en-Val' Motshwarateu wins the 12 km Excella SA men's cross-country senior title in a time of 37'11 and Elana Meyer the women's 6 km event in 20'44 (Nelspruit, 1/9); Zola Pieterse beats Elana Meyer in the Excella Prestige women's 6 km event with Simon Meli winning the men's 12 km race in 36'26 (Port Elizabeth, 8/9); Matthews Temane wins the 10 km Matthews Temane Metropolitan Life race in 29'30 and Zola Pieterse the women's race in 33"05 (Potchefstroom); Steven Moloko wins the 80 km Karoo road race in a time of 5:30'09" (Laings-burg).

Rugby: History is made when the WP League wins the Sport Pienaar Trophy for the first time by beating E-Tvl 22-16, WP wins the Gold Cup by beating Northern Free State 43-10 (Paarl, 29/9).

Show-jumping Peter Gotz on *Noble Cut* wins the Samsung International competition at the Kyalami Equestrian Centre (Johannesburg, 9/9).

Snooker: Terry Reilly (E-Tvl) becomes the new United SA champion by beating Schalk Mouton (SAP) 5-3 (Pretoria, 15/9).

Soccer: S-Tvl wins the Xeratech SA Currie Cup championships when they beat SA Defence 1-0 (NFL, 15/9).

Squash: Tvl's Claire Nitch regains her title as SA's leading women's player (Johannesburg, 18/9); Gunner Way (WP) wins the Gillette SA men's singles title when he defeats top-seeded Paul Symonds 15-10, 15-4, 7-15, 15-7 (Johannesburg, 28/9).

Tennis: Pieter Aldrich and Danie Visser win the US Open doubles title beating Paul Anacone and David Wheaton (US) 6-2, 7-6, 6-2 (New York, 9/9); Amanda Coetzer scores a surprising victory by beating top-seeded Dinky van Rensburg 6-4, 6-4 to win the Triumph International SA Open women's championships for the first time (Johannesburg, 15/9); OFS's Amanda Coetzer is voted most improved player of the year and Dinky van Rensburg singles player of the year (Johannesburg, 22/9); Stefan Kruger and Christo van Rensburg take the doubles title of the Swiss Indoor tournament, beating third seeds Neil Broad and Gary Muller 4-6, 7-6 (7/3), 6-3 (Basel, 30/9).

Triathlon: Tvl's SA champion Rockley Montgomery wins the Bushman's River championship in a record time of 2:32'20" (Port Elizabeth, 22/9).

Unity talks: A unity pact is signed by SA's three major controlling soccer bodies, the Soccer Association of South Africa, the SA Soccer Federation and the Football Association of South Africa (Johannesburg, 23/9).

Volleyball: WP wins the men's section of the Trek SA championships by beating Tvl 3-1, and Natal the women's section by beating Tvl 3-1 (Bloemfontein, 29/9).

October

Angling: S-Tvl (525 points) wins the SA National Freshwater Championships (Vaaldam, 4/10).

Badminton: Natal wins the SA Masters tournament (Pietermaritzburg, 13/10).

Body-building: Pierre van der Westhuizen wins the World Championships (Melbourne, 15/10).

Boxing: The SA National Boxing Board of Control is invited to attend meetings of the WBA (Johannesburg, 5/10); At a special meeting of the SA Boxing Coordinating Council it is decided to send delegations to meetings of the WBC and WBA (Umtata, 7/10); Charles Oosthuizen retains his SA middleweight title beating Donald Ngomane with a knockout in the 2nd round (Johannesburg, 8/10); Sugarboy Malinga wins the SA light heavyweight title by outpointing champion Sakkie Horn over 12 rounds (Johannesburg, 11/10); Light heavyweight Hein van Bosch wins the Best Boxer award at the SA Amateur championships (Johannesburg, 20/10); Derrick Whiteboy retain his SA bantamweight title beating Victor Sonaba on points (Johannesburg, 22/10); Jacob Matlala becomes the SA junior flyweight champion defeating Wele Maqolo on points over 12 rounds (Port Elizabeth, 28/10).

Bowls: Team Campbell, skipped by Spring-bok Kevin Campbell, wins the Prestasi 1990 World Fives bowls tournament (Johannesburg, 21/10).

Canoeing: Junior Robbie Herreveld and Sharon Manning (Tvl) become the new SA K2 champions by covering the 25 km from the Vaaldam to Pumphouse in 1:53'05" (Vaaldam, 20/10).

Cricket: University of Port Elizabeth (161/4) wins the Benson & Hedges Trophy for SA Universities cricket after a draw against Stellenbosch University (228/5) (Stellenbosch, 3/10); Adrian Kuiper (WP), John Maguire, Rod McCurdy (EP), Mike Gatting (captain of the English side) and Roy Pienaar (Tvl) are voted SA Cricketers of the Year (Cape Town, 5/10); WP (185/4) retains the Protea Assurance challenge trophy by beating Transvaal (181/9) by 6 wickets (Cape Town, 10/10).

Golf: The Rest of South Africa beats the Springbok women's team 3-1 (Cape Town, 4/10); Kevin Stone (99) wins his third title on the Sharp Winter Tour by winning the 27 hole Bophuthatswana Classic tournament (Mafikeng, 14/10); Springbok Retief Goosen (205) wins the Kempton Park Classic tournament (Kempton Park, 19/10); An 11-year-old girl, Amelia Moses, wins the Hendler Hart Southern Transvaal Bronze women's championships by an amazing 12 shots with a 36-hole total of 174 (Johannesburg, 24/10); Steve Burnett fires the lowest round in the Winter Tour and a new Nigel Golf Club course record of 62 in the first round of the South African Players Championships (Nigel, 25/10); Graeme Watson (267) wins the playoff with Tony Louw in the SA Players Challenge (Nigel, 28/10).

Horse-racing: *Honey Chunk* wins the R750 000 OK Gold Bowl (Turffontein, 6/10).

Icehockey: The German Fischer Invitation team wins the series against the South Africans 2-1 (Johannesburg, 7/10).

Ice-skating: S-Tvl's Debbie Crow wins the junior women's title in the Aegis national championships (Cape Town, 13/10); SA champions Clinton King and Fiona Kirk become the first SA ice skaters ever to achieve a perfect six for their free style performance (Cape Town, 14/10).

Motorcycling: A ban on South Africans competing in international events overseas is lifted by the International Motorcycle Federation (FIM) at its annual congress (Budapest, 23/10).

Motor sport: Jannie Habig and Douglas Judd win the WesBank International Rally (Pretoria, 20/10); The winners of the 1990 Stannic Group N National Championships are Michael Briggs, Terry Moss, Mike White, Neil Stephen and Grant McCleery (Johannesburg, 28/10).

Power-lifting: Gerrit Badenhorst retains his super-heavyweight world title bettering his own world record with 1 103,5 kg (London, 14/10).

Road running: Willie Mtolo (2:21'5") and Helene Joubert (2:56'25") won the men's and women's Ford Johannesburg marathon (Johannesburg, 10/10); Michael McDermott won his ninth Harrismith mountain race in 55'19 (Harrismith); Frith van der Merwe set a new half-marathon record when she won the Foot of Africa event in 1:11'42" (Bredasdorp, 13/10).

Rugby: The Currie Cup, SA's premier rugby competition, will be sponsored for a record amount of nearly R88 million over the next six years (Johannesburg, 3/10); Natal wins the Currie Cup by beating champions N-Tvl 18-12, OFS becomes the new Midas Cup under 20 champions by beating WP 18-9 (Pretoria, 6/10); Natal's Joel Stransky (314 points) and Christie Noble (18 tries) are the 1990 top-scorers in South African first-class rugby (Johannesburg, 16/10).

SA Sportsman of the Year: The Rand Sports Writers' Society nominates world boxing champions Brian Mitchell, Dingaan Thobela and Welcome Ncita, cricketer Jimmy Cook, athlete Yvette de Klerk and tennis doubles pair Pieter Aldrich and Danie Visser as finalists for the Fedlife Sportsman of the Year Award (Johannesburg, 28/10).

Snooker: Pierre Mans wins the SA Open title beating Jimmy van Rensburg 8-5 (Germiston, 24/10).

Soccer: The Currie Cup XI beats the Football Association of Bophuthatswana's national amateur team 2-1 (Cape Town, 20/10); De Beers FC are the 1990 NPSL champions after their 2-1 victory over AmaZulu (Tembisa, 20/10).

SA National Olympic Committee (SANOC): Johan du Plessis is re-elected chairman unopposed (Johannesburg, 27/10).

Squash: SS win the Protea SA men's club championships by beating Camps Bay 6-0 and Welgemoed the women's section by beating Pietermaritzburg Collegians 5-1 (Durban, 16/10).

Tennis: Natal and champion N-Tvl share the honours of the Nashua SA senior interprovincial championships (Pietermaritzburg, 13/10).

Tenpin bowling: Spike Knowles retains his Anchor Life South African scratch singles title beating Springbok Phillip Philippou 177-189 and 244-218 (Johannesburg, 24/10).

Tug of war: SA beats Switzerland 2-0 (Worcester, 30/10).

Wrestling: Danie Voges recaptures his SA professional Super-heavyweight title by beating champion Danie Britz 2-1 (Port Elizabeth, 6/10).

November

Athletics: Wickus Olivier (RAU) shatters the SA triple jump record with a distance of 16,56 m

(Johannesburg, 24/11); Sponsorship of R50 000 is announced for a summer series (Cape Town, 30/11).

Bowls: Border wins the interprovincial tournament for women by beating SN 22-15 (Uvongo, 15/11).

Boxing: Vuyani Bungu retains his SA junior featherweight title crown on a unanimous points decision over challenger Zolani Makhubalo (East London, 4/11); Aron Kabi beats Luvuyo Kakaza on a TKO in the 5th round to retain his SA welterweight title (Johannesburg, 25/11); Welcome Ncita appointed Border's Sportsman of the Year (East London, 28/11).

Cycling: Willie Engelbrecht of the Southern Sun/M-Net team won the 18th Rapport Tour in a time of 37:34'20" (Krugersdorp, 3/11); Willie Engelbrecht won the Pick a Pay and Natal Mercury 100 km race between Pietermaritzburg and Durban in 2:33'22" (Durban, 11/11); Willie Engelbrecht sped to another victory in the Voltaren Emulgel 160 km ultra-cycle classic race in 4:24'07" (Johannesburg, 25/11).

Gliding: Johan Anderson betters the world record from 233 km to 258 km (Hartebeespoortdam, 31/11).

Golf: Andrew Rice wins the Florida Inter-collegiate championships (Florida, US, 4/11); Joe Dlamini pips Robbie Chapman on the first hole of a sudden death play-off to win the Inter-Sport Pro-Am on the new Fish River Sun golf course (Ciskei, 8/11); Tvl wins the interprovincial women's tournament by beating WP 14-4 (Johannesburg, 10/11); John Bland strolls to an easy 70-75 victory over Hugh Baiocchi in the Minolta Matchplay tournament (Pilanesberg, 17/11); Fulton Allem (276) wins the TJ Masters tournament (Stellenbosch, 24/11).

Horse-racing: Cape colt *Phantom Robber* wins the R300 000 South African Invitation Stakes over 1 600 m at Scottsville (Pietermaritzburg, 10/11); *State Treasure* wins the Gosforth Park Fillies Guineas over 1 600 m (Gosforth Park, 17/11); *Senor Santa* wins the First National Bank Handicap over 1 600 metres (Turffontein, 24/11); Dr Nic Labuschagne, president of the Natal Rugby Union, is appointed chairman of the Durban Turf Club (Durban, 30/11).

Motor sport: Michael Briggs becomes the first driver to win the Castrol Challenge endurance race twice in a row (Cape Town, 11/11).

Road running: Zola Pieterse wins the 15 km Pick a Pay road race in a record time of 51'05"5 sec (Bloemfontein); Elana Meyer clocks 33'03" in the Truworths 10 km Women's Fashion Run (Cape Town, 10/11); Johan Landsman (4'01"14) and Elana Meyer (4'33"77), both of Stellen-

bosch, win the men's and women's underground mile (Middelbult Mine, 17/11); Adam Motlagale scores a major upset when he pips Springbok David Tsebe at the post to win with a time of 43'16, Gert Thys (junior — 43'32), George Mosweu (veterans — 45'58), Elana Meyer (women's — 48'17) and Danny Shongwe (masters — 49'40) better SA records (SA Ohlsson's 15 km road championships, Bellville, 3/11); Springbok Lawrence Peu wins the 15 km Jeppe Quondam and Auto-Atlantic road race in 47'32 (Johannesburg, 10/11); Rami Tsebe (N-Tvl) wins in a SA record time of 28'20 and Elana Meyer (WP) the women's section in 32'22 (SA 10 km Challenge, Durban, 24/11).

Rugby: N-Tvl's Springbok hooker Uli Schmidt is voted Player of the Year (Pretoria, 12/11).

SA Defence Force sport: Eugene van der Merwe (Power lifting) and Elinda Vorster (Athletics) are voted Sportsman and Sportswoman of the Year (Pretoria, 21/11).

Saltwater fishing: Far N-Tvl wins the 1990 Bols SA National Game Fish championships (Saldanha Bay, 2/11).

SA Sportsman of the year: The world's number one doubles tennis pair, Danie Visser and Pieter Aldrich, make history by becoming the first pair to be named together for this prestigious award (Johannesburg, 29/11).

Show-jumping: The General Accident championships of SA is won by defending champion Gonda Betrix and *Structural Projects Flaunt* (Johannesburg, 3/11).

Snooker: Francois Ellis retains his South African professional singles title defeating Pierre Mans 7-3 (Johannesburg, 8/11); The Springboks and the President's team share the honours 5-5 (Kempton Park, 23/11); The President team beats the Springboks 12-11 (Johannesburg, 24/11); The Springbok and Junior Springbok teams draw five-all against the President and Prestige teams (Pretoria, 25/11).

Soccer: Double Action Sundowns draw 0-0 against Moroko Swallows to win the Castle League (NSL, 17/11); Jomo Midas Cosmos wins their first major national soccer league knockout cup defeating AmaZulu in the Bob Save Super Bowl final (Durban, 18/11).

Tennis: Danie Visser and Pieter Aldrich ranked first as doubles pair by the International Tennis Federation (Sydney, 7/11); Ross Fairbank-Nideffer ranked 20th women's player in the world (Miami); Wayne Ferreira becomes the 1990 champion by beating Byron Talbot 6-3, 6-1 and Free Stater Amanda Coetzer wins the women's title by beating champion René Mentz 4-6, 6-4, 6-3 (SA Closed Championships, Johannesburg, 16/11); Mark Kaplan beats Gary Muller (6-4), 6-4) and Wayne Ferreira beats Christo van Rensburg (6-3, 7-6, 10-8), and Ferreira/Pietie Norval beat Pieter Aldrich/Danie Visser, 6-4, 6-4 (SA Open, Johannesburg, 30/11).

Triathlon: Hannele Steyn wins in a world class time of 2:02'28" (Gordon's Bay, 24/11).

Tug of war: SA wins the third test against Switzerland (Welkom, 7/11).

Unity talks: South African Track and Field Association's Danie Malan is pleased with the outcome of the Harare sports summit where, for the first time, the SA Amateur Athletics Union met with all the other athletics bodies in the Republic (Port Elizabeth); The South African Softball Association (SASA) and the South African Softball Federation (SASF) agree to set their unification goal for August 1991 (Johannesburg, 17/11).

Yachting: SA scores two 'firsts' at the assembly of the International Yacht Racing Union held in Britain; John Sully is the first South African to be honoured for his services to the sport, while Geoff Myburgh is the first to be appointed to the International Youth Committee.

December

Angling: SA wins the World Cup Marlin competition (Mauritius, 27/12).

Athletics: Tukkies retains their title in the men's section and Potchefstroom takes the women's Roger Dyason trophy; Chris Britz (RAU) collects another SA 10 km road walk record (43'27) (FNB SA University championships, Port Elizabeth, 8/12); Johan Landsman (4:05'60") and Elana Meyer (4:30'70") of Stellenbosch University win the annual Kohler Street Mile (Port Elizabeth, 23/12).

Bowls: Kevin Campbell (NT) is ranked no 1 by the SA Bowling Association, followed by Dave Kempthorne (SOFS) (Johannesburg, 3/12).

Boxing: WBO lightweight champion Dingaan Thobela's world title challenge victory against Maurice Acevas in Brownville is voted WBO's Fight of the Year (Miami); Junior heavyweight champion Freddie Rafferty retains his title by beating Gideon Hlongwa in the second round (Durban); Pierre Coetzer scores a 10th round TKO victory over American Kimmuel Odum (Rome, 15/12).

Canoeing: Men: Neil Viljoen/Pierre van der Merwe (Tvl — 8:29'56"6); Women: Marinda Hartzenberg/Suzette Vallenduuk (OFS — 10:14'08") (SA K2 Championships over 11 km, Parys, 8/12).

Cricket: University of Port Elizabeth wins the SA Universities tournament (Cape Town, 7/12);

Kepler Wessels (EP) is named Man of the Series, and Philip Amm's 430 runs is a new series record (Nissan Shield final, Port Elizabeth, 15/12).

Cycling: Gary Beneke wins the final 165 km leg of the Voltaren Emulgen Super Series in a time of 4:25'20" (Durban, 2/12); Fransie Kruger (Tvl) is voted most outstanding rider at an open meeting (Paarl, 26/12).

Golf: Simon Hobday (271) wins the US Seniors Tour final qualifying tournament (California, 1/12); Wayne Westner smashes John Bland's year-old Durbanville Country Club course record with a 9 under par 63 (Cape Town, 1/12); David Frost birdies the last two holes to win the Million Dollar Challenge with a score of 284 (Sun City, 9/12); John Bland (273) wins the Bloemfontein and Spoornet Classic (Bloemfontein, 15/12); Fulton Allem (277) wins the Goodyear Classic (Port Elizabeth, 22/12).

Horse-racing: *Miss Averof* wins the R150 000 White Horse Dingaans handicap (Turffontein, 8/12).

Jukskei: OFS wins the overall SA Schools Championships (Kroonstad, 15/12).

Paddleski: Springbok lifesaver Herman Chalupsky, who led the 244 km Marix Challenge Paddleski marathon from Port Elizabeth to East London from the start, wins in an overall record time of 19:19'22" (East London, 16/12).

Show-jumping: Tony Lewis wins the Mercedes-Benz SA championship, followed by Ronnie Lawrence and SA Grand Prix titleholder Anneli Wucherpfennig (Inanda, 2/12).

Soccer: Bennett Masinga of Double Action Sundowns is presented with the trophy as well as R5 000 for finishing the season as leading goalscorer (20 goals) in the Castle League (Johannesburg, 5/12).

Squash: Grant Way becomes the new SA closed champion by beating Paul Symonds 3-1 (Johannesburg, 10/12).

Surfing: Vince King wins the AA-rated Surfers — The Movie Classic, the final event of the 1990 SA Surfing Series (Umhlanga Rocks, 16/12).

Swimming: Stellenbosch wins the South African Universities Jubilee overall swimming trophy (Bloemfontein, 8/12).

Tennis: Wayne Ferreira is the youngest SA tennis player to win the Altech Xerox SA Open singles championship by beating Mark Kaplan 6-3, 7-5, 7-6 (8/6) and with Pietie Norval in the doubles beating Stefan Kruger/Christo van Rensburg 6-3, 6-7 (5/7), 7-6 (7/4) (Johannesburg, 1/12); Alana Bakos/Salli van Rensburg (ST) win the Spar Women's Doubles Club championships beating Christine Kotze/Marette van Schoor (Boland) by a single point after nine games of round robin matches between 12 provincial champions (Johannesburg, 1/12); Bo Erikssen of Sweden appointed full-time coach at Kingswood College in Grahamstown (Grahamstown, 3/12); Wayne Ferreira beats Mark Kaplan 6-2, 3-6, 6-3 and in the men's doubles final first-seeded Pieter Aldrich/Danie Visser beat De Beer/Honey 6-7 (7/5), 6-3, 7-6 (7/4) (Standard Bank Challenge, 8/12).

Triathlon: Double Springbok Henk Watermeyer retains his Prestige Indocid Gel canoe triathlon title in an aggregate time of 3:52'45" (Johannesburg, 16/12).

Yachting: John Martin finishes first in the second leg of the BOC single-handed race around the world (Sydney, 20/12); Greg Davis beats seven times winner Geoff Meek in the Rothmans Regatta (Cape Town, 23/12).

Water polo: E-Tvl and Natal share the Kramer interprovincial trophy (Benoni, 11/12); Border wins the 1990 Penny Pinchers SA Schools championships (Boksburg, 15/12).

Acknowledgements:

Frikkie van Rensburg, *Die Volksblad*, Bloemfontein

South Africa remains one of the world's most rewarding holiday destinations. Visitors have an amazing variety of options, ranging from magnificent beaches to some of the world's most famous game parks and nature reserves; massive mountain ranges guarding verdant valleys; vast inland plains, forests, waterfalls, mineral and hot springs; a rich mosaic of peoples with widely different customs and all the amenities of First World cities.

Hints for the tourist

Tourists must have valid passports and, in some instances, visas. Enquiries can be directed to South African diplomatic representatives abroad or the Department of Home Affairs in Pretoria.

Tourists must satisfy passport control officers that they have the means to support themselves during their stay. They must also have valid international health certificates. Visitors from the yellow fever belt in Africa and America, as well as those who travel through or disembark in these areas, have to be inoculated against the disease.

Accommodation facilities in SA are the best developed on the African continent. Tourists have a choice between simple, adequate country inns in the rural areas and luxury five-star hotels in the cities. The country's mild climate is ideal for caravanning and camping holidays. There are more than 600 caravan parks, some of which also offer camping facilities.

The transport infrastructure — airlines, railroads, luxury tour buses and self-drive cars — is such that the tourist can travel comfortably and quickly from his port of entry to any other part of the country. International airlines, including the South African Airways, also operate regular scheduled flights to and from the country.

Apart from many main-line trains to all parts of the country, Transnet (the national carrier) and some private companies operate regular tours to all major tourist attractions. Tours are planned by experts to suit individual requirements. The inclusive booking system enables the tourist to pay the full cost of a holiday in advance.

General tourist information is obtainable abroad at any of the South African Tourism Board's (Satour) branch offices and at any of the board's regional offices in South Africa.

Wildlife

Because of the abundance and variety of its plant and animal life and its widely varied types of country, South Africa has been described as 'the greatest wildlife show on earth'.

Despite the wasteful and often cruel 'overkill' of game in the 19th century, which caused near extinction of most of the world's plains game, fairly large remnants of South Africa's game have survived.

Unfortunately three species unique to the Cape, the quagga (*Equus quagga*), the blue buck (*Hippotragus leucophaens*) and the Cape lion, did not survive the hunters' guns. Others, such as the white rhino (*Ceratotherium simum*) and the Cape mountain zebra (*Equus zebra*), were threatened with extinction for many years. The elephant totally disappeared from some of its natural haunts. The cheetah, sable and the rare white-tailed gnu (or black wildebeest) all but disappeared, but are quite common today.

Wildlife in South Africa is protected by the National Parks Board, the provincial administrations, the Department of Environment Affairs, the self-governing states, private organisations and individuals, including farmers.

SA is a member of the Washington Convention for the Protection of Endangered Wildlife Species and signatory to the Convention on Trade in Endangered Species (Cites) of Wild Fauna and Flora and the Convention on the Conservation of Wetlands of international importance, especially the waterfowl habitat (Ramsar).

Fauna

Game is so prolific in SA's national parks and other protected areas that animals have to be culled regularly to prevent destruction of their own environment.

The major species are the following:
– Elephant, rhinoceros (two species), Cape buffalo, giraffe, zebra (two species), hippopotamus, warthog, bushpig.

– *Antelope*: eland, roan, sable, gemsbok (*oryx*), wildebeest (two species), red hartebeest, tses-sebe, waterbuck, kudu, springbok, impala, bontebok, suni, blesbok, reedbuck (two species), rhebok, bushbuck, nyala, duiker (three species), oribi, steenbok, grysbok (two species), klipspringer.
– *Cats*: lion, leopard, cheetah, lynx (caracal), serval, black-footed cat, wild cat.
– *Primates*: baboon, monkey (two species), bushbaby (two species).
– *Others*: hyena (two species), Cape wild dog, zebra (two species), genet (two species); mongoose (11 species); civet, honey badger (ratel), otter (two species), aardvark, aardwolf, jackal (three species), fox (two species), hyrax (three species), pangolin, porcupine, hare and rabbit (six species), squirrel (three species), hedgehog, as well as various species meerkat, rat, mole and other small mammals.
– *Reptiles*: crocodile, monitors (two species), snakes (about 98 species of which only 16 are potentially dangerous to man), tortoise (11 species), marine turtle (five species).

There are 800 butterfly species in SA and new species are discovered almost every year. Destruction of their natural habitat is the main reason for the decline of SA's butterfly population. Two South African species are already extinct, another two are on the list for endangered insects, 102 species are vulnerable and 91 species are classified as rare.

The golden copper butterfly (*Poecilmitis aureus*), all species of double tail butterflies (*Charaxes* spp.) and the rare copper butterfly (*Aloeides dentatis*) are protected invertebrae in the Transvaal.

In the Cape the following invertebrae are classified as being protected or endangered: all species *Peripatus genus peripatopsis* and *genus opistthopatus* (endangered), 12 species of the family *Lycaenidae*, two species of the family *Nymphalidae,* one specie of the family *Satgridae* and one specie of the family *Hepialidae*.

SA's first butterfly reserve was established at Ruimsig, Transvaal, in 1984 to protect a colony of the rare copper butterfly. In total 98 other species butterflies are found in the 12 ha reserve.

Plant life

SA is only one seventh the size of the United States, yet it has many more plant species — more than 22 000. Even Russia, which extends over one seventh of the earth's land surface, has fewer species than South Africa.

South Africa is also the only country in the world with an entire floral kingdom within its boundaries. This is the Cape kingdom of '*fynbos*', world famous for its spectacular flowers. In the Cape Peninsula — an area the size of the Isle of Wight — there are more kinds of wild plants than in the entire British Isles.

A Cape wild flower which was considered extinct 20 years ago, has reappeared. This discovery is considered to be the first success of the Search and Save project which was established jointly by the Botanical Association and the SA Nature Foundation in 1988 to save extremely endangered plant species. The *Serruria foeniculacea* is related to the blushing bride (*Serruria florida*).

A new hybrid protea with a beautiful reddish-brown flower was discovered near Clanwilliam. The plant is a cross between the *Protea glabra* and the *Protea laurifolia*. A hybrid protea has also been discovered in the mountains at Fish Hoek.

The seven-week fern (*Rumohra adiantiforme*) is a protected plant which is found in indigenous forests in the southern and western Cape. Also known as 'green gold' because its leaves remain fresh for up to seven weeks, it is easily transported and can repeatedly be used in flower arrangements.

South Africa has more than 1 000 tree species, some of them exceptional. The wood of the leadwood tree (*Combretum imberbe*) is so hard that it hardly leaves a mark when chopped with a sharp axe. One such tree in the eastern Transvaal was carbon-dated at 1 100 years. These hardwoods are so strong that they do not rot but merely erode like rocks.

The yellowwood tree (*Podocarpus* species) is the country's national tree. Yellowwood trees can grow to a height of more than 40 m. The Big Tree near the Storms River bridge (46 m), the King Edward VII in the Knysna forest (46 m) and the Eastern Monarch in the Amatola mountains (44 m) are well-known.

The most prolific tree in South Africa is the sweet-thorn tree (*Acacia karroo*), which is known to send taproots down 65 m to seek out water. Its sweet gum was used by pioneers for confectionery, its bark for rope, its wood for wagon parts and its leaves and pods for fodder.

One of the strangest trees is the *naboom* (*Euphorbia ingens*), a cactus-like plant that 'bleeds' a white, poisonous, milk-like latex when injured. Some Black inhabitants toss 'bleeding' branches into shallow pools to stupefy fish so that they can be easily caught.

One of the natural wonders of South Africa is the annual blossoming of Namaqualand's wild flowers which transforms the semi-desert of the north-western Cape near Springbok into a fairy-land. After rain the grey landscape is suddenly covered with a multi-coloured carpet from horizon to horizon (August to October, depending on rainfall).

Among South Africa's plant curiosities are a number of species of cycads (family *Cycadaceae*) — fossil plants — which grew on earth long before the advent of today's trees and the 'resurrection bush' (*Myrothamnus flabellifolius*), a shrub that appears to be dead one day but, after a shower of rain, will suddenly be vibrantly alive.

Two cycad species in South Africa are already extinct, four are on the verge of extinction in their natural habitat, while seven more are on the endangered list. Of the 28 species indigenous to South Africa, 16 are found in the Transvaal. Several species do not have enough trees left in nature to form viable colonies.

In the desert areas plants have adopted peculiar ways to avoid being eaten and to ensure that reproduction takes place. Some look like stones, while others smell similar to rotting meat to attract passing insects (the carrion-flower), or their colours are so bright that insects cannot miss them (*mesembryanthemum*).

National parks

The flagship of the National Parks Board is the Kruger National Park which is internationally renowned for both its management of wildlife and for being one of the world's most impressive national parks.

Since 1926 a number of national parks and a national lake area have been established in SA. They are the Kruger National Park, the Kalahari Gemsbok National Park, the Addo Elephant National Park, the Bontebok National Park, the Mountain Zebra National Park, the Golden Gate Highlands National Park, the Augrabies Falls National Park, the Tsitsikamma National Park, the Wilderness National Park, the Knysna National Lake Area, the Karoo National Park, the Vaalbos National Park, the West Coast National Park, the Zuurberg National Park, the Tankwa Karoo National Park and the Kransberg National Park (still to be proclaimed).

The Parks Board manages the 1 million ha Kalahari Gemsbok National Park and controls an additional 2,5 million hectares in collaboration with the Botswana government. These two parks together constitute one of the last regions on earth where large migrations, such as those of eland, can still take place in an area considerably larger than the Kruger National Park.

The establishment of the Mountain Zebra , the Addo Elephant and Bontebok national parks saved these species from extinction.

The Mountain Zebra National Park was established in 1937 with only six animals but it now has a population of 235. In 1931 there were only 11 Addo elephants in existence. Now there are 160 in the Addo Elephant Park, while the bontebok population increased from 22 to 300 animals.

Upgrading of proclaimed areas is a matter of high priority, and the possibility of further expanding existing parks is constantly studied. Wildlife management is based on thorough research, and contributions have been made by the Parks Board in various fields. Scientists employed by the board are supported in their research by co-ordinated research programmes carried out all over the world by institutes, universities and other experts.

From time to time new models for establishing national parks are studied and put into effect by the board, in accordance with the guidelines laid down by the World Conservation Union (IUCN) in the national interest. Thus the Knysna Lagoon is at present managed as a national lake area and the West Coast National Park, as well as the Augrabies Falls National Park, are being enlarged by means of contractual agreements with the owners of adjacent land.

The National Parks Board today controls 16 conservation areas — 15 national parks and one national lake area — with a total land area of some 3,1 million ha. Its budget, of which about 80 per cent is self-generated, amounts to R130 million each year. Its staff exceeds 5 000.

Inquiries for reservations should be addressed to the Chief Director, National Parks Board, PO Box 787, 0001 Pretoria, or PO Box 7400, 8012 Rogge Bay or PO Box 774, 6530 George.

Places of interest

In addition to South Africa's fauna en flaura there are many other places of interest for the tourist.

Aquariums
Well-known aquariums are found in Durban and Port Elizabeth while the aquarium at the National Zoological Gardens of South Africa in Pretoria is the only one in South Africa which is able to cultivate its own sea water.

Bird sanctuaries
In the Transvaal the Melrose Bird Sanctuary in Johannesburg has been kept in as natural a con-

dition as possible and suitable shrubs and trees have been planted to provide food for the birds of which about 150 species have been identified. Natural conditions have also been maintained at the Florence Bloom Bird Sanctuary and suitable food sources, trees and shrubs have been added. The sanctuary is partly open to the public. The Paradise Bird Sanctuary in Sandton has the largest variety birds in Southern Africa. In Pretoria, the 11 ha Austin Roberts Bird Sanctuary in Nieuw Muckleneuk attracts both city and country birds. The most important aspect of this sanctuary is its large number of heron and egret. The Korsman Bird Sanctuary in Benoni attracts migratory waterfowl, including ibis and flamingo. More than 300 species of fowl have been spotted in the Marievale Bird Sanctuary located on a large vlei near Nigel. The Rondebult Bird Sanctuary on the outskirts of Germiston protects more than 150 species of bird. Most of the waterfowl species breeding in southern Africa have been spotted here.

In Natal the Pietermaritzburg Bird Sanctuary is known for its snow-white cattle egrets, apart from a variety of smaller birds. The Amanzimtoti Bird Sanctuary is a haven for exotic and indigenous birds. A lake-like stretch of calm water framed by palms forms an ideal environment for a large number of waterbirds. The Mitchell Park Aviaries, Durban, house a small collection of indigenous and exotic birds, including waterfowl. The Umgeni Bird Sanctuary is situated 1,5 km north of Durban and has about 2 000 birds representing some 300 species.

One of the best bird-watching areas in the Cape Peninsula is provided by the Rondevlei Bird Sanctuary. To date, 222 species of local and European migratory birds have been spotted. The Rietvlei Bird Sanctuary in Milnerton is the largest breeding area for waterfowl in the Cape. There are more than 146 species including the migratory Arctic tern.

Botanical gardens
During 1990 the former Botanical Research Institute and the National Botanic Gardens amalgamated into the National Botanical Institute (NBI) with its head office at Kirstenbosch National Botanical Garden, Cape Town.

The NBI is an autonomous state-aided institute which collects and cultivates plants indigenous to Southern Africa in botanical gardens; undertakes and promotes research in connection with plants and related matters and makes plant material available for research; studies and cultivates endangered plant species; promotes the utilisation of the economic potential of in-

digenous plants and establishes non-indigenous plants for comparative studies and educational purposes.

The eight national botanical gardens controlled by the NBI are Kirstenbosch in Cape Town, Karoo in Worcester, Harold Porter in Betty's Bay, OFS in Bloemfontein, Natal in Pietermaritzburg, Lowveld in Nelspruit, Witwatersrand in Roodepoort and that of Pretoria.

Some local authorities also have botanical gardens which are not controlled by the NBI. Important municipal botanical gardens include The Wilds and Melville Koppies in Johannesburg and the Municipal Botanical Gardens in Durban.

Caves
There are many caves the tourist can visit. Of these the Cango, Echo, Sterkfontein and Sudwala caves are the most spectacular.

The Cango caves near Oudtshoorn are world famous. They were discovered in three phases, of which only one section, Cango I, is accessible to the public. Cango III was discovered in 1975. The longest cave in this section equals the length of three rugby fields.

The Echo caves are situated at the top of the Molopong Valley in the eastern Transvaal. Implements and tools from the Middle and Late Stone Age and the earlier Iron Age were discovered here. The largest chamber is 100 m in length and 40 m high.

The Sterkfontein caves near Krugersdorp comprise six large rooms connected by passages and a subterranean lake. The skull of a woman (Mrs Ples), estimated to be about 1,5 million years old, was discovered here earlier this century.

The Sudwala caves are situated in the Mankelekele mountain near Nelspruit in the eastern Transvaal. The P R Owen room, a natural amphitheatre, is 67 m in diameter and 37 m high. The room has been used for concerts and choir recordings. In early times the Sudwala caves were used as a shelter.

The Miracle Cave near Daniëlskuil is in the northern Cape. Bushmen paintings dating back 10 000 years have been discovered on the walls of the cave.

Cultural attractions
The Durban tattoo is annually presented by the Durban City Council and First National Bank. A tattoo is also presented at the annual Goodwood Show held in Goodwood near Cape Town.

The Roodepoort Eisteddfod is the only international arts festival in the Southern Hemisphere. In 1989, 40 countries outside Africa inquired about taking part.

The Cape Coons had their origin in a group of Negro vocalists who visited the Cape in the last century. The first Malay group, the Cherry Pickers, was established in 1890 and since then the Cape Coons have entertained Capetonians and tourists on the first two days of each new year.

Gold Reef City is a fully operational theme park depicting Johannesburg during the gold rush. Gold Reef City was established to preserve a disappearing cultural heritage and to educate and entertain at the same time. The Chamber of Mines' Gold Mine Museum has been incorporated here. The mine dancers especially attract a large audience.

Similar conservation projects have also been undertaken at Kimberley's big hole. Visitors can travel to the museum in a traditional tram. Gold rushes are staged and visitors can 'mine' diamonds by buying a bucket filled with gravel — in some of which the real thing can be found!

A golf-course in barren Namaqualand turned into a flower garden after good rain had fallen

Pilgrim's Rest in the eastern Transvaal is an authentic diggers' village restored to its former glory. Visitors can stay in typical diggers' homes.

The hamlet of Matjiesfontein in the Cape Province developed along the railway lines on James Logan's farm at the end of the 19th century. Initially he sold water to the trains and its passengers, but later he built the Lord Milner Hotel. In 1975 the entire hamlet was declared a national monument and has become a very popular place to stay. Today the railway line still runs through Matjiesfontein.

Verwoerdburg City near Pretoria boasts a water organ. Six hundred nozzles, 144 lights and 34 pumps spout water in five colours as high as 30 m. Concerts, opera, musicals and overtures are presented regularly. A similar organ exists at Wemmer Pan, near Johannesburg.

The Rand Show, an annual event during Easter, is the largest of its kind in the country and attracts visitors from all over the world.

The Cape Festival is also held in April.

Routes
A new development in South African tourism has been the introduction of various routes. Apart from the well-known wine routes in various regions and a Crayfish Route along the West Coast, visitors can also follow the Northern Natal Battlefield Route, which includes Newcastle, Vryheid, Dundee, Ladysmith and neighbourings towns. This route covers numerous Anglo-Boer and Zulu war fields.

A Succulent Plant Route was opened on the Knersvlakte near Vanrhynsdorp, Cape. More than 100 succulent plant species, some of which are found only in South Africa, can be seen here.

Captour, the Cape tourism association, has introduced a Whale Route along the Cape west and south coasts. It includes observation posts at places along the coast where whales are regularly seen.

Snake parks
The Hartbeespoort Dam Snake and Animal Park on the northern boundary of the Hartbeespoort Dam, has a fine reptile collection.

The Transvaal Snake Park at Halfway House between Johannesburg and Pretoria, houses up to 150 species of snakes, other reptiles and amphibians from southern Africa and elsewhere.The emphasis is on the development of programmes for the breeding of animals in captivity.

In Durban, the Fitz-Simons Snake Park represents more than 100 exotic and indigenous species.

The Port Elizabeth Snake Park maintains the traditional open pit for exhibiting snakes, common in the area. Other snakes may be seen in glass-fronted cases, while exotic and indigenous constrictors can be seen in the Python House.

Zoological gardens
The National Zoological Gardens of South Africa in Pretoria, which is the only member in Africa of the American Association for Zoological Parks and Aquaria and is also a member of the International Union of Directors of Zoological Gardens and Aquariums (IUDZG), has taken the lead in establishing the Pan-African Association for Zoological Gardens, Aquaria and Botanic Gardens in 1989 (PAAZAB). The zoo is also a founder member of the International Union of Zooculturists.

The zoo is considered one of the 10 best in the world and about one million people visit it each year. The area of the National Zoological Gardens comprise about 60 ha.

The National Zoological Gardens has considerable success in breeding highly endangered species such as the Waldrapp Ibis, Przewalski horse, European bison, addra gazelle, Pére Davids deer, Arabian oryx, red forest buffalo, and others. Southern African endangered species such as the roan antelope, riverine rabbit and the wild dog are also successfully bred here. The zoo has also launched a black rhino breeding programme at its Potgietersrus Game Breeding Centre.

The aquarium and reptile park of the National Zoolgical Gardens exhibits valuable king penguins and rare dwarf crocodiles.

The insectarium was officially opened in December 1990. It includes exhibitions of ants, water insects and an observation beehive as well as beetles, grasshoppers and a termitarium. It also has a collection of non-insects like spiders and scorpions.

The zoo's collection includes 900 specimens of 137 mammal species, 1 350 specimens of 198 bird species, 6 343 specimens of 275 fish species and 665 specimens of 136 reptile species.

The Zoological Gardens has a breeding centre for game in Potgietersrus and Lichtenburg where especially endangered animal species are bred. The zoo's successful breeding programme for cheetah at the De Wildt Cheetah Research and Breeding Centre has been extended to the Potgietersrus Game Breeding Centre.

The National Zoological Gardens have a Friends of the Zoo Society and an 'Adopt-an-animal' scheme. Several educational courses and night tours are also offered.

The Johannesburg Zoological Gardens have an animal collection which include about 300 species represented by some 1 900 specimens. The animals are in open-air enclosures separated from the public by dry or water moats. This include the internationally acclaimed gorilla complex, pachyderm section and the section for large carnivores. Of particular interest are the African elephants, golden lion tamarins, sitatunga, fossa and the selection of big apes. The Johannesburg Zoo was the first to breed the white lion successfully.

The Bloemfontein Zoological Gardens have had notable successes in breeding 'ligers', a cross between a lion and a tiger.

Hunting

Southern Africa has become one of the most popular big game hunting regions in the world. It offers a great variety for trophy hunters, including the white rhinoceros, black wildebeest, nyala, eland, buffalo and other rare trophies. Strict regulations exist regarding all rare game.

Hunting is regulated on a provincial basis. All four provinces have nature conservation ordinances regulating the hunting of game. Hunting proclamations of the various provinces differ and are promulgated annually.

The hunting season for the different provinces also differs, but normally runs during the winter months from 1 May to 31 July.

Dangerous game (lion, leopard, elephant and buffalo) is mainly restricted to game parks, where no hunting is permitted, and to private game reserves such as Sabi-Sand, Timbavati and Klaserie where these species may be hunted only on a limited scale and by special permit obtained from the Transvaal Directorate Nature and Environmental Conservation.

Most species may be hunted legally by non-landowners during the hunting season, provided they have the written consent of the landowner and a valid hunting permit issued by the appropriate conservation authority. Game such as impala, kudu, wildebeest (gnu), zebra, duiker and warthog are mainly concentrated on farms in the Transvaal and the Natal bushveld regions, while springbok, blesbok and the rare white-tailed gnu are found in the Transvaal highveld regions, the OFS and the northern Cape.

Sportsmen have organised themselves into hunters' associations, some of which concentrate mainly on bird-shooting. The South African Hunters' and Game Preservation Association is the best known. The South African Professional Hunters' Association represents professional hunters and hunting enterprises in the RSA.

Hiking

Organised hiking — that is along trails defined and administered by the National Hiking Way Board — is extremely popular in South Africa. Sections of the National Hiking Way System have been gradually extended and developed so that the entire system will follow an almost unbroken line from the Soutpansberg range in the northern Transvaal to the Cedarberg Wilderness area in the Cape Province.

The National Hiking Way System is managed and developed in terms of the Forest Act of 1984. The Act also provides for a National Hiking Way Board and a National Hiking Way Fund.

The National Hiking Way Board operates under the auspices of the Forestry Branch of the Department of Water Affairs and Forestry and its membership includes representatives of major conservation, recreational and educational organisations, as well as knowledgeable individuals.

The National Hiking Way Fund is financed by donations and revenue earned from routes open to the public.

The National Hiking Way System consists of various hiking way trail sections (20 at present), with overnight facilities, and eight trails for a few hours' leisurely walk.

Overnight huts are usually equipped with sleeping bunks and foam mattresses, cooking utensils, firewood, water, latrines and basic washing facilities. Hikers carry their own food, sleeping bags, clothes and other personal equipment and requisites. No guides, cooks or carriers are provided.

The National Hiking Way Board issues a brochure whenever a new route is opened. This brochure contains information on aspects such as the geology, trees and other plantlife, animals and birds found in that area, the history and the management goals of the area through which the route passes as well as a route map.

There are also many opportunities for hikers other than the trails and walks under the control of the National Hiking Way Board. There are about 60 other hiking way trails administered by conservation authorities, town councils and farmers as well as about 300 one-day walks. In some private and state game reserves hikers can join a hiking tour under the guidance of a game ranger.

Further details on hiking clubs, brochures for

hiking way trails and books on hiking are available at tel. (012) 310-3839.

Nature conservation

Nature conservation is a provincial function and each province has promulgated its own ordinances to deal with hunting, fishing and the protection of fauna and flora. The provinces also establish game and nature reserves which are managed in accordance with the primary purpose for which they were created. The provinces have also been charged with management of mountain catchment areas and wilderness regions. The same applies to the self-governing states.

Cape Province
The Cape Province is the largest of the four provinces and has the most varied topography. It has a great variety of game. The flora is particularly impressive and includes the Cape Floristic Kingdom, one of the world's six floral kingdoms.

The authority responsible for conservation in the Cape is the Chief Directorate: Nature and Environmental Conservation of the Cape Provincial Administration.

In addition to 130 conservation areas under its control the chief directorate subsidises and coordinates the management of 85 nature reserves under the control of local authorities and is also responsible for proclamation and management of protected natural environments such as the Cape Peninsula. The chief directorate also manages wilderness areas, drift-sand areas and state-owned mountain catchment land and is involved in the management of 613 937 ha of privately owned mountain catchment areas.

Functions of the chief directorate include control over hunting, buying, selling and keeping in captivity of wild animals, problem animal control, game and wild-flower utilisation, outdoor recreation at nature reserves, state dams and provincial public resorts, professional hunting and angling and bait collecting in inland waters and estuaries. It also controls issuing of permits to exploit marine resources and exercises control in five marine reserves. It is responsible for seven patrol boats, 13 fishing harbours, 33 offshore islands and the use of the shore below the high-water mark. All islands are nature reserves while only a few are used for collection of guano.

The chief directorate runs a comprehensive programme of environmental education from some reserves. Its research section undertakes ecological surveys of potential conservation areas and areas endangered by development. In this field it works with other organisations and is involved in several programmes designed to save endangered ecosystems and species.

A total of 90 nature reserves, state forests and wilderness areas with a total area of about 1,24 million ha are under the control of the chief directorate.

Natal
Not only are the oldest proclaimed game reserves in Africa — Umfolozi, St Lucia and Hluhluwe — found in Natal but the Natal Parks Board has earned an international reputation, especially for its efforts in the conservation of the white rhinoceros (*Ceratotherium s. simum*), which was on the verge of extinction.

The reserves in Natal are well-known for their scenic variety, including mountain forest, thornveld, mangrove swamps, coastal and marine reserves. Rest camps can be found in almost all the reserves managed by the Natal Parks Board, while visitors can enjoy camping facilities in other reserves. Visitors to the Umfolozi, St Lucia and Itala nature reserves can go on wilderness hiking trips under the supervision of a ranger.

The Natal Parks Board probably controls the largest and most popular wildernesses in South Africa, namely those in the Natal Drakensberg and also about 118 000 ha proclaimed wilderness areas in the rest of the province and about 50 000 ha nature reserve.

In March 1989 the conservation component of the Natal Parks Board received an amount of R250 000 from the Southern African Nature Foundation (SANF), a branch of the World Wide Fund for Nature (WWF), in recognition of the province's role in conservation both in and outside South Africa. The WWF has its head office in Switzerland.

Today the Natal Parks Board controls and develops 80 parks, nature reserves and resorts in Natal. The most important are: Hluhluwe Game Reserve, 51 km from Mtubatuba; Umfolozi Game Reserve, joined to Hluhluwe; Mkuzi Game Reserve, 95 km north of Mtubatuba; St Lucia Game Reserve, including Lake St Lucia; Itala Nature Reserve near Louwsberg in the Pongola River Valley; Giant's Castle Game Reserve; and the Royal Natal National Park in the Drakensberg range.

The board's St Lucia Marine Reserve contains fine examples of the most southernly coral reef systems off the shores of South Africa. Along with the Maputaland Marine Reserve, this area shares the distinction of being the only protected breeding area in Africa for the endangered loggerhead and leatherback marine turtles.

The chapter on game of the Natal Conservation Ordinance, 1974, makes provision for schedules of ordinary, protected and specially protected game. Ordinary game may be hunted under licence during an open season. Protected game may only be hunted under permit and licence, the fee depending on the species. Specially protected game, which includes grysbok, klipspringer, red hartebeest, giraffe, black rhinoceros, pangolin and antbear, may not be hunted at all.

The board, with the Natal Wildlife Conservancy Association, runs a very successful conservancy system on privately owned farmland in Natal.

The ordinance and its regulations also provide for closed seasons for certain marine and freshwater fish; limitations on the capture and keeping in captivity of wild birds and mammals and on the gathering of wild flowers; the regulation of professional hunting and control of the activities of visitors to reserves.

Transvaal

The Chief Directorate: Nature and Environmental Conservation of the Transvaal Provincial Administration is responsible for conservation and utilisation of fauna and flora in the province. Apart from those farms or reserves with special exemption permits, all forms of utilisation and movement of fauna and flora are controlled by this authority through the Nature Conservation Ordinance, 1983. The four main functions include natural resource management, management oriented research, environmental education and outdoor recreation. Apart from normal reserve management and law enforcement, commonly associated with nature conservation activities, the status of various plant and animal species are continually being researched and monitored. Of increasing importance is promotion of sustainable development within industry, commerce and the government sector. For this reason the chief directorate screens impact assessments where development might adversely affect a natural resource. To promote the ethic of sustainable utilisation and the necessity for biotic diversity, a variety of education programmes are being developed for schools and adult groups. Nature recreation activities are also provided for those who enjoy outdoor life.

The Chief Directorate: Nature and Environmental Conservation manages 54 conservation areas. These range from large reserves which have a high species diversity to small areas which are set aside for specific species which are identified as threatened. Large reserves include the Blyderivierspoort Nature Reserve (22 664 ha) and Serala Wilderness Area (22 009 ha), both forming part of the Transvaal Drakensberg Escarpment. Cythna Letty, which is only seven hectares in extent, was established to protect *Aloe vryheidensis*. Reserves carrying large herbivores include Hans Merensky in the lowveld, Loskop Dam with its large white rhino population which is situated in mixed bushveld, Suikerbosrand on the highveld and Langjan in the arid northwestern corner of the province. The total area covered by all provincial reserves is 242 870 ha. Species currently deserving special conservation attention include various cycad species, roan and sable, the blue swallow and a variety of the province's smaller fish species which are found in the Drakensberg Escarpment streams. These fish are threatened as a result of injudicious forestry activities. Two reserves, Barberspan near Delareyville and Marievale near Springs, are recognised by Ramsar as wetlands of international importance.

There are 557 private nature reserves with a combined area of about 1 290 000 ha belonging to municipalities, corporate bodies and private individuals in the Transvaal.

In addition to this there are 1 400 privately-owned game farms who actively manages their wildlife resource while also promoting an environmental understanding through their various safari operations. Although these areas are privately owned, trading, hunting and transporting of game is regulated by the Provincial Ordinance for conservation. A number of support services are provided for these landowners by the chief directorate.

Orange Free State

The Directorate: Nature and Environmental Conservation of the Orange Free State Provincial Administration was established in 1969. The Ordinance imposes restrictions on indiscriminate taking of plants and animals, including fish, from their natural environment but provides for utilisation of the more abundant species.

This directorate controls less than 1 per cent of the OFS's surface area. Continued attempts are made to persuade landowners to manage their land as private nature reserves or conservancies. A conservancy consists of one or more farms where the farmers work together to conserve nature in the area. At present there are 14 private nature reserves and 24 conservancies in the OFS.

Boating and fishing opportunities are created

to encourage outdoor recreation, while game viewing is made possible in reserves.

The directorate manages 14 nature reserves with a total surface area of 158 179 ha. The most important are the Willem Pretorius Game Reserve (12 000 ha) and the reserves Tussen die Riviere (22 000 ha), Sandveld (37 735 ha) and Sterkfontein Dam (14 470 ha).

Accommodation is available at the Willem Pretorius Game Reserve, the Tussen die Riviere Nature Reserve and the Sterkfontein Dam Nature Reserve.

The total game population in the provincial nature reserves number more than 19 000. To maintain a healthy balance between the available grazing and the number of animals, game is regularly removed from the reserves. A public game auction is held annually while the public is also given an opportunity to hunt game in the reserves. This service is very popular.

Research on the habits, occurrence and needs of animals and plants is undertaken regularly. The Special Services Division regularly looks into ways and means to solve administrative problems on nature reserves and to promote conservation of private land.

Development impact studies are undertaken in order to examine the effect development projects have on the environment. Development projects are evaluated and an environment advice and information service are provided for developers.

The nursery for indigenous plants outside Bloemfontein distributes thousands of plants annually, while the fish hatchery beneath the bank of the Hendrik Verwoerd Dam hatches fish and distributes it among landowners.

Guidance and information regarding environmental conservation are presented constantly. About 2 500 pupils and prospective teachers are for instance taken on field trips on a regular basis. There is a modern outdoor education centre at the Willem Pretorius Game Reserve where groups of up to 140 people can be accommodated at any given time.

SA Nature Foundation

The Southern African Nature Foundation (SANF), which represents the World Wide Fund for Nature (WWF), was established in 1968. Since then the SANF has collected nearly R40 million for 250 conservation projects in South Africa and 12 other countries, including Malawi, Botswana and Zimbabwe.

Some of the SANF's most important projects were the establishment of five national parks; the creation or enlargement of more than 30 nature reserves; the establishment of five chairs and various research programmes for nature conservation and environmental management at South African universities; co-ordinated attempts to protect more than 35 species (including the black rhinoceros, riverine rabbit, roan antelope, wattled crane and jackass penguin) which are threatened with extinction, as well as plant protection programmes and the development of educational environmental programmes and strategies.

The administrative costs of the SANF are covered by the interest on specific trust funds, which means that the total amount of each donation received is used for conservation work.

Interesting facts

The number of elephants in South Africa has increased from less than 200 during the previous century to a constant 8 200 since 1981.

South Africa has the world's biggest land mammal (elephant), second biggest (white rhino) and third biggest (hippo), the tallest (giraffe), the fastest (cheetah) and smallest (pygmy shrew).

It has 10 per cent of the world's known species of birds, including the largest (ostrich) and the largest flying bird, the *gompou* or kori bustard, which can weigh up to 20 kg.

Three of the world's 15 crane species are found in South Africa. The wattled crane is an endangered species of which only three hundred are left in South Africa.

Approximately 100 cricket species are found in South Africa.

South Africa boasts four rabbit species. One is the rare and shy riverine rabbit — one of the country's and the world's most endangered mammal species. They are found only between Deelfontein and Calvinia in the Karoo.

The Johannesburg Botanical Garden owns one of the biggest collections of lithops in the world. Lithops are found only in the southern regions of Africa.

The wild dog is an endangered species mainly because of the destruction of its natural habitat and its being killed especially by farmers. There are only about 350 left in the Kruger National Park.

The Egyptian vulture which became extinct in South Africa more than 50 years ago, has returned. In 1989 three of these birds were noticed in the Langjan nature reserve in the north-western Transvaal. The birds were last seen in 1932 when they were breeding in Transkei.

It is estimated that up to half of all water-birds along the southern coast of the Cape have a home in the Wilderness Lake Area. A total of 79 of South Africa's 95 species water-birds can be found here. There are about 15 species wild geese in the area.

One of the earth's four known leatherback turtle breeding grounds is on the Maputaland coast in northern Zululand, where four of the world's seven species of turtles breed. The leatherback turtles which come here to breed have increased from five in 1963 to 100 in 1984.

A total of 396 reptile and amphibian species are found in South Africa, Swaziland and Lesotho. About half of these are found nowhere else in the world. More than 20 of the 33 endangered species are found in the Cape Peninsula and Maputaland in Natal.

In the eastern Transvaal the Timbavati, Sabi-Sand and Klaserie group of unfenced private game reserves are allegedly the largest in the world.

Three of Southern Africa's four ibis species can be observed at the Rondebult Bird Sanctuary near Germiston.

News items: 1990

The oak tree was SA's Tree of the Year in 1990. Although it is not an indigenous tree, it was planted in the Cape as early as the 17th century.

The first ever bongo pair in the Southern Hemisphere arrived at the Johannesburg Zoo in January. The National Zoological Gardens of South Africa in Pretoria received three bongos in June as well as six barasinghas, another first for Africa.

South Africa's issue of permits for international trade in African elephant products was suspended for a year in January.

A Mandril baboon born in captivity at the Johannesburg Zoo in January made history by being the first to survive in Africa in the past ten years. The survival of this endangered species depends on reproduction in zoos.

The government approved the creation of a Greater St Lucia conservation area — at 275 000 ha the third-largest in the country — in February. It will involve the consolidation of an area that includes a large section of privately owned farmland, to link Mkuze Game Reserve with the St Lucia area.

An elephant calf born more than a year ago in the Knysna forest was seen for the first time in February. Apparently only four elephants are left in the Knysna forest.

The South African branch of the International Council for Animal and Nature Conservation (CIC) was founded in March.

The Mazda Wildlife Fund was launched in April and donated R5 million — available in instalments of R1 million every year for the next five years — for wildlife conservation.

South African Airways launched the African Wildlife Heritage Trust in April. The first of two annual contributions was presented to the main beneficiaries of the trust: the Southern African Nature Foundation and the International Wilderness Foundation.

Ten women completed Total's Drakensberg Expedition for Women, a hike of 350 km in the Drakensberg, in April in an attempt to draw attention to raptors and to collect money for the African Raptor Information Centre (Aric). They collected R25 000.

In a world first, five black rhino were put up for auction by the Natal Parks Board in June. They were sold for R2,2 million.

South Africa won the 1990 International Wildlife Conservation Award, which is awarded by Safari Club International annually.

A rare Madagascar Boa has been bred for the first time in South Africa by a private owner. The snake produced six young.

Anglo American and De Beers donated R2,6 million for urgent conservation projects to the SA Nature Foundation.

A chair in Hotel and Tourism Management has been established at the University of Pretoria following collaboration between the Southern Sun Hotel Group and the university's Graduate School of Management.

The following South African hotels received the 1990 M-Net Hospitality Awards: Royal Hotel, Durban (city hotels), Fish River Sun (casinos), Hotel Camps Bay, Cape Town (suburban hotels), Drakensberg Sun (resort hotels) and Coach House (country hotels).

A researcher from the Botany Department of the University of the North, Mr Larry Leach, was chosen as the first recipient from Africa of the Golden Cactus Award of the International Organisation for Succulent Plant Study.

Game ranger Mr Jon Maltby has been awarded the Purple Bar Award, the Natal Parks Board's highest award for bravery, after physically intervening between game guards and a group of ambushers.

A Braille hiking trail was introduced in the Karoo National Botanical Garden at Worcester in August. A similar hiking trail was opened in Kirstenbosch in 1982. A trail for handicapped people is available at the Natal Parks Board's Kenneth Stainbank Nature Reserve in Durban. This trail caters for the blind and may easily be used by people in wheelchairs.

Nearly 300 animals, including kudu, impala, waterbucks and two elephants, died in an outbreak of anthrax in the Kruger National Park in September.

The National Zoological Gardens of South Africa in Pretoria received Africa's first pair of giant ant-eaters from Argentina in September.

Public resorts countrywide were opened to all races on 15 October.

The elephant and rhinoceros were classified as 'specially protected game' in the Transvaal during the year.

A commercial fisherman was arrested for allegedly harpooning a rare Heaviside's dolphin near Saldanha Bay in November. Heaviside's dolphins are endemic to the West Coast and Namibia and only about 1 000 of them are believed to exist.

The presence of Hartmann's mountain zebra in the Richtersveld was confirmed when one carcass and tracks of seven others were found.

Success was achieved in combating offences related to cycads. One investigation led to Johannesburg where hundreds of cycads originating from the eastern Cape were confiscated.

Acknowledgements:

Cape Provincial Administration
Department of Environment Affairs
Natal Parks Board
National Parks Board
National Zoological Gardens of South Africa
Provincial Administration of the Orange Free State
SA Nature Foundation
SA Tourism Board
Transvaal Provincial Administration

Despite devolution of many conservation functions to the provincial administrations, large areas of state and privately-owned land are still controlled and managed by the Department of Environment Affairs and the Forestry Branch of the Department of Water Affairs and Forestry to preserve wildlife and indigenous vegetation. This implies overall co-ordination of nature conservation, management of conservation areas (including indigenous forests, drift-sands and mountain catchment areas), administration of legislation on control of veld fires, protection of rare plants, promotion of tree planting and tree conservation, outdoor recreation in state forests, control of invasive species, coastal conservation and conservation and utilisation of marine life. Several other government departments and bodies are also involved in preserving the general environment and keeping it as life-supporting as possible for man and beast.

Among other things, conservation areas are managed to maintain species and genetic diversity of flora and fauna, to preserve endangered and rare fauna and flora, to maintain ecologically viable habitats, restore ecologically degraded habitats, conserve wilderness areas and scenic landscapes, preserve cultural-historic phenomena such as rock art and historical buildings, conserve areas to counter erosion (or as water catchments or recreation areas) and undertake research on fauna and flora. Management's emphasis is chiefly on maintenance of ecological processes, life-support systems and sustainable utilisation of species and ecosystems.

The South African Plan for Nature Conservation was initiated in 1975 to identify and place rare or endangered species or endangered areas under conservation management. The plan aims to co-ordinate all nature conservation objectives; maintain a register of conserved areas, classifying them according to the purposes for which they are conserved and to collate and map all information needed for planning purposes. Information on the plans of individual nature conservation organisations is stored to co-ordinate national planning and make information available to all organisations involved in conservation, including government departments, so that important natural areas may be included in development plans at national and regional levels.

Only low-density non-intensive recreational use by a limited number of persons is permitted of conservation areas. Wilderness areas and nature reserves of the Forestry Branch of the Department of Water Affairs and Forestry are integral parts of state forests. Not all state forest land enjoys the special conservation status of proclaimed conservation areas, but the multiple-use principle ensures application of sound conservation principles on all land. State forest land covers a total area of 1,6 million ha, of which 9 per cent is under indigenous forest, 18 per cent under plantations, 72 per cent under mountain catchment areas and 1 per cent under driftsand.

Environmental conservation

The Committee for Environmental Management is a statutory body established to advise the Director-general of the Department of Environment Affairs on any matter regarding the protection and utilisation of the environment. This promotes co-ordination of conservation actions in the country.

Wilderness areas are declared in terms of the Forest Act of 1984, and enjoy the highest status of all conservation areas. They are large undeveloped and uninhabited areas with an intrinsically wild character. These areas may not be violated by development such as roads, buildings or mining. Eight wilderness areas with a total area of 231 966 ha have been proclaimed. These include the popular Cedarberg near Clanwilliam and extensive areas in the Natal Drakensberg.

Sixteen **mountain catchment areas** totalling 599 598 ha in area have been proclaimed on private land. This permits the department to undertake conservation work on private land in the public interest. Private farmers cannot afford this. High-quality water discharge is the main object of conservation of these areas.

To curtail undesirable development in natural areas with high aesthetic and conservational potential, **nature areas** in private ownership are proclaimed and managed in terms of the Environmental Conservation Act, 1989.

The **South African Natural Heritage**

Programme, initiated by the Department of Environment Affairs and sponsored by private enterprise, is designed to register and conserve important natural sites in private ownership. In this the owner plays an indispensable role. Areas of special plant communities, good examples of aquatic habitats, sensitive catchment areas, habitats of endangered species and outstanding natural features qualify for registration. Ownership is not affected and the owner may request financial and technical assistance to manage the site.

The department plays an important role in **environmental education**. It publishes a variety of magazines, brochures, information pamphlets and posters as well as audio-visual programmes to promote an awareness of environmental conservation among the general public.

South Africa also observes World Environment Day on 5 June, Arbor Day (the first Friday in August) and National Marine Day every year.

South Africa is faced with many of the same kind of **problems** as other developing countries where rapid industrialisation, population growth and urbanisation are posing a threat to the quality of the environment. Because the need to protect the environment while permitting a degree of development and urbanisation that will satisfy the requirements of a growing population is a complicated issue, Parliament in 1980 approved a White Paper on a national policy for environmental conservation. The White Paper proposed various guidelines for striking a balance between development and conservation.

After thorough investigation of the various environmental impact assessment (EIA) systems applied by developed nations, it was decided that EIA should be introduced on a voluntary basis in SA. The general objective is to ensure that the environment is considered in both planning and implementation of physical development projects. The Department of Environment Affairs actively promotes this approach.

An Integrated Environmental Management Procedure (IEM) has been developed by the Council for the Environment (CE), through which observance of environmental considerations and public participation can be intregrated in planning. The Department is at present investigating methods of applying IEM in existing planning procedures.

Pollution control

Various bodies have organised symposiums dealing with, among other, air pollution control,

solid waste management and recycling, wildlife protection, oceanography, transportation and the environment and planning for environmental conservation to stimulate public interest.

Air pollution

The Atmospheric Pollution Prevention Act, 1965, is directed at prevention of air pollution or reducing it to a minimum.

The National Air Pollution Advisory Committee advises the Minister of National Health and Population Development on all matters related to control, prevention and abatement of air pollution. Controlled areas, i.e. areas where certain stringent control measures apply, are designated by the Minister on the advice of this committee. A study is made of anti-pollution measures introduced in other countries to determine their applicability to South African conditions.

The industrial sector contributes considerably to air pollution. Eighty per cent of the energy used is coal based. It is estimated that fly-ash from power stations is emitted at a rate of about one million tons a year. Another one million tons of sulphur dioxide may be emitted into the atmosphere yearly by power stations, refineries and the sulphide ore-smelting industry. Another 10 000 tons of iron oxides derived from iron and steel works pollute the air. These pollutants are usually emitted at considerable height through tall stacks and are greatly diluted before reaching ground level. However, research and countermeasures take due account of the possibility that some of the pollutants, like sulphur dioxide, can be carried over long distances and eventually cause 'acid rain'. No evidence of acid rain has as yet been proved by scientific methods.

Low-level atmospheric pollution is derived mainly from smaller installations in cities, such as coal stoves in residential areas without electricity and coal-heated boilers in factories and hospitals. It has been estimated that all these emit some 50 000 tons of sulphur dioxide into the atmosphere annually. On the eastern Transvaal highveld about 300 tons of hydrocarbons are discharged into the air each year.

The whole country has been declared a controlled area in respect of **noxious or offensive gases**. The objective is to minimise industrial emission into the atmosphere by using available technology with due regard to economic implications. A system of registration and provisional registration certificates authorises operation of industrial processes which evolve noxious or offensive gases. A registration certificate is issued by the Chief Air Pollution Control Officer when he is satisfied that the 'best practicable means' are used to prevent or reduce to a minimum pollutants caused by such a process. At present 69 processes are listed in the Act.

An agreement has been entered into between the governments of the Republic of South Africa and Transkei on consultation, co-operation and reciprocal assistance in management of air pollution and maintenance of adequate standards.

Three levels of **smoke** pollution control are utilised, i.e. simple or direct control (in terms of which local authorities are authorised to inspect plans for installation of fuel-burning appliances, stacks, etc. and to act in the case of complaints); regulatory powers (which enable local authorities to prescribe smoke pollution limits for light industries and to act in the case of infringements) and, finally, smoke-control zones for private dwellings, where control measures are more stringent.

The locally-designed and developed minimum-smoke stove has meant considerable improvement in combustion of volatiles and smoke which would otherwise have been emitted into the atmosphere.

South Africa has a unique problem in the sand dumps and slimes dams formed by waste from mines. On the Witwatersrand, **dust** blown from these dumps presents a serious problem to nearby residential areas. Various methods have been applied to cut down the dust problem — the most successful being vegetation of the dumps. The research laboratory of the Chamber of Mines has evolved a method of establishing vegetation on mine dumps and large tracts of land previously plagued by dust have been grassed. Both the Witwatersrand and OFS gold fields have been declared dust control areas. Waste coal dumps also cause a pollution problem when the waste coal ignites spontaneously. The Government Mining Engineer acts as chief air pollution officer in these areas.

The Government Mining Engineer is also responsible for the combating of asbestos dust in the atmosphere, resulting from the exploitation, milling, packing and transport of asbestos fibre.

Regulations on **vehicle emissions** have been made applicable only to emissions of diesel-powered vehicles. They require a very low concentration of smoke or free carbon in the exhaust and are designed to enforce proper engine maintenance. However, few municipalities enforce the law on diesel emissions. The regulations are based on the use of the Hartridge-BP smoke meter. Three limits are prescribed, i.e. at an altitude of less than 600 m, 65 Hartridge Units (HU); at an altitude of between 600 m and 1 200 m, 70 HU and at altitudes above 1 200 m, 75 HU.

Though pollution from petrol-driven motor cars is much lower than in cities such as New York, Tokyo and Los Angeles, it is a problem of growing proportions and contributes to photochemical smog in certain areas. Concentrations of carbon monoxide, hydrocarbons, nitrous oxide and lead emitted by motor vehicles are monitored. However, statistics do not show significant increases over the years. The concentration of airborne lead in the country's major cities is generally much lower than the two micrograms of lead per m^3 of air at present accepted by most countries as an ambient air quality standard. A programme to decrease the lead content of petrol gradually has already been put into operation.

Water pollution

In terms of the Water Act of 1956, the Department of Water Affairs and Forestry is primarily responsible for control of water pollution. Also involved in preventive and other measures are the Departments of National Health and Population Development, Agriculture, Mineral and Energy Affairs, Environment Affairs, the four provincial administrations, local authorities and water boards, which can apply preventive measures and pollution control within their statutory powers. The Department of Water Affairs and Forestry is also responsible for registration and classification of all water care works, which comprise works for purification of water to potable standards and sewage and effluent treatment works. It is also responsible for the operators of these works, which are required to employ minimum numbers of qualified operators of certain classes, according to the size and sophistication of the works.

Because of South Africa's limited water supplies, re-use of purified effluents is essential. In terms of the Water Act, effluents must be purified to specified standards and returned to their respective sources. The CSIR has pioneered work to reclaim pure water from industrial and sewage effluents in South Africa. Proven techniques can be applied to supplement drinking water from this source, if necessary.

Progressively more time and attention are being devoted to surveys and research, especially with regard to water quality management in catchment areas in urban, mining, agricultural and industrial areas. Despite application of quality standards which effluents must satisfy before they can be discharged into the environment, increasing concentrations of pollutants still occur and constitute a threat to the utilisation of water and the health of the consumer.

Cases for real concern exist where treated effluents are discharged into rivers and re-used indirectly. A new management strategy is therefore being developed within the Department of Water Affairs and Forestry. This determines quality needs for the various consumer sectors for every catchment area. The assimilative capacity of the water source for effluents determines the quantity and quality of effluents that may be discharged in the vicinity of the source. Toxic and dangerous effluents may be banned completely or partially.

The most serious forms of water pollution are mineralisation through dissolved solids, eutrophication, acid mine drainage, silt, toxic substances (for example heavy metals, agricultural agents, such as fertilisers and pesticide residues and also carcinogens) and pathogens

The industrial sector contributes largely to air pollution

(viruses, bacteria and parasites). Mineralisation, eutrophication and siltation must receive preferential attention because of their economic implications and the effects they have on physical development and utilisation of water resources.

Acid water filtering from piles of stored coal is probably the biggest ground water pollution problem in South Africa.

Coal and gold mines, various other industries, thermal energy generation, the agricultural sector, irrigational backflow as well as natural run-off which leaches mineral salts, are the major sources of mineralisation.

Water boards, local governments and other water-supplying organisations devote their attention to the removal of pollutants from water at purification plants before supply to the consumer.

The effects of acid mine drainage and leakage from active and disused coal and gold mines are countered by recycling, evaporation, neutralisation or desalination.

In co-ordination with the Division of Water Technology of the CSIR, universities, consultants, mining companies and others, the Water Research Commission investigates existing technology and methods of water treatment and management to ensure that all water consumers are assured of water quality which is acceptable for its different uses.

Besides provincial ordinances and regulations, there are about 20 Acts of Parliament in terms of which industries and other operators of polluting installations and processes can be obliged to develop alternative methods and techniques which will cause as little pollution as possible.

Marine pollution

Marine pollution from land-based sources is mainly controlled by the Department of Water Affairs and Forestry (Water Act, 54 of 1956). Various other national statutes regarding marine pollution are administered by the Department of Transport, Environment Affairs, National Health and Population Development, etc. Preventive measures are largely the responsibility of the Department of Transport, while the Department of Environment Affairs is concerned with cleaning up of oil pollution once it has occurred.

The most important cause of marine pollution is oil spilt by tankers. Certain parts of the sea are declared prohibited dumping areas and the master (or owner) of any ship is prosecuted if any oil is discharged from his ship in such an area. A port captain may withhold clearance for the departure of a ship if he has reason to believe that oil may be discharged in a prohibited area if it is allowed to sail. Laden tankers must maintain a distance of not less than 20 km off the South African coast.

A coastal sensitivity atlas was compiled for Southern Africa following an assessment of sensitivity to oil of the entire coast and its resources. The atlas is an invaluable aid in preparation of contingency plans in the event of an oil spill.

The Department of Environment Affairs has four vessels and one aircraft equipped to combat oil pollution at sea. All pilots flying over the sea or near the coastline are asked to report oil slicks or ships discharging oil at sea.

The Department accepts full financial responsibility for countermeasures at sea, irrespective of identification of the source of the oil slick. If the offending ship can be identified, the Department pays for the removal of oil from a beach. If the source of the pollution cannot be identified and if that beach falls within the area of jurisdiction of a local authority, the Department contributes 50 per cent of the cost of cleaning the beach. The decision whether or not the beach should be cleaned, rests with the local authority. Once it has decided to clean a beach polluted by an unidentified source, the decision is conveyed to the marine division in whose area the beach falls.

Any person exporting or importing oil may be instructed to procure and maintain material and equipment to combat pollution of the sea by oil.

Other sources of marine pollution are chemical substances and other wastes discharged by ships, pollutants such as industrial effluents (heavy metals and organic substances) originating on land and washed to sea by rivers, agricultural pesticides, fertilizers, silt and solid wastes and cooling water discharged into the sea by power stations along the coast. A considerable number of coastal communities cannot afford conventional sewage purification plants to handle the increase in effluent load during peak holiday times. In the past this has led to health risks because inadequately purified sewage effluent was discharged into coastal rivers, river mouths and along the coasts. These discharges are not dispersed safely into the sea but tend rather to gather near the beach. Sewage and other solid wastes from coastal cities and towns are sometimes discharged directly into the sea. Bacteria and viruses in this sewage contaminate water and marine organisms. The CSIR is actively involved in design and location of marine-treatment schemes (ocean outfalls) to minimize the detrimental effect of marine discharge and thus to create an acceptable method of sewage disposal.

Hazardous and noxious substances

Dangerous substances, which are extensively used in agriculture and industry, are controlled mainly by the Department of National Health and Population Development and the Department of Agriculture.

Pesticides are controlled in terms of the Fertilisers, Farm Feeds, Agricultural Remedies and Stock Remedies Act, 1947. There are regulations for the sale and compulsory registration of veterinary remedies as well as for agricultural remedies, while certain standards are set for pesticidal residues on export fruit. The Department of Agriculture administers the Conservation of Agricultural Resources Act, under which various measures are implemented to prevent or contain soil erosion.

The Hazardous Substances Act empowers the Department of National Health and Population Development to take action to prevent the misuse or abuse of chemicals and other products which could be directly or indirectly hazardous to man. The Act provides for prohibition or control of importation, manufacture, sale, use, operation, application, disposal or dumping of substances which by reason of their toxic, corrosive, irritant, strongly sensitising or inflammable nature may cause injury to or the death of human beings.

The Hazardous Substances Act also provides for control of electronic product radiation. Initially one set of regulations was promulgated to control use of electronic products while diagnostic, therapeutic and industrial X-ray machines, electron and heavy particle accelerators and neutron generators have been declared Group III hazardous substances. In terms of these regulations the Department issues licences for the use of electronic products and the premises on which they are operated, subject to the findings of inspections carried out in situ.

Various departments are represented on the standing Interdepartmental Advisory Committee safeguarding Man against Poisons (Indac). The committee advises the Registrar of the Ferlisisers, Farm Feeds, Agricultural Remedies and Stock Remedies Act, 1947, on registration of poisonous agricultural remedies, toxicology of such substances, registration and control of veterinary remedies and chemical products used in agriculture.

Recently a second set of regulations was promulgated to extend further control over electronic products to include the manufacture and sales. Prescribed standards and manufacture practices prevent hazardous electronic products being placed on the market. At the same time the list of electronic products declared hazardous products was extended to include industrial and medical apparatus emitting non-ionising radiation. Only electronic products declared safe after investigation by the department and subsequently licensed, may be sold.

Through its Radiation Control Division, the department runs a radiation control programme aimed at reducing human exposure to radiation to a level as low as reasonably achievable (the Alara principle). This is in line with the latest recommendations made by the International Commission for Radiological Protection (ICRP). This programme includes the control of man-made radioactive nuclides (not within the confines of nuclear installations). The South African Atomic Energy Corporation (AEC) took over this controlling function in 1986. It is still being applied in terms of Section 50 of the Nuclear Energy Act.

Waste and pollution control

The Department of Environment Affairs has commissioned the CSIR to

— report on the position (situation) of waste management and pollution control, the relevant organisations and their present actions and responsibilities in SA
— investigate and report on legislation, legislative enforcement and judgement. Deficiencies in these areas with respect to waste management and pollution control are to be identified and remedial measures to be recommended.

Areas excluded from the study are noise and radioactive wastes. The study includes all other waste disposal and management practices related to the marine, land and atmospheric environments. The present study is seen as the first phase of a larger study which will include further investigation into areas where shortcomings and deficiencies are identified.

Hazardous waste

Hazardous waste includes a wide spectrum of non-radioactive materials such as polluted dissolvents, chlorinated hydrocarbons, PCBs, pesticides, toxic and carcinogenic (mutagenic, carcinagenic, terratogenic substances etc) compounds and other by-products of chemical manufacturing and mineral processing plants.

The Foundation for Research Development of

the CSIR investigates production, processing and storage of hazardous waste in the RSA to draw up a strategy, management plan and regulations for hazardous waste. Such a strategy, management plan and regulations will be compiled in collaboration with other government institutions.

Noise control

The Environment Conservation Act allows for the establishment of the Council for the Environment, which can name committees to address different aspects of environmental pollution and conservation. This council was established in 1983 and the committee for noise pollution, namely the Committee for Noise, Vibration and Shock, started operating in 1984.

One of the committee's first priorities was to formulate national noise control regulations. These concept regulations were published in the Government Gazette of 27 April 1990. Local governments wishing to implement the regulations and with the trained manpower and aids at their disposal can request that the regulations be made applicable in their respective areas.

The regulations provide for noise control over a wide area and contain preventive as well as remedial mechanisms. One of the most important planning measures is the concept of a 'controlled area', that is an area in which noise levels are above a certain level and where certain control measures apply. Examples are noise contours surrounding airports, roads and industries.

These areas are determined on the basis of calculations or measurements to instructions of procedures as reflected in SABS standards. After such areas have been identified, limitations can be placed on development in those areas or conditions can be laid down with regard to buildings erected in such areas.

This mechanism is very handy where new Black residential areas are developed, roads are planned or modified, land use is rezoned or residential developments are planned.

Because it is difficult to measure the disturbance value of noise, the regulations provide for subjective as well as objective methods of evaluation.

Objective evaluation takes place by means of noise measurements where the criteria, procedures and instrumentation have been standardised nationally and internationally.

In cases where noise measurements are not possible, there must be subjective evaluation and the regulations solve this problem by means of moderation tests.

Provision is also made to control vehicle noise by means of noise measurements. This method has certain advantages from the point of view of law enforcement.

In affiliation with the proposed policy of Integrated Environmental Management of the Council for the Environment, these regulations provide for implementation of noise impact studies. These have cost benefits where big development projects with a significant impact on the environment occur.

News items: 1990

Average recorded atmospheric lead levels in all major urban areas increased for inland areas, the Minister of National Health and Population Development said in 1990.

In 1989 damage amounting to at least R399 million was caused by fires in South Africa — an increase of 52,5 per cent on 1988.

People causing pollution of the sea by oil can be fined up to R200 000 and/or five years imprisonment in terms of the Prevention and Combating of Pollution of the Sea by Oil Act.

A controversial mercury recycling plant at Cato Ridge in Natal was ordered to suspend all operations producing mercury effluents until problems with the plant's waste disposal system could be controlled. The plant has resumed operation after implementing various pollution control options on advice from an independent firm of consultants. Only low mercury levels are present in rivers downstream from the plant. Sediment levels are much lower but still not acceptable and further steps are being investigated.

An international conference on air pollution was held in Pretoria in October.

A new 'Green' range of nearly 30 environment friendly domestic products was introduced by one of South Africa's biggest supermarket groups on Earth Day (22 April).

South Africa was one of 60 signatories to the Montreal Protocol for protection of the ozone layer, prescribing stricter use of chlorofluorocarbons (CFCs) adopted in London in June. A national action plan to protect the ozone layer was announced in October.

A special balloon fitted with instruments to measure ozone concentrations was sent into the atmosphere on 5 June (World Environment Day). This was the first time such a balloon had ever been sent up in Africa south of the equator.

The Department of Environment Affairs appointed the University of Cape Town's Environmental Evaluation Unit to co-ordinate a comprehensive environmental impact study in the coastal dunes at Lake St Lucia, where the Richards Bay Minerals mining company seeks to mine titanium for 30 years.

The CSIR has appointed a 'green man' to keep an eye on SA's environment. Dr D Grobler heads the environmental programme.

The Department of Water Affairs and Forestry approved, in principle, construction of a Class 1 toxic waste containment site three kilometres from Krugersdorp on the West Rand. No permit has yet been issued.

The Department of Environmental Affairs published wide-ranging regulations in terms of which persistent noise offenders can be fined up to R20 000 or be jailed for two years. By the end of 1990, 10 local authorities had already adopted and were in the process of implementing these regulations in their respective areas of jurisdiction.

The government announced a complete ban on importation of hazardous waste from other countries in August.

A survey by the Foundation for Research Development, the Department of Environment Affairs and the Department of National Health and Population Development, has found that sea and marine life pollution along the Cape coast is spreading at an alarming rate.

The President's Council is investigating a National Environmental Management System for the RSA.

Acknowledgements:
CSIR
Department of Environmental Affairs
Department of National Health and Population Development
Department of Transport
Department of Water Affairs
SABS

List of useful addresses

A

Advertising Standards Authority (ASA), PO Box 2560, 2000 Johannesburg

Africa Institute of SA, PO Box 630, 0001 Pretoria

Afrikaanse Handelsinstituut (AHI), PO Box 1741, 0001 Pretoria

Afrikaanse Sakekamer, PO Box 2164, 0001 Pretoria

Afrikaanse Taal- en Kultuurvereniging (ATKV), PO Box 4585, 2000 Johannesburg

Anglo American Corporation, PO Box 61587, 2107 Marshalltown

Anglovaal, PO Box 62379, 2107 Marshalltown

Animal and Dairy Science Research Institute, Private Bag X2, 1675 Irene

Argus Printing & Publishing Company, PO Box 1014, 2000 Johannesburg

Armscor, Private Bag X337, 0001 Pretoria

Atlas Aircraft Corporation of SA, PO Box 11, 1620 Kempton Park

Atomic Energy Corporation (AEC), PO Box 582, 0001 Pretoria

B

Banana Board, Private Bag X243, 0001 Pretoria

Baragwanath Hospital, PO Box, 2013 Bertsham

Barlow Rand, PO Box 782248, 2146 Sandton

Boeresportgilde, PO Box 9424, 0001 Pretoria

Boskop Training Centre, Private Bag X500, 2528 Boskop

Boy Scouts of South Africa, 21 Troye Street, 0002 Sunnyside

Bureau for Heraldic, Private Bag X236, 0001 Pretoria

C

Canning Fruit Board, PO Box 426, 7620 Paarl

Cape Performing Arts Board (Capab), PO Box 3579, 8000 Cape Town

Cape Technikon, PO Box 652, 8000 Cape Town

Cedara College of Agriculture, Private Bag X9059, 3200 Pietermaritzburg

Central Economic Advisory Service (CEAS), Private Bag X455, 0001 Pretoria

Chamber of Mines of SA, PO Box 809, 2000 Johannesburg

Chicory Board, PO Box 41, 6185 Alexandria

Citrus Board, PO Box 1158, 0001 Pretoria

Cosatu, PO Box 2409, 2000 Johannesburg

Cotton Board, PO Box 4387, 0001 Pretoria

Council for Mineral Technology, Private Bag X3015, 2125 Randburg

CSIR, PO Box 395, 0001 Pretoria

D

Dairy Board, PO Box 1284, 0001 Pretoria

De Beers Consolidated Mines, PO Box 62349, 2107 Marshalltown

Deciduous Fruit Board, PO Box 1801, 7530 Bellville

Development Bank of Southern Africa (DBSA), PO Box 1234, 1685 Halfweghuis

Dried Fruit Board, PO Box 508, 7655 Wellington

Dry Bean Board, Private Bag X135, 0001 Pretoria

E

East Rand Gold and Uranium Co Ltd, PO Box 980, 2000 Johannesburg

Egg Board, Private Bag X176, 0001 Pretoria

Endangered Wildlife Trust, PO Box X11, 2122 Parkview

Eskom, PO Box 1091, 2000 Johannesburg

European Immigration Company, PO Box 2556, 0001 Pretoria

F

Federasie van Afrikaanse Kultuurvereniginge (FAK), PO Box 91050, 2006 Auckland Park

Federated Union of Black Artists (Fuba), PO Box 4202, 2000 Johannesburg

Foundation for Education, Science and Technology, PO Box 1758, 0001 Pretoria

G

Genmin, PO Box 61820, 2107 Marshalltown

Geological Survey, 280 Pretoria Street, 0184 Silverton

Girl Guides Association of SA, 987 Park Street, 0083 Hatfield

Glen Agriculture College, Private Bag X01, 9360 Glen

Goldfields of SA, PO Box 1167, 2000 Johannesburg

Grain Crops Research Institute, Private Bag X1251, 2520 Potchefstroom

Graslands Research Centre, Private Bag X05, Lynn East, 0039 Pretoria

Grootfontein College of Agriculture, Private Bag X529, 5900 Middelburg (CP)

H

Hartbeesthoek Radio Astronomy Observatory (hartRao), Mokomtek, PO Box 395, 0001 Pretoria

Hiking Federation of SA, PO Box 17247, Groenkloof, 0027 Pretoria

Hospice Association, PO Box 87600, 2041 Houghton

Human Sciences Research Council (HSRC), Private Bag X41, 0001 Pretoria

Hydrological Research Institute (HRI), Roodeplaat Dam, Private Bag X313, 0001 Pretoria

I

Industrial Development Corporation, PO Box 784055, 2146 Sandton

Iscor, PO Box 450, 0001 Pretoria

J

Johannesburg Chamber of Commerce and Industry, Private Bag 34, 2006 Auckland Park

Johannesburg Stock Exchange (JSE), PO Box 34, 2006 Auckland Park

K

Kontreisportfederasie, PO Box 9423, 0001 Pretoria

L

Land and Agricultural Bank of SA, PO Box 375, 0001 Pretoria

Law Society of SA, PO Box 40542, 0007 Arcadia

Lucerne Seed Board, PO Box 185, 6620 Oudtshoorn

M

Magnetic Observatory, PO Box 32, 7200 Hermanus

Maize Board, PO Box 669, 0001 Pretoria

Meat Board, PO Box 40051, 0001 Pretoria

Medical Association of SA (MASA), PO Box 20272, 0005 Alkantrant

Medical Research Council (MRC), PO Box 70, 7505 Tygerberg

Medical University of Southern Africa (Medunsa), PO Box 203, PO Medunsa 0204

Minerals Bureau, Private Bag X4, 2017 Braamfontein

Mohair Board, PO Box 2243, 6000 Port Elizabeth

N

NALN, Private Bag X20543, 9300 Bloemfontein

Natal Preforming Arts Council, PO Box 5353, 4000 Durban

National Advisory Committee on Air Pollution, Department of National Health and Population Development, Private Bag X63, 0001 Pretoria

National Botanical Gardens of South Africa, Private Bag X7, 7735 Claremont

National Botanical Institute, Private Bag 101, 0001 Pretoria

National Council for Child & Family Welfare SA, PO Box 30990, 2017 Braamfontein

National Cultural History and Open-air Museum, P O Box 3300, 0001 Pretoria

National Energy Council, Private Bag X03, 0040 Lynnwood Ridge

National Film Archives, Private Bag X236, 0001 Pretoria

National Hiking Way Board, Private Bag X447, 0001 Pretoria

National Institute for Crime Prevention & Rehabilitation of Offenders (Nicro), PO Box 1005, 7905 Caledon Square

National Maize Producers' Organisation (Nampo), PO Box 88, 9660 Bothaville

National Media (Nasmedia), PO Box 2271, 8000 Cape Town

National Monuments' Council (NMC), PO Box 26018, 0007 Arcadia/PO Box 4637, 8000 Cape Town

National Occupational Safety Association (NOSA), PO Box 26434, 0007 Arcadia

National Parks Board, PO Box 787, 0001 Pretoria

National Road Safety Council (NRSC), Private Bag X147, 0001 Pretoria

National Sea Rescue Institute of South Africa (NSRI), PO Box 6085, 8012 Rogge Bay

National Transport Commission (NTC), Private Bag X193, 0001 Pretoria

National Zoological Gardens of South Africa, PO Box 754, 0001 Pretoria

Nuclear Fuel Corporation of South Africa (Nefcor), PO Box 61453, 2107 Marshalltown

O

Oilseeds Board, PO Box 211, 0001 Pretoria

Audit Bureau of Circulation, PO Box 31559, 2017 Braamfontein

P

Pan African Association for Zoological Gardens, Aquaria and Botanic Gardens (PAAZAB), PO Box 754, 0001 Pretoria

Parliament, P O Box 15, 8000 Cape Town

Performing Arts Council of the OFS, PO Box 1292, 9300 Bloemfontein

Performing Arts Council of the Transvaal (Pact), PO Box 566, 0001 Pretoria

Perskor van Suid-Afrika, PO Box 845, 2000 Johannesburg

Phosphate Development Corporation, PO Box 8098, 2000 Johannesburg

Plant Biotechnology Research Centre, Private Bag X293, 0001 Pretoria

Plant Protection Research Institute, Private Bag X134, 0001 Pretoria

Potato Board, Private Bag X135, 0001 Pretoria

Potchefstroom Agricultural College, Private Bag X804, 2520 Potchefstroom

Potchefstroomse Universiteit vir Christelike Hoër Onderwys, Private Bag X6001, 2520 Potchefstroom

R

Rand Afrikaans University (RAU), PO Box 524, 2000 Johannesburg

Research Institute for Citrus and Subtropical Fruit, Private Bag X11208, 1200 Nelspruit

Research Institute for Fruit and Fruit Technology, Private Bag X82075, 0300 Rustenburg

Research Institute for Oenology and Viticulture, Private Bag X5026, 7600 Stellenbosch

Research Institute for Sea Fisheries, Private Bag X2, 8012 Roggebaai

Rhodes University, PO Box 94, 6140 Grahamstown

Rooibos Tea Board, PO Box 64, 8135 Clanwilliam

S

SA Agricultural Union (SAAU), PO Box 1508, 0001 Pretoria

SA Airways, PO Box 7778, 2000 Johannesburg

SA Akademie vir Wetenskap & Kuns, PO Box 538, 0001 Pretoria

SA Art Association, PO Box 1024, 0001 Pretoria

SA Associated Health Service Professions Board, PO Box 17055, 0027 Groenkloof

SA Association for Sport Science, Physical Education and Recreation (Saassper), PO Box 13206, 0014 Clubview

SA Association of Industrial Editors (SAAIE), PO Box 70398, 0041 The Willows

SA Association of Municipal Employees, PO Box 35343, 0102 Menlo Park

SA Astronomical Observatory (SAAO), PO Box 32, 7935 Observatory

SA Blood Transfusion Service, PO Box 9326, 2000 Johannesburg

SA Broadcasting Corporation (SABC), Private Bag X1, 2006 Auckland Park

SA Bureau for Racial Affairs (Sabra), PO Box 2768, 0001 Pretoria

SA Bureau for Standards (SABS), Private Bag X191, 0001 Pretoria

SA Business Chamber, PO Box 91267, 2006 Auckland Park

SA Confederation of Labour, PO Box 19299, 0117 Pretoria West

SA Council for Alcoholism and Drug Dependence, PO Box 1324, 8000 Cape Town

SA Council for Social Work, Private Bag X55877, 0007 Arcadia

SA Council of Churches, Queens Bridge Building, Juta Street, 2001 Braamfontein

SA Cricket Union (SACU), PO Box 55009, 2116 Northlands

SA Cultural History Museum, PO Box 645, 8000 Cape Town

SA Development Trust Corporation (SADTC), PO Box 213, 0001 Pretoria

SA First Aid League, PO Box 295, 0001 Pretoria

SA Forest Research Institute, PO Box 727, 0001 Pretoria

SA Foundation for Organ Donors, 801 Nedbank Centre, Foreshore, 8001 Cape Town

SA Foundation, PO Box 7006, 2000 Johannesburg

SA Housing Trust, PO Box 3316, 2125 Randburg

SA Institute for Librarianship and Information Science, PO Box 36575, 0102 Menlo Park

SA Hunters' and Game Preservation Association, 266 Schoeman Street, 0001 Pretoria

SA Institute for Medical Research (SAIMR), PO Box 19300, 0117 Pretoria West

SA Institute for Racial Affairs (SAIRA), PO Box 31044, 2017 Braamfontein

SA Institute for International Affairs, PO Box 31596, 2017 Braamfontein

SA Law Commission, Private Bag X668, 0001 Pretoria

SA Library, PO Box 496, 8000 Cape Town

SA Marine Corporation (Safmarine), PO Box 40336, 0007 Arcadia

SA Media Council, PO Box 5222, 8000 Cape Town

SA Medic Alert Foundation, PO Box 4841, 8000 Cape Town

SA Medical and Dental Council (SAMDC), PO Box 205, 0001 Pretoria

SA Mint, Private Bag X66, 0001 Pretoria

SA Music Rights Organisation, PO Box 9292, 2000 Johannesburg

SA National Olimpic Committee, PO Box 87780, 2041 Houghton

SA Nature Foundation, PO Box 456, 7600 Stellenbosch

SA Nursing Association, PO Box 1280, 0001 Pretoria

SA Nursing Council, PO Box 1123, 0001 Pretoria

SA Pharmacy Board, PO Box 40040, 0007 Arcadia

SA Red Cross, PO Box 8726, 2000 Johannesburg

SA Reserve Bank, PO Box 427, 0001 Pretoria

SA Script Writers' Association, PO Box 91792, 2006 Auckland Park.

SA Tourism Board (Satour), Private Bag X164, 0001 Pretoria

SA Trimgym Association, PO Box 1438, 0001 Pretoria

SA Typographical Union, PO Box 1993, 0001 Pretoria

Saasveld School of Forestry, Private Bag X6531, 6530 George

Safto, PO Box 9039, 2000 Johannesburg

Sapa (SA Press Association), PO Box 7766, 2000 Johannesburg

Sasol, PO Box 5486, 2000 Johannesburg

Secretariat of the Economic Community, Private Bag X321, 0001 Pretoria

Simon van der Stel Foundation, PO Box 1743, 0001 Pretoria

Small Business Development Corporation (SBDC), PO Box 7780, 2000 Johannesburg

Soekor, PO Box 307, 7500 Parow

Soil and Irrigation Research Institute, Private Bag X79, 0001 Pretoria

Southern African Black Taxi Association (Sabta), PO Box 269, 0001 Pretoria

SPCA, PO Box 912/185, 0127 Silverton

St John Ambulance Association, PO Box 35, 0001 Pretoria

State Archives and Heraldic Services, Private Bag X236, 0001 Pretoria

State Library, PO Box 397, 0001 Pretoria

State Security Council (SSC), Private Bag X87, 0001 Pretoria

T

Tobacco Board, PO Box 26100, 0007 Arcadia

Technikon Mangosuthu, PO Box 12363, 4026 Jacobs

Technikon ML Sultan, PO Box 1334, 4000 Durban

Technikon Natal, PO Box 953, 4000 Durban

Technikon Northern Transvaal, Private Bag X07, 0116 Pretoria North

Technikon OFS, Private Bag X20539, 9300 Bloemfontein

Technikon Peninsula, PO Box 1906, 7530 Bellville

Technikon Port Elizabeth, Private Bag X6011, 6000 Port Elizabeth

Technikon Pretoria, 420 Church Street, 0002 Pretoria

Technikon RSA, Private Bag 7, 2017 Braamfontein

Technikon Vaal Triangle, Private Bag X021, 1900 Vanderbijlpark

Technikon Witwatersrand, PO Box 3293, 2000 Johannesburg

The Federation of Salaried Staff Associations of SA, PO Box 2096, 2000 Johannesburg

Times Media, PO Box 1138, 2000 Johannesburg

U

United Workers' Union of SA (Uwusa), PO Box 261136, 2023 Excom

University of Cape Town, Private Bag, 7700 Rondebosch

University of Durban-Westville, Private Bag X54001, 4000 Durban

University of Natal, PO Box 375, 3200 Pietermaritzburg

University of Port Elizabeth, PO Box 1600, 6000 Port Elizabeth

University of Pretoria (UP), 0001 Pretoria

University of South Africa (Unisa), PO Box 392, 0001 Pretoria

University of Stellenbosch, Private Bag X5018, 7600 Stellenbosch

University of the OFS, PO Box 339, 9300 Bloemfontein

University of the Western Cape, Private Bag X17, 7535 Bellville

University of the Witwatersrand, Private Bag 3, 2050 Wits

University of Zululand, Private Bag 10, 4110 Isipingo

V

Veterinary Research Institute, Private Bag X5, 0110 Onderstepoort

Vista University, Private Bag X634, 0001 Pretoria

Voortrekkers, PO Box 23442, 0031 Innesdale

W

Water Research Commission, PO Box 824, 0001 Pretoria

Wheat Board, PO Box 908, 0001 Pretoria

Wildlife Society of South Africa, PO Box 44189, 2104 Linden

Wool Board, Private Bag X245, 0001 Pretoria

World Trade Centre, PO Box 500, 1620 Kempton Park

Index

A

accommodation 233
adspend 127
adult education 178
advertising 123, 127
advertising organisations 127
 – Advertising Standards Authority 127
 – Association of Advertising Agencies 127
 – Association of Marketers 127
 – SA Advertising Research Foundation 127
 – SA Market Research Association 127
advocates 56
AEC 19, 105, 250
aerospace industry 113
Africa 71
 – population growth rate 72
African Indigenous Churches 215
African languages 25
 – colloquial 25
 – fanakalo 25
 – foreign influences 25
 – literature 205
African National Congress 11, 19, 43, 67, 123
Africana 208
 – museum 208
Afrikaans 10, 24, 123
 – churches 216
 – literature 203
Afrikaanse
 – Handelsinstituut 149
 – Taal- en Kultuurvereniging 201
 – Volksang- en Volkspelebeweging 202
Afrikaner Broederbond 15
Afrikaner-Weerstandsbeweging 44
Afrikaners 9, 31
aggregate real inventories 145
agribusiness 84
agriculture 79
 – co-operatives 151
 – credit 84
 – field crops 79
  – barley 80
  – citrus 80
  – deciduous fruit 80
  – maize 79
  – potato crop 80
  – small grains 79
  – sorghum 80
  – subtropical fruit 80
  – sugar 80
  – sunflower seed 80
  – tomatoes, onions and cabbages 80, 81

 – vineyards 80
 – wheat 80
 – livestock 81
  – beef cattle farming 81
  – dairy farming 81
  – feedlot industry 81
  – poultry and pig 82
  – sheep farming 81
  – stock breeding 81
 – production 79
 – research 168
 – training 83
agricultural co-operatives 149
Agulhas current 3
Aids 188
Aids Training and Information Centres 188
air pollution 246
air traffic control 113
airports (state) 112
 – B J Vorster 112
 – Ben Schoeman 112
 – D F Malan 112
 – H F Verwoerd 112
 – Jan Smuts 112
 – J B M Hertzog 112
 – Louis Botha 112
 – P W Botha 112
 – Pierre van Ryneveld 112
airports (ports of entry) 112
 – D F Malan 112
 – Louis Botha 112
 – Rand Airport 112
 – Jan Smuts 112
 – Komatipoort 112
 – Wonderboom 112
 – Lanseria 112
 – Grand Central 112

Akademie vir Taal, Lettere en Kuns 25
Alara principle 250
alcohol abuse 191
alumino-silicates 102
amateur radio 120
 – licences 120
ambulance services 186
ANC 11, 19, 43, 67, 123
andalusite 95
Anglo-Boer War 11, 15
Animal and Dairy Science Research Institute 168
antelope 234
antimony 95, 99
apartheid 11
Appellate Division 53
aquaculture 83
aquariums 235, 238
architecture 209

archives 208
Argus Printing and Publishing Company 124
Armaments Corporation of SA 63
Armenians 33
Armscor 63
artisans and apprentices 134
asbestos 95, 102
Asians 24, 34
associated health service professions 185
Associated Scientific and Technical Societies of SA 165
Atlas Aircraft Corporation 18, 113
Atomic Energy Corporation 19, 105, 250
attorneys 56
Attorneys-General 53
automatic international telephone exchange 119
Autonet 109
auxiliary school services 174
Ayrshires 81

B

Balfour Declaration 11
ballet 202
Baragwanath hospital 186, 187
barley 80
Barlow Rand Foundation 133
Bartholomeu Dias 9, 12
barytes 103
beef breeds 81
 – Bonsmara 81
 – Drakensberger 81
 – Nguni 81
Beltel 119
Benguela system 1, 3
bentonite 104
big game hunting 239
Big hole 98, 237
bird sanctuaries 235
 – Austin Roberts 236
 – Florence Bloom 236
 – Korsman 236
 – Marievale 236
 – Melrose 235
 – Mitchell Park Aviaries 236
 – Paradise 236
 – Pietermaritzburg 236
 – Rietvlei 236
 – Rondebult 236, 243
 – Rondevlei 236
Black Consciousness Movement 43
black granite 102
Black People's Convention 43
Black population 9, 27, 195
Blacks